The Motor Racing yearbook 1994-95

Phil Bradley

Photographs:
Bryn Williams and Colin McMaster

W·O·R·D·S·O·N Sport
SPORT FOR ALL

Contents...

FIA Formula 1 Grand Prix

PPG IndyCar World Series

2

British Touring Car Championship

Le Mans 24-hour Race

AUTHOR'S ACKNOWLEDGEMENTS

Many thanks to all those people who, in one way or another, have made this book possible.
In particular, I would like to thank Bruce Smith and everybody at *Words on Sport* for making it happen.
I would also like to thank both Mike Durcan and my daughter, Erica Bradley, for their invaluable input whilst Bryn Williams and Colin McMaster's photographs speak for themselves.
Finally, I would like to dedicate the hours I have spent in preparing the book to my wife, Carole, as a token of my appreciation of her patience and understanding.

Publisher's Note

Words on Sport would like to say a special thank-you to Kelvin Clarke at Ford Graphics and the staff of Bruce Smith Books for all aspects of this book's production.

Text © Phil Bradley 1994.
Photographs © Bryn Williams and Colin McMaster 1994.

First published in November 1994 by Words on Sport Limited.

Typeset by Martin at Bruce Smith Books Limited.

Reprographics by Ford Graphics Ltd, Fordingbridge, Hants.
Contact: Kelvin Clarke – Telephone: (01425) 655657.

Printed and bound in England by:
Ashford Colour Press Ltd, Gosport, Hants.

Words on Sport Limited, PO Box 382, St Albans, Herts, AL2 3JD.

Registered Office:
Worplesdon Chase, Worplesdon, Guildford, Surrey, GU3 3LA.
Registered in England No. 2917013.

FIA Formula 1
Grand Prix
year

Preview...

The season promised to be one of excitement and change. No one was prepared for the tragedy to come.

Not for many years had a season of F1 motor racing been so eagerly awaited as the 1994 campaign. Sadly, it was all to pale into insignificance with the deaths of Ayrton Senna and Roland Ratzenberger and severe injuries to Karl Wendlinger. But that the changes made to F1's rules on computer aids, down-force and re-fuelling had re-awakened public interest was not in doubt. Behind the changes had been a drop of some 12.5% in TV viewing figures thus making the sport less attractive to would-be sponsors and the new rules were observed by the public as making the Championship more open and therefore more interesting. On the subject of refuelling, Damon Hill's pre-season view was to prove prophetic as he said *"No pun intended but we are playing with fire. I don't know whether it is more dangerous or not because I simply sit in the car at refuelling but if there is a spillage it can obviously catch fire and the prospects of a spillage increase when people are working flat out".* Benetton's Verstappen was to find out to his cost that Hill's words were to come true at Hockenheim.

The major players were still thought to be Williams, McLaren, Benetton, and Ferrari, although the latter were known to be starting the season with a balancing problem and were not expected to come on strong until the half way stage of the campaign. Ferrari would have one of the most experienced driver teams with Alesi and Berger having contested some 250 Grand Prix's between them, although it remained a mystery to

The Pacific Grand Prix would present a new track for Formula 1 in picturesque settings.

The 'class' of '94.

most observers how Alesi was still to win a race. That left Williams, McLaren and Benetton, whose expected challenge to the top two in 1993 never quite materialised except in Portugal. Benetton's number one driver would be the ever improving German, Michael Schumacher, and in 1994 he would quickly more than double his previous two Grand Prix wins. Benetton team boss Flavio Briatore had dropped Riccardo Patrese from the driver line-up but the second spot was still to prove a problem with neither J.J. Lehto nor Jos Verstappen getting anywhere near the same performance from their cars as Schumacher.

> *"No pun intended but we are playing with fire. I don't know whether it is more dangerous or not because I simply sit in the car at refuelling but if there is a spillage it can obviously catch fire and the prospects of a spillage increase when people are working flat out"*
> *– Damon Hill*

Williams, on their form during the nineties, had to start favourites especially with Ayrton Senna (winner of more than one in four of his 158 Grand Prix starts) having switched from rivals McLaren. With Damon Hill (three wins in 18 Grand Prix's before the season began) as second driver, Williams seemed to be well equipped to land a hat-trick of Constructors' Championships if the car was good enough under the newly introduced regulations. McLaren, on the other hand, looked to have it all to do if they were to retain their remarkable record of only finishing outside the top two once in the previous eleven years. In addition to losing Senna, they had a new engine in the Peugeot V10 and they would line up with a driver team that had the most unlike McLaren statistics of not one pole or win between them. Mika Hakkinen, who won the British F3 Championship with West Surrey Racing in 1990, was retained from 1993 whilst Martin Brundle had the difficult task of following Senna. This would be the seventh Grand Prix outfit that Brundle had driven for following a debut for Tyrrell in 1984 and, despite the fact that he had not won a GP in over a century of starts, Brundle had amassed an impressive 51 points during 1992 and 1993 with Benetton and Ligier.

There were two new teams in the 1994

Sparks were about to start flying for Damon Hill.

Championship, Simtek and Pacific with the former having originally been the brainchild of FIA President Max Mosley in 1989 when he established Simtek Research with 22 year old Nick Wirth. On his elevation to FIA President, Mosley sold his 50% stake to Wirth because of conflict of interest and Wirth has done magnificently to get a F1 racing outfit on the track. With former Champion Sir Jack Brabham involved, it was no surprise to see David Brabham at the wheel of one car but the team were to be hit by tragedy early in the season when Roland Ratzenberger crashed and died at Imola. That the outfit carried on took great courage and it was a credit to Wirth that his cars were almost always running at the end. The other new boys were Pacific and, given that they had been successful at every level of racing up to F3000 prior to turning to F1, it was something of a surprise to see them consistently out-qualified by Simtek.

Of the other teams, Tyrrell would have been hoping for a recovery from their dreadful 1993 effort when neither of their drivers finished any of the first five races and the best position achieved was tenth by de Cesaris in Monaco and Katayama in Hungary leaving the outfit pointless for the first time since entering Formula 1 in 1968. Katayama kept his drive but de Cesaris was replaced by Mark Blundell who scored Brabham's only point in 1991 and notched up 10 points in 1993 for Ligier.

Many people's idea of the team most likely to cause a surprise was the British outfit of Jordan. In 1993 Rubens Barrichello had been their only regular driver with the second car being driven at various times by Capelli, Boutsen, Naspetti and, finally, Eddie Irvine. The young Brazilian had shown considerable promise in 1993, the high spot being a fifth place in Japan and, with Irvine's aggressive attitude, Jordan appeared to have a nice little team.

Footwork, now owned by Japanese conglomerate magnate Wataru Ohashi after being founded in 1978 as Arrows by Jackie Oliver and Alan Rees, has had its ups and downs in recent years. In 1991 the team experienced its worst ever season when it failed to register a solitary point but, in 1992, it bounced back to be one of only two teams that managed to finish every GP whilst one of their drivers, Michele Alboreto completed more laps than any other driver in the competition. There was, however, more disappointment in 1993 with just four points and the team lost its Honda engine deal to Lotus for 1994. The engine was replaced by Ford and drivers Derek Warwick and Aguri Suzuki by Christian Fittipaldi and Gianni Morbidelli who had been team mates before at Minardi.

Lotus were looking to its newly acquired Honda engine to restore some of its past glory when it provided Jim Clark, Graham Hill, Jochen Rindt, Emerson Fittipaldi and Mario Andretti with Championship winning cars. Lotus started the season in third place in the all time winners list behind only Ferrari and McLaren but hadn't tasted victory for six years. Herbert was rumoured for a long time to be departing to McLaren but the move never went ahead whilst Pedro Lamy's season was to come to a quick halt with a testing accident. They looked to have it all to do if they were to get back in the points consistently.

Elsewhere, Sauber had enjoyed a good debut in 1993 with a final total of 12 points putting them level with Lotus in sixth place. Wendlinger, who was in the points at Montreal, Budapest, Monza and Estoril kept his drive but Lehto was replaced by F1 debutant Heinz Harald Frentzen. Sadly, Wendlinger's season would come to a premature end at Monaco but, thankfully, he made a

The glare of the media spotlight fell upon David Coulthard. Could he adequately fill Ayrton Senna's seat in '94?

remarkable recovery from his extremely serious injuries. By contrast, Larrousse had probably its most disappointing campaign in 1993 when Comas scored the team's only point at Monza. The outfit had dropped Lamborghini for 1994 to revert to a Ford Cosworth engine and were hoping to improve on their record of just 21 points in 111 Grand Prixs. The other French outfit to compete in 1994 were Ligier who came fifth behind the big four the previous year. Although Ligier had gone close to capturing the title in 1979, 1980 and 1981, their efforts in 1993 represented a big improvement in recent form which they would be looking to maintain. Team Director and founder Guy Ligier is, as a matter of interest, a former French Rugby international and a national rowing champion. The remaining team, Minardi, were badly hit by the recession in 1993 and they joined forces with BMS Scuderia Italia (who themselves failed to appear in the final two races of 1993) for 1994. As might be expected, the team relied on Italians Alboreto and Martini as its drivers.

The saddest season for many years was about to begin ❖

Ayrton Senna

Brazil

Let the battle commence

Interlagos – 27 March 1994

Michael Schumacher celebrates his victory over Damon Hill – the two would become bitter rivals by the end of the season.

The pre-race talk was all about how the new rules would stand up to the actual test under race conditions. The other sideshow was when Goodyear, sole suppliers of tyres to the F1 circuit, let it be known that they were far from happy with their reduced allocation of passes issued under Grand Prix boss Bernie Ecclestone's instructions. By way of retaliation, Goodyear racing supremo, Leo Mahl threatened to halt the supply of tyres unless more passes were forthcoming. They were.

When qualification got underway, there were major shocks – none more so than Damon Hill completing just three laps before his fire extinguisher went off due to an electrical fault. As much of a shock as Hill doing so badly was the sight of Christian Fittipaldi's Arrows car in third and Mark Blundell's Tyrrell in fourth. The second

Arrows car with Gianni Morbidelli was in seventh but Verstappen guessed wrong with his tyre pressures and found himself down in fourteenth. New boy Heinz-Harald Frentzen made an impressive debut in his Sauber but it was Senna and Schumacher who dominated. On the second day, Hill made up lost ground to take fourth place on the grid, but couldn't stop team mate Senna claiming his 63rd pole position,

Sauber Mercedes in only their second season had the satisfaction of having two cars in the first seven grid places but Jordan were disappointed with local hero Barrichello only 14th and Irvine 16th. Morbidelli had his best ever qualifying placing of sixth but the shock was seeing McLaren in 8th and 18th with Hakkinen and Brundle respectively. The back row was shared by the two new teams who each only got one car into the race, Pacific with Bertand Gachot and David

Brabham's Simtek. Pacific's other driver, Paul Belmondo, experienced nothing but mechanical trouble and didn't register a time whilst Simtek's Roland Ratzenberger had both driver error and mechanical faults to blame for his absence

When the action got underway for real, Senna made most of pole to take the lead from Alesi whose start quickly saw him past Schumacher. At the rear, Pacific's bad luck continued as Bernard Gachot became the first retirement of the 1994 season when he was unable to miss Beretta's Larrouse as that car frantically tried to avoid Bernard's Ligier after completing just one circuit! Berretta carried on for one more lap before joining Gachot in the pits. Schumacher, meanwhile, had overtaken Alesi but the field was quickly thinning with Berger's Ferrari being hit by valve failure and Morbidelli's Arrows Ford beset by gearbox trouble which was also to account for team-mate Fittipaldi on lap 21. Before then, however, Alboreto had been sunk by engine failure and Frentzen's debut came to an untimely end after only 16 laps as he spun off.

The first refueller proved to be Martin Brundle after 15 laps but he was quickly joined by several others including Alesi, Verstappen and Barrichello. But the most crucial refuel was yet to come and when it did, the race took on a fresh complexion. Senna arrived just under a second in front of Schumacher but it was the German who was first away and within a lap he was two and half seconds in front.

Blundell was next to exit the race when he had a wheel collapse on lap 22 as Schumacher increased his lead to some five seconds over Senna with Hill a good 30 seconds down without having made a pit stop. Also without a pit stop was Martini's Minardi which was in fifth with Alesi separating him from Hill. Lap 35 saw a potentially fatal accident when Brundle's engine shut down and Bernard, who was right behind him, moved left to escape. Unfortunately, Irvine and Verstappen were also on Brundle's tail and as Bernard exited on to the grass, Irvine and Verstappen collided, with the latter becoming airborne before landing virtually on top of Brundle who had his helmet split as he was knocked unconscious. Irvine was later adjudged to have been the culprit and had a hefty fine and suspension slapped on him.

As the race continued, Senna stayed within five seconds of Schumacher but couldn't get any closer. In attempting to do so, he blew his chance on lap 56 when he spun his car and stalled the engine. Schumacher now was a full lap ahead of second place Hill and the crowd,

Third place Jean Alesi puts a foot on the armco at Interlagos.

Interlagos

An anti-clockwise track which therefore strains drivers necks more than the conventional clockwise circuits over 71 twisting laps.

Lap Distance: 2.687 miles/4.323 km
Race Distance: 190.777 miles/306.933 km

1	Senna's	Second gear entry, third gear exit
2	Curva Do Sol	Flat out
3	Subida Do Lago	There is a bumpy entrance to this tight left hander and a lot of cars manage to spin here.
4	Curva do Laranja	Double apex right hander with an extremely bumpy entrance. Probably the most difficult corner on the circuit as arrival at it is downhill at speed. After going through the first apex in fourth, the car drifts out for the second apex and, on exiting at the top in third, another right hander is on top of you almost immediately as Pinnetrinmo approaches.
5	Pinheirinho	Very tight left hander that should only be taken in second, exited in third and then up to fourth.
6	Cotovello	No time to get into fifth as the car approaches Cotovello, a tight right hander that is taken in second, exited in third, climbing to fifth as the car makes for a left hander prior to turning for Mergulho.
7	Mergulho	Taken in fourth before accelerating upto Subida (8) and Arquebancada (9) corners. These are both left handed, banked, and uphill before emerging on to the finishing straight.

Brazilian Grand Prix – 5 Year Record

Year	1st	2nd	3rd	4th	5th	6th
1989	Mansell (Ferrari)	Prost (McLaren)	Gugelmin (March)	Herbert (Benetton)	Warwick (Arrows)	Nannini (Benetton)
1990	Prost (Ferrari)	Berger (McLaren)	Senna (McLaren)	Mansell (Ferrari)	Boutsen (Williams)	Piquet (Benetton)
1991	Senna (McLaren)	Patrese (Williams)	Berger (McLaren)	Prost (Ferrari)	Piquet (Benetton)	Alesi (Benetton)
1992	Mansell (Williams)	Patrese (Williams)	Schumacher (Benetton)	Alesi (Ferrari)	Capelli (Ferrari)	Alboreto (Footwork)
1993	Senna (McLaren-Ford)	Hill (Williams-Ren't)	Schumacher (Benetton-Ford)	Herbert (Lotus-Ford)	Blundell (Ligier-Renault)	Zanardi (Lotus-Ford)

1994 Grid Positions and Qualifying Times

Grid	No	Driver	1st Session	2nd Session	Diff	Grid	No	Driver	1st Session	2nd Session	Diff
1	2	A. Senna	1'16.386	1'15.962	–	16	15	E. Irvine	1'19.269	1'18.751	2.789
2	5	M. Schumacher	1'16.575	1'16.290	0.328	17	28	G. Berger	1'18.931	1'18.855	2.893
3	27	J. Alesi	1'17.772	1'17.385	1.423	18	8	M. Brundle	1'18.864	No Time	2.902
4	0	D. Hill	1'18.270	1'17.554	1.592	19	26	O. Panis	1'19.304	1'19.533	3.342
5	30	H.H. Frentzen	1'18.144	1'17.806	1.844	20	25	E. Bernard	1'19.396	1'19.633	3.434
6	10	G. Morbidelli	1'18.970	1'17.866	1.904	21	12	J. Herbert	1'19.798	1'19.483	3.521
7	29	K. Wendlinger	1'17.982	1'17.927	1.965	22	24	M. Alboreto	1'19.517	No Time	3.555
8	7	M. Hakkinen	1'18.122	1'19.576	2.160	23	19	O. Biretta	1'19.922	1'19.524	3.562
9	6	J. Verstappen	1'18.787	1'18.183	2.221	24	11	P. Lamy	1'21.029	1'19.975	4.013
10	3	U. Katayama	1'19.519	1'18.194	2.232	25	34	B. Gachot	1'22.495	1'20.729	4.767
11	9	C. Fittipaldi	1'18.730	1'18.204	2.242	26	31	D. Brabham	1'22.266	1'21.186	5.224
12	4	M. Blundell	1'19.045	1'18.246	2.284						
13	20	E. Comas	1'18.990	1'18.321	2.359			**Non-Qualifiers**			
14	14	R. Barrichello	1'18.759	1'18.414	2.452	27	32	R. Ratzenberger	1'22.707	1'23.109	6.745
15	23	P. Martini	1'18.659	No Time	2.697	28	33	P. Belmondo	No time	No time	

with the race a foregone conclusion and their hero not a part of it, streamed out of the track in their thousands. After Hill came Alesi with a good home performance in fourth from Barrichello. Katayama, having grabbed his best ever grid position promptly converted it in to his first ever Grand Prix points in fifth with Wendlinger in sixth. Of the twelve finishers, amazingly there were eleven different teams with nine different outfits filling the first nine places – something almost unheard of and gave a seal of approval to Bernie Ecclestone's plans for making the sport more interesting from a spectator point of view ⚑

At the after race party, drivers like to unwind, slip into something more comfortable and let their hair down with a Samba!

The Championship

Race Placing and Points

Drivers' Points		Constructors' Points	
10	M. Schumacher	10	Benetton
6	D. Hill	6	Williams
4	J. Alesi	4	Ferrari
3	R. Barrichello	3	Jordan
2	U. Katayama	2	Tyrrell
1	K. Wendlinger	1	Sauber

Race Placings

Pos	No	Driver	Team	Time	Diff	Grid	
1	5	M. Schumacher	Mild Seven Benetton Ford	1;35'38.759	–	2	
2	0	D. Hill	Rothmans Williams Renault	–	1 lap down	4	
3	27	J. Alesi	Ferrari	–	1 lap down	3	
4	4	R. Barrichello	Sasol Jordan	–	1 lap down	14	
5	3	U. Katayama	Tyrrell	–	2 laps down	10	
6	9	K. Wendlinger	Broker Sauber Mercedes	–	2 laps down	7	
7	12	J. Herbert	Team Lotus	–	2 laps down	21	
8	23	P. Martini	Minardi Scuderia Italia	–	2 laps down	15	
9	20	E. Comas	Tourtel Larrousse F1	–	3 laps down	13	
10	11	P. Lamy	Team Lotus	–	3 laps down	24	
11	26	O. Panis	Ligier Gitanes Blondes	–	3 laps down	19	
12	3	D. Brabham	MTV Simtek Ford	–	4 laps down	26	

Failed to Finish

Pos	No	Driver	Team	Time	Diff	Grid	
13	2	A. Senna	Rothmans Williams Renault	–	55 laps	1	(Spin)
14	8	M. Brundle	Marlboro McLaren Peugeot	–	34 laps	18	(Accident)
15	15	E. Irvine	Sasol Jordan	–	34 laps	16	(Accident)
16	6	J. Verstappen	Mild Seven Benetton Ford	–	34 laps	9	(Accident)
17	25	E. Bernard	Ligier Gitanes Blondes	–	33 laps	20	(Accident)
18	4	M. Blundell	Tyrrell	–	21 laps	12	(Accident)
19	9	C. Fittipaldi	Footwork Arrows Ford	–	21 laps	11	(Gearbox)
20	30	H. Frentzen	Broker Sauber Mercedes	–	15 laps	5	(Spin)
21	7	M. Hakkinen	Marlboro McLaren Peugeot	–	13 laps	8	(Electrical)
22	24	M. Alboreto	Minardi Scuderia Italia	–	7 laps	22	(Electrical)
23	10	G. Morbidelli	Footwork Arrows Ford	–	5 laps	6	(Gearbox)
24	28	G. Berger	Ferrari	–	5 laps	17	(Air valve leak)
25	19	O. Berreta	Tourtel Larrousse F1	–	2 laps	23	(Accident)
26	34	B. Gachot	Pacific Grand Prix	–	.	1 lap	25	(Accident)

Fastest Lap: M. Schumacher – 1'18.455 – (123.230mph/198.4kph)

Average Speed of Winner: 192.6kph

Pacific

War in the Pacific

TI Circuit, Aida, Japan – 17 April 1994

Roland Ratzenberger's MTV Simtek Ford finished 11th.

Jean Alesi, third in the opening Brazilian Grand Prix, was missing from the line up in Japan, having suffered crushed vertebrae whilst testing at Mugello on 30th March. Also missing was Eddie Irvine who had been found to be the culprit in the big smash at Interlagos and earned himself a rest. Replacing Alesi was Ferrari test driver Nicola Larini but Jordan went for local boy, Aguri Suzuki with money apparently playing a big part as both Fuji Television and Japanese tobacco giants, Mild Seven, were reported as paying substantial amounts to get the driver involved.

Apart from Suzuki the only driver to have experience of this first time Grand Prix track was Roland Ratzenberger who had raced in Japanese Touring Cars but, ironically, he was the first driver to spin when testing began on the Thursday prior to the race. But the burning question was

whether Benetton's first place in Brazil was a one-off or a real threat to the supremacy Williams had held. The first session saw Senna fastest but right behind was Schumacher confirming that he would definitely be posing problems to the Williams team. A bigger surprise, however, was Erik Comas' Larrousse in third ahead of Damon Hill. The battle for pole continued throughout the two days with first Schumacher setting a new target and then Senna wiping it away but by the end of qualifying, Schumacher had failed to dislodge Senna.

If the masses were looking for the answer as to whether Schumacher's Brazilian win would earn a quick riposte from Senna they were to be bitterly disappointed only seconds after the start. Schumacher got away quicker than Senna forcing the Brazilian to back off slightly which resulted in Hakkinen giving a slight touch to the Rothmans car in front of him. Senna began to spin as Hakkinen got through a gap but Larini couldn't evade Senna and hit him with sufficient force to render both cars out of the contest. In a separate incident at the start, Comas seemed to land his undertray on the kerb causing him to crash into Blundell's Tyrrell and putting the Briton out of the race. Comas pitted for repairs and went on to finish but the number of competitors was therefore down to 23 within moments of the start and it was only quick work by the marshals in clearing the debris that prevented a restart.

By the start of the second lap, Schumacher was already seconds ahead and the race as a spectacle was soon to be over as he gradually increased his superiority and stamped his Benetton's authority over the rest of the field. Hill, when challenging Hakkinen for second, spun off at Revolver Corner (a repeat of his qualifying experience) on lap four and was down to tenth by the time he rejoined. In a marvellous piece of aggressive driving, the Briton within the next nine laps had overtaken Morbidelli, Verstappen, Frentzen, Fittipaldi, Brundle and Barrichello. Gerhard Berger, however, proved to be made of sterner stuff and although Hill twice got alongside the Austrian, he couldn't finish the manoeuvre successfully. The first pit stops were now required

and Hill came in at the end of the 18th circuit to emerge back in tenth but as others were forced to refuel he was quickly back in business making in-roads and by lap 25 was in fifth. Hakkinen, meanwhile, having played a part in depriving the race of Senna was forced to retire almost immediately after his pit stop when his gears packed up. The Finn thus became the sixth casualty of the race as both Brabham and Beretta had also gone with engine problems.

There was little more incident for some time with Katayama's Tyrrell being next to incur engine trouble after completing 42 laps but he was quickly joined by Suzuki. Schumacher, meanwhile, was making the best of his way home and was looking uncatchable bar a catastrophe. Berger was still second but the battle for third between Barrichello and Brundle was preventing Hill making further progress. However, when Berger, Barrichello and Brundle all made belated pit stops for both fuel and tyres, Hill was up to second, albeit over forty seconds down on Schumacher. With only the Briton seemingly able to mount any sort of challenge to Schumacher, the German's victory was virtually assured on the 50th lap when Hill ground slowly to a halt.

Hill's demise put Berger into second, Barrichello third whilst British interest was main-

Pedro Lamy's Lotus on its way to eighth place.

TI Circuit, Aida

More used to motorbike races, this was the first time the clockwise track was used for Grand Prix races, over 83 unfamiliar laps.

Lap Distance	2.314 miles/3.723 km
Race Distance	192.06 miles/309.027 km

A brand new track in terms of Grand Prix racing and used domestically as a private track for anybody wealthy enough to pay a reputed £90,000 a head to join. Its inaugural race was a Sports Car race in 1990 and it has since hosted some Formula 3 and Touring Car races. It was widely reported that the billionaire owner, Hajima Tanaka, had paid almost £3m for the privilege of staging a Grand Prix at his private track. It is built in a wilderness and, with only one road serving it, the crowd was restricted to 70,000 from the 100,000 capacity. Children were given three days off school so as not to add to the road congestion but, super efficient as the Japanese are, the youngsters had the commensurate amount of time docked from their school holidays!

1. First Corner	4. Attwood Curve	7. Piper Corner	10. Mike Knight Corner
2. Williams Corner	5. Hair Pin Corner	8. Redman Corner	11. Last Corner
3. Moss S	6. Revolver Corner	9. Hobbs Corner	

1994 Grid Positions and Qualifying Times

Grid	No	Driver	1st Session	2nd Session	Diff	Grid	No	Driver	1st Session	2nd Session	Diff
1	2	A. Senna	1'10.218	1'19.304	–	16	20	E. Comas	1'13.111	1'13.550	2.893
2	5	M. Schumacher	1'10.440	No time	0.222	17	23	P. Martini	1'13.529	1'13.756	3.311
3	0	D. Hill	1'10.771	1'12.048	0.553	18	25	E. Bernard	1'13.613	1'14.204	3.395
4	7	M. Hakkinen	1'11.683	No time	1.465	19	29	K. Wendlinger	1'13.855	1'14.163	3.637
5	28	G. Berger	1'11.744	1'12.184	1.526	20	15	A. Suzuki	1'13.855	1'14.163	3.714
6	8	M. Brundle	1'12.351	No time	2.133	21	19	O. Beretta	1'14.101	1'14.271	3.883
7	27	N. Larini	1'12.372	5'32.428	2.154	22	26	O. Panis	1'14.106	1'14.667	3.888
8	14	R. Barrichello	1'12.409	1'13.172	2.191	23	12	J. Herbert	1'14.538	1'14.424	4.206
9	9	C. Fittipaldi	1'13.169	1'12.444	2.226	24	11	P. Lamy	1'14.657	1'15.146	4.439
10	6	J. Verstappen	1'12.554	1'12.681	2.336	25	31	D. Brabham	1'14.946	1'14.748	4.530
11	30	H. H. Frentzen	1'12.686	1'12.797	2.468	26	32	R. Ratzenberger	No time	1'16.356	6.138
12	4	M. Blundell	1'13.013	1'12.751	2.533						
13	10	G. Morbidelli	1'12.866	1'13.090	2.648	**Non-Qualifiers**					
14	3	U. Katayama	1'13.013	1'13.411	2.795	27	34	B. Gachot	1'16.927	1'18.571	6.709
15	24	M. Alboreto	1'13.342	1'13.016	2.798	28	33	P. Belmondo	1'18.671	1'17.450	7.232

Aguri Suzuki takes his Sasol Jordan for a spin — again!

tained by Brundle in fourth, which was to become third when the Brazilian pitted on lap 62. With less than ten miles to go, however, and his first points for McLaren seemingly in the bag, Brundle's engine began to overheat and he was forced to retire at the end of the 67th lap. A crash between Alboreto and Wendlinger with less than two laps remaining plus Morbidelli's retirement on the same circuit, catapulted Frentzen and Comas into the points. In the case of Comas it gave the Larrousse outfit their first point since Patrick Tambay became a partner ▪

Senna and Hill have a bit of a chin wag.

The Championship

Race Placing and Points

Drivers' Points		Constructors' Points	
10	M. Schumacher	10	Benetton
6	G. Berger	6	Ferrari
4	R. Barrichello	4	Jordan
3	C. Fittipaldi	3	Footwork
2	H. H. Frentzen	2	Sauber
1	E. Comas	1	Larrousse

Leaderboard after Round Two

Drivers' Points		Constructors' Points	
20	M. Schumacher	20	Benetton
7	R. Barrichello	10	Ferrari
6	D. Hill	7	Jordan
6	G. Berger	6	Williams
4	J. Alesi	3	Footwork
3	C. Fittipaldi	3	Sauber
2	U. Katayama	2	Tyrrell
2	H. H. Frentzen	1	Larrousse
1	K. Wendlinger		
1	E. Comas		

Race Placings

Pos	No	Driver	Team	Time	Diff	Grid	
1	5	M. Schumacher	Mild Seven Benetton Ford	1:46'01.693	–	2	
2	8	G. Berger	Ferrari	1:47'16.993	1'15.30	5	
3	14	R. Barrichello	Sasol Jordan	–	1 lap down	8	
4	9	C. Fittipaldi	Footwork Arrows Ford	–	1 lap down	9	
5	30	H. H. Frentzen	Broker Sauber Mercedes	–	1 lap down	11	
6	20	E. Comas	Tourtel Larrousse F1	–	3 laps down	16	
7	12	J. Herbert	Team Lotus	–	3 laps down	23	
8	11	P. Lamy	Team Lotus	–	4 laps down	24	
9	26	O. Panis	Ligier Gitanes Blondes	–	5 laps down	22	
10	25	E. Bernard	Ligier Gitanes Blondes	–	5 laps down	18	
11	32	R. Ratzenberger	MTV Simtek Ford	–	5 laps down	26	

Failed to Finish

12	10	G. Morbidelli	Footwork Arrows Ford	–	69 laps	13	(Engine)
13	29	K. Wendlinger	Broker Sauber Mercedes	–	69 laps	19	(Accident)
14	24	M. Alboreto	Minardi Scuderia Italia	–	69 laps	15	(Accident)
15	8	M. Brundle	Marlboro McLaren Peugeot	–	67 laps	6	(Engine)
16	23	P. Martini	Minardi Scuderia Italia	–	63 laps	17	(Spin)
17	6	J. Verstappen	Mild Seven Benetton Ford	–	54 laps	10	(Spin)
18	0	D. Hill	Rothmans Williams Renault	–	49 laps	3	(Transmission)
19	15	A. Suzuki	Sasol Jordan	–	44 laps	20	(Spin)
20	3	U. Katayama	Tyrrell	–	42 laps	14	(Engine)
21	7	M. Hakkinen	Marlboro McLaren Peugeot	–	19 laps	4	(Transmission)
22	19	O. Beretta	Tourtel Larrousse F1	–	14 laps	21	(Engine)
23	31	D. Brabham	MTV Simtek Ford	–	2 laps	25	(Engine)
24	2	A. Senna	Rothmans Williams Renault	–	0 laps	1	(Accident)
25	4	M. Blundell	Tyrrell	–	0 laps	12	(Accident)
26	27	N. Larini	Ferrari	–	0 laps	7	(Accident)

Fastest Lap: M. Schumacher – 1'14.023 (111.801 mph/180 kph)

Average Speed of Winner: 173.9kph

San Marino

Motor Racing's Blackest Day

The start of the San Marino Grand Prix

mola proved to be the blackest weekend Formula One has known. By the end of the actual race, the previous 72 hours carnage had claimed three lives and ten injured in five separate accidents. If Grand Prix followers had lapsed into a false sense of security with eight years having passed since Elio de Angelis was killed in testing at Paul Ricard and twelve since Gilles Villeneuve and Riccardo Paletti were killed in race or qualifying action, then they were to be brought to their senses in the most tragic way imaginable.

Roland Ratzenberger in reply to a question about the speed of the Imola track replied that this was merely a game. The real world, he observed, was a couple of hundred miles away in war-torn Bosnia. There was little hint of what was to befall Formula One when the drivers set out on their qualifying session on Friday morning but the first sign of trouble came early in the afternoon and everybody feared the worst when Rubens Barrichello had an almighty accident at Variante Bassa chicane. His car seemed to hit the kerb and take off towards a wall. Fortunately, indeed it probably saved another fatality, the car did not get quite high enough to miss the tyre wall altogether with the bottom of the car clipping the top of the tyres. It was sufficient to reduce the impact with the concrete by possibly 20mph before it landed nose first and rolled. Medical assistance was on the spot and badly needed by the Brazilian whose breathing tubes were blocked by his injuries. He had had a lucky escape and when he awoke in hospital he found countryman, Ayrton Senna, at his bedside. Once satisfied that Barrichello was going to survive, the World Champion returned not only to claim pole but to lower Mansell's 1992 qualifying record.

Saturday was even bleaker. Ratzenberger's Simtek seemed to go out of control at Villeneuve having looked to shed some of its body at high speed. The debris appeared then to go under the car and launch it in to the air at nearly 200mph. The car smashed into the concrete wall and slowed down with very little left of it. Ratzenberger's game had claimed his life as surely as a Serbian shell claiming the lives of children in the Bosnian enclaves. The Formula One fraternity were numbed into silence. Williams, Benetton and Sauber packed up for the day, others felt they had to carry on. Whichever decision was made, it was taken with tears.

If Saturday had been worse than Friday, then Sunday was tragically worse still. David Brabham, Ratzenberger's team mate, decided to race but Alboreto almost missed it by default. He was still in the pits when the exit road was closed ready for the off and had to start from the pit lane once the other cars were on their way. Unfortunately, two weren't as Lehto stalled on the grid. An unsighted Lamy, who went from right to left across the track to try to find a gap as cars in front of him swerved round the stricken Lehto, ploughed straight into the Benetton. A wheel and

debris flew from the Lotus high into the air, landing amongst spectators, four of whom were taken to hospital. Sadly, a 28 year old from the Italian ski resort of Courmayeur later died.

The safety car was sent out to pace the cars whilst the track was cleared and the drivers remained in convoy for four laps. When the fifth lap began, Senna was leading Schumacher followed by Berger, Hill, Frentzen and Hakkinen as the race began again in earnest. But on lap six, Senna's car simply went straight on at Tamburello and smashed into the wall at about 180mph. When the car came to a standstill, Senna could be seen slumped motionless in the cockpit but it seemed an eternity before any help could be got to him as the rest of the field thundered by. It was clearly serious but just how serious was in doubt for several hours as the World Champion clung to life until his heart finally stopped at 6.40pm.

Amazingly, the race was ordered to be restarted. Berger was in front in the new race but behind Schumacher with the two parts added together. The German pitted on lap six of the restarted race but Berger lost the advantage when he also had to stop with suspension problems leaving Hakkinen in front. He, too, lost the

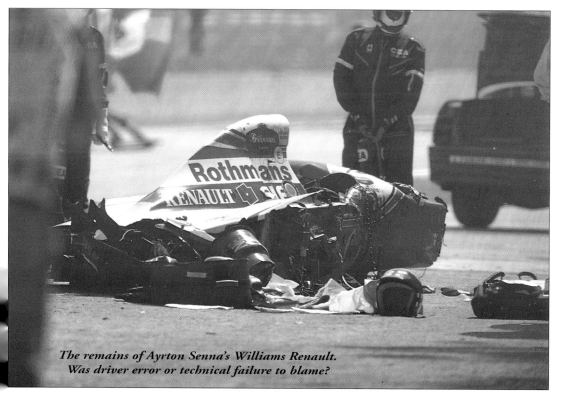

The remains of Ayrton Senna's Williams Renault.
Was driver error or technical failure to blame?

Imola

Another of the anti-clockwise tracks that tend to cause drivers problems with their necks over 61 laps.

Lap Distance   3.132 miles/5.026 km
Race Distance   191.034 miles/307.439 km

1. Tamburello   First corner from the start. A left hander taken at speed, often still in sixth gear. Gained notoriety with the death of Ayrton Senna.

2. Villeneuve   No slower than Tamburello except that on exiting the car needs to be on the other side of the track with the driver beginning to get down through the gears to second ready for a sharp left hander. The combined change of speed and direction often finds drivers heading for the gravel trap at the left hander following Villeneuve.

3. Piratella   A somewhat blind left hander that is taken in fourth before changing quickly up to fifth to approach the bumpy left hander, downhill to Acque Minerale.

4. Acque Minerale   A very bumpy and uncomfortable chicane negotiated in second.

5. Variante Alfa   Fast chicane that can be tackled in third and certainly requires a third gear exit. Drivers tend to take more chance at this chicane because it does have a safe run-off area.

6. Rivazza   Requires hard braking down from sixth to second in order to tackle this right hander which is downhill and is taken in second. It opens out straight into a sharp left hander.

7. Variante Bassa   A very tricky right-left switchback which leads into Traguardo.

8. Traguardo   Almost as soon as the previous right-left flick is accomplished, Traguardo looms up as a left-right chicane that feeds the pits straight.

San Marino Grand Prix – 5 Year Record

Year	1st	2nd	3rd	4th	5th	6th
1989	Senna (McLaren)	Prost (McLaren)	Nannini (Benetton)	Boutsen (Williams)	Warwick (Arrows)	Palmer (Tyrrell)
1990	Patrese (Williams)	Berger (McLaren)	Nannini (Benetton)	Prost (Ferrari)	Piquet (Benetton)	Alesi (Tyrrell)
1991	Senna (McLaren)	Berger (McLaren)	Lehto (Dallara)	Martini (Minardi)	Hakkinen (Lotus)	Bailey (Lotus)
1992	Mansell (Williams)	Patrese (Williams)	Senna (McLaren)	Brundle (Benetton)	Alboreto (Footwork)	Martini (Dallara)
1993	Prost (Williams)	Schumacher (Benetton)	Brundle (Ligier)	Lehto (Sauber)	Alliot (Larrousse)	Barbazza (Minardi)

1994 Grid Positions and Qualifying Times

Grid No	Driver	1st Session	2nd Session	Diff	Grid No	Driver	1st Session	2nd Session	Diff
1	2	A. Senna	1'21.548	No time	–	16	9	C. Fittipaldi	1'24.655	1'24.472	2.924
2	5	M. Schumacher	1'21.885	1'21.885	0.337	17	25	E. Bernard	1'24.678	1'40.411	3.130
3	28	G. Berger	1'22.113	1'21.226	0.565	18	20	E. Comas	1'26.295	1'24.852	3.304
4	0	D. Hill	1'23.199	1'22.168	0.620	19	26	O. Panis	1'24.996	1'25.160	3.448
5	6	J.J. Lehto	1'22.717	1'24.029	1.169	20	12	J. Herbert	1'25.114	1'25.141	3.566
6	27	N. Larini	1'22.841	1'23.006	1.293	21	15	A. de Cesaris	1'25.234	1'25.872	3.686
7	30	H. H. Frentzen	1'23.119	No Time	1.571	22	11	P. Lamy	1'26.453	1'25.295	3.747
8	7	M. Hakkinen	1'23.611	1'23.140	1.592	23	19	O. Beretta	1'27.179	'25.991	4.443
9	3	U. Katayama	1'24.000	1'23.322	1.774	24	31	D. Brabham	1'27.607	1'26.817	5.269
10	29	K. Wendlinger	1'23.788	1'23.347	1.799	25	34	B. Gachot	1'27.732	1'27.143	5.595
11	10	G. Morbidelli	1'23.663	1'24.682	2.115	26	32	R. Ratzenberger	1'27.657	1'27.584	6.036
12	4	M. Blundell	1'23.703	1'23.831	2.155						
13	8	M. Brundle	1'24.443	1'23.858	2.310		**Non-Qualifiers**				
14	23	P. Martini	1'24.078	1'24.423	2.530	27	33	P. Belmondo	1'28.361	1'27.881	6.333
15	24	M. Alboreto	1'24.276	1'24.780	2.728	28	14	R. Barrichello	No time	No time	No time

lead in the pits on lap 21 leaving Larini clear in the latest race but still behind Schumacher on aggregate. By lap 26, the issue was clearer as Schumacher overtook Larini on the road. Brundle lost a great slice of time on his pit stop when he stalled after a visit on lap 39 and by the time Schumacher paid his last visit on lap 46 the race was all but won. It was, however, in the pits that the next accident was to occur as Alboreto accelerated out to rejoin the race after a pit stop on lap 49. Going past the McLaren pit, his right rear wheel nut flew off causing mayhem. The wheel arced high into the air before bouncing at random down the pit lane to hit a Lotus mechanic whilst the Minardi car slewed through the Ferrari mechanics hitting three of them. The stretchers were back in full use but the race was still allowed to continue.

The race reached its meaningless conclusion and, for the record, Schumacher took his third consecutive victory but it meant nothing to him, or the thousands who watched the whole ill-fated weekend unfurl 🏁

The Championship

Race Placing and Points

Drivers' Points		Constructors' Points	
10	M. Schumacher	10	Benetton
6	N. Larini	8	Ferrari
4	M. Hakkinen	4	McLaren
3	K. Wendlinger	3	Sauber
2	U. Katayama	2	Tyrrell
1	D. Hill	1	Williams

Leaderboard after Round Three

Drivers' Points		Constructors' Points	
30	M. Schumacher	30	Benetton
7	R. Barrichello	16	Ferrari
7	D. Hill	7	Jordan
6	G. Berger	7	Williams
6	N. Larini	6	Sauber
4	J. Alesi	4	Tyrrell
4	K. Wendlinger	4	McLaren
4	U. Katayama	3	Footwork
4	M. Hakkinen	1	Larrousse
3	C. Fittipaldi		
2	H.H. Frentzen		
1	E. Comas		

Race Placings

Pos	No	Driver	Team	Time	Diff	Grid	
1		M. Schumacher	Mild Seven Benetton Ford	1:28'28.642	–	2	
2		N. Larini	Ferrari	1:29'23.584	54.942s	6	
3		M. Hakkinen	Marlboro McLaren Peugeot	1:29'39.321	1'10.679	8	
4		K. Wendlinger	Broker Sauber Mercedes	1:29'42.300	1'13.658	0	
5		U. Katayama	Tyrrell	–	1 lap down	9	
6		D. Hill	Rothmans Williams Renault	–	1 lap down	4	
7		H. H. Frentzen	Broker Sauber Mercedes	–	1 lap down	7	
8		M. Brundle	Marlboro McLaren Peugeot	–	1 lap down	13	
9		M. Blundell	Tyrrell	–	2 laps down	12	
10		J. Herbert	Team Lotus	–	2 laps down	20	
11		O. Panis	Ligier Gitanes Blondes	–	2 laps down	19	
12		E. Bernard	Ligier Gitanes Blondes	–	3 laps down	17	
13		C. Fittipaldi	Footwork Arrows Ford	–	3 laps down		

Failed to Finish

Pos	No	Driver	Team	Time	Diff	Grid	
14		A. de Cesaris	Sasol Jordan	–	49 laps	21	(Spin)
15		M. Alboreto	Minardi Scuderia Italia	–	44 laps	15	(Loose wheel)
16		G. Morbidelli	Footwork Arrows Ford	–	40 laps	11	(Engine)
17		P. Martini	Minardi Scuderia Italia	–	37 laps	14	(Spin)
18		D. Brabham	MTV Simtek Ford	–	27 laps	24	(Gearbox)
19		B. Gachot	Pacific Grand Prix Ltd	–	23 laps	25	(Oil Pressure)
20		O. Beretta	Tourtel Larrousse F1	–	17 laps	23	(Engine)
21		G. Berger	Ferrari	–	16 laps	3	(Loose wheel)
22		A. Senna	Rothmans Williams Renault	–	5 laps	1	(Accident)
23		E. Comas	Tourtel Larrousse F1	–	5 laps	18	(Accident)
24		J.J. Lehto	Mild Seven Benetton Ford	–	0 laps	5	(Accident)
25		P. Lamy	Team Lotus	–	0 laps	22	(Accident)

Fastest Lap: D. Hill – 1'24.335 (215.100kph/133.602mph)

Average Speed of Winner: No average speed due to the race being stopped.

Monaco

Circuit de Monaco – 15 May 1994

Martin Brundle's McLaren negotiates Monaco's tight corners.

It was not the usual high spirited get together that is normally associated with Monaco. Imola was too recent an experience for that and a stark reminder of the tragic events there was the Brazilian flag that flew over the Williams pit at half mast. But, incredibly, there was still more grim news waiting to unfurl. Towards the end of the first qualifying session, Karl Wendlinger's Sauber went off line at the exit from the tunnel and data suggested that he braked too late for the chicane, causing the car to hit the barriers which separate the escape road from the chicane itself. The Austrian was in a critical condition and his life hung in the balance for some days. A controlled coma, however, was used to ease the pressure on a cerebral injury and brain swelling and the racing world was saved another fatality. Traditionally, Friday is a day off as it is a local holiday but there was no time to spare for most of the Grand Prix entourage. There was a meeting of Grand Prix drivers, the Sauber team declared it would not race and the FIA announced sweeping reforms to the rules, leaving the engineers the task of analysing what problems the new regulations would cause.

By Saturday, although in subdued mood, racing began again with Schumacher capturing Mansell's 1992 qualifying record time to take pole and then, to show he really meant business, he went out again and smashed the lap record with a time of 1'18.560. Hakkinen and Berger had an almighty duel for second place on the grid with the only Williams driver, Hill, in fourth. Alesi, returning from his lay-off, was a creditable fifth whilst the two Arrows were next best. Bouncing straight back into action after his dice with death at San Marino was Rubens Barrichello but he was down in fifteenth, two places behind a disappointed Comas who had been as high as fourth at one stage. Bringing up the rear were the two Pacific Grand Prix cars but at least their 23rd and 24th were the highest qualifying places they had yet attained, albeit by default!

The start of the race was reserved for the drivers to pay their respects to Ayrton Senna and Roland Ratzenberger. Where pole would have been was a Brazilian flag painted on the track with the Austrian flag painted on second slot. The cars then moved onto the parade, leaving a stalled Lamy behind. He would now have to start from the back of the grid but there was no such problem for Schumacher who used his pole position to advantage and pulled straight away from Hakkinen. Hill went even faster to pass Berger and then he tackled Hakkinen at Virage St Devote. However, as Hill tried to pass the Finn on the left, the gap closed and the cars collided putting both out of the race after a matter of yards rather than miles. Indeed, the incident only served to increase Schumacher's lead, as Berger, and the following entourage had to slow down to bypass Hill and Hakkinen. The lead was almost four seconds at the end of the first circuit, nearly

six by the end of the third and a whopping 16 seconds after ten laps. The race was over, barring accidents, almost before it had begun. St Devote also claimed the two Italians, Morbidelli and Martini, on the first lap so only twenty cars made it to the end of the first tour. The race was largely uneventful in the early stages apart from Schumacher lapping everybody up to eighth place by lap 21. This lap also witnessed the first pit stop as Brundle pulled in early on a well calculated move that was to pay handsome dividends later in the race. The Briton did not stop again, apart from having rubbish cleared from the radiator intakes, and he overtook all the front runners bar Schumacher and Berger, as they all made their stops. In fact Barrichello never resumed once he had pitted, his engine simply packing up. Comas had gearbox problems from an early stage and, although he finished, the Larrouse never figured whilst Bernard's exit in a spin at the harbour chicane heralded a chain of cars departing for the afternoon. Katayama's gearbox failed and Blundell slid up the escape road at St Devote with his brakes jammed and spilling oil as he went.

Karl Wendlinger receives treatment from trackside medics

Circuit de Monaco

The "glamour" race of the Grand Prix
season over 78 laps, it is also one of
the most demanding. At the start it
is almost impossible to overtake so a
good grid position is essential.

Lap Distance	2.068 miles/3.328 km
Race Distance	161.298 miles/259.583 km

1	Virage de Sainte Devote	Approached from the pits in sixth but then it's down into third or fourth into this right hander.
2	Montee du Beau Rivage	Past Rosie's Bar in sixth and then it's over the crest of the hill and down to fourth as Virage Massenet beckons.
3	Virage Massenet	A long left hander, the car must be kept close to the inside kerbs all the way into...
4	Casino Square	A quick right hander that is taken in third before taking the downhill exit.
5	Virage Mirabeau	Approached downhill in fifth, the gear changes have to be fast to get into second for this bumpy right hander before exiting in third towards...
6	Virage Ancienne Gare	A left hand hairpin negotiated in second, the steering turned full lock, then right into...
7	Virage du Portier	Another sharp right hander cleared in second, and then into...
8	Lowens Tunnel	With frightening noise and sparks, the cars change up to sixth to re-emerge into...
9	Nouvelle Chicane	Left-right chicane taken in second.
10	Tabac	The most spectacular and glamourous part of the course alongside the harbour.
11	Swimming Pool	Lots of gear changes slow the cars towards...
12	Virage de la Rascasse	The slowest corner on the circuit which is taken in second, and then uphill to...
13	Virage Antony Noghes	Quickly up into third gear and back on to the pit straight.

Monaco Grand Prix – 5 Year Record

Year	1st	2nd	3rd	4th	5th	6th
1989	Senna (McLaren)	Prost (McLaren)	Modena (Brabham)	Caffi (Dallara)	Alboreto (Tyrrell)	Brundle (Brabham)
1990	Senna (McLaren)	Alesi (Tyrrell)	Berger (McLaren)	Boutsen (Williams)	Caffi (Arrows)	Bernard (Lola)
1991	Senna (McLaren)	Mansell (Williams)	Alesi (Ferrari)	Moreno (Benetton)	Prost (Ferrari)	Pirro (Dallara)
1992	Senna (McLaren-Ford)	Mansell (Williams)	Patrese (Williams)	Schumacher (Benetton)	Brundle (Benetton)	Gachot (Larrousse)
1993	Senna (McLaren)	Hill (Williams)	Alesi (Ferrari)	Prost (Williams)	Fittipaldi (Minardi)	Brundle (Ligier)

1994 Grid Positions and Qualifying Times

Grid No		Driver	1st Session	2nd Session	Diff	Grid No		Driver	1st Session	2nd Session	Diff
1	5	M. Schumacher	1'20.230	1'18.560	–	15	14	R. Barrichello	1'24.731	1'22.359	3.799
2	7	M. Hakkinen	1'21.881	1'19.488	0.928	16	12	J. Herbert	1'24.103	1'22.375	3.815
3	28	G. Berger	1'22.038	1'19.958	1.398	17	6	J.J. Lehto	1'23.885	1'22.679	4.119
4	0	D. Hill	1'22.605	1'20.079	1.519	18	19	O. Beretta	1'24.126	1'23.025	4.465
5	27	J. Alesi	1'22.521	1'20.452	1.892	19	11	P. Lamy	1'25.859	1'23.858	5.298
6	9	C. Fittipaldi	1'23.588	1'21.053	2.493	20	26	O. Panis	1'25.115	1'24.131	5.571
7	10	G. Morbidelli	1'23.580	1'21.189	2.629	21	25	E. Bernard	1'27.694	1'24.377	5.817
8	8	M. Brundle	1'21.580	1'21.222	2.662	22	31	D. Brabham	1'26.690	1'24.656	6.096
9	23	P. Martini	1'23.162	1'21.288	2.728	23	34	B. Gachot	1'48.173	1'26.082	7.522
10	4	M. Blundell	1'23.522	1'21.614	3.054	24	33	P. Belmondo	1'29.984	8'36.897	11.424
11	3	U. Katayama	1'24.488	1'21.731	3.171						
12	24	M. Alboreto	1'25.421	1'21.793	3.233	**Non-Qualifiers**					
13	20	E. Comas	1'23.514	1'22.211	3.651	25	30	H.H. Frentzen	Broker Sauber Mercedes		
14	15	A. de Cesaris	1'24.519	1'22.265	3.705	26	29	K. Wendlinger	Broker Sauber Mercedes		

This saw Berger lose his second place as he spun on the greased surface to allow Brundle in and that's the way it stayed to the finish leaving Schumacher to claim his fourth successive victory and open up a commanding lead in the race for the title ⚑

Schumacher and Brundle take home the silverware

The Championship

Race Placing and Points

Drivers' Points		Constructors' Points	
10	M. Schumacher	10	Benetton
6	M. Brundle	6	McLaren, Ferrari
4	G. Berger	3	Jordan
3	A. de Cesaris	1	Minardi
2	J. Alesi		
1	M. Alboreto		

Leaderboard after Round Four

Drivers' Points		Constructors' Points	
40	M. Schumacher	40	Benetton
10	G. Berger	22	Ferrari
7	R. Barrichello	10	Jordan
	D. Hill		McLaren
6	N. Larini	7	Williams
	J. Alesi	6	Sauber
	M. Brundle	4	Tyrrell
4	K. Wendlinger	3	Footwork
	U. Katayama	1	Larrouse
	M. Hakkinen		Minardi
3	C. Fittipaldi		
	A. de Cesaris		
2	H. H. Frentzen		
1	E. Comas, M. Alboreto		

Race Placings

Pos	No	Driver	Team	Time	Diff	Grid	
1	5	M. Schumacher	Mild Seven Benetton Ford	1:49'55.372	–	1	
2	8	M. Brundle	Marlboro McLaren Peugeot	1:50'32.650	37.278	8	
3	28	G. Berger	Ferrari	1:51'12.196	1'16.824	3	
4	15	A. de Cesaris	Sasol Jordan	–	1 lap down	14	
5	27	J. Alesi	Ferrari	–	1 lap down	5	
6	24	M. Alboreto	Minardi Scuderia Italia	–	1 lap down	2	
7	6	J.J. Lehto	Mild Seven Benetton Ford	–	1 lap down	17	
8	19	O. Beretta	Tourtel Larrousse F1	–	2 laps down	8	
9	26	O. Panis	Ligier Gitanes Blondes	–	2 laps down	20	
10	20	E. Comas	Tourtel Larrousse F1	–	3 laps down	13	
11	11	P. Lamy	Team Lotus	–	5 laps down	19	

Failed to Finish

12	12	J. Herbert	Team Lotus	–	68 laps	16	(Gearbox)
13	33	P. Belmondo	Pacific Grand Prix Ltd	–	63 laps	24	(Driver fatigue)
14	34	B. Gachot	Pacific Grand Prix Ltd	–	49 laps	23	(Gearbox)
15	9	C. Fittipaldi	Footwork Arrows Ford	–	47 laps	6	(Gearbox)
16	31	D. Brabham	MTV Simtek Ford	–	5 laps	22	(Accident)
17	4	M. Blundell	Tyrrell	–	40 laps	10	(Engine)
18	3	U. Katayama	Tyrrell	–	38 laps	11	(Gearbox)
19	25	E. Bernard	Ligier Gitanes Blondes	–	34 laps	21	(Spin)
20	14	R. Barrichello	Sasol Jordan	–	27 laps	15	(Electrical)
21	0	D. Hill	Rothmans Williams Renault	–	0 laps	4	(Accident)
22	7	M. Hakkinen	Marlboro McLaren Peugeot	–	0 laps	2	(Accident)
23	10	G. Morbidelli	Footwork Arrows Ford	–	0 laps	7	(Accident)
24	23	P. Martini	Minardi Scuderia Italia	–	0 laps	9	(Accident)

Fastest Lap: M. Schumacher – 1'21.078 (91.784mph/147.772kph).

Average Speed of Winner: 141.690kph

Spain

Triumph in the heat and dust

Gerhard Berger's problems started and ended with the Ferrari's Achilles heel – the gearbox.

The grim toll of casualties in F1 continued just prior to the Spanish Grand Prix when Pedro Lamy had a horrific crash in testing at Silverstone. The Portuguese driver's Lotus failed to take the left hand Abbey Curve, spun across the road and hit the top of the outer wall before cutting through the safety fencing and coming to rest in the spectator exit tunnel. Lamy fractured both knees, and received various other injuries to wrist, thumb and head but, fortunately, was not in a critical condition. Other changes saw Eddie Irvine back from his suspension to take back the ride for Jordan which seemed ill luck on Andrea de Cesaris after he had got the car home in fourth at Monaco whilst David Coulthard was promoted from his test driving role at Williams to make his F1 debut for the stricken team. Simtek replaced the ill fated Roland Ratzenberger with 29 year old Italian Andrea Montermini but they must have shuddered in disbelief when the replacement driver had a horrific crash in qualifying at the exit to the last corner before the main straight. The Italian got his wheels on the grass but when his right hand wheels regained grip on the tarmac the car was thrown towards a wall at over 200kph. Incredibly, although the bulkhead off the Simtek was ripped off along with the front wheels, Montermini suffered nothing more serious than mild concussion, a broken toe on his right foot and a cracked left heel.

New boy David Coulthard was only 16th after the first session but improved to ninth in the second whilst up front it was still the big names of Schumacher and Hill that dominated the front line. At the back it was also a familiar sight with the two Pacific cars once more well off the pace but with only one Sauber car in the field and

Montermini in hospital everybody qualified only for Beretta to have the embarrassment of his Larrousse packing up on the pre-parade! When the race did get underway, it was the usual sight of Schumacher setting off and giving everybody a distant view of his rear end. Hill retained his second place from the grid and Hakkinen likewise in third but the McLaren team had opted for three pit stops to everybody else's two and when the Finn came in on lap 15 he dropped to eighth. Hill pitted four laps later and then it was Schumacher's turn. That pit stop was almost disastrous for the Championship leader as when he re-emerged he had serious problems selecting gears. Hakkinen was now rushing through the field as the others made their stops and on lap 23 he overtook the German to go into the lead with Hill chasing hard after dropping to fourth following his visit to the pits. First out of the race after Beretta was Belmondo who spun his Pacific on the fourth lap when already in last place and Alboreto quickly followed with engine problems a lap later.

Debutant Coulthard was enjoying a fine race, having made a great start which saw him jump three places at the off to sixth but, like Schumacher, he was to pay dearly for his first pit stop. When he attempted to leave the pits, his Williams stalled due to an electrical problem and took an eternity to fire again and he rejoined in a

Coulthard's race Rothmans *short by an electrical problem – with his gearbox*

desperately disappointing 20th place. On the 17th lap Ukyo Katayama would have been hoping for a better birthday present than having his engine fail on him and Comas soon joined him with a water leak. By the half way stage, the field had thinned out substantially with Frentzen, Morbidelli, Berger and Gachot all having retired. Coulthard, too, couldn't stay out as his electrical problems became too great and it was a sad end to what had been an extremely promising debut and it was quickly confirmed by Williams that the Scot would retain the drive for Canada.

Damon Hill had more gearbox trouble to thank for his win – that of Michael Schumacher

Circuit de Catalunya

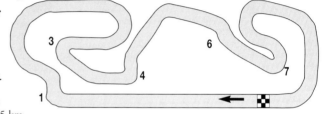

A purpose built track on the site of the Montjuich Park overlooking the Olympic city. As it is a new track it is not only fast but safe with well positioned gravel traps over its 65 laps.

Lap Distance	2.949 miles/4.747 km
Race Distance	191.727 miles/308.855 km

1. Elf — The approach to Elf is downhill until almost the corner itself when it rises. This corner is taken in third on the inside so that the car can drift out to the left for the next bend before taking on the long right hander in fourth and fifth.

2. Repsol — This continues looping back on itself until the car hits the left hairpin at Seat (3) which has to be taken in second. Then it's time to accelerate up to fifth on a short straight.

4. Wurth — The car has to slow down to third for this sharp left hander.

5. Camposa — This right hander is blind but can be navigated safely in fourth leading to a fifth gear right-left chicane at Nissan.

6. Nissan — For this race the drivers, after the carnage of the previous few weeks, insisted a temporary tyre chicane was put up to slow the cars down on the run into the chicane.

7. La Caixa — Another short straight beckons before taking this left hander that keeps on sweeping left before changing direction into a long right hander.

8. Banc de Savadell — This is exited in fourth as the car accelerates towards the penultimate corner, another right hander that turns into a short straight leading to the final bend which is taken almost flat out in fifth. Then it's on to the home straight at about 150mph.

Spanish Grand Prix – 5 Year Record

Year	1st	2nd	3rd	4th	5th	6th
1989	Senna (McLaren)	Berger (Ferrari)	Prost (McLaren)	Alesi (Tyrrell)	Patrese (Williams)	Alliot (Lola)
1990	Prost (Ferrari)	Mansell (Ferrari)	Nannini (Benetton)	Boutsen (Williams)	Patrese (Williams)	Suzuki (Lola)
1991	Mansell (Williams)	Prost (Ferrari)	Patrese (Williams)	Alesi (Ferrari)	Senna (McLaren)	Schumacher (Benetton)
1992	Mansell (Williams)	Schumacher (Benetton)	Alesi (Ferrari)	Berger (McLaren)	Alboreto (Footwork)	Martini (Dallara)
1993	Prost (Williams)	Senna (McLaren)	Schumacher (Benetton)	Patrese (Benetton)	Andretti (McLaren)	Berger (Ferrari)

1994 Grid Positions and Qualifying Times

Grid No	Driver	1st Session	2nd Session	Diff	Grid No	Driver	1st Session	2nd Session	Diff
1	5	M. Schumacher	1'23.426	1'21.908	–	16	20	E. Comas	1'26.097	1'25.050	3.142
2	0	D. Hill	1'24.716	1'22.559	0.651	17	19	O. Beretta	1'28.011	1'25.161	3.253
3	7	M. Hakkinen	1'24.580	1'22.660	0.752	18	23	P. Martini	1'25.502	1'25.247	3.339
4	6	J.J. Lehto	1'25.587	1'22.983	1.075	19	26	O. Panis	1'27.872	1'25.577	3.669
5	14	R. Barrichello	1'25.990	1'23.594	1.686	20	25	E. Bernard	1'28.289	1'25.766	3.858
6	27	J. Alesi	1'24.957	1'23.700	1.792	21	9	C. Fittipaldi	1'27.631	1'26.084	4.176
7	28	G. Berger	1'26.121	1'23.715	1.807	22	12	J. Herbert	1'59.009	1'26.397	4.489
8	8	M. Brundle	1'26.614	1'23.763	1.855	23	11	A. Zanardi	1'30.379	1'27.685	5.777
9	2	D. Coulthard	1'27.428	1'23.782	1.874	24	31	D. Brabham	1'30.797	1'28.151	6.243
10	3	U. Katayama	1'27.017	1'23.969	2.061	25	34	B. Gachot	1'34.318	1'28.873	6.965
11	4	M. Blundell	1'25.863	1'23.981	2.073	26	33	P. Belmondo	1'31.750	1'30.657	8.749
12	30	H. H. Frentzen	1'25.115	1'24.254	2.346	**Non-Qualifiers**					
13	15	E. Irvine	1'26.368	1'24.930	3.022	27	32	A. Montermini	1'31.111	No Time	
14	24	M. Alboreto	1'26.595	1'24.996	3.088						
15	10	G. Morbidelli	1'27.459	1'25.018	3.110						

Schumacher was by now coming to grips with his gearbox trouble but Hill had taken over in front at Hakkinen's pit stop which dropped the Finn to third behind the Brit and German. In fourth was Lehto, followed at a safe distance by Brundle. Schumacher retook the lead on lap 41 when Hill made his final pit stop but the Brit was back in the lead four laps later when the German and Hakkinen pitted. The Finn's race was now almost over for, on lap 49, a great black cloud of oily smoke erupted from the McLaren and it was left to Hill and Schumacher to coast home virtually unchallenged. With both the leaders taking it easy and with others retiring, Blundell was able to make it on to the podium followed by Alesi and Martini although the happiest of all, bar Hill, may just have been the back from suspension Irvine in sixth. But, 26 years after Graham Hill's victory in the Spanish Grand Prix lifted the souls after Jimmy Clark's untimely death, so his son, Damon, emulated the feat by giving the Williams team the sort of boost they must have been very badly in need of following the Senna tragedy at Imola ❖

The Championship

Race Placing and Points

Drivers' Points		Constructors' Points	
10	D. Hill	10	Williams
6	M. Schumacher	6	Benetton
4	M. Blundell	4	Tyrrell
3	J. Alesi	3	Ferrari
2	P. Martini	2	Minardi
1	E. Irvine	1	Jordan

Leaderboard after Round Five

Drivers' Points		Constructors' Points	
46	M. Schumacher	46	Benetton
17	D. HIll	25	Ferrari
10	G. Berger	17	Hill
9	J. Alesi	11	Jordan
7	R. Barrichello	10	McLaren
6	N. Larini, M.Brundle	8	Tyrrell
4	K. Wendlinger	6	Sauber
	U. Katayama	3	Footwork
	M. Hakkinen		Minardi
	M. Blundell	1	Larrousse
3	C. Fittipaldi		
	A. de Cesaris		

Drivers with 2 points or less not included.

Race Placings

Pos	No	Driver	Team	Time	Diff	Grid	
1	0	D. Hill	Rothmans Williams Renault	1:36'14.374	–	2	
2	5	M. Schumacher	Mild Seven Benetton Ford	1:36'38.540	24.166	1	
3	4	M. Blundell	Tyrrell	1:37'41.343	1'26.969	11	
4	27	J. Alesi	Ferrari	–	1 lap down	6	
5	23	P. Martini	Minardi Scuderia Italia	–	1 lap down	18	
6	15	E. Irvine	Sasol Jordan	–	1 lap down	13	
7	26	O. Panis	Ligier Gitanes Blondes	–	2 laps down	19	
8	25	E. Bernard	Ligier Gitanes Blondes	–	3 laps down	20	
9	11	A. Zanardi	Team Lotus	–	3 laps down	23	
10	31	D. Brabham	MTV Simtek Ford	–	4 laps down	24	
11	8	M. Brundle	Marlboro McLaren Peugeot	–	6 laps down	8	

Failed to Finish

Pos	No	Driver	Team	Time	Diff	Grid	
12	6	J.J. Lehto	Mild Seven Benetton Ford	–	53 laps	6	(Engine)
13	7	M. Hakkinen	Marlboro McLaren Peugeot	–	48 laps	3	(Engine)
14	12	J. Herbert	Team Lotus	–	41 laps	22	(Spin)
15	14	R. Barrichello	Sasol Jordan	–	39 laps	5	(Engine)
16	9	C. Fittipaldi	Footwork Arrows Ford	–	35 laps	21	(Engine)
17	2	D. Coulthard	Rothmans Williams Renault	–	32 laps	9	(Gearbox)
18	34	B. Gachot	Pacific Grand Prix Ltd	–	32 laps	25	(Wing damage)
19	28	G. Berger	Ferrari	–	27 laps	7	(Gearbox)
20	10	G. Morbidelli	Footwork Arrows Ford	–	24 laps	5	(Fuel valve)
21	30	H.H. Frentzen	Broker Sauber Mercedes	–	21 laps	12	(Gearbox)
22	20	E. Comas	Tourtel Larrousse F1	–	19 laps	16	(Water)
23	3	U. Katayama	Tyrrell	–	16 laps	10	(Engine)
24	24	M. Alboreto	Minardi Scuderia Italia	–	4 laps	14	(Engine)
25	33	P. Belmondo	Pacific Grand Prix Ltd	–	3 laps	26	(Spin)
26	19	O. Beretta	Tourtel Larrousse F1	–	0 laps		(Engine problem on parade lap)

Fastest Lap: M. Schumacher – 1'25.155 (124.648mph/200.683kph)

Average Speed of Winner: 192.366kph.

Canada

Team talk problems

Circuit Gilles Villeneuve – 12 June 1994

Jean Alesi on his way to an impressive third place in the ever improving Ferrari.

After Schumacher's first defeat of the season in Spain, this race was eagerly awaited to see whether his opponents could impose another set back on the German and thus instill some vestige of competition for the title which seemed to be heading inexorably his way.

For three of the four practice sessions, it seemed as though perhaps the bubble may have burst with Alesi's Ferrari dominating proceedings as Schumacher's engine blew up. The Saturday afternoon final qualifying session became a battle of the *Birthday Boys* as Benetton engineer Pat Symonds worked through the day getting the set ups right on Schumacher's new engine whilst Alesi hoped to celebrate his 30th birthday with pole. In the end, it was Symonds who was celebrating the most as Schumacher captured his third successive pole, but Alesi was a creditable second with team mate Berger in third, ahead of Hill and the second Williams driven by Coulthard. Minardi brought their new M194's to Canada but Martini opted for the old M193 for his first practice before quickly changing to the new car for the rest of the qualifying sessions. Team mate Michele Alboreto went straight into the M194 but suffered both an oil leak and clutch failure leaving the new motors in 15th and 18th places. Bringing up the rear was David Brabham in the lone Simtek whilst the Pacific's, despite modifications, were again last with Gachot grabbing the final place to leave team mate Paul Belmondo as the non-qualifier.

If there had been any doubts as to whether Schumacher could quickly regain his number one spot, they disappeared within seconds of the start as the Benetton raced ahead at the off and stayed there for the following 190 miles. As early as the first corner, there was clear daylight between the German and Alesi whilst Coulthard also made a great getaway to overtake team-mate, Damon Hill.

The first retirement came on the fourth lap when Brundle's engine cut out with Frentzen quickly joining him as he misjudged a chicane to hit the kerb and spin into the tyre wall. Sauber's other car didn't last much longer either, as De Cesaris retired on lap 25 with falling oil pressure. But up front it was Schumacher from Alesi with Berger in third. The second Ferrari, however, was making life very difficult for the chasing pack to get near Alesi and was to provoke a major row between the Williams drivers. Coulthard was in fourth but couldn't get past Berger which was obviously upsetting Hill, who clearly fancied his chances but was unable to mount a challenge on third because of his own team mate. Eventually Coulthard was instructed from the pits to allow Hill to pass and the Scot waved the second Williams through, only to get a different sort of hand gesture back from the Englishman!

Once on Berger's tail, Hill closed quickly and on lap 15 took third spot. Berger pitted on lap 22 which enabled Coulthard to go fourth but Schumacher seemed to be running for ever as Alesi went in the pits on lap 31 and Hill two laps later. The Englishman got the better of these pit exchanges to eventually emerge in second but Schumacher had built up such a commanding lead that, by the time he finally stopped for fuel on his 40th circuit, he still held a comfortable cushion when he returned to the race.

Pit stops were to prove the undoing, however, of Katayama for his first took over a minute when a rear wheel nut locked and then his front wheel nuts gave the same problem on his second. Irvine went out on lap 41 when he spun trying to lap Zanardi at the left-right flick that opens on to the pit straight. He went backwards in to the wall and then Katayama was also out, spinning on lap 46. A circuit later Comas, having earned two *stop and go* ten second penalties for speeding in the pit lanes, retired with clutch problems and just when it seemed that Pacific may get a finish, Gachot came in with falling oil pressure.

Meanwhile, following his pit stops, Coulthard had dropped to seventh but was chasing Barrichello hard. The Brazilian was experiencing great problems with his gears and was to fall away but gained a place when Morbidelli dropped out of the race when holding fourth place. The Italian's high position had been achieved on the strength of one pit stop against most of the other drivers' two and he looked capable of holding on to his position before his gearbox packed in on his 52nd circuit.

Michael Schumacher at speed.

Circuit Gilles Villeneuve

A clockwise track situated on Notre Dame Island, across the St. Lawrence river from Montreal, its 69 laps seem all the harder on a narrow and twisty track.

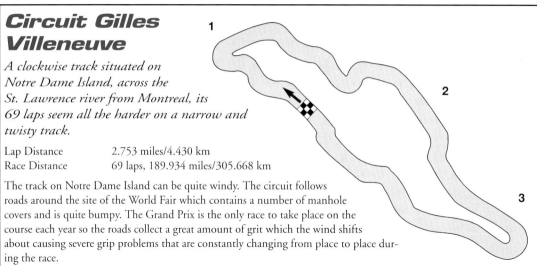

Lap Distance	2.753 miles/4.430 km
Race Distance	69 laps, 189.934 miles/305.668 km

The track on Notre Dame Island can be quite windy. The circuit follows roads around the site of the World Fair which contains a number of manhole covers and is quite bumpy. The Grand Prix is the only race to take place on the course each year so the roads collect a great amount of grit which the wind shifts about causing severe grip problems that are constantly changing from place to place during the race.

The start/finish straight runs alongside the Olympic Rowing Basin towards Island Hairpin(1) which is taken in second and sometimes even first gear. Out of Island Hairpin there is just time to get up to fifth before a right-left chicane is taken in third. There is then a big right-hander to be taken in fifth. Almost immediately the cars are dropped into second for the next chicane, a left-right combination before the long back straight which runs adjacent to the St Lawrence River (2). Then a right-left chicane, which can be taken in third, beckons and then its flat out towards the second hairpin.

Pits Hairpin (3) is a long loop which often sees a lot of overtaking action as it is quite wide. Out of Pits Hairpin the cars have yet another chicane to negotiate before they can approach the home straight which is guarded by one final chicane.

Canadian Grand Prix – 5 Year Record

Year	1st	2nd	3rd	4th	5th	6th
1989	Boutsen (Williams)	Patrese (Williams)	De Cesaris (Dallara)	Piquet (Lotus)	Arnoux (Ligier)	Caffi (Dallara)
1990	Senna (Williams)	Piquet (Benetton)	Mansell (Ferrari)	Berger (McLaren)	Prost (Ferrari)	Warwick (Lotus)
1991	Piquet (Benetton)	Modena (Tyrrell)	Patrese (Williams)	De Cesaris (Jordan)	Gachot (Jordan)	Mansell (Williams)
1992	Berger (McLaren)	Schumacher (Benetton)	Alesi (Ferrari)	Wendlinger (March)	De Cesaris (Tyrrell)	Comas (Ligier)
1993	Prost (Williams)	Schumacher (Benetton)	Hill (Williams)	Berger (Ferrari)	Brundle (Ligier)	Wendlinger (Sauber)

1994 Grid Positions and Qualifying Times

Grid No		Driver	1st Session	2nd Session	Diff	Grid No		Driver	1st Session	2nd Session	Diff
1	5	M. Schumacher	1'26.820	1'26.178	–	16	9	C. Fittipaldi	1'29.493	1'28.882	2.704
2	27	J. Alesi	1'26.277	1'26.319	0.099	17	12	J. Herbert	1'30.063	1'28.889	2.711
3	28	G. Berger	1'27.652	1'27.059	0.881	18	24	M. Alboreto	1'29.597	1'28.903	2.725
4	0	D. Hill	1'28.011	1'27.094	0.916	19	26	O. Panis	1'29.530	1'28.950	2.772
5	2	D. Coulthard	1'28.636	1'27.211	1.033	20	6	J.J. Lehto	1'29.580	1'28.993	2.815
6	14	R. Barrichello	1'28.612	1'27.554	1.376	21	20	E. Comas	1'29.653	1'29.039	2.861
7	7	M. Hakkinen	1'27.616	1'27.851	1.438	22	19	O. Beretta	1'31.167	1'29.403	3.225
8	15	E. Irvine	1'28.843	1'27.780	1.602	23	11	A. Zanardi	1'31.698	1'30.160	3.982
9	3	U. Katayama	1'27.827	1'27.953	1.649	24	25	E. Bernard	1'30.806	1'30.493	4.315
10	30	H. H. Frentzen	1'28.048	1'27.977	1.799	25	31	D. Brabham	1'32.273	1'31.632	5.454
11	10	G. Morbidelli	1'28.730	1'27.989	1.811	26	34	B. Gachot	1'32.838	1'32.877	6.660
12	8	M. Brundle	1'28.451	1'28.197	2.019						
13	4	M. Blundell	1'29.108	1'28.579	2.401	**Non-Qualifiers**					
14	29	A. De Cesaris	1'29.793	1'28.694	2.516	27	33	P. Belmondo	1'33.291	1'33.006	6.828
15	23	P. Martini	1'29.691	1'28.847	2.669						

With Morbidelli's defection, Coulthard was now up to sixth, behind Hakkinen but in front of Fittipaldi and Lehto. Schumacher remained well out in front, followed by Hill who, in turn, had a comfortable margin to spare over Alesi. Berger, a respectful distance behind Alesi, was being challenged by Hakkinen for fourth and the flying Finn looked like celebrating his McLaren team's 400th Grand Prix start with points when his engine failed after 62 laps. Alesi very nearly didn't make it to the line as he was stuck in second gear with the box jammed solid and, had he not been so close to the finish, his race would have been over. As it was, he hung on to four points by just two seconds from Berger with Coulthard emulating the late Jim Clark by finishing fifth in only his second Grand Prix.

Several hours after the race ended, however, it was announced that Christian Fittipaldi's Footwork had been disqualified as his car was found to be 2.5kg underweight which gave the promoted Lehto his first point of the season for the second Benetton. But the race had effectively followed the path of qualifying with the first five home occupying the first five grid places, albeit not in the same order. There was no doubting the qualities of the first Benetton, however, whose win in Canada left Schumacher a mighty 33 points clear after his fifth win in six starts ▩

The Championship

Race Placing and Points

Drivers' Points		Constructors' Points	
10	M. Schumacher	11	Benetton
6	D. Hill	8	Williams
4	J. Alesi	7	Ferrari
3	G. Berger		
2	D. Coulthard		
1	J.J. Lehto		

Leaderboard after Round Six

Drivers' Points		Constructors' Points	
56	M. Schumacher	57	Benetton
23	D. Hill	32	Ferrari
13	G. Berger, J. Alesi	25	Williams
7	R. Barrichello	11	Jordan

NB Drivers with 6 points or less not listed.

Race Placings

Pos	No	Driver	Team	Time	Diff	Grid	
1	5	M. Schumacher	Mild Seven Benetton Ford	1:44'31.887	–	1	
2	0	D. Hill	Rothmans Williams Renault	1:45'11.547	0'39.660	4	
3	27	J. Alesi	Ferrari	1:45'45.275	1'13.388	2	
4	28	G. Berger	Ferrari	1:45'47.496	1'15.609	3	
5	2	D. Coulthard	Rothmans Williams Renault	–	1 lap down	5	
6	6	J.J. Lehto	Mild Seven Benetton Ford	–	1 lap down	20	
7	14	R. Barrichello	Sasol Jordan	–	1 lap down	6	
8	12	J. Herbert	Team Lotus	–	1 lap down	17	
9	23	P. Martini	Minardi Scuderia Italia	–	1 lap down	15	
10	4	M. Blundell	Tyrrell	–	2 laps down	13	
11	24	M. Alboreto	Minardi Scuderia Italia	–	2 laps down	18	
12	26	O. Panis	Ligier Gitanes Blondes	–	3 laps down		
14	31	D. Brabham	MTV Simtek Ford	–	4 laps down		

Failed to Finish

Pos	No	Driver	Team	Time	Diff	Grid	
15	11	A. Zanardi	Team Lotus	–	62 laps	23	(Engine)
16	7	M. Hakkinen	Marlboro McLaren Peugeot	–	61 laps	7	(Engine)
17	19	O. Beretta	Tourtel Larrousse F1	–	57 laps	22	(Engine)
18	10	G. Morbidelli	Footwork Arrows Ford	–	50 laps	11	(Gearbox)
19	34	B. Gachot	Pacific Grand Prix	–	47 laps	26	(Oil Pressure)
20	20	E. Comas	Tourtel Larrousse F1	–	45 laps	21	(Clutch)
21	3	U. Katayama	Tyrrell	–	44 laps	9	(Spin)
22	15	E. Irvine	Sasol Jordan	–	40 laps	8	(Spin)
23	29	A. De Cesaris	Sauber Mercedes-Benz	–	24 laps	14	(Oil leak)
24	30	H. H. Frentzen	Sauber Mercedes-Benz	–	5 laps	10	(Spin)
25	4	M. Brundle	Marlboro McLaren Peugeot	–	3 laps	12	(Electrical)

Disqualified

–	9	C. Fittipaldi	Footwork Arrows Ford – Finished sixth but car did not meet minimum weight regulation				

Fastest Lap: M. Schumacher – 1'28.927 (111.939mph/180.147kph)

Average Speed of Winner: 176.243kph

France
Past master returns

Mika Hakkinen, his engine ablaze, drives around the circuit to the nearest fire point to have the flames extinguished by awaiting marshals.

F1 (or to be more precise, Williams and a reported £1m) had finally tempted the 1992 Champion, Nigel Mansell, back from his sojourn on the other side of the Atlantic and Indy Car racing. Indeed, if anybody was going to break the stranglehold that Schumacher had on the 1994 title, it was thought by many that this one-off appearance by the Briton might just be the occasion as the Williams car had never lost at Magny-Cours and neither had Mansell, who won in both 1991 and 1992 whilst Williams had taken 1-2 in the last two seasons.

Benetton replaced J.J. Lehto by giving the drive in their second car to the recalled Jos Versteppan who had deputised for Lehto in Brazil and Japan earlier in the Championship whilst, at the other end of the scale, Jean-Marc Gounon made his debut for Simtek.

Mansell eased himself back in to F1 with a test drive at Brands Hatch on the Tuesday prior to Magny-Cours and was astonished to find a five figure crowd turn up just to watch him get used to the car! If people were expecting big things from the Indy Car Champion, they were to be initially disappointed when, in the Friday qualifying session, Mansell found no fewer than six drivers finishing in front of him with Schumacher in his accustomed lead role.

However, Saturday was to prove, perhaps, the most exciting qualifying session for years with Mansell playing his part to the full. Alesi took the pole away from Schumacher but the German quickly regained it before losing it to Mansell. In the middle of all this action, Versteppan had an accident that could have resulted in very serious consequences when he failed to handle the Lycee and smacked into the pit wall, sending debris flying into the McLaren pit and fortunately destroying only television monitors rather than the engineers who were in the pit. A very near miss indeed.

When qualifying resumed, Hill dislodged his new team-mate from the lead with Berger then coming into the reckoning by depositing Mansell into third. But pole changed yet again when Nigel hit back only for Hill to do better still with just six minutes remaining. So, after having been first and second in the last two runnings of the French GP at Magny-Cours, Williams now found themselves first and second on the grid to give themselves real hope of stopping Schumacher.

There was other good news for British followers with Oxford based new boys, Simtek out qualifying an *established* car for the first time. Any pretentions Williams had of dominating the race from the front line of the grid, however, were quickly dispelled when Hill was amazed to find Schumacher going past him by the first corner after the Englishman had made, in his own words, *"My second best start of the season"*! The German, however, described his own getaway as *"Perfect – it really couldn't have been better"*. Mansell, meanwhile, was down to third whilst an early pit stop soon saw him drop to fifth but Schumacher, having assumed the lead, did not manage to drive away into the distance as in the earlier rounds.

By the fifteenth lap both Hill and Schumacher had lapped Verstappen in the second Benetton following a trip into the gravel by Lehto's replacement on lap 11 and only 0.6 seconds separated the two leaders. The first retirement came on lap 20 when Zanardi's Lotus caught fire whilst Alboreto quickly joined him two laps later. Irvine, having out-qualified team-mate Rubens Barrichello for the first time since the Irishman's debut race in Suzuki, went out on lap 25 with gearbox problems and a lap later Verstappen called it a day when he visited the gravel for a second time. Lap 29 saw more retirements with Brabham's transmission failing but Panis was even unluckier when his Ligier was involved in a collision with Morbidelli putting both out of the contest and almost taking out Schumacher, who was about to lap them. Brundle continued the high casualty rate when he quit whilst racing in a comfortable seventh, saying the car simply was not handling properly.

Up front, the two leaders powered ever onwards and by lap 31, Katayama, de Cesaris, Martini, Fittipaldi, Beretta, Herbert, Blundell, Bernard, Comas and newcomer, Gounon, had all been lapped. Within another ten laps it didn't make much difference to three of them as Beretta, Blundell and Bernard had all joined the sidelines and on lap 42 Barrichello and Alesi went also. The Brazilian was looking good for a top

Spot the driver! Nigel Mansell's "guest" appearance at Magny-Cours fuelled speculation about his return to Formula 1 for 1995.

Circuit Magny-Cours

The 72 lap clockwise track is known for its flat surface and few long straights making overtaking difficult.

Lap Distance   2.640 miles/4.289 km
Race Distance   190.139 miles/
                    305.998 km

Since staging its first Grand Prix in 1991 it has gained a reputation for acting quickly to demands for change. It was no surprise then to learn that following serious accidents at other venues the Magny-Cours circuit installed an additional 10,000 safety tyres, 3,000 metres of additional fencing, and 9,000 tonnes of extra gravel as well as demolishing some 960 metres of concrete walling.

1. Grande Courbe   Because the bend leading to this long right hander is a left hander taken in sixth, it is difficult to get the car on the right line entering the bend, itself negotiated in fourth, before exiting to...
2. Estoril   The long back straight, usually taken flat out.
3. Adelaide   The straight finishes abruptly at Adelaide which is a 180 degree, second gear hairpin taking the vehicle back in the direction from which it has just come, towards...
4. Nurburgring   A fast right-left that is cleared in fourth leads to Nurburgring which itself is not as tight as Adelaide but, nevertheless, is taken in second gear despite it being long and wide.
5. Imola   From Nurburgring it's up quickly through the gears to fifth before changing down to meet the challenge of Imola, a right-left that protects...
6. Chateaux d'Eau   A virtual 90 degree turn entered in second and exited in third on to a straight that allows the car to accelerate towards a second gear chicane.
7. Lycee   Immediately following the chicane is the sharp Lycee right hander taken in third that opens into the pits straight.

French Grand Prix – 5 Year Record

Year	1st	2nd	3rd	4th	5th	6th
1989	Prost (McLaren)	Mansell (Ferrari)	Patrese (Williams)	Alesi (Tyrrell)	Johansson (Onyx)	Grouillard (Ligier)
1990	Prost (Ferrari)	Capelli (March)	Senna (McLaren)	Piquet (Benetton)	Berger (McLaren)	Patrese (Williams)
1991	Mansell (Williams)	Prost (Ferrari)	Senna (McLaren)	Alesi (Ferrari)	Patrese (Williams)	de Cesaris (Jordan)
1992	Mansell (Williams)	Patrese (Williams)	Brundle (Benetton)	Hakkinen (Lotus)	Comas (Ligier)	Herbert (Lotus)
1993	Prost (Williams)	Hill (Williams)	Schumacher (Benetton)	Senna (McLaren)	Brundle (Ligier)	Andretti (McLaren)

1994 Grid Positions and Qualifying Times

Grid	No	Driver	1st Session	2nd Session	Diff	Grid	No	Driver	1st Session	2nd Session	Diff
1	0	D. Hill	1'17.539	1'16.282	–	16	23	P. Martini	1'20.084	1'18.248	1.966
2	2	N. Mansell	1'18.340	1'16.359	0.077	17	4	M. Blundell	1'20.001	1'18.381	2.099
3	5	M. Schumacher	1'17.085	1'16.707	0.425	18	9	C. Fittipaldi	1'20.801	1'18.568	2.286
4	27	J. Alesi	1'17.855	1'16.954	0.672	19	12	J. Herbert	1'20.108	1'18.715	2.433
5	28	G. Berger	1'17.441	1'16.959	0.677	20	20	E. Comas	1'20.576	1'18.811	2.529
6	15	E. Irvine	1'19.463	1'17.441	1.159	21	24	M. Alboreto	1'20.097	1'18.890	2.608
7	14	R. Barrichello	1'20.108	1'18.715	1.200	22	10	G. Morbidelli	1'20.707	1'18.936	2.654
8	6	J. Verstappen	1'18.669	1'17.645	1.363	23	11	A. Zanardi	1'20.122	1'19.066	2.784
9	7	M. Hakkinen	1'19.041	1'17.768	1.486	24	31	D. Brabham	1'22.527	1'19.771	3.489
10	30	H.H. Frentzen	1'19.318	1'17.830	1.548	25	19	O. Beretta	1'21.964	1'19.863	3.581
11	29	A. de Cesaris	1'20.145	1'17.866	1.584	26	32	J.M. Gounon	1'23.264	1'21.829	5.547
12	8	M. Brundle	1'18.112	1'18.031	1.749						
13	26	O. Panis	1'19.967	1'18.044	1.762	**Non-Qualifiers**					
14	3	U. Katayama	1'19.969	1'18.192	1.910	33		P. Belmondo	1'24.637	1'21.952	5.670
15	25	E. Bernard	1'19.292	1'18.236	1.954	34		B. Gachot	1'24.008	1'23.004	6.722

four placing when Alesi made a mess of the chicane before Lycee causing him to spin wildly out of control and in to the gravel. On rejoining the race he didn't appear to see Barrichello and moved straight in to the path of the oncoming Jordan which put both cars out.

The accident put Mansell up to fourth in his comeback race but it was not to last much longer as he coasted to a stop on lap 46 at Adelaide with his transmission having failed. The former was a long time getting out of the car which fuelled suggestions that he had found his return a bit more exhausting than he had allowed for.

Hill was now losing ground on Schumacher until the German pitted on lap 55 which reduced his advantage to about 15 seconds but the race, with the pit stops exhausted, was now over bar accidents. Berger was a lonely third and Frentzen's Sauber, promoted when Hakkinen retired on lap 49, fourth. Next came Martini but Sauber breathed a sigh of relief as de Cesaris hung on to sixth by literally inches from the fast finishing Herbert to get both their cars in the

points whilst an absolutely delighted Gounon came home in ninth on his debut for Simtek. But, once more, the Schumacher band-wagon rolled on up front to make it six out of seven ▓

The Championship

Race Placing and Points

Drivers' Points		Constructors' Points	
10	M. Schumacher	10	Benetton
6	D. Hill	6	Williams
4	G. Berger	4	Ferrari, Sauber
3	H.H. Frentzen	2	Minardi
2	P. Martini		
1	A. de Cesaris		

Points after Round Seven

Drivers' Points		Constructors' Points	
66	M. Schumacher	67	Benetton
29	D. Hill	36	Ferrari
17	G. Berger	31	Williams
13	J. Alesi	11	Jordan
7	R. Barrichello	10	McLaren
6	Larini		Sauber
	Brundle	8	Tyrrell

Race Placings

Pos	No	Driver	Team	Time	Diff	Grid	
1	5	M. Schumacher	Mild Seven Benetton Ford	1:38'35.704	–	3	
2	0	D. Hill	Rothmans Williams Renault	1:38'48.346	12.642	1	
3	28	G. Berger	Ferrari	1:39'28.469	52.765	5	
4	30	H.H. Frentzen	Sauber	–	1 lap	10	
5	23	P. Martini	Minardi Scuderia Italia	–	2 laps	16	
6	29	A. de Cesaris	Sauber	–	2 laps	11	
7	12	J. Herbert	Team Lotus	–	2 laps	19	
8	9	C. Fittipaldi	Footwork Arrows Ford	–	2 laps	18	
9	32	J.M. Gounon	Simtek Ford	–	4 laps	26	
10	4	M. Blundell	Tyrrell	–	5 laps	17	

Failed to Finish

11	20	E. Comas	Tourtel Larrousse	–	66 laps	20	(Engine)
12	3	U. Katayama	Tyrrell	–	53 laps	14	(Spin)
13	7	M. Hakkinen	Marlboro McLaren Peugeot	–	48 laps	9	(Engine)
14	27	J. Alesi	Ferrari	–	41 laps	4	(Accident)
15	14	R. Barrichello	Sasol Jordan	–	41 laps	7	(Accident)
16	25	E. Bernard	Ligier Gitanes Blondes	–	40 laps	15	(Gearbox)
17	19	O. Beretta	Tourtel Larrousse	–	36 laps	25	(Engine)
18	8	M. Brundle	Marlboro McLaren Peugeot	–	29 laps	12	(Engine)
19	10	G. Morbidelli	Footwork Arrows Ford	–	28 laps	22	(Accident)
20	26	O. Panis	Ligier Gitanes Blondes	–	28 laps	13	(Accident)
21	31	D. Brabham	Simtek Ford	–	28 laps	24	(Gearbox)
22	6	J. Versteppan	Mild Seven Benetton Ford	–	25 laps	8	(Spin)
23	15	E. Irvine	Sasol Jordan	–	24 laps	6	(Gearbox)
24	24	M. Alboreto	Minardi Scuderia Italia	–	21 laps	21	(Engine)
25	11	A. Zanardi	Team Lotus	–	19 laps	23	(Engine)

Fastest Lap: D. Hill – 1'19.678 (119.318mph)

Average Speed of Winner: ??kph

Silverstone – 10 July 1994

Damon Hill delivers the result the crowd wanted – first place in his home Grand Prix.

Could Hill extend the Williams sequence of victories in the British Grand Prix to four or would Schumacher turn his domination of the 1994 Championship into a first success in Britain after finishing in the top four in each of the previous two seasons?

When qualifying began it was the new Ferrari's of Alesi and Berger that initially showed they could well be a threat to the ambitions of both Schumacher and Hill. Indeed, the Briton had a hair raising experience when the front of his car began to come apart as he hurtled towards Becketts but he managed to just about keep the car on the road and brought it to a grinding halt. *"We had a problem with the suspension and it was fortunate that it broke where it did,"* Hill said afterwards in the pits adding *"It was a very nasty shock"*.

Schumacher began to get closer to the Ferrari's and took provisional pole ahead of them with Hill in fourth, Frentzen fifth and Coulthard sixth at the end of the Friday session as Irvine took the question of equality with his Jordan team mate, Ruben Barrichello, to its extreme by finishing with an identical time. A crowd of 12,000 had been attracted to the Friday qualifying session

If the qualifying for the French GP had been the most exciting for years then Saturday's session of the British equivalent was not far behind with the lead swapping several times before Hill grabbed the fourth pole of his career by just three thousandths of a second from his arch rival, Schumacher, but not before an almighty tussle. Hill set the ball rolling in the second session by immediately ducking below provisional pole but was then relieved of the lead himself by Gerhard

Berger. Then Schumacher took over before Hill put in a storming 1'24.960. With less than a minute remaining, Schumacher made one last effort but just failed to dislodge the Briton. Once again the cars to fail to qualify were the Pacifics whilst the last row belonged to Simtek.

The race got underway in controversial circumstances when Schumacher overtook Hill on the parade lap, an incident that was to see him given a stop-go penalty, black flagged for not adhering to it, then allowed to continue when he did pit and finally fined £17,000 for not complying with the original instruction. Undeterred by the controversy surrounding his rival Hill drove serenely on to give the crowd the victory they were sought in the hot afternoon sun. The Briton therefore achieved not only his fifth GP victory but also managed what his father never did in a 176 race career in taking his home country's GP.

The start was also notable for the failure of both Brundle and Irvine to move off which undermined the remote hopes of Britons filling the first five positions as they had done in 1965 when they also claimed pole and fastest lap. Brundle's engine blew up at the off leaving him stranded whilst Irvine went out even earlier as his engine seized up on the formation lap. Also in trouble on the formation lap was Coulthard who stalled and had to start from the back of the grid after originally qualifying in seventh. Others to have a short day out were Zanardi, whose throttle jammed on the warm up lap, finally causing his engine to call it a day on the fourth lap whilst Morbidelli scarcely lasted any longer with a fractured fuel pipe.

Hill made a superb start and led for the first fifteen laps before pitting and regained his position when Schumacher stopped for the second time on the 27th lap. Berger had led briefly for four laps in his Ferrari following Schumacher's first pit stop but it was to be his summit as he was forced to retire after 32 laps with engine failure leaving Alesi to battle on to third place for the Italian manufacturer. The Austrian had further bad news when it was announced he had been fined $10,000 for exceeding 80kph in the pit lane during practice. But a tight race up front was dramatically tilted in favour of Hill when Schumacher's punishment was finally delivered via a stop-go penalty of five seconds which effectively counted for about fifteen given the fact that

he had to leave the track and slow down in the pit lane before even beginning his penalty. Given the size of the winning margin it was clearly a decisive factor in the outcome of the race but, nevertheless, it has to be said that once given the advantage, the Briton never put a foot wrong.

Verstappen probably had the unluckiest drive of the day, suffering from cramp from the half way mark and was visibly distressed when eventually managing to finish ninth. But the finish, a predictable one from a long way out, took a new lease of life when Barrichello and Hakkinen experienced a completely needless collision at the last corner of the race which resulted in them being given suspended one race bans. So, the honour that eluded Graham Hill throughout his long career eventually joined the family heirlooms courtesy of his son and let nobody take anything away from Damon because of Schumacher's problems with the rules. The Briton had taken pole and then led from the off until his first pit stop, all of which was prior to the German losing his time at the *stop and go.*

But the matter was not to rest there. Some sixteen days later, FIA announced that Schumacher had been disqualified, a two race

Damon Hill, victorious on the Podium, would have to watch his back for the rest of the season to carry off the championship.

Silverstone

After the Imola tragedy over £1 million was spent in alterations to make this 59 lap clockwise circuit one of the safest in the world.

Lap Distance   3.142 miles/5.23 km
Race Distance   188.52 miles/313.80 km

1.	Copse	Previously negotiated in fifth at 250kph, it is now taken in third at approximately 150kph after safety alterations, with quick changes back to sixth before...
2.	Maggotts	Dropping down to fifth for Maggotts which guards the entrance to...
3.	Becketts	A left hander entered in fourth at 280 kph dropping to about 175kph for the exit to...
4.	Chapel	The last of the series of left-right-left-right-left bends leading to...
5.	Hangar Straight	The fastest part of the circuit at 300kph.
6.	Stowe	Previously taken at about 175kph it has been slowed to about 120kph as a result of being made much tighter.
7.	Vale	The cars go through at something like 260kph with good overtaking opportunities and a second gear, sharp left into...
8.	Club	A right hand corner with very good overtaking opportunities.
9.	Abbey	Previously taken flat out, alterations make this a third gear left-right bend.
10.	Bridge Corner	Now taken in fifth and about 250kph, 50kph slower than previously.
11-13.	Priory/Brooklands/Luffield	A series of flicks coming so close on one another that ensures it is the slowest part of the circuit before the cars emerge into...
14.	Woodcote	A quick dash to the finishing straight.

British Grand Prix – 5 Year Record

Year	1st	2nd	3rd	4th	5th	6th
1989	Prost (McLaren)	Mansell (Ferrari)	Nannini (Benetton)	Piquet (Lotus)	Martini (Minardi)	Perezsala (Minardi)
1990	Prost (Ferrari)	Boutsen (Williams)	Senna (McLaren)	Bernard (Lola)	Piquet (Benetton)	Suzuki (Lola)
1991	Mansell (Williams)	Berger (McLaren)	Prost (Ferrari)	Senna (McLaren)	Piquet (Benetton)	Gachot (Jordan)
1992	Mansell (Williams)	Patrese (Williams)	Brundle (Benetton)	Schumacher (Benetton)	Berger (McLaren)	Hakkinen (Lotus)
1993	Prost (Williams)	Schumacher (Benetton)	Patrese (Benetton)	Herbert (Lotus)	Senna (McLaren)	Warwick (Footwork)

1994 Grid Positions and Qualifying Times

Grid No		Driver	1st Session	2nd Session	Diff	Grid No		Driver	1st Session	2nd Session	Diff
1	0	D. Hill	1'26.894	1'24.960	–	16	10	G. Morbidelli	1'28.159	1'27.886	2.926
2	5	M. Schumacher	1'26.323	1'24.963	0.003	17	24	M. Alboreto	1'29.403	1'28.100	3.140
3	28	G. Berger	1'26.738	1'24.980	0.020	18	29	A. de Cesaris	1'30.034	1'28.212	3.252
4	27	J. Alesi	1'26.891	1'25.541	0.581	19	11	A. Zarnadi	1'29.240	1'28.225	3.265
5	7	M. Hakkinen	1'27.983	1'26.268	1.308	20	9	C. Fittipaldi	1'28.816	1'28.231	3.271
6	14	R. Barrichello	1'27.890	1'26.271	1.311	21	12	J. Herbert	1'29.268	1'28.340	3.380
7	2	D. Coulthard	1'27.698	1'26.337	1.377	22	24	E. Comas	1'30.274	1'28.519	3.559
8	3	U. Katayama	1'27.936	1'26.414	1.454	23	25	E. Bernard	1'30.058	1'28.519	3.995
9	8	M. Brundle	1'28.224	1'26.768	1.808	24	21	O. Beretta	1'29.971	1'29.299	4.339
10	6	J. Verstappen	1'29.142	1'26.841	1.881	25	31	D. Brabham	1'31.437	1'30.690	5.730
11	4	M. Blundell	1'28.510	1'26.920	1.960	26	32	J.M. Gounon	1'31.225	1'30.722	5.762
12	15	E. Irvine	1'27.890	1'27.065	2.105						
13	30	H.H. Frentzen	1'27.284	1'28.231	2.324	**Non-Qualifiers**					
14	23	P. Martini	1'28.517	1'27.522	2.562	34		B. Gachot	1'31.496	1'31.877	6.536
15	26	O. Panis	1'29.381	1'27.785	2.825	33		P. Belmondo	1'34.631	1'32.507	7.547

ban issued and his Silverstone points deducted along with the imposition of a Draconian £330,000 fine on Benetton for failing to bring in their driver when instructed to do so. To complete Benetton's day of woe, FIA also fined them, along with Marlboro McLaren, a further £70,000 for failing to hand over computer software for examination when requested to do so. With over 120,000 tickets sold for the German GP now just days away, Schumacher immediately lodged an appeal so that he could drive in his home race ▓

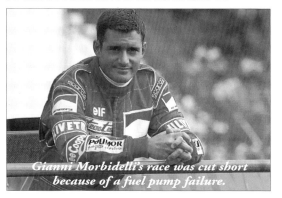

Gianni Morbidelli's race was cut short because of a fuel pump failure.

The Championship

Race Placing and Points

Drivers' Points		Constructors' Points	
10	D. Hill	11	Williams
6	M. Schumacher*	6	Benetton
4	J. Alesi	4	Ferrari
3	M. Hakkinen	3	McLaren
2	R. Barrichello	2	Jordan
1	D. Coulthard		

Points after Round Seven

Drivers' Points		Constructors' Points	
72	M. Schumacher	73	Benetton
39	D. Hill	42	Williams
17	G. Berger	40	Ferrari
	J. Alesi	13	McLaren
9	R. Barrichello		Jordan
7	M. Hakkinen	10	Sauber
6	N. Larini	8	Tyrrell
	M. Brundle	5	Minardi
5	H.H. Frentzen	3	Footwork
		1	Larrousse

*NB – Schumacher was later disqualified and the points gained in the race deducted.

Race Placings

Pos	No	Driver	Team	Time	Diff	Grid	
1	0	D. Hill	Rothmans Williams Renault	1:30'03.640	–	1	
2	5	M. Schumacher	Mild Seven Benetton Ford	1:30'22.418	18.778	2	
3	27	J. Alesi	Ferrari	1:31'11.768	1'08.128	4	
4	7	M. Hakkinen	Marlboro McLaren Peugeot	1:31'44.299	1'40.659	5	
5	14	R. Barrichello	Sasol Jordan	1:31'45.391	1'41.751	6	
6	2	D. Coulthard	Rothmans Williams Renault	–	1 lap down	7	
7	3	U. Katayama	Tyrrell	–	1 lap down	8	
8	30	H.H. Frentzen	Sauber	–	1 lap down	13	
9	6	J. Verstappen	Mild Seven Benetton Ford	–	1 lap down	0	
10	9	C. Fittipaldi	Footwork Arrows Ford	–	2 laps down	20	
11	23	P. Martini	Minardi Scuderia Italia	–	2 laps down	14	
12	12	J. Herbert	Team Lotus	–	2 laps down	21	
13	26	O. Panis	Ligier Gitanes Blondes	–	2 laps down	15	
14	25	E. Bernard	Ligier Gitanes Blondes	–	2 laps down	23	
15	19	O. Berretta	Tourtel Larrousse F1	–	2 laps down	24	
16	31	D. Brabham	Simtek Ford	–	3 laps down	25	
17	32	J.M. Gounon	Simtek Ford	–	3 laps down	26	

Failed to Finish

Pos	No	Driver	Team	Time	Diff	Grid	
18	28	G. Berger	Ferrari	–	32 laps	3	(Engine)
19	4	M. Blundell	Tyrrell	–	20 laps	11	(Electrical)
20	20	E. Comas	Tourtel Larrousse	–	11 laps	22	(Engine)
21	29	A. de Cesaris	Sauber	–	11 laps	18	(Engine)
22	10	G. Morbidelli	Footwork Arrows Ford	–	5 laps	16	(Fuel Pump)
23	11	A. Zanardi	Team Lotus	–	4 laps	19	(Engine)

Did not Start

Pos	No	Driver	Team	Time	Diff	Grid	
–	15	E. Irvine	Sasol Jordan	–	–	12	(Engine)
–	4	M. Brundle	Marlboro McLaren	–	–	9	(Engine)

Fastest Lap: D. Hill – 1'27.100 (129.822mph/209.014kph)
Average Speed of Winner: 202.143kph

The Ferrari of Gerhard Berger avoided early skirmishes to coast home in later laps.

The days leading up to the Hockenheim race saw a new row now brewing over *launch control* systems with an inquiry into Benetton's ability to use a computerised aid reporting *"In order to enable launch control, a menu with ten options has to be selected on the PC screen. Launch control is not visible amongst those ten options. Nothing else appears but if the operator of the PC scrolls down to an invisible option 13 then launch control can be activated"*. Benetton's defence to the allegation was that the option had been deliberately made invisible so that it could not be activated by error and Ross Brawn, Benetton's technical director, said the aid had been simply used to help Schumacher practice his starts as *"By his own admission, Michael had been pretty useless at the start in 1993"*. There was also considerable interest into how the cars would perform with the new stepped bottoms created by the regulation: 10mm x 300mm wooden planks fitted to reduce downforce and so reduce cornering speeds.

Once the actual action got underway, it quickly became apparent that Schumacher could struggle to beat the Williams and Ferrari's as the first qualifying session came to a close with Hill in provisional pole by some half a second from Berger's Ferrari. But their task was made easier by Benetton surprising everybody by allowing Verstappen out in Schumacher's car after the championship leader had posted the third fastest time. The Finn's own car had been made inoperable by fire extinguisher fluid but he then put Schumacher's into the gravel at the second chicane. A hot day on Saturday gave the Ferrari's the advantage they sought over Williams and for the first time since the Portuguese GP at Estoril in 1990 the front row belonged to the red Italian car. This time it was Berger and Alesi, four years earlier it had been Mansell and Prost. Williams had to be content with Hill in third and Coulthard in sixth whilst Schumacher was fourth ahead of Katayama's Tyrrell whose other car, driven by Martin Brundle, lined up seventh. As usual, the

Pacifics of Belmondo and Gachot did not make the cut but the former at least had some small consolation in the fact that he outqualified Gachot for the first time.

It had been four years since an all Ferrari front row, and not since the 1973 British Grand Prix has almost half of the cars failed to complete the first lap. The start comprised virtually four separate incidents. At the back of the grid de Cesaris, Zanardi, Martini, and Alboreto were involved in a major skirmish which took all four cars out of the race leaving the innocent Minardi team without a runner. Towards the front, Hakkinen seemed to try to get a flyer and moved in between Coulthard and the pit wall to try to get past the Briton. He then cut back across the Williams car giving it quite a stiff clip shunting both vehicles immediately in front of Blundell's Tyrrell which then took out both Jordans and Frentzen. The only car from this episode to get back in the race was Coulthard but the incident was to have a dramatic effect on Hill's chances of making ground on Schumacher. Elsewhere, Herbert and Brundle disputed the same piece of road which resulted in Herbert's afternoon being over and when Alesi's engine inexplicably cut out, eleven cars had failed to complete a lap. It seemed like the race must be stopped but instead of red flags, yellow ones appeared.

As the cars cruised round under the yellow flag, it was time to take stock and there were some surprises such as Katayama in third, Panis fourth, Verstappen fifth and Bernard sixth. But where was Hill? In his own words he *"missed a golden opportunity today"* when he attempted to pass Katayama at the third chicane on the first circuit. He touched the Japanese driver incurring structural damage. But disaster befell Hill when he drove up the pit road to find team mate Coulthard already in the pit having his damaged car from the start line incident repaired. By the time Hill got back out, he was out of contention and merely hoping for retirements elsewhere.

Up front it was Berger from Schumacher and when the German pitted as early as lap 12 it was obvious that Benetton were carrying a light fuel load as against Ferrari's one stop heavy load. Berger was therefore now under pressure in the knowledge that both cars now had just one pit stop each to make but that Schumacher's car would have the lighter fuel load. But, just as Berger was to pit on lap 20, the race tilted significantly in his path when a little puff of blue smoke appeared from the Benetton. A lap later the German flags that had been waving all afternoon were down as Schumacher headed slowly in to the pits and out of his home GP. Also out by now was Katayama after his early third place showing

Olivier Panis achieved a surprise second place, perhaps more through attrition than skill as the Legiers came home second and third.

Hockenheim

Over 45 laps and situated in the middle of a forest, its long, high speed straights make for potentially fatal shunts, putting it low on the list of favourite tracks.

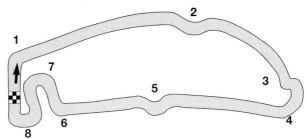

Lap Distance	4.235 miles/6.815 km
Race Distance	190.559 miles/306.675 km

It is a particularly daunting track in the rain when the long straights produce huge amounts of spray which convert quickly in to mist which cannot disperse because of the surrounding trees. The crowd is housed in permanent massive stands in a purpose built stadium area where the pits and most of the corners are housed.

1. Turn One   A fast right hander that is taken in fourth and exited in fifth ready to move up to sixth and approximate 200mph for the long run to the first chicane.
2. Bremskurve 1   Slowing to second gear for the right-left-right chicane. Prior to the race this chicane was re-named in memory of Jim Clark, the driver who died at the track.
3. Bremskurve 2   The drivers are very busy on this particular stretch. The previous straight turns into a long right hand bend about 350 metres before...
4. Ostkurve   The chicane which is a right-left taken in second gear leading into a long, fast right hander and on to the next straight.
5. Bremskurve 3   Very bumpy and fast (fourth gear) at the approach and middle section, it is exited in fifth to get back into sixth for the next straight. Re-named after Ayrton Senna prior to the race.
6. Agip kurve   A fast right hander that is taken at high speed, often still in fifth.
7. Sachs kurve   Quickly down to second for the hairpin that has a well earned reputation for being slippy.
8. Opel kurve   The final section in the stadium that leads back to the startline, the Opel kurve is a double apex hairpin taken in third and fourth before exiting on to the pits straight in

German Grand Prix – 5 Year Record

Year	1st	2nd	3rd	4th	5th	6th
1989	Senna (McLaren)	Prost (McLaren)	Mansell (Ferrari)	Patrese (Williams)	Piquet (Lotus)	Warwick (Arrows)
1990	Senna (McLaren)	Nannini (Benetton)	Berger (McLaren)	Prost (Ferrari)	Patrese (Williams)	Boutsen (Williams)
1991	Mansell (Williams)	Patrese (Williams)	Alesi (Ferrari)	Berger (McLaren)	de Cesaris (Jordan)	Gachot (Jordan)
1992	Mansell (Williams)	Senna (McLaren)	Schumacher (Benetton)	Brundle (Benetton)	Alesi (Ferrari)	Comas (Ligier)
1993	Prost (Williams)	Schumacher (Benetton)	Blundell (Ligier)	Senna (McLaren)	Patrese (Benetton)	Berger (Ferrari)

1994 Grid Positions and Qualifying Times

Grid No		Driver	1st Session	2nd Session	Diff	Grid No		Driver	1st Session	2nd Session	Diff
1	28	G. Berger	1'44.616	1'43.582	–	16	10	G. Morbidelli	1'47.814	1'46.817	3.235
2	27	J. Alesi	1'45.272	1'44.012	0.430	17	9	C. Fittipaldi	1'47.150	1'47.102	3.520
3	0	D. Hill	1'44.026	1'44.131	0.444	18	29	A. de Cesaris	1'47.745	1'47.235	3.653
4	5	M. Schumacher	1'44.875	1'44.268	0.686	19	6	J. Verstappen	40'34.496	1'47.316	3.734
5	3	U. Katayama	1'46.534	1'44.718	1.136	20	23	P. Martini	1'47.831	1'47.402	3.820
6	2	D. Coulthard	1'45.477	1'45.146	1.564	21	11	A. Zanardi	1'47.678	1'47.425	3.843
7	4	M. Blundell	1'45.814	1'45.474	1.892	22	20	E. Comas	1'48.770	1'48.229	4.647
8	7	M. Hakkinen	1'45.487	1'45.878	1.905	23	24	M. Alboreto	1'48.402	1'48.295	4.713
9	30	H.H. Frentzen	1'46.488	1'45.893	2.311	24	19	O. Beretta	1'48.681	1'48.875	5.099
10	15	E. Irvine	1'45.911	1'45.942	2.329	25	31	D. Brabham	1'50.685	1'48.870	5.288
11	14	R. Barrichello	1'45.962	1'45.939	2.357	26	32	M. Gounon	1'50.361	1'49.204	5.622
12	26	O. Panis	1'47.925	1'46.165	2.583						
13	8	M. Brundle	1'46.644	1'46.218	2.636			**Non-Qualifiers**			
14	25	E. Bernard	1'47.531	1'46.290	2.708	27	33	J. Belmondo	1'51.916	1'51.122	7.540
15	12	J. Herbert	1'48.621	1'46.330	3.048	28	34	B. Gachot	1'52.839	1'51.292	7.710

and there had been an amazing escape for Verstappen in the pits. The Finn had been re-fuelling when fuel spilled and ignited swallowing up Verstappen and several mechanics in a fireball. With the fire extinguished in four seconds, it at least proved that emergency measures worked. Coulthard, and then Brundle's retirement left Hill in eleventh and gaining on the Simteks.

Berger was now clearly able to coast home but there was the unusual sight of two Ligiers in the first three, followed by the two Footwork cars, followed by the two Larrousse's. Although both Simtek's were to disappear late in the day, it wasn't enough to get Hill into the points and the day belonged to Berger. It was the Austrian's first GP success since Adelaide in 1992 when he was with McLaren and it was Ferrari's first win since the Spanish GP of 1990. But if Berger was celebrating, there were some who were not. Hakkinen was given a one race ban for careless driving whilst Barrichello was given a suspended one race ban for leaving the track before reporting to the Stewards after being involved in an accident ∎

The Championship

Race Placing and Points

Drivers' Points		Constructors' Points	
10	G. Berger	10	Ferrari
6	O. Panis		Ligier
4	E. Bernard	5	Footwork
3	C. Fittipaldi	1	Larrousse
2	G. Morbidelli		
1	E. Comas		

Points after Round Eight

Drivers' Points		Constructors' Points	
66	M. Schumacher	67	Benetton
39	D. Hill	52	Ferrari
27	G. Berger	43	Williams
17	J. Alesi	14	Jordan
10	R. Barrichello		McLaren
8	M. Hakkinen	10	Ligier
6	O. Panis		Sauber
	N. Larini	9	Tyrrell
	M. Brundle	8	Footwork
	C. Fittipaldi	5	Minardi
5	H.H. Frentzen	1	Larrousse
	U. Katayama		

Race Placings

Pos	No	Driver	Team	Time	Diff	Grid	
1	28	G. Berger	Ferrari	1:22'37.272	–	1	
2	26	O. Panis	Ligier Gitanes Blondes	1:23'32.051	54.779	12	
3	25	E. Bernard	Ligier Gitanes Blondes	1:23'42.314	1'05.042	14	
4	9	C. Fittipaldi	Footwork Arrows	1:23'58.881	1'21.609	17	
5	10	G. Morbidelli	Footwork Arrows	1:24'07.816	1'30.544	16	
6	20	E. Comas	Tourtel Larrousse	1:24'22.717	1'45.445	22	
7	19	O. Beretta	Tourtel Larrousse	–	1 lap down	24	
8	0	D. Hill	Rothmans Williams Renault	–	1 lap down	3	

Failed to Finish

Pos	No	Driver	Team	Time	Diff	Grid	
9	32	J.M. Gounon	Simtek Ford	–	39 laps	26	(Engine)
10	31	D. Brabham	Simtek Ford	–	37 laps	25	(Clutch)
11	5	M. Schumacher	Mild Seven Benetton Ford	–	20 laps	4	(Engine)
12	8	M. Brundle	Marlboro McLaren Peugeot	–	19 laps	13	(Engine)
13	2	D. Coulthard	Rothmans Williams Renault	–	17 laps	6	(Electrics)
14	6	J. Verstappen	Mild Seven Benetton Ford	–	16 laps	19	(Pit Fire)
15	3	U. Katayama	Tyrrell	–	6 laps	5	(Throttle)
16	4	M. Blundell	Tyrrell	–	0 laps	7	(Accident)
17	7	M. Hakkinen	Marlboro McLaren Peugeot	–	0 laps	8	(Accident)
18	11	A. Zanardi	Team Lotus	–	0 laps	21	(Accident)
19	12	J. Herbert	Team Lotus	–	0 laps	15	(Accident)
20	14	R. Barrichello	Sasol Jordan	–	0 laps	11	(Accident)
21	15	E. Irvine	Sasol Jordan	–	0 laps	10	(Accident)
22	23	P. Martini	Minardi Scuderia Italia	–	0 laps	20	(Accident)
23	24	M. Alboreto	Minardi Scuderia Italia	–	0 laps	23	(Accident)
24	27	J. Alesi	Ferrari	–	0 laps	2	(Engine)
25	29	A. de Cesaris	Sauber	–	0 laps	18	(Accident)
26	30	H.H. Frentzen	Sauber	–	0 laps	9	(Accident)

Fastest Lap: D. Coulthard – 1'46.211 (143.642mph/231.264kph)

Average Speed of Winner: 222.970kph

Michael Schumacher in the Benetton keeps ahead of Damon Hill.

In the time since the German Grand Prix, F1 in general, and Benetton in particular, had again been involved in controversy. FIA alleged that the pit lane fire that had engulfed Verstappen's car at Hockenheim had been caused by Benetton removing a filter from the fuel lines which enabled the car to be refuelled some 12% faster. Benetton said they had been given permission by a FIA official to do so but this was vehemently denied by FIA. Controversy was certainly following Benetton about.

The slowness of the track was expected to be more to the liking of Benetton than Williams or Ferrari but Williams did have history on their side with four wins in the eight runnings of the Hungarian GP including four poles in the previous five seasons. In the event, the writing was on the wall for Williams after the qualifying sessions with pole occupied by Schumacher half a second in front of Hill but some 3.6 seconds slower than the previous season's time despite the fact that the track remained unaltered.

With Hakkinen banned for this race, McLaren turned to the services of Frenchman Phillippe Alliot who hadn't driven in a GP since the 1993 Portuguese race. The newcomer faced a difficult task as McLaren had achieved just five finishes from their eighteen starts with just three point scoring races, form not exactly expected from an outfit that shared with Ferrari the most number of GP victories (104). Another under pressure was Verstappen, for whom a string of disappointing performances were putting question marks over his place. Footwork confirmed they were still running Gianni Morbidelli at Hungororing despite his sponsors backing out whilst rumours abounded that Zanardi was about to be replaced at Lotus by the Belgian Philippe Adams, which meant he was another to be racing under pressure.

During qualifying, Verstappen again failed to endear himself to the Benetton camp when he damaged his car in the second session which left him in midfield whilst Peugeot boss, Jean Pierre Jabouille, known to want Brundle out of the McLaren and Alliott in, berated the Briton's sixth place on the grid by saying *"It is a pity Brundle could not sustain his times otherwise he would have been third. Phillippe improved his times consistently but just lacks time in the car to do himself justice".* Alliott lined up fourteenth.

Zanardi tried hard with his Lotus and actually outqualified Herbert but the car was simply not suited to the many bends in the circuit whilst Morbidelli's efforts to impress would-be sponsors was severely hampered by a visit to the gravel trap. Down at the bottom end, Simtek's David Brabham managed to climb ahead of Herbert and Beretta's Larrousse. It was the first time in 1994 that Simtek had outqualified another team other than Pacific. But the most disappointed driver surely had to be Alesi who struggled to 13th.

When the race got underway, all eyes were on Schumacher to see if he could make his customary fast start but it was Panis on the fifth row that captured most of the attention. He swerved out from behind Irvine and positively flew down the middle of the track. Another to make ground quickly was Alesi, who was obviously determined to make up for lost time during qualifying. But at the front, Hill got away well and appeared to be heading Schumacher in to the first corner and

the Briton had the inside line. Incredibly, Schumacher went relentlessly round Hill on the outside and in to the lead from which, pit stops apart, he would not be headed. The overtaking of Schumacher at that first corner was probably the spectacle of the race but the second corner also produced excitement as Katayama, Irvine and Barrichello all arrived together. Barrichello had the inside, Katayama the outside whilst Irvine was sandwiched in between. Amazingly the ensuing shunt gave Irvine the rare statistic of failing to survive the first lap in each of his last four Grand Prix! But there was worse news for his Jordan team as, for the second race running, neither of their cars completed a lap!

Zanardi's attempt to keep his drive lost ground on the fifth circuit when a blown cylinder cost him three laps sat in the pits but Schumacher had no such trouble and was by now some five seconds up on Hill. As the race unravelled it became apparent that Benetton had decided on a light fuel load for Schumacher with three pit stops and this gave him an advantage that he was to make the most of. Hill was secure in second but his team mate, Coulthard was anything but safe in third as Brundle closed to make it three Britons in the first four. Alliott, meanwhile had been forced out on lap 22 and Morbidelli joined the sidelines when he tangled with de Cesaris.

McLaren mechanics scrawl over the car of Martin Brundle in the pits.

Hungaroring

Over 77 laps and with a lack of lengthy straights it is known as the slowest circuit outside of Monaco and is notoriously difficult to overtake on.

| Lap Distance | 2.47 miles/3.975 km |
| Race Distance | 189.851miles/305.535 km |

1. Turn One — A long right-hand downhill bend entered in third, exited in fourth with just time to get up to fifth before slowing immediately to third for...
2. Turn Two — There is a choice of two lines here but whether the car turns in early or late makes little difference to the amount of oversteer experienced as this long left hander begins to sweep right, which can be taken in fifth on to one of the few bumpy straights.
3. Turn Three — Leaving the straight the driver cannot see the exit, but can still take it in fifth.
4. Turn Four — Another long right hander entered in third, accelerated through fourth and exited in fifth.
5. Turn Five — A right-left chicane that is entered in second gear, exited in third.
6. Turn Six — A left hander where the approach is extremely bumpy.
7. Turn Seven — This right hander is exited in fifth with the gentle left hander towards Eight taken flat out.
8. Turn Eight — Not as fast as it looks as the corner suddenly tightens, with everybody using the exit kerb.
9. Turn Nine — An off camber and downhill right-left chicane which always seems to gather particles of grit, whilst a high kerb awaits the unsuspecting at the second apex.
10. Turn Ten — Almost hairpin like corner situated directly behind the pits and taken in second.
11. Turn Eleven — A long right hander that guards the pit straight. Plenty of action here as the cars first oversteer, turning to understeer by the time they exit on to the straight via the kerb.

Hungarian Grand Prix – 5 Year Record

Year	1st	2nd	3rd	4th	5th	6th
1989	Mansell (Ferrari)	Senna (McLaren)	Boutsen (Williams)	Prost (McLaren)	Cheever (Arrows)	Piquet (Lotus)
1990	Boutsen (Williams)	Senna (McLaren)	Piquet (Benetton)	Patrese (Williams)	Warwick (Lotus)	Bernard (Lola)
1991	Senna (McLaren)	Mansell (Williams)	Patrese (Williams)	Berger (McLaren)	Alesi (Ferrari)	Capelli (Leyton House)
1992	Senna (McLaren)	Mansell (Williams)	Berger (McLaren)	Hakkinen (Lotus)	Brundle (Benetton)	Capelli (Ferrari)
1993	Hill (Williams)	Patrese (Benetton)	Berger (Ferrari)	Warwick (Footwork)	Brundle (Ligier)	Wendlinger (Sauber)

1994 Grid Positions and Qualifying Times

Grid No		Driver	1st Session	2nd Session	Diff	Grid No		Driver	1st Session	2nd Session	Diff
1	5	M. Schumacher	1'19.479	1'18.258	–	16	9	C. Fittipaldi	1'22.375	1'21.873	3.615
2	0	D. Hill	1'19.700	1'18.824	0.566	17	29	A. de Cesaris	1'23.573	1'21.946	3.688
3	2	D. Coulthard	1'20.395	1'20.205	1.947	18	25	E. Bernard	1'23.269	1'22.038	3.780
4	28	G. Berger	1'21.009	1'20.219	1.961	19	10	G. Morbidelli	1'22.311	1'30.262	4.053
5	3	U. Katayama	1'21.877	1'20.232	1.974	20	24	M. Alboreto	1'22.379	1'22.379	4.121
6	8	M. Brundle	1'20.819	1'20.629	2.371	21	20	E. Comas	1'22.754	1'22.487	4.229
7	15	E. Irvine	1'21.406	1'20.698	2.440	22	11	A. Zanardi	1'23.361	1'22.513	4.255
8	30	H.H. Frentzen	1'22.268	1'20.858	2.600	23	31	D. Brabham	1'24.187	1'22.614	4.356
9	26	O. Panis	1'23.244	1'20.929	2.671	24	12	J. Herbert	1'23.306	1'22.705	4.447
10	14	R. Barrichello	1'21.498	1'20.952	2.694	25	19	O. Beretta	1'24.645	1'22.899	4.641
11	4	M. Blundell	1'21.731	1'20.984	2.726	26	32	J.M. Gounon	1'26.678	1'24.191	5.933
12	6	J. Verstappen	1'21.141	9'03.939	2.883						
13	27	J. Alesi	1'21.280	1'21.206	2.948			**Non Qualifiers**			
14	7	P. Alliott	1'22.915	1'21.498	3.240	27	34	B. Gachot	1'26.521	1'24.908	6.650
15	23	P. Martini	1'24.440	1'21.837	3.579	28	33	P. Belmondo	1'28.334	1'26.275	8.017

Little of note occurred until the 59th circuit when fifth placed Alesi departed and then Coulthard, who was now holding Brundle at a distance of half a second, saw his first podium position disappear in a cloud of dust as he went skidding in to the safety wall. This left Brundle with visions of a podium spot but, due to the retirements, Verstappen had appeared in fourth. Schumacher had things so much under control that he allowed both Brundle and Verstappen to unlap themselves as the race for the third place unfolded. Brundle was visibly slowing with electrical problems, whilst Verstappen was closing quickly but, at the start of the last circuit, it still seemed Brundle would just last home. Sadly, he didn't, as his car packed in at the top end of the track to allow an overjoyed Verstappen his first ever podium finish. Blundell drove a good race to bring his Tyrrell home in fifth (three Brits in the top five) and Panis saw to it that Ligier's new found form was rewarded with a second successive appearance in the points.

But for one man and one team, after all the recent tensions, this was exactly the result Schumacher and Benetton wanted ▩

The Championship

Race Placing and Points

Drivers' Points		Constructors' Points	
10	M. Schumacher	14	Benetton
6	D. Hill	6	Williams
4	J. Verstappen	3	McLaren
3	M. Brundle	2	Tyrrell
2	M. Blundell	1	Ligier
1	O. Panis		

Points after Round Ten

Drivers' Points		Constructors' Points	
76	M. Schumacher	81	Benetton
45	D. Hill	52	Ferrari
27	G. Berger	49	Williams
17	J. Alesi	17	McLaren
10	R. Barrichello	14	Jordan
9	M. Brundle	11	Ligier
8	M. Hakkinen		Tyrrell
7	O. Panis	10	Sauber
6	N. Larini	8	Footwork
	C. Fittipaldi	5	Minardi
	M. Blundell	2	Larrousse
5	H.H. Frentzen		
	U. Katayama		

Race Placings

Pos	No	Driver	Team	Time	Diff	Grid	
1	5	M. Schumacher	Mild Seven Benetton Ford	1:48'00.185	–	1	
2	0	D. Hill	Rothmans Williams Renault	1:48'21.012	21.012	2	
3	6	J. Verstappen	Mild Seven Benetton Ford	1:49'10.514	1'10.329	12	
4	8	M. Brundle	Marlboro McLaren Peugeot	–	1 lap down	6	(Alternator failure)
5	4	M. Blundell	Tyrrell	–	1 lap down	11	
6	26	O. Panis	Ligier Gitanes Blondes	–	1 lap down	9	
7	24	M. Alboreto	Minardi Scuderia Italia	–	2 laps down	20	
8	20	E. Comas	Tourtel Larrousse	–	2 laps down	21	
9	19	O. Beretta	Tourtel Larrousse	–	2 laps down	25	
10	25	E. Bernard	Ligier Gitanes Blondes	–	2 laps down	18	
11	31	D. Brabham	MTV Simtek Ford	–	3 laps down	23	
12	28	G. Berger	Scuderia Ferrari	–	4 laps down	4	(Electrical)
13	11	A. Zanardi	Team Lotus	–	5 laps down	22	

Failed to Finish

Pos	No	Driver	Team	Time	Diff	Grid	
14	9	C. Fittipaldi	Footwork	–	69 laps	16	(Transmission)
15	2	D. Coulthard	rothmans Williams Ford	–	59 laps	3	(Accident)
16	27	J. Alesi	Scuderia Ferrari	–	58 laps	13	(Transmission)
17	23	P. Martini	Minardi Scuderia	–	58 laps	15	(Spin)
18	30	H.H. Frentzen	Sauber Mercedes	–	39 laps	8	(Transmission)
19	12	J. Herbert	Team Lotus	–	34 laps	24	(Electrical)
20	29	A. de Cesaris	Sauber Mercedes	–	30 laps	17	(Accident)
21	10	G. Morbidelli	Footwork	–	30 laps	19	(Accident)
22	7	P. Alliott	Marlboro McLaren	–	21 laps	14	(Water leak)
23	32	J.M. Gounon	MTV Simtek	–	9 laps	26	(Steering)
24	3	U. Katayama	Tyrrell	–	0 laps	5	(Accident)
25	14	R. Barrichello	Sasol Jordan	–	0 laps	10	(Accident)
26	15	E. Irvine	Sasol Jordan	–	0 laps	7	(Accident)

Fastest Lap:　　M. Schumacher – 1'20.881 (109.699mph/176.615kph)
Average Speed of Winner:　169.737kph

Belgium
On the skids

Johnny Herbert demonstrates how smoking can damage your health, tyres, brakes, nerves, etc, etc.

Team Lotus, having a desperate season, announced that local boy Philippe Adams would take over Alessandro Zanardi's drive for Spa with the Italian returning for his home Grand Prix. Adams had been European Opel Lotus Champion in 1988 before turning to F3 where he finished second in the British Championship to Gil de Ferran before winning a poorly supported British F2 Championship in 1993. During the 1994 season he had won five of the nine rounds in the Belgian Touring Car Championship in which he had competed prior to making his F1 debut. The decision, however, could hardly have been timed worse for Adams' father, a leading politician, was declared Belgium's largest ever bankrupt just days prior to the GP and several companies besieged the Lotus pit demanding that sponsorship logo's be removed in a desire to distance themselves from the bankruptcy. The problems for Lotus also continued off the track when they were refused permission to appeal against a High Court ruling that they must pay Cosworth £400,000 following a long running dispute.

Over at the Tourtel Larrousse camp there were two glum faces and two happy ones. Amidst rumours that Phillippe Alliott would take over the Erik Comas car following his one off appearance at Spa as stand in for the suspended Hakkinen, it was decided that Alliott would displace Olivier Berretta leaving Eric van de Poele, who had raised sufficient sponsorship for a drive himself, overlooked. A spokesman said *"Olivier's money ran out it's as simple as that".*

Schumacher, meanwhile, presumably approached the race with some confidence as Spa had seen some significant landmarks in the young German's life. The nearest track to his home town of Korpen just over the border had been the scene of his F1 debut in 1991 and the 1992 race had seen him set a fastest lap for the first time as well as his first ever Grand Prix victory. But he also knew that his appeal against his two race ban was due to be heard two days after Spa thus making it imperative for him to score well as a safeguard against things going badly at the appeal. Hill was also in confident mood having won here twelve months earlier and happy in the knowledge that the circuit should suit the Williams car better than most bar, perhaps, Ferrari. On the statistical side it was Arrows' 250th Grand Prix and Minardi's 150th.

The first qualifying session, however, was to throw up a major, indeed mega surprise. Jordan, having achieved a feat in not completing a single lap with either of its two cars in the previous two rounds now saw Barrichello plonk himself in provisional pole and to complete a great morale boosting day for the team, Irvine grabbed fourth! Elsewhere, David Brabham celebrated the birth of his son by outqualifying no fewer than seven cars whilst Adams failed to improve the Lotus lot finishing only in front of a stricken Fittipaldi and the two Pacifics. Brabham took great delight, in particular, at outqualifying Comas who, earlier in the season, had said he would pack in racing if he was ever outqualified by a Simtek. Stepping out of his car at Spa Brabham said *"I would just like to wish Erik a very happy retirement"!*

Although it had rained prior to the first qualifying session, the track had dried out to allow drivers to push the cars through their paces but Saturday's rains showed no abatement with the result that few drivers ventured out with any serious intentions. Certainly Jordan did not see any point in risking their cars in the wet but Fittipaldi's Friday performance left him with no option other than to hope to post a time below that of the two Pacific's in order to just get in to the race. In the event he did so comfortably. So Barrichello not only took his first ever pole but also became the youngest driver at the age of 22 ever to do so in the history of Grand Prix racing.

The race itself, over 195 miles, was decided by just about the smallest margin possible – 1.6 millimetres! That was the amount by which the plank of Schumacher's car was adjudged illegal some five hours after the event had finished to cause yet another uproar. The skidblock, introduced earlier in the season to reduce speeds, must be 10mm thick although a 10% wear rate is allowable during a race making the minimum

legal thickness effectively 9mm. The post race inspection of the winning Benetton car revealed the plank to be only 7.4mm thick in one part resulting in Schumacher's disqualification from a race he had won with some considerable authority. Another appeal by Benetton was on the cards.

Despite being behind Barrichello's surprise pole position, the German, as always, took on the leader from the green light. Remembering that the Jordan team had failed to complete a full lap in either of their cars in the previous two races, Schumacher immediately pressured Barrichello intensely at the first corner, La Source, diving left and right before opting to go left again to try and go past on the outside. Barrichello, to his credit, just repulsed this first attack but was powerless, quite literally, to do anything about the next assault on the straight leading to Les Combes. The Brazilian was running a one stop strategy and his heavy fuel load deprived him of any chance of dealing with the Benetton.

By the end of the first lap, Alesi had also passed Barrichello and the two Williams cars did likewise on the second circuit but on lap three he surprisingly regained a place when Alesi's engine folded. A lap later saw Comas' weekend deteriorate even further when his engine did likewise. Frentzen was now chasing Barrichello hard but couldn't get past with the status quo holding up for several tours until, having by now completed eleven laps, the German's patience ran out and he tried too hard at Eau Rouge and spun off. Just one lap later Berger was next to retire and in

Barrichello won pole but still failed to finish.

Spa-Francorchamps

The longest circuit on the calendar endears itself to drivers who never get bored of its 44 laps which makes use, in parts, of local roads.

Lap Distance   4.33 miles/6.968 km
Race Distance   190.671 miles/306.854 km

Spa is many driver's favourite track with one of the most challenging corners in motor racing – Eau Rouge.

1. La Source   The corner comes very quickly after the start of the race and is a sharp right hander taken in second.
2. Eau Rouge   Entered in sixth gear, it went sharply downhill and then uphill left, right, and left. In its modified form it cuts sharp left at the bottom of the hill, curving back on a right hander for the long Kemmel straight.
3. Les Combes   Good overtaking possibilities exist at this right-left chicane due to the good run-off areas. The right-left combination is taken in third and exited in fourth.
4. Malmedy   A virtual hairpin which, due to being off camber, causes cars all sorts of steering problems. Taken in second, exited in third.
5. Le Pouhon   Also off camber, this double left hander is entered in fifth and exited in sixth.
6. Les Fanges   A right left chicane where the entry is made in third, up to fourth in the middle section and exited via the use of the kerb.
7. Stavelot   A double right hander that is fast as it is downhill. Entered in third with fourth being engaged in the middle but it is bumpy and cars tend to skip about a bit.
8. Blanchimont   A long sweeping lefthander leading to...
9. Bus Stop   A sharp right, left, right that slows the cars right down before emerging on to the pit straight.

Belgian Grand Prix – 5 Year Record

Year	1st	2nd	3rd	4th	5th	6th
1989	Senna (McLaren)	Prost (McLaren)	Mansell (Ferrari)	Boutsen (Williams)	Nannini (Benetton)	Warwick (Arrows)
1990	Senna (McLaren)	Prost (Ferrari)	Berger (McLaren)	Nannini (Benetton)	Piquet (Benetton)	Gugelmin (March)
1991	Senna (McLaren)	Berger (McLaren)	Piquet (Benetton)	Moreno (Benetton)	Patrese (Williams)	Blundell (Brabham)
1992	Schumacher (Benetton)	Mansell (Williams)	Patrese (Williams)	Brundle (Benetton)	Senna (McLaren)	Hakkinen (Lotus)
1993	Hill (Williams)	Schumacher (Benetton)	Prost (Williams)	Senna (McLaren)	Herbert (Lotus)	Patrese (Benetton)

1994 Grid Positions and Qualifying Times

Grid	No	Driver	1st Session	2nd Session	Diff	Grid	No	Driver	1st Session	2nd Session	Diff
1	14	R. Barrichello	2'21.163	No time	–	16	25	E. Bernard	2'26.044	2'31.025	4.881
2	5	M. Schumacher	2'21.494	2'25.501	0.331	17	26	O. Panis	2'26.079	2'31.501	4.916
3	0	D. Hill	2'21.681	2'25.570	0.518	18	24	M. Alboreto	2'26.738	2'32.286	5.575
4	15	E. Irvine	2'22.074	No time	0.911	19	11	P. Alliott	2'26.901	2'31.350	5.738
5	27	J. Alesi	2'22.202	2'25.099	1.039	20	12	J. Herbert	2'27.155	2'32.610	5.992
6	6	J. Verstappen	2'22.218	2'28.576	1.055	21	31	D. Brabham	2'27.212	2'41.593	6.049
7	2	D. Coulthard	2'22.359	2'27.180	1.196	22	20	E. Comas	2'28.156	2'30.524	6.993
8	7	M. Hakkinen	2'22.441	2'28.997	1.278	23	3	U. Katayama	2'28.979	2'29.925	7.816
9	30	H.H. Frentzen	2'22.634	2.28.026	1.471	24	9	C. Fittipaldi	16'56.162	2'30.931	9.768
10	23	P. Martini	2'23.326	2'30.896	2.163	25	32	J.M. Gounon	2'31.755	2'40.280	10.592
11	28	G. Berger	2'23.895	2'29.391	2.732	26	11	P. Adams	2'33.885	2'34.733	12.722
12	4	M. Blundell	2'24.048	2'28.164	2.885			**Non-Qualifiers**			
13	8	M. Brundle	2'24.117	2'28.428	2.954						
14	10	G. Morbidelli	2'25.114	2'31.403	3.951	27	34	B. Gachot	2'34.582	2'34.951	13.419
15	29	A. de Cesaris	2'25.695	2'30.475	4.532	28	33	P. Belmondo	2'35.729	No time	14.566

moving his car to safety from a dangerous position the Austrian received a suspended one race ban for taking what seemed to most onlookers to be a sensible precaution for other people's safety.

Alliott and Adams also became casualties with Gianni Morbidelli picking up a suspended $10,000 fine for ignoring a yellow flag at the scene of Adams misadventure. Katayama's spectacular rise of thirteen places from 23rd on the grid came to grief after completing 18 laps whilst Barrichello and Brundle were soon to join him on the sidelines. Up front there was little danger to Schumacher but the two Williams were in interesting positions with Coulthard in front of Hill! Just when everybody was wondering whether Coulthard would be ordered to give way, he was called in by his team as he had a wing moving on the rear of the car. Hill, however, did not have sufficient time left to catch Schumacher who coasted home with Verstappen coming in third to add to the Benetton joy which was soon to be shattered by the disqualification of the winner ⬛

The Championship

Race Placing and Points

Drivers' Points		Constructors' Points	
10	D. Hill	13	Williams
6	M. Hakkinen	6	McLaren
4	J. Verstappen	4	Benetton
3	D. Coulthard	2	Tyrrell
2	M. Blundell	1	Footwork
1	G. Morbidelli		

Points after Round Eleven

Drivers' Points		Constructors' Points	
76	M. Schumacher	85	Benetton
55	D. Hill	62	Williams
27	G. Berger	52	Ferrari
19	J. Alesi	23	McLaren
14	M. Hakkinen	14	Jordan
10	R. Barrichello	13	Tyrrell
9	M. Brundle	11	Ligier
8	J. Verstappen	10	Sauber
	M. Blundell	9	Footwork
7	D. Coulthard	5	Minardi
	O. Panis	2	Larrousse

NB – Drivers with less than seven points not shown.

Race Placings

Pos	No	Driver	Team	Time	Diff	Grid	
1	0	D. Hill	Rothmans Williams Ford	1:28'47.170	–	3	
2	7	M. Hakkinen	Marlboro McLaren Peugeot	1:29'38.551	51.381	8	
3	6	J. Verstappen	Mild Seven Benetton Ford	1:29'57.623	1'10.453	6	
4	2	D. Coulthard	rothmans Williams Ford	1:30'32.957	1'45.787	7	
5	4	M. Blundell	Tyrrell	–	1 lap down	12	
6	10	G. Morbidelli	Footwork	–	1 lap down	14	
7	26	O. Panis	Ligier Gitanes Blondes	–	1 lap down	17	
8	23	P. Martini	Minardi Scuderia Italia	–	1 lap down	10	
9	24	M. Alboreto	Minardi Scuderia Italia	–	1 lap down	18	
10	25	E. Bernard	Ligier Gitanes Blondes	–	2 laps down	16	
11	32	J.M. Gounon	Simtek	–	2 laps down	25	
12	12	J. Herbert	Team Lotus	–	3 laps down	20	

Failed to Finish

Pos	No	Driver	Team	Time	Diff	Grid	
13	15	E. Irvine	Sasol Jordan	–	40 laps	4	(Battery)
14	9	C. Fittipaldi	Footwork	–	33 laps	24	(Engine)
15	31	D. Brabham	Simtek	–	29 laps	21	(Wheel came off)
16	29	A. de Cesaris	Sauber	–	27 laps	15	(Throttle)
17	8	M. Brundle	Marlboro McLaren Peugeot	–	24 laps	13	(Accident)
18	14	R. Barrichello	Sasol Jordan	–	19 laps	1	(Accident)
19	3	U. Katayama	Tyrrell	–	18 laps	23	(Engine)
20	11	P. Adams	Team Lotus	–	15 laps	26	(Accident)
21	28	G. Berger	Ferrari	–	11 laps	11	(Engine)
22	19	P. Alliott	Tourtel Larrousse	–	11 laps	19	(Engine)
23	30	H.H. Frentzen	Sauber	–	10 laps	9	(Spin)
24	20	E. Comas	Tourtel Larrousse	–	3 laps	22	(Engine)
25	27	J. Alesi	Ferrari	–	2 laps	5	(Engine)

Disqualified:

–	5	M. Schumacher	Mild Seven Benetton Ford – Contravention of technical regulations			2	

Fastest Lap: D. Hill – 01'57.117 (133.665mph/215.200kph)

Average Speed of Winner: 208.170kph

Autodromo di Monza – 11 September 1994

Johnny Herbert's luck ran out on the fourteenth lap despite a good start.

There would be no Schumacher in the Monza race due to the commencement of his two race ban for his misdeeds in the British GP and his place went to J.J. Lehto for whom it seemed this might well be a last chance. Another driver to make his F1 comeback at the Italian track was Yannick Dalmas, whose career was thus coming full circle as it had been for Larrousse that he had made his GP debut in Mexico in 1987.

Lotus made two changes from Belgium with Zanardi returning in place of Adams as promised whilst Herbert would debut a new Mugen engine. Much to the delight of the Italian crowd, qualifying saw Alesi set fastest lap after fastest lap to put Ferrari on pole and he was joined on the front row by team mate Gerhard Berger during the second session. But, without doubt, the major surprise was that of Herbert whose new engine had obviously made a quite incredible improvement to his Lotus as he ended the first day in sixth place. There was more to come from the

likeable Briton in the second session and, with only five minutes left, he was amazingly in third place behind only the two Ferrari's. Then Damon Hill, who caused a minor stir by asking for, and being granted, a swop of engineers with Coulthard's, pulled a quick lap out of the hat to push Herbert down to fourth but still ahead of the second Williams driven by Coulthard. Benetton without their German ace were nowhere to be seen with Verstappen in tenth and Lehto an even more disappointing 20th. Dalmas in his comeback was a lowly 23rd but ahead of team-mate Comas whilst the unluckiest driver was Irvine who had a good first day time wiped out when he drove one more lap than the permitted twelve.

The day of the race started badly for Ferrari when Berger had a hefty bump in practice. He was taken from the track to hospital but then declared himself fit to race. He wouldn't, however, be racing in his car as that was too badly damaged and it was into the spare that Berger stepped as did Hill with Williams. The Briton's own car had developed an oil leak just before the start and the Didcot team got their spare car out on to the track with only five minutes breathing space. But that was an age compared to McLaren who, as they fired up Brundle's engine with the driver already strapped in the cockpit, found a water pressure problem. Brundle made it with literally seconds to spare.

As if that wasn't enough tension for the start, more quickly followed when the green light went on with, once again, the culprit appearing to be Irvine. Alesi and Berger held their positions at the off but Herbert had made a fast start to catch and pass Hill as they approached the first chicane. Behind Herbert, however, Irvine had made an even faster getaway and was positively flying down the right hand side of the track which had cleared as most drivers moved to the left for the approach to the chicane. Irvine appeared to brake too late and smacked into the back of Herbert spinning him and causing mayhem. One of the results of this was that Herbert's new car was out of the race and the Briton had to return to the old uncompetitive vehicle and start from the pit lane. Irvine was banished to the back of the grid and was given a one race suspension suspended for three races which, in view of his three race ban earlier in the campaign, had most observers thinking the Irishman had got off lightly. Of the other casualties Coulthard now began the second race in Hill's discarded motor which had

now been repaired, Comas watched as his Larrousse was towed back to the grid and Panis was yet another to have to resort to his team's spare car.

When the race restarted there were three more casualties with Morbidelli spinning off as a result of contact with Zanardi who claimed somebody had hit him into Morbidelli. It seemed likely that the person to hit Zanardi was Verstappen, who also claimed he had received a push which caused him to hit Zanardi and puncture the Italian's tyre. Whatever, the race field was now down to 23 and on lap fourteen it became one less when Herbert called it a day. He was quickly joined a lap later by the race leader Alesi who came in on lap 15 for the first of what, presumably, would have been a two stop race for the Ferrari ace. But when he set off, or rather tried to set off, to rejoin the race there was no power. Alesi threw his gloves down as he climbed out of the car an obviously very disenchanted man after having held a twelve second lead.

The new race leader was now Berger in the second Ferrari but he was only a second up as opposed to the big margin that Alesi had built up. The problems that had beset Ferrari in their home Grand Prix continued when Berger pitted on lap 24. Just as he was about to rejoin the race, Panis came along the pit road, slowing in to the next pit which prevented Berger making a swift getaway. By the time he was back in the race he was

Herbert and Irvine come together at the start.

Autodromo di Monza

Since its start nearly all of the Italian GPs have been held here, over 53 super-fast laps.

| Lap Distance | 3.602 miles/5.794 km |
| Race Distance | 191.009 miles/307.398 km |

1. Variante Goodyear This is approached at some 190mph due to the long, wide pit straight that precedes it. It is a very fast but bumpy left-right-left-right second gear chicane.
2. Curva Grande A very bumpy longish right hander that is hard work on the steering. Drivers invariably use the kerb at its exit.
3. Variante della Roggia The breaking area prior to entering this left-right chicane is both bumpy and slippy.
4. Curvo di Lesmos Contentious sharp right handers that Damon Hill criticised as *"Too dangerous even for a F3000 car because there is not a sufficient run off area due to it being a part of the Royal Park"*. Invariably taken at speed in fifth and exited in sixth gear.
5. Curva del Serraglio A long straight that means the driver approaches the next chicane at speeds approaching 200mph.
6. Curva del Vialone Drivers hope their brakes are in good order as they approach this left hander braking from 200 mph in sixth gear to fourth gear at the 100 metre board. Then onto...
6. Variante Ascari The second part of the chicane quickly flicking right, then left. Exited in fifth on to the Rettifilio Centro straight.
7. Curvo Parabolica A long, looping right hander that is entered from the Rettifilio straight in fourth before moving in to fifth gear as the bend begins to open up and exited in sixth. Known for generating a great deal of understeer.

Italian Grand Prix – 5 Year Record

Year	1st	2nd	3rd	4th	5th	6th
1989	Prost (McLaren)	Berger (Ferrari)	Boutsen (Williams)	Patrese (Williams)	Alesi (Tyrrell)	Brundle (Brabham)
1990	Senna (McLaren)	Prost (Ferrari)	Berger (McLaren)	Mansell (Ferrari)	Patrese (Williams)	Nakajima (Tyrrell)
1991	Mansell (Williams)	Senna (McLaren)	Prost (Ferrari)	Berger (McLaren)	Schumacher (Benetton)	Piquet (Benetton)
1992	Senna (McLaren)	Brundle (Benetton)	Schumacher (Benetton)	Berger (McLaren)	Patrese (Williams)	De Cesaris (Tyrrell)
1993	Hill (Williams)	Alesi (Ferrari)	Mi.Andretti (McLaren)	Wendlinger (Sauber)	Patrese (Benetton)	Comas (Larrousse)

1994 Grid Positions and Qualifying Times

Grid	No	Driver	1st Session	2nd Session	Diff	Grid	No	Driver	1st Session	2nd Session	Diff
1	27	J. Alesi	1'24.620	1'23.844	–	16	14	R. Barrichello	1'27.034	1'25.946	2.102
2	28	G. Berger	1'24.915	1'23.978	0.134	17	10	G. Morbidelli	1'27.939	1'26.002	2.158
3	0	D. Hill	1'24.734	1'24.158	0.314	18	23	P. Martini	19'42.320	1'26.056	2.212
4	12	J. Herbert	1'26.365	1'24.374	0.530	19	9	C. Fittipaldi	1'27.675	1'26.337	2.493
5	2	D. Coulthard	1'24.869	1'24.502	0.658	20	5	J.J. Lehto	1'27.611	1'26.384	2.540
6	26	O. Panis	1'26.958	1'25.455	1.611	21	4	M. Blundell	1'26.574	1'26.697	2.730
7	7	M. Hakkinen	1'26.004	1'25.528	1.684	22	24	M. Alboreto	1'27.623	1'26.832	2.988
8	29	A. de Cesaris	1'27.188	1'25.540	1.696	23	19	Y. Dalmas	1'29.525	1'27.846	4.002
9	15	E. Irvine	No Time	1'25.568	1.724	24	20	E. Comas	1'30.530	1'27.894	4.050
10	6	J. Verstappen	1'27.361	1'25.618	1.774	25	32	J.M. Gounon	1'29.594	1'28.353	4.509
11	30	H.H. Frentzen	1'26.406	1'25.628	1.784	26	31	D. Brabham	1'30.691	1'28.353	4.775
12	25	E. Bernard	1'27.387	1'25.718	1.874						
13	11	A. Zanardi	1'27.617	1'25.733	1.889			**Non-Qualifiers**			
14	3	U. Katayama	1'26.525	1'25.889	2.045	27	34	B. Gachot	1'31.549	1'31.387	7.543
15	8	M. Brundle	1'26.899	1'25.933	2.089	28	33	P. Belmondo	1'32.035	No time	8.191

down to fourth behind Coulthard, Hill and Hakkinen. Coulthard was driving a quite brilliant race but, as he approached half way, Coulthard moved to the side in the pit straight to allow Williams team-mate Hill through and into the lead. Coulthard now rode shotgun for Hill and little was going to get past him but, as the race progressed, it became apparent that nothing could get past for Berger was now some fifteen seconds adrift in third. With retirements having reduced the cars still running to just ten, what appeared to be heading for an uneventful finish suddenly became eventful as the bad luck that had dogged Coulthard's finishes all season struck yet again. On the final lap and with a second place virtually assured, the second Williams ran out of fuel and was classified sixth. But Hill had done what he had to do and that was win the race and reduce the absent Schumacher's title lead to just eleven points with the German still due to miss one more race as a result of his suspension. A British victory in Italy, but it didn't seem quite the same without the German ace ▰

The Championship

Race Placing and Points

Drivers' Points		Constructors' Points	
10	D. Hill	11	Williams
6	G. Berger	6	Ferrari
4	M. Hakkinen		McLaren
3	R. Barrichello	3	Jordan
2	M. Brundle		
1	D. Coulthard		

Points after Twelve Rounds

Drivers' Points		Constructors' Points	
76	M. Schumacher	85	Benetton
65	D. Hill	73	Williams
33	G. Berger	58	Ferrari
19	J. Alesi	29	McLaren
18	M. Hakkinen	17	Jordan
13	R. Barrichello	13	Tyrrell
11	M. Brundle	11	Ligier
8	J. Verstappen	10	Sauber
	D. Coulthard	9	Footwork
	M. Blundell	5	Minardi
7	O. Panis	2	Larrousse

Race Placings

Pos	No	Driver	Team	Time	Diff	Grid	
1	0	D. Hill	Rothmans Williams Renault	1:18'02.754	–	3	
2	28	G. Berger	Ferrari	1:18'07.684	4.93	2	
3	7	M. Hakkinen	Marlboro McLaren Peugeot	1:18'28.394	25.64	7	
4	14	R. Barrichello	Sasol Jordan	1:18'53.388	50.634	16	
5	8	M. Brundle	Marlboro McLaren Peugeot	1:19'28.329	1'25.575	15	
6	2	D. Coulthard	Rothmans Williams Renault	–	1 lap down	5	(Out of fuel)
7	25	E. Bernard	Ligier Gitanes Blondes	–	1 lap down	12	
8	20	E. Comas	Tourtel Larrousse	–	1 lap down	24	
9	5	J.J. Lehto	Mild Seven Benetton Ford	–	1 lap down	20	
10	26	O. Panis	Ligier Gitanes Blondes	–	1 lap down	6	

Failed to Finish

Pos	No	Driver	Team	Time	Diff	Grid	
11	31	D. Brabham	Simtek	–	46 laps	26	(Brakes)
12	3	U. Katayama	Tyrrell	–	45 laps	14	(Brakes)
13	9	C. Fittipaldi	Footwork	–	43 laps	19	(Engine)
14	15	E. Irvine	Sasol Jordan	–	41 laps	9	(Engine)
15	4	M. Blundell	Tyrrell	–	39 laps	21	(Brakes)
16	23	P. Martini	Minardi Scuderia Italia	–	30 laps	18	(Spin)
17	24	M. Alboreto	Minardi Scuderia Italia	–	28 laps	22	(Gearbox)
18	30	H.H. Frentzen	Sauber	–	22 laps	11	(Engine)
19	29	A. de Cesaris	Sauber	–	20 laps	8	(Engine)
20	32	J.M. Gounon	Simtek	–	20 laps	25	(Gearbox)
21	19	Y. Dalmas	Tourtel Larrousse	–	18 laps	23	(Spin)
22	27	J. Alesi	Ferrari	–	14 laps	1	(Transmission)
23	12	J. Herbert	Team Lotus	–	13 laps	4	(Alternator)
24	6	J. Verstappen	Mild Seven Benetton Ford	–	0 laps	10	(Puncture)
25	10	G. Morbidelli	Footwork	–	0 laps	17	(Spin)
26	11	A. Zanardi	Team Lotus	–	0 laps	13	(Puncture)

Fastest Lap: D. Hill – 1'25.930 (150.987mph/242.988kph)

Average Speed of Winner: 236.322kph

Damon Hill's skillful passing of David Coulthard spared him having to obey team orders.

Damon Hill and the Williams team headed for Estoril under greater pressure than any other team, as they desperately needed a good show in Portugal to set up a shoot-out over the last three races when Schumacher would be back for a Benetton outfit who simply did not look the same without the young German maestro. Indeed, a win for Hill would see him just one point behind the Championship leader whilst a British 1-2 for the first time in 25 years could see the Williams team take over the lead from Benetton in the race for the Manufacturer's title.

The omens for Hill were good as the previous year he had taken pole and set the fastest time whilst neither of the drivers to finish in front of him in the actual race, Michael Schumacher and Alain Prost, would be on show in the 1994 version. Williams, too, enjoyed a good track record at Estoril and went into this race on the back of two wins and a second in the previous three runnings. Standing in the way of Hill and Williams would be Benetton regular driver Jos Verstappen and Schumacher's replacement J.J. Lehto but their performances hitherto left the critics betting against either of the pair being able to continue Benetton's fine record of finishing in the points at Estoril in every season since 1987. But whilst the top two teams were battling it out, there was also some interest just behind them as Ferrari's third place was now coming under a slight threat from McLaren after the Italians had earlier held a comfortable second, ahead of Williams, for the first seven races of the campaign.

Johnny Herbert found himself in the spotlight and quite literally was fighting for the life of Lotus who were in the hands of administrators and had been given this race, and the following one at Jerez, to prove they were capable of competing at this level and thus have a chance of returning to financial viability.

Qualifying saw Hill challenging Berger hard for

pole when he suffered his accident which could have had far more serious implications than, in fact, it did. Hill's car turned upside down with his head taking a close inspection of the contents of a gravel trap after his left hand wheels hit – guess who – a spinning Eddie Irvine! The Ulsterman must not have been able to believe his bad luck. Racing under the threat of suspension following his Monza misdemeanour, Irvine would have been extremely grateful to Hill for exonerating him from any blame.

Strangely, the incident occurred at the newly modified Turn Seven which the majority of drivers now ranked as the slowest at any Grand Prix track and all complained of vast amounts of wheel spin. With Hill's challenge out of the way, Berger was able take his total number of poles into double figures whilst just behind Hill, and equalling his best qualifying performance thus far in his short career, was David Coulthard. Berger's top spot was Ferrari's third pole of the season but McLaren, their challengers for third in the Manufacturer's table, were not far behind. Hakkinen had outqualified team-mate Ayrton Senna in the 1993 version at this track and he put in another good performance to line up fourth ahead of the other Ferrari driven by Alesi. Williams, meanwhile, must have been rubbing their hands with glee as they saw the Benetton cars struggle round to 10th and 14th!

Suffering no ill effects and with his car in equally fine fettle following the escapade with Irvine, Hill took his place on the front row but was slowly away allowing not only Berger to extend his pole advantage but also Coulthard to get up to second by the first corner. Berger, planning three pit stops, had a light load of fuel and began pulling away from the two Brits but, after completing seven laps, the Austrian was out when his gearbox's hydraulic pump broke. This piece of good fortune left Coulthard in the lead but who began to put some distance between himself and his Championship contending team mate at a rate approaching a second a lap.

Hill's deficit at the end of twelve circuits was 3.4secs but three tours later, it was up to almost six seconds. But Hill's pit stop was much briefer than Coulthard's and the two Brit's were not far apart when Hill rejoined. After Alesi and Barrichello had completed their pit stops, the Williams pair were back in tandem at the head of affairs and their cause was to be further aided on Alesi's 39th lap as he tried to lap David Brabham for the second time when in a comfortable third. Views on whose fault it was differed with some saying Brabham simply did not use his mirrors to see Alesi's advance but others thought Alesi took an unnecessary risk by going for a gap that was never really there. The Stewards supported the former view and issued a one race ban suspended for three races on Brabham. With Alesi gone, the race was now a formality barring mechanical failure or accident befalling the Williams pair.

Just prior to this incident, Hill had taken the lead when Coulthard came up to lap Dalmas. The Larrousse slowed dramatically at the scene of Hill's qualifying crash causing the Scot to back off. Hill was far enough away not to be involved

About to prove a little race experience...   *Hill chases Coulthard for first place*

Autodromo do Estoril

With slow, tight corners and short fast straights its 71 laps are very demanding.

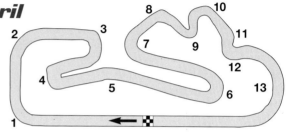

Lap Distance	2.709 miles/4.350 km
Race Distance	192.339 miles/ 308.848 km

In between the old turns Seven and Eight, two more corners were inserted increasing the number of turns from eleven to thirteen and slowing the cars down.

1. Pirelli Bridge — Approached at high speed this corner is entered in fifth and exited with the help of a low kerb.
2. Martini Bridge — Almost immediately the cars enter into the second right hander which is taken flat out. Considered by most drivers to be more dangerous than the former Turn Eight, the barriers here are not far from the track and the corner tightens up very quickly.
3. Turn Three — A very bumpy right hander taken in third with a late entry and apex causing bad understeer.
4. Turn Four — With little or no grip, the cars get through in third before changing up to fourth at the exit.
5. Turn Five — More a kink than a corner it can be taken flat out but it does have a huge bump in the middle.
6. Turn Six — Taken in third, this favours well balanced cars as it has two apexes and tightens quickly.
7. Turn Seven — An off-camber, downhill right hander that is negotiated in third.
8. Turn Eight — Modified so that the cars arrive at the corner much earlier than previously, it is a 120 degree turn followed by a straight of just 200 metres.
9. Turn Nine — A new, very tight left hander taken in second. Many drivers have complained it is too slow.
10. Turn Ten — The track climbs quite steeply to this long, open right hander bringing it back to the old track.
11. Turn Eleven — A fast right hander that is taken in fourth as it is entered blind and tightens up quickly.
12. Turn Twelve — A very sharp left hander that is taken in second.
13. Turn Thirteen — A punishing right hand corner that seems to go on for ever before bringing the cars back on to the main straight. Re-named Senna in memory of the great Brazilian.

Portuguese Grand Prix – 5 Year Record

Year	1st	2nd	3rd	4th	5th	6th
1989	Berger (Ferrari)	Prost (McLaren)	Johansson (Onyx)	Nannini (Benetton)	Martini (Minardi)	Palmer (Tyrrell)
1990	Mansell (Ferrari)	Senna (McLaren)	Prost (Ferrari)	Berger (McLaren)	Piquet (Benetton)	Nannini (Benetton)
1991	Patrese (Williams)	Senna (McLaren)	Alesi (Ferrari)	Martini (Minardi)	Piquet (Benetton)	Schumacher (Benetton)
1992	Mansell (Williams)	Berger (McLaren)	Senna (McLaren)	Brundle (Benetton)	Hakkinen (Lotus)	Alboreto (Footwork)
1993	Schumacher (Benetton)	Prost (Williams)	Hill (Williams)	Alesi (Ferrari)	Wendlinger (Sauber)	Brundle (Ligier)

1994 Grid Positions and Qualifying Times

Grid	No	Driver	1st Session	2nd Session	Diff	Grid	No	Driver	1st Session	2nd Session	Diff
1	28	G. Berger	1'20.608	1'20.863	–	16	10	G. Morbidelli	1'22.974	1'22.756	2.148
2	0	D. Hill	1'20.803	1'20.766	0.158	17	29	A. de Cesaris	1'22.885	1'22.888	2.277
3	2	D. Coulthard	1'21.120	1'21.033	0.425	18	23	P. Martini	1'23.243	1'23.464	2.635
4	7	M. Hakkinen	1'21.251	1'21.700	0.643	19	24	M. Alboreto	1'23.364	1'24.186	2.756
5	27	J. Alesi	1'21.517	1'22.086	0.909	20	12	J. Herbert	No time	1'23.408	2.800
6	3	U. Katayama	1'21.590	4'03.441	0.982	21	25	E. Bernard	1'25.039	1'23.699	3.091
7	8	M. Brundle	1'21.656	1'22.035	1.048	22	20	E. Comas	1'24.192	1'24.306	3.584
8	14	R. Barrichello	1'21.839	1'21.796	1.188	23	19	Y. Dalmas	1.24.438	1.24.920	3.830
9	30	H.H. Frentzen	1'22.795	1'21.921	1.313	24	31	D. Brabham	1'24.527	1.24.514	3.906
10	6	J. Verstappen	1'22.614	1'22.000	1.392	25	11	P. Adams	1'25.313	1'25.708	4.705
11	9	C. Fittipaldi	1'22.636	1'22.132	1.524	26	32	J.M. Gounon	1'25.686	1'25.649	5.041
12	4	M. Blundell	1'22.288	1'22.971	1.680						
13	15	E. Irvine	1'23.411	1'22.294	1.686	**Non-Qualifiers**					
14	5	J.J. Lehto	1'22.613	1'22.369	1.761	27	34	B. Gachot	1'25.686	1'25.649	6.777
15	26	O. Panis	1'23.711	1'22.672	2.064	28	33	P. Belmondo	1'32.706	1'29.000	8.392

but close enough to see his opportunity and seize it and effectively take the race, to reduce Schumacher's Championship lead to a solitary point and, with Benetton only managing two points courtesy of Vertappen's fifth place, Williams went into the Manufacturer's lead for the first time in 1994. Hakkinen came home third, ahead of Barrichello, and with the second McLaren in the hands of Martin Brundle sixth, Ferrari's third place lead was down to 24 points. Life for Lotus, however, appeared grim after all that Monza had promised. Adams had a poor race whilst all that Herbert could drag out of his car was a twelfth place, one lap down on Hill.

There was no doubt, however, to whom the day belonged as the Williams team celebrated overtaking Benetton, Hill celebrated cutting Schumacher's lead to one point, Coulthard celebrated his first podium finish and the British fans celebrated their nation's first one-two since the 1994 winner's father, Graham, brought home Piers Courage at Monaco in 1969 ▓

The Championship

Race Placing and Points

Drivers' Points		Constructors' Points	
10	D. Hill	11	Williams
6	G. Berger	6	Ferrari
4	M. Hakkinen		McLaren
3	R. Barrichello	3	Jordan
2	M. Brundle		
1	D. Coulthard		

Points after Twelve Rounds

Drivers' Points		Constructors' Points	
76	M. Schumacher	89	Williams
75	D. Hill	87	Benetton
33	G. Berger	58	Ferrari
22	M. Hakkinen	34	McLaren
19	J. Alesi	20	Jordan
16	R. Barrichello	13	Tyrrell
14	D. Coulthard	11	Ligier
12	M. Brundle	10	Sauber
10	J. Verstappen	9	Footwork
8	M. Blundell	5	Minardi
7	O. Panis	2	Larrousse

Race Placings

Pos	No	Driver	Team	Time	Diff	Grid	
1	0	D. Hill	Rothmans Williams Renault	1:41'10.165	–	2	
2	2	D. Coulthard	Rothmans Williams Renault	1:41'10.768	0.603	3	
3	7	M. Hakkinen	Marlboro McLaren Peugeot	1:41'30.358	20.193	4	
4	14	R. Barrichello	Sasol Jordan	1:41'38.168	28.003	8	
5	6	J. Verstappen	Mild Seven Benetton Ford	1:41'39.550	29.385	10	
6	8	M. Brundle	Marlboro McLaren Peugeot	1:42'02.867	52.702	7	
7	15	E. Irvine	Sasol Jordan	–	1 lap down	13	
8	9	C. Fittipaldi	Footwork	–	1 lap down	11	
9	26	O. Panis	Ligier Gitanes Blondes	–	1 lap down	15	
10	10	G. Morbidelli	Footwork	–	1 lap down	16	
11	25	E. Bernard	Ligier Gitanes Blondes	–	1 lap down	21	
12	12	J. Herbert	Team Lotus	–	1 lap down	20	
13	23	P. Martini	Minardi Scuderia Italia	–	2 laps down	18	
14	24	M. Alboreto	Minardi Scuderia Italia	–	2 laps down	19	
15	19	Y. Dalmas	Tourtel Larrousse	–	2 laps down	23	
16	32	J.M. Gounon	Simtek	–	4 laps down	26	
17	11	P. Adams	Team Lotus	–	4 laps down	25	

Failed to Finish

Pos	No	Driver	Team	Time	Diff	Grid	
18	4	M. Blundell	Tyrrell	–	61 laps	12	(Engine)
19	5	J.J. Lehto	Mild Seven Benetton Ford	–	60 laps	14	(Accident)
20	29	A. de Cesaris	Sauber	–	54 laps	17	(Differential)
21	27	J. Alesi	Ferrari	–	38 laps	5	(Accident)
22	31	D. Brabham	Simtek	–	36 laps	24	(Accident)
23	30	H.H. Frentzen	Sauber	–	31 laps	9	(Gearbox)
24	20	E. Comas	Tourtel Larrousse	–	27 laps	22	(Suspension)
25	3	U. Katayama	Tyrrell	–	26 laps	6	(Gearbox)
26	28	G. Berger	Ferrari	–	7 laps	1	(Gearbox)

Fastest Lap: D. Coulthard – 1'22.446 (118.297mph/190.379 kph)

Average Speed of Winner: 183.589 kph

Second Coming
European

Schumacher stops in the pit lane at Jerez as marshals visually check the Benettons tyres prior to the warm-up lap.

With Schumacher back from suspension, this was the big one for Hill and and the German maestro. Adding further intrigue was the return to F1 of Nigel Mansell but there were several other drivers who would remember the European Grand Prix at Jerez, re-routed and re-named from the original destination of Argentina. Larrousse, who had sent an invitation to F3000 driver Emmanuel Clerico to take over from Yannick Dalmas but had their overtures rejected, turned to Hideki Noda to make his F1 debut. Also in for a first drive was 26 year old Italian Domenico Schiattarella at Simtek where he took over from Jean Marc Gounon.

At Lotus, whose future was still seriously in doubt, there was a 100% turn round in driving personnel as Zanardi returned in place of Phillippe Adams but the major surprise was the defection of Johnny Herbert to Ligier. Replacing him at Lotus in a direct swop was Ligier's Eric Bernard in a deal that had been kept very quiet.

Schumacher, having been measured in his comments all season, made a quite amazing verbal assault on Hill in the run up to the race. His description of Hill as *"not a number one driver"* was obviously designed to upset Hill but the Briton threw it straight back in the German's face by taking provisional pole in the first qualifying session. But if that made it one round each, Schumacher fought back in the next session to take pole from Hill who would line up second in a race where pole was thought to be a tremendous advantage because of the limited overtaking opportunities at the narrow Spanish track. But the big two names did not have it all to themselves as four other drivers, Barrichello, Mansell, Berger and, interestingly, Johnny Herbert, all had top spot at one time or another. Mansell was quietly impressive in a final third place despite the fact that he was *"still in the wrong time zone"*.

Herbert's switch to Ligier was rewarded with a seventh place on the grid after his top spot proved to be only temporary but even more impressive was Frentzen's fourth spot, his best to date. The major surprise was finding Alesi down amongst the also rans whilst McLaren would not have been over the moon with Brundle's fifteenth place, only one better than Alesi.

One driver just grateful to get through qualifying was Mark Blundell whose Tyrrell smashed into the tyres at Curva Angel Nieto. The two newcomers Noda and Schiattarella qualified in the last two places thus depriving Pacific of a start yet again but Noda incurred the wrath of the Stewards when he failed to stop at a pit lane red light weight check and earned himself a suspended one race ban. Also during qualifying, Tyrrell were awarded a $10,000 suspended fine for entering parc femme and putting a tarpaulin over Blundell's damaged car.

Come race day, there was a nasty fright for Brundle whose car developed a water leak on the grid leaving his mechanics barely time to get the car sorted. They won their race against time only to find their efforts go completely unrewarded when the Marlboro car became the first retirement before the thirty mile mark. With the start thought to play an important part, British fans were overjoyed to see Hill zoom off when the lights went green with Schumacher making his worst get away of the season.

Another to make a very poor grid exit was Mansell who was overtaken by Frentzen, Barrichello and Berger before the first corner. But Hill and Schumacher imposed their authority on the race and were soon clear with the Williams driver holding an advantage over the German that fluctuated between one and two seconds for the first fifteen laps at which stage Schumacher pulled in for his first of a three stop strategy.

Hill's increased lead was to prove no more than an optical illusion for when he pitted, on lap 18, his stop was significantly longer due, so the Williams team thought at the time, to taking on more fuel as he intended only one more pit call and the Benetton was back in the lead. Even more devastating was the ease with which the lightly loaded Schumacher pulled away from Hill opening up such a gap that it soon became obvi-

Mansell talks mechanics.

ous the time lost by the extra pit stop Benetton were planning would be easily affordable.

By now, Noda's debut had ended with electrical problems on his eleventh lap, a fault that was to beset the second Larrousse of Comas on lap 38, and also gone was Verstappen in the second Benetton when he spun off on lap 16. Mansell, too, was having problems as he had his front wing clipped by Noda and when he eventually stopped for repairs on lap 15 he rejoined more than a lap behind the leaders in 23rd.

When Schumacher made his second stop on lap 33, Hill retook the lead but then surprisingly was called into the pits himself two laps later. This was definitely not in the script but it transpired that the Williams team thought they had not loaded enough fuel at the first stop due to a problem with the re-fuelling equipment. It was decided to put on board enough fuel to take him to the finish with the consequence that the much heavier Williams car couldn't keep pace. In fact, it was not surprising that Hill could not cope with Schumacher for the Williams team had loaded sufficient fuel in the first place only for malfunctioning equipment to show otherwise, leaving Hill now loaded with much more fuel than he needed!

Mansell, meanwhile, had climbed back up to

Hakkinen finished third.

Jerez

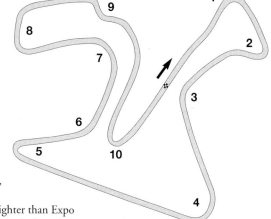

Jerez is a very narrow, twisting, tight track of 69 laps more suitable to motor-cycle racing than Formula One. It is virtually impossible to overtake giving paramount importance to a good grid position.

Lap Distance	2.750 miles/4.428 km
Race Distance	189.75 miles/305.532 km

1. **Expo 92**   Approached at 180 mph in sixth gear with the drivers having to break hard and drop into third gear to complete the right hander, into...

2. **Michelin**   Another right hander but much tighter than Expo with the cars dropping to second gear before exiting at 60mph.

3. **Turn Three**   150mph left hander taken in fifth or sixth exerting tremendous *G* force on the drivers.

4. **Sito Pons**   Big right hander entered at 130mph and exited at 150mph ready for the longest straight on the circuit.

5. **Dry Sack**   This very tight right hander is approached at 185mph, braking hard down to 60mph.

6. **Turn Six**   Left hander taken in fourth at 120mph.

7. **Turn Seven**   A looping left hander that is approached at 130mph and exited at 90mph with gear change from fourth to third.

8. **Angel Nieto and Peluqui**   Two tight right handers that follow on from one another taken at about 90mph.

9. **Ayrton Senna Chicane**   Originally a 90 degree right hander, it was revised and is now a right-left chicane that can only be taken in second. An extremely slow part of the track.

10. **Ducados**   Slowing from sixth to second, this tight left-hander guards the start/finish line.

European Grand Prix – 4 Meeting Record

Year	1st	2nd	3rd	4th	5th	6th
1983	Piquet (Brabham)	Prost (Renault)	Mansell (Lotus)	De Cesaris (Alfa)	Warwick (Toleman)	Giacomelli (Toleman)
1984	Prost (McLaren)	Alboreto (Ferrari)	Piquet (Brabham)	Lauda (McLaren)	Arnoux (Ferrari)	Patrese (Alfa)
1985	Mansell (Williams)	Senna (Lotus)	Rosberg (Williams)	Prost (McLaren)	De Angelis (Lotus)	Boutsen (Arrows)
1993	Senna (McLaren)	Hill (Williams)	Prost (Williams)	Herbert (Lotus)	Patrese (Benetton)	Barbazza (Minardi)

1994 Grid Positions and Qualifying Times

Grid	No	Driver	1st Session	2nd Session	Diff	Grid	No	Driver	1st Session	2nd Session	Diff
1	5	M. Schumacher	1'24.207	1'22.762	–	16	27	J. Alesi	1'25.182	1'44.801	2.420
2	0	D. Hill	1'24.137	1'22.892	0.130	17	23	P. Martini	1'25.812	1'25.294	2.532
3	2	N. Mansell	1'24.971	1'23.392	0.630	18	29	A. De Cesaris	1'25.407	1'25.411	2.645
4	30	H.H. Frentzen	1'24.184	1'23.431	0.669	19	9	C. Fittipaldi	1'26.094	1'25.427	2.665
5	14	R. Barrichello	1'24.700	1'23.455	0.693	20	24	M. Alboreto	1'26.744	1'25.511	2.749
6	28	G. Berger	1'25.079	1'23.677	0.915	21	11	A. Zanardi	1'26.973	1'25.557	2.795
7	25	J. Herbert	1'26.241	1'24.040	1.278	22	12	E. Bernard	1'28.047	1'25.595	2.833
8	10	G. Morbidelli	1'26.048	1'24.079	1.317	23	31	D. Brabham	1'28.388	1'26.055	3.293
9	7	M. Hakkinen	1'25.275	1'24.122	1.360	24	20	E. Comas	1'28.042	1'26.272	3.510
10	15	E. Irvine	1'24.207	1'24.157	1.395	25	19	H. Noda	1'29.041	1'27.168	4.439
11	26	O. Panis	1'25.384	1'24.432	1.670	26	32	D. Schiattarella	1'30.069	1'27.976	5.214
12	6	J. Verstappen	1'35.441	1'24.643	1.881						
13	3	U. Katayama	1'26.304	1'24.738	1.976	**Non-Qualifiers**					
14	4	M. Blundell	1'25.995	1'24.770	2.008	27	34	B. Gachot	1'30.099	1'29.488	6.726
15	8	M. Brundle	1'25.942	1'25.110	2.348	28	33	P. Belmondo	1'31.162	1'30.324	7.472

16th by lap 48 but then spun into the gravel to end a disappointing come back. No doubt the fan who had brought a flag proclaiming *"Nige, we love you – but give the keys to Coulthard"* felt justified. Behind the leaders, who had the race to themselves, Frentzen was keeping up his good qualifying form and a one stop strategy paid dividends with sixth place just behind Berger. But there was a good scrap for the final podium placing between Hakkinen and Irvine, who was having the best Grand Prix drive of his career.

The Jordan was in fact running third until the second stops, all round the forty lap mark, when his advantage of five seconds turned to a deficit of a similar margin once everybody was back out on the track. Thereafter, at one point, Irvine was back on Hakkinen's tail but couldn't get past and, doubtless thinking of his reputation with the authorities and fearful of causing any more trouble, backed off to finish fourth.

But the headlines were made, once more, by the German wonder boy whilst for Hill, it was just about the only result acceptable bar a win. At least it kept him in with a shout going in to the last two races. ◼

The Championship

Race Placing and Points

Drivers' Points		Constructors' Points	
10	M. Schumacher	10	Benetton
6	D. Hill	6	Williams
4	M. Hakkinen	4	McLaren
3	E. Irvine	3	Jordan
2	G. Berger	2	Ferrari
1	H.H. Frentzen	1	Sauber

Points after Thirteen Rounds

Drivers' Points		Constructors' Points	
86	M. Schumacher	97	Benetton
81	D. Hill	95	Williams
35	G. Berger	60	Ferrari
26	M. Hakkinen	38	McLaren
19	J. Alesi	23	Jordan
16	R. Barrichello	13	Tyrrell
14	D. Coulthard	11	Sauber
12	M. Brundle	11	Ligier
10	J. Verstappen	9	Footwork

NB Drivers with less than 10 points not shown.

Race Placings

Pos	No	Driver	Team	Time	Diff	Grid
1	5	M. Schumacher	Mild Seven Benetton Ford	1:40'26.689	–	1
2	0	D. Hill	Rothmans Williams Renault	1:40'51.378	00'24.689	2
3	7	M. Hakkinen	Marlboro McLaren Peugeot	1:41'36.337	01'09.648	9
4	15	E. Irvine	Sasol Jordan	1:41'45.135	01'18.466	10
5	28	G. Berger	Ferrari	–	1 lap down	6
6	30	H.H. Frentzen	Sauber	–	1 lap down	4
7	3	U. Katayama	Tyrrell	–	1 lap down	13
8	25	J. Herbert	Ligier Gitanes Blondes	–	1 lap down	7
9	26	O. Panis	Ligier Gitanes Blondes	–	1 lap down	11
10	27	J. Alesi	Ferrari	–	1 lap down	16
11	10	G. Morbidelli	Footwork	–	1 lap down	8
12	14	R. Barrichello	Sasol Jordan	–	1 lap down	5
13	4	M. Blundell	Tyrrell	–	1 lap down	14
14	24	M. Alboreto	Minardi Scuderia Italia	–	2 laps down	20
15	23	P. Martini	Minardi Scuderia Italia	–	2 laps down	17
16	11	A. Zanardi	Team Lotus	–	2 laps down	21
17	9	C. Fittipaldi	Footwork	–	3 laps down	19
18	12	E. Bernard	Team Lotus	–	3 laps down	22
19	32	D. Schiattarella	Simtek	–	5 laps down	26

Failed to Finish

–	2	N. Mansell	Rothmans Williams Renault	–	47 laps	3	(Spin)
–	31	D. Brabham	Simtek	–	43 laps	25	(Engine)
–	29	A. de Cesaris	Sauber	–	37 laps	18	(Throttle)
–	20	E. Comas	Tourtel Larrousse	–	37 laps	23	(Electrical)
–	6	J. Verstappen	Mild Seven Benetton Ford	–	15 laps	12	(Spin)
–	19	H. Noda	Tourtel Larrousse	–	10 laps	24	(Electrical)
–	8	M. Brundle	Marlboro McLaren Peugeot	–	8 laps	15	(Engine)

Fastest Lap: M. Schumacher – 1'25.040 (116.477mph/187.450kph)

Average Speed of Winner: 182.507kph

Japan

Cliffhanger
in the rain

Suzuka, Japan – 6 November 1994

*Few drivers come much sharper than
Johnny Herbert in the Benetton.*

After the large number of driver changes for the European Grand Prix there were more to come in the Japanese race as the smaller teams ran out of budget and welcomed anybody who had the financial backing for a drive. One driver change those remarks did not apply to was Johnny Herbert, to whom Benetton turned after the Briton had driven in the previous race for Ligier. The reason given was that Verstappen was being rested because of a neck injury but few believed it.

So Hill entered the first qualifying session aware that if Schumacher won the race then he would have to finish at least runner-up in order to take his challenge to the final race. On paper, it was thought that the quick Suzuka track would favour the likes of the Williams and Ferrari machines but Schumacher had shown at Spa that he could compete with the straight line speed cars on the fastest of circuits. The German

was to reiterate the point in the first qualifying session when he left Hill trailing by almost half a second to take what would later be converted to pole position by the weather. Hill, normally unflappable, was quite clearly perturbed by the German's pace and pointedly brushed past reporters commenting only *"I have nothing to say"*. Schumacher, on the other hand, would talk to anybody: *"I am completely satisfied. I would say all the pressure is with somebody else"*.

The weekend's qualifying was yet to take an even bigger turn for the worse as far as Hill was concerned for, after his team mate Nigel Mansell had posted the fastest time of the practice that preceded the second day's qualifying, heavy rain intervened. Brundle posted the fastest time of the few who got underway but it was a startling twenty seconds down on Friday's times and, after Herbert and Barrichello had both spun off, the authorities abandoned the session to leave Hill without the opportunity to get back at the

German. Another German to be pleased the rains came was H.H. Frentzen who went one better than Jerez with third ahead of Mansell.

The rain had not abated by the time the race was due to get underway and there was a real prospect of it being called off. But a start was ordered and pole assumed an importance of great magnitude as Schumacher pulled to the front without the handicap of any spray. Hill, in second place, and the rest of the field were virtually driving in a fog such was the amount of water rearing up at them. Lehto's comeback was short lived as he spun off on the first circuit, a fate which also befell Noda. Frentzen moved quickly up to third past Mansell but he, too, spun off on the first lap although he was able to rejoin in sixth as Herbert went fourth.

But Hill was almost two seconds down on Schumacher at the start of the second tour as the German made the most of his huge advantage from the clear road in front of him. A ten second gap had appeared by the fourth lap but the weather became even worse with hailstones turning the fog like spray into a white sheet. But as the pace car came out so Herbert, Inoue and Katayama departed, victims of aquaplaning.

Six laps later, the rain eased and the Safety Car moved off to let the cars resume a race that was now effectively reduced to 43 laps but within minutes Lagorce, Alboreto, Martini and Berger all came off the track. When Morbidelli couldn't straighten up for a corner and had his car cut in half the Stewards at last decided enough was enough but they were extremely fortunate that Morbidelli was not badly hurt. As the race was stopped, Brundle became the next casualty in conditions that were farcical. After a delay of thirty minutes, the race was restarted with times being aggregated but it was still Schumacher and Hill who were pulling away at the front.

By lap eighteen, Schumacher pitted for what seemed to be a two stop strategy and Hill took over the lead. The German's stop left him in second overall but it put him down to seventh on the track and amongst some traffic whilst Hill, on the other hand, now had the benefit of an open road. With this newly acquired advantage, Hill increased his lead over his rival to some thirty seconds until the Williams came in for its only pit stop on lap 24. Hill rejoined in the overall lead but was now behind Alesi and Mansell, who were having a tremendous tussle for overall third, on the track. Neither of these cars, however, had pitted and when they did, on lap 26, Hill was back in front both overall and on the track. Schumacher, though, was eating away at the gap which had been fourteen seconds on lap 26. By lap 33 the lead had been reduced by ten seconds as Schumacher lapped consistently a second or so faster than Hill. But the Brit's trump card was, of course, that his arch rival would still have to make another stop whereas the Williams didn't. By lap 35, the lead was reduced to just 0.4 secs and on lap 37 the German went into the overall lead by 1.1 secs.

Alarmingly, for Hill at least, there was absolutely no sign of the Benetton pit crew getting ready to receive their driver. Lap forty came and went with Schumacher's lead now 3.782 seconds and the thought came that perhaps the Benetton was not going to stop. If that was indeed the case, then Hill was in big trouble. Just as Hill's hopes were diminishing, however, came the dramatic sight of the Benetton crew getting their pit ready but even a lightning seven second stop was not enough to prevent Hill regaining a lead of fifteen seconds by the time Schumacher had cleared the pit lane. Schumacher now knew the chips were down and proceeded to charge after Hill.

With seven laps to go, the deficit was down to 11.5 secs and closed relentlessly. Hill was now coming up behind Comas which slowed him slightly and the lead was down to seven seconds

Mansell leads Frentzen, Brundell and Hakkinen.

Suzuka

With 53 twisting laps Suzuka's layout is very challenging.

Lap Distance	3.64 miles/ 5.858km
Race Distance	193.117 miles/310.791km

1. Turn One — Approached from the short start/finish straight flat out in sixth with a change down to fifth.
2. Turn Two — Much tighter than the first corner and can only be negotiated in fourth.
3. The S Curves — Left-right-left-right combination that severely taxes any car that is not well balanced. Can usually be taken in fourth.
4. Dunlop Curve — On exiting the S Curves it is immediately up to fifth for a long left hander. It is extremely bumpy and drivers experience plenty of understeer.
5. Degner Curve — A very tight right hander that is entered in fourth, down to third as the second part of the corner becomes tighter still and then generally exited with the use of the kerb. Then it is up to fourth and fifth to go under the bridge where the course crosses itself.
6. Hairpin — Is guarded by a short right hander which somewhat slows the cars but then they have to get down very quickly to second gear for the hairpin.
7. Spoon Curve — Approached via a long looping right hander in sixth gear before entering the actual left hander in fourth. It tightens up forcing the cars to take third gear as they drift to the outside. The cars tend to understeer but it is important to get the exit right as it leads on to the fastest part of the track over the bridge.
8. "130 R" — A very fast left hander which only slows the cars down to fifth gear.
9. Chicane — The Chicane guards the entrance to the finishing straight. The right-left combination is taken in second before third gear is snatched for the final right hander.

Japanese Grand Prix – 5 Year Record

Year	1st	2nd	3rd	4th	5th	6th
1989	Nannini (Benetton)	Patrese (Williams)	Boutsen (Williams)	Piquet (Lotus)	Brundle (Brabham)	Warwick (Arrows)
1990	Piquet (Benetton)	Moreno (Benetton)	Suzuki (Lola)	Patrese (Williams)	Boutsen (Williams)	Nakajima (Tyrrell)
1991	Berger (McLaren)	Senna (McLaren)	Patrese (Williams)	Prost (Ferrari)	Brundle (Brabham)	Modena (Tyrrell)
1992	Patrese (Williams)	Berger (McLaren)	Brundle (Benetton)	de Cesaris (Tyrrell)	Alesi (Ferrari)	Fittipaldi (Minardi)
1993	Senna (McLaren)	Prost (Williams)	Hakkinen (McLaren)	Hill (Williams)	Barrichello (Jordan)	Irvine (Jordan)

1994 Grid Positions and Qualifying Times

Grid	No	Driver	1st Session	2nd Session	Diff	Grid	No	Driver	1st Session	2nd Session	Diff
1	5	M. Schumacher	1'37.209	1'57.128	–	16	23	P. Martini	1'39.548	2'01.929	2.339
2	0	D. Hill	1'37.696	1'57.278	0.487	17	11	A. Zanardi	1'39.721	2'02.077	2.512
3	30	H.H. Frentzen	1'37.742	1'56.935	0.533	18	9	C. Fittipaldi	1'39.868	2'00.084	2.659
4	2	N. Mansell	1'37.768	2'00.963	0.559	19	26	O. Panis	1'40.042	2'00.575	2.833
5	6	J. Herbert	1'37.828	1'59.729	0.619	20	25	F. Lagorce	1'40.557	2'02.780	3.348
6	15	E. Irvine	1'37.880	1'57.760	0.671	21	24	M. Alboreto	1'40.652	2'02.219	3.443
7	27	J. Alesi	1'37.907	1'58.204	0.698	22	20	E. Comas	1'40.979	2'01.035	3.769
8	7	M. Hakkinen	1'37.998	1'58.204	0.789	23	19	H. Noda	1'40.990	2'05.354	3.781
9	8	M. Brundle	1'38.076	1'56.876	0.867	24	31	D. Brabham	1'41.659	2'09.453	4.450
10	14	R. Barrichello	1'38.533	2'01.905	1.324	25	12	H. Salo	1'41.805	2'01.637	4.596
11	28	G. Berger	1'38.570	1'58.926	1.361	26	32	T. Inoue	1'45.004	No time	7.795
12	10	G. Morbidelli	1'39.030	2'07.293	1.821			**Non-Qualifiers**			
13	4	M. Blundell	1'39.266	2'02.266	2.057						
14	3	U. Katayama	1'39.462	2'04.187	2.253	27	34	B. Gachot	1'46.374	No time	9.165
15	29	J.J. Lehto	1'39.483	1'59.943	2.274	28	33	P. Belmondo	1'46.629	No time	9.420

with four laps remaining. Once clear of Comas, Hill had a clear road in front of him to the next back marker, Fittipaldi, but with three laps to go there was just 5.242 secs in it. At this rate, Schumacher looked as if he would just catch Hill who was now rapidly catching Fittipaldi. The Brazilian, however, waved Hill through.

It was a cliffhanger as Hill started the final tour with an overall lead of 2.457 seconds, but fortune shone on the Williams camp as Schumacher came across Salo. The Finn moved quickly out of the German's way but there was an inevitable slight time loss and Hill was home, the German's overall Championship lead reduced to one point going to the final race in Australia. Mansell's nip and tuck battle with Alesi continued all the way to the last chicane where the Brit overtook the Ferrari in a spectacular manoeuvre that, although it didn't give him third place overall, seemed to be Mansell's way of saying *"I'm back"*. Schumacher, for once without a smile on his face, said *"I had no traffic problems, everybody was very good. Our strategy has won us several races but today it lost us the race"*. The first and fourth placings for the Williams were enough to send them to

The Championship

Drivers' Points		Constructors' Points	
10	D. Hill	13	Williams
6	M. Schumacher	6	Benetton
4	J. Alesi	4	Ferrari
3	N. Mansell	2	Jordan
2	E. Irvine	1	Sauber
1	H.H. Frentzen		

Leaderboard after Round 15

Drivers' Points		Constructors' Points	
92	M. Schumacher	108	Williams
91	D. Hill	103	Benetton
35	G. Berger	64	Ferrari
26	M. Hakkinen	38	McLaren
23	J. Alesi	25	Jordan
16	R. Barrichello	13	Tyrrell
14	D. Coulthard	12	Sauber
12	M. Brundle	11	Ligier
10	J. Verstappen	9	Footwork
8	M. Blundell	5	Minardi
		2	Larrousse

Australia in the lead for the constructor's Championship but the final word belonged to Hill who declared *"It's going to be tough, but it's going to be exciting"*. 🏁

Race Placings

Pos	No	Driver	Team	Time	Diff	Grid	
1	0	D. Hill	Rothmans Williams Renault	1:55'53.530	–	2	
2	5	M. Schumacher	Mild Seven Benetton Ford	1:55'56.895	3.365s	1	
3	27	J. Alesi	Ferrari	1:56'45.575	52.045s	7	
4	2	N. Mansell	Rothmans Williams Renault	1:56'49.604	56.074s	4	
5	15	E. Irvine	Sasol Jordan	1:57'35.637	1'42.107	6	
6	30	H.H. Frentzen	Sauber	1:57'53.393	1'59.863	3	
7	7	M. Hakkinen	Marlboro McLaren Peugeot	1:57'56.488	2'02.958	8	
8	9	C. Fittipaldi	Footwork	–	1 lap down	18	
9	20	E. Comas	Tourtel Larrousse	–	1 lap down	22	
10	12	M. Salo	Team Lotus	–	1 lap down	25	
11	26	O. Panis	Ligier Gitanes Blondes	–	1 lap down	19	
12	31	D. Brabham	MTV Simtek Ford	–	2 laps down	24	
13	11	A. Zanardi	Team Lotus	–	2 laps down	17	

Failed to Finish

Pos	No	Driver	Team	Time	Diff	Grid	
–	4	M. Blundell	Tyrrell	–	26 laps	13	(Spin)
–	14	R. Barrichello	Sasol Jordan	–	16 laps	10	(Electrical)
–	8	M. Brundle	Marlboro McLaren Peugeot	–	13 laps	9	(Spin)
–	10	G. Morbidelli	Footwork	–	13 laps	12	(Spin)
–	28	G. Berger	Ferrari	–	10 laps	11	(Electrical)
–	23	P. Martini	Minardi Scuderia Italia	–	10 laps	16	(Spin)
–	24	M. Alboreto	Minardi Scuderia Italia	–	10 laps	21	(Spin)
–	25	F. Lagorce	Ligier Gitanes Blondes	–	10 laps	20	(Spin)
–	3	U. Katayama	Tyrrell	–	3 laps	14	(Spin)
–	6	J. Herbert	Mild Seven Benetton Ford	–	3 laps	5	(Spin)
–	32	T. Inoue	MTV Simtek Ford	–	3 laps	26	(Spin)
–	19	H. Noda	Tourtel Larrousse	–	0 laps	23	(Spin)
–	29	J.J. Lehto	Sauber	–	0 laps	15	(Spin)

Fastest Lap: D. Hill - 1'56.597 (113.17mph/182.124kph) **Average Speed of Winner:** 152.674kph

A sporting win?
Australia

Schumacher held the lead in Adelaide – for 35 laps at least.

So the championship arrived at the final showdown in Australia with Hill's late season charge of four victories in the previous five races having brought him to within a point of Schumacher who stood not only between the Briton and the Championship but between Hill and history. For if the Williams man took the title he would become the first son of a former World Champion to do so. It was the first time since 1986, and only the second occasion in its history, that the Australian Grand Prix would decide the destiny of the title. But in the run up to Adelaide, tension began to show as Hill came out with a quite amazing tirade against his team bosses Frank Williams and Patrick Head, alleging in a television interview that they had not shown him a great deal of support. Away from the main contestants, Jean-Denis Deletraz made his Formula 1 debut by replacing Erik Comas at Larrousse whilst the only

other change from the Japanese line up was the return of Schiattarella to partner Aussie David Brabham at Simtek.

But all eyes were on Hill, Schumacher and, to a lesser degree, Nigel Mansell who on his return to Grand Prix racing had warned everybody not to expect anything from him until Australia. A strange statement given he had never won down under! When qualifying got underway, both Schumacher and Mansell were very fortunate to escape serious injury before taking the front row ahead of Hill. Mansell's incident came as he tried to catch Schumacher's leading time and he drove round a corner at full speed to find Herbert's car stalled and lying sideways across the road. An instinctive piece of driving saw Mansell spin but miss the stationary Benetton. With four minutes of the first session left, Mansell took over provisional pole leaving the German time only for a couple of laps to try and regain the lead. Pushing hard, Schumacher lost control at the chicane and hit the wall, losing two wheels in the process. The German, incredibly, walked away unhurt but his car was badly damaged and the Benetton team were left to work long into the night to get the replacement chassis ready. From Hill's point of view, there must have looked to be a big a gap to make up as he was six-tenths of a second behind in third.

As in Japan, however, the weather intervened to ruin Hill's second session chance of pole with torrential ran ensuring nobody improved their first session times. But the day of reckoning arrived with the rain gone and the weather set fair for a dry race. Schumacher made his customary good start and Mansell his customary bad one leaving the German in the lead from Hill with Mansell down to fifth by the end of the first lap. Schumacher's advantage of some two seconds, however, did not grow as in previous races with Hill digging in hard behind his rival. By the time the two leaders lapped new boy Deletraz as early as the tenth circuit, Hill had cut Schumacher's lead to about 1.3 seconds with the Briton himself clear of Hakkinen in third by some twenty seconds. The Benetton outfit lost their second car

when Herbert, who had been struggling in fifteenth, pulled into the pits after just thirteen circuits and Irvine quickly followed. Retirements now came thick and fast with Morbidelli, Noda, Katayama and Schiattarella all disappearing before a quarter of the race distance.

Up front Schumacher and Hill were giving the crowd a thrilling exhibition of Grand Prix driving at its very best with Hill harrying the German at every conceivable opportunity. Lap 19 saw both cars in the pits together and there was just 0.7 seconds in it when they rejoined the race still first and second.

The two leaders now began to catch the backmarkers and, although both went past Alboreto without any time loss, it seemed that Schiattarella held Hill up for a shade longer than he had Schumacher. Blundell, Salo, Martini, Fittipaldi and Zanardi were all lapped as the two Championship contenders blitzed round but there was no doubting the traffic was delaying Hill as the gap grew to 2.8 secs by lap 33. Once clear of the backmarkers Hill began creeping nearer and nearer to the German and was right back on his tail by lap 35 when the anti-climax of the sporting year arrived.

Every picture tells a story. Race winner Nigel Mansell jokes with Micheal Schumacher as a dejected Damon Hill reflects on what might have been.

Adelaide

With 81 bumpy laps, a car's set-up plays a major part in the result.

Lap Distance	2.349 miles/ 3.780 km
Race Distance	190.155 miles/ 306.180 km

1. **Turn One** — From the startline, this fast left-right-left chicane is approached on a flying lap in fifth before being taken in fourth.
2. **Wakefield Road** — The cars enter close to the wall before straightening up and accelerating into fifth.
3. **Wakefield Corner** — This is guarded by a series of bumps on the approach making this sharp right hander a very uncomfortable proposition for the drivers, taken in second gear.
4. **Flinders Street** — This short straight is entered from a left hander that is equally as sharp as the previous right hander. Exited via another tight right hander in second gear.
5. **East Terrace** — After the slow entrance in second gear, the cars change quickly up to fourth before hitting a fast left flick followed immediately by a difficult right hander.
6. **Rundle Road** — Approached from a tight right hander in third, this is the second longest straight in the race.
7. **Dequetteville Terrace** — Otherwise known as Brabham Straight, this is the circuit's longest straight although overtaking opportunities are usually limited to the furthest end approaching the hairpin.
8. **Roundabout** — The slowest corner on the circuit. Taken in second gear, the approach contains several big bumps.
9. **Racecourse** — A fast but very bumpy right sweep that brings the cars back towards the finishing straight.
10. **Fosters Corner** — A right hand hairpin that slows the cars down into second gear guards the finishing straight.

Australian Grand Prix – 5 Year Record

Year	1st	2nd	3rd	4th	5th	6th
1989	Boutsen (Williams)	Nannini (Benetton)	Patrese (Williams)	Nakajima (Lotus)	Pirro (Benetton)	Martini (Minardi)
1990	Piquet (Benetton)	Mansell (Ferrari)	Prost (Ferrari)	Berger (McLaren)	Boutsen (Williams)	Patrese (Williams)
1991	Senna (McLaren)	Mansell (Williams)	Berger (McLaren)	Piquet (Benetton)	Patrese (Williams)	Morbidelli (Ferrari)
1992	Berger (McLaren)	Schumacher (Benetton)	Brundle (Benetton)	Alesi (Tyrrell)	Boutsen (Ligier)	Modena (Jordan)
1993	Senna (McLaren)	Prost (Williams)	Hill (Williams)	Alesi (Ferrari)	Berger (Ferrari)	Brundle (Legier)

1994 Grid Positions and Qualifying Times

Grid	No	Driver	1st Session	2nd Session	Diff	Grid	No	Driver	1st Session	2nd Session	Diff
1	2	N. Mansell	1'16.179	1'33.988	–	18	24	M Alboreto	1'18.755	1.36.498	2.576
2	5	M. Schumacher	1'16.197	1'32.627	0.018	17	29	J.J. Lehto	1'18.806	1.36.257	2.627
3	0	D. Hill	1'16.830	1'33.792	0.651	18	23	P. Martini	1'18.957	1'36.257	2.778
4	7	M. Hakkinen	1'16.992	1'35.432	0.813	19	9	C. Fittipaldi	1'19.061	1'35.790	2.882
5	14	R. Barrichello	1'17.537	1'37.610	1.358	20	25	F. Lagorce	1'19.153	1'37.393	2.974
6	15	E. Irvine	1'17.667	No time	1.488	21	10	G. Morbidelli	1'19.610	1'35.136	3.431
7	6	J Herbert	1'17.727	1'35.712	1.584	22	12	M. Salo	1'19.844	1'43.071	3.665
8	27	J. Alesi	1'17.801	1'33.905	1.622	23	19	H. Noda	1'20.145	1'47.569	3.966
9	8	M. Brundle	1'17.950	1'36.246	1.771	24	31	D. Brabham	1'20.442	No time	4.263
10	30	H.H. Frentzen	1'17.962	1'35.623	1.783	25	20	J.D. Deletraz	1'22.422	1'44.155	6.243
11	28	G. Berger	1'18.070	1'33.818	1.891	26	32	D. Schiattarella	1'22.529	No time	6.350
12	26	O. Panis	1'18.072	1'36.222	1.893						
13	4	M. Blundell	1'18.237	1'35.462	2.058	**Non-Qualifiers**					
14	11	A. Zanardi	1'18.331	1'39.179	2.152	27	33	P. Belmondo	1'24.087	No time	7.908
15	3	U. Katayama	1'18.411	1'36.628	2.232	28	34	B. Gachot	No time	No time	–

Schumacher, under considerable pressure from Hill, misjudged his line out of Flinders Street and hit the right hand wall hard. The badly damaged car veered across the track to the left which manufactured a gap on the inside for Hill to drive through. It then appeared the German quite ruthlessly shut the door on the Briton as he slewed his car back across the track, taking out the Williams car in the process. That Schumacher was out of the contest was not in doubt but Hill, sporting a puncture and body damage, rolled round to the pits hoping for the best but fearing the worst. The puncture was no problem but the bent front wishbone certainly was and the German took the World Championship whilst standing waiting for a lift back to the pits.

Mansell was now left in the lead from Berger, Hakkinen, Barrichello, Brundle and Panis with the first two some way clear. They proceeded to have a great battle with Berger regaining the lead by 0.4 secs after the last pit stops from the 1992 Champion but, on lap 64, Alboreto probably unsighted Berger at a corner and the Austrian slid

The Championship

Drivers' Points		Constructors' Points	
10	N. Mansell	10	Williams
6	G. Berger	7	Ferrari
4	M. Brundle	4	McLaren
3	R. Barrichello	3	Jordon
2	O. Panis	2	Ligier
1	J. Alesi		

well wide allowing Mansell to capitalise. The Briton's cause was further aided by Frentzen, who appeared to allow him through but then raced against Berger who, at one stage, gesticulated wildly at the German before eventually getting past. His chance was now gone, however, and Mansell came to win the race he would have liked to have won in 1986 when his retirement at Adelaide cost him the World title. Back in third, Brundle was making it a hat-trick of points scoring finishes at Adelaide whilst Barrichello finished the season as he had started it in Brazil with a fourth place. But it was an unfortunate end to a sad season. ■

Race Placings

Pos	No	Driver	Team	Time	Diff	Grid	
1	2	N. Mansell	Rothmans Williams Renault	1:47'51,480	–	1	
2	28	G. Berger	Ferrari	1:47'53.991	2.511s	11	
3	8	M. Brundle	Marlboro McLaren Peugeot	1:48'43.867	52.487s	9	
4	14	R. Barrichello	Sasol Jordan	1:49'02.010	70.530s	5	
5	26	O. Panis	Ligier Gitanes Blondes	–	1 lap down	12	
6	27	J. Alesi	Ferrari	–	1 lap down	8	
7	30	H.H. Frentzen	Sauber	–	1 lap down	10	
8	9	C. Fittipaldi	Footwork	–	1 lap down	19	
9	23	P. Martini	Minardi Scuderia Italia	–	2 laps down	18	
10	29	J.J. Lehto	Sauber	–	2 laps down	17	
11	25	F. Lagorce	Ligier Gitanes Blondes	–	2 laps down	20	
12	7	M. Hakkinen	Marlboro McLaren Peugeot	–	5 laps down	4	

Failed to Finish

	No	Driver	Team			Grid	
–	24	M. Alboreto	Minardi Scuderia Italia	–	69 laps	16	(Suspension)
–	4	M. Blundell	Tyrrell	–	66 laps	13	(Accident)
–	20	J.D. Deletraz	Tourtel Larrousse	–	56 laps	25	(Gearbox)
–	12	M. Salo	Team Lotus	–	49 laps	22	(Electircs)
–	31	D. Brabham	MTV Simtek Ford	–	49 laps	24	(Engine)
–	11	A. Zanardi	Team Lotus	–	40 laps	14	(Throttle Cable)
–	5	M. Schumacher	Mild Seven Benetton Ford	–	35 laps	2	(Accident)
–	0	D. Hill	Rothmans Williams Renault	–	35 laps	3	(Wishbone)
–	32	D. Schiattarella	MTV Simtek Ford	–	21 laps	26	(Gearbox)
–	3	U. Katayama	Tyrrell	–	19 laps	15	(Spin)
–	19	H. Noda	Tourtel Larrousse	–	18 laps	23	(Oil leak)
–	10	G. Morbidelli	Footwork	–	17 laps	21	(Oil Pump)
–	15	E Irvine	Sasol Jordan	–	15 laps	6	(Spin/fire)
–	6	J. Herbert	Mild Seven Benetton Ford	–	13 laps	7	(Gearbox)

Fastest Lap: M. Schumacher – 1'17.140 (109.616 mph/176.372 kph)

Average Speed of Winner: 170.290kph

Review

1994 turned out to be a year of change and of tragedy, the Championship decided by guts and by guile.

It was a season that began in controversy, quickly moved on to tragedy, engaged itself in dispute, returned to controversy and ended in anti-climatic style just when the intense rivalry between Michael Schumacher and Damon Hill threatened to at least give back Formula 1 some of its former glory. Indeed, as the German and British contenders for the title fought tooth and nail throughout the rain sodden penultimate race in Japan and the first thirty-five laps of the final Grand Prix in Australia, it even began to look as though the 1994 campaign would actually be remembered for some top class racing as well as the tragedy and altercations.

Sadly, it was not to be, for the 1994 title fight once more became contentious as Schumacher took the Championship stood by the roadside following a manoeuvre that, at best, was a hor-

rendous mistake, at worst an unbelievable piece of gamesmanship. Only Michael Schumacher will ever know for certain the answer to that but, if his shunting of Hill after the German himself had crashed in Adelaide was deliberate, then Schumacher can a least console himself in he knowledge that most people considered the title, in the end, landed up with its rightful owner although not in the way they would have liked.

For a man whose trade mark all season had been an infectious grin, there was noticeably no smile from the newly installed World Champion at the post Adelaide press conference. A quite remarkable state of affairs, given his triumph over so much adversity throughout 1994, which suggested, perhaps, more than some regret at how the title had finally been captured. He explained his solemn attitude away by saying he felt his

Benetton, the team behind World Champion Michael Schumacher, pose for a team photograph with Schumacher and Johnny Herbert.

Berger led an encouraging year for Ferrari by racing his way into third place in the Drivers World Championship.

success had been devalued by the absence of Ayrton Senna. The German immediately dedicated his triumph to the Brazilian and then proceeded to apologise to Hill for the comments he had made about the Briton from the time things began to get tight at the top of the leaderboard. Was this the scent of remorse?

For his part Hill, just as he had done throughout a long and difficult season, kept his dignity and did not once criticise the move that prevented him becoming the first son of a former World Champion to win the title. After eight months on the circuit Hill, for one tenth of one second in Adelaide, had his hands on the title but was brushed aside in a moment of madness from his rival. Yes, it would have been very easy for him to have cried *"Foul"* but it spoke volumes for the character of the man that he remained calm and positive about it all, saying simply *"That's motor racing"* when he must surely have wanted to say a great deal more. Some people become winners in defeat and Damon Hill certainly became just that.

Back in March, the season had got underway in Brazil with nobody quite sure what lay ahead. The new regulations, especially regarding re-fuelling, computer aids and downforce, were viewed by many teams with some apprehension but the first race seemed to vindicate the

Authorities' stance in pressing ahead with the unpopular measures against most teams' expressed fears. Martin Brundle went down in the record books as the first driver to re-fuel under the new laws whilst Pacific's Bernard Gachot became the first retirement of 1994. Unfortunately for the debutant team, that was almost the highlight of their year as Pacific rarely appeared thereafter due to only *qualifying* when other teams had non-runners. But with nine different teams filling the first nine places, and eleven different teams in the twelve finishers, FIA chief Bernie Ecclestone seemed to have been proved right in his decision to press ahead with the changes. The lasting memory, however, of that Brazilian Grand Prix was the sight of the vast crowd streaming out well before the finish once their hero, Ayrton Senna, had spun off. They were not to know that they would never see their champion race on home soil again.

If the season had begun with the unknown, it continued in that vein when the entourage moved on to Japan for the Pacific Grand Prix, introduced to the calendar at the whim of billionaire Japanese businessman, Hajima Tanaka, who was reported to have paid a vast sum of money to stage a race at his private track. The unknown was now becoming clearer with Aida throwing up several similarities to Brazil. Schumacher won for

Final Placing and Points

Drivers' Points

92	M. Schumacher	7	H.H. Frentzen
91	D. Hill	6	N. Larini
41	G. Berger	6	C. Fittipaldi
26	M. Hakkinen	6	E. Irvine
24	J. Alesi	5	U. Katayama
19	R. Barrichello	4	K. Wendlinger
16	M. Brundle	4	A. de Cesaris
14	D. Coulthard	4	P.L. Martini
13	N. Mansell	4	E. Bernard
10	J. Verstappen	3	G. Morbidelli
9	O. Panis	2	E. Comas
8	M. Blundell	1	J.J. Lehto

Constructors' Points

118	Williams	13	Tyrrell
103	Benetton	12	Sauber
71	Ferrari	9	Footwork
42	McLaren	5	Minardi
28	Jordan	2	Larrousse
13	Ligier		

the second consecutive race and Senna failed to finish for the second successive time whilst Barrichello followed up his fourth in Brazil by going one better in Japan.

So Williams moved into the European tour with just the six points gleaned by Damon Hill in Brazil and the pressure was mounting on the team's new signing, Ayrton Senna, to perform in a car that was acknowledged as unlikely to be competitive until later in the season. That pressure may, or may not, have led to the Imola tragedy that saw the great man lose his life but there were terrible things happening out on the track that went unheeded prior to the race itself.

Barrichello's superb start to the campaign came to a halt with a frightening crash on the Friday at Variante Bassa chicane but Saturday proved to be fatal as Roland Ratzenberger lost his young life. Sunday saw yet more carnage as an Italian spectator was killed by flying debris from a start-line collision between Lehto and Lamy and then, after just six laps of the restarted race, Senna was killed at Tamburello to complete the blackest weekend that motor-racing has ever known. Incredibly, the decision was taken to have another restart following which Schumacher extended his lead to 23 points over Barrichello and Hill.

The Monaco Grand Prix took place amid emotional scenes not helped by another crash which almost cost Karl Wendlinger his life. Hill raced alone for Williams following the death of his team mate but he didn't drive far as Hakkinen put the Briton out on the first circuit, leaving Schumacher to turn the Championship into a one horse race with his fourth successive victory giving him a thirty point lead over Gerhard Berger. But the two mysteries of the season were the mighty Williams outfit languishing with just seven points and the second Benetton car having failed to score a single point whilst Schumacher was piling up his maximum.

The second question was never satisfactorily answered but Hill began to make some inroads for Williams when he captured the Spanish Grand Prix but even then the sceptics were quick to point out that Schumacher would surely have won but for being stuck in fifth gear for much of the race. Spain, incidentally, threw up another factor that would grow into a contentious issue

Roland Ratzenberger (1962-1994)

"*M*otor Racing is dangerous" is the caption frequently used around racing tracks to make fans aware of the dangers and to deter them from getting too close to the action. Formula One had seemingly become steadily safer, certainly there had been accidents and, yes, there have been spectacular spills, but no driver had been killed for twelve years. The death of Roland Ratzenberger at Imola during qualifying sadly

brought the dangers back into sharp perspective in the cruelest way possible.

Nobody deserves to die for their sport, human life is too precious a commodity, but if a driver has reached the pinnacle and become a household name, the memories may just ease the pain of those left behind. Sadly with Roland he had not been in the top echelon of the sport long enough to leave his mark as a winner.

Born in Saltzburg in 1962, Roland began by establishing his name, like so many others, in the

Brundle leads Hakkinen at Adelaide, but the flying Finn ended the season in a creditable fourth position in the Drivers World Championship.

before the season's end for it saw the debut of David Coulthard who was to perform extremely well for Williams only to lose his place to Nigel Mansell when the former champion was free of Indy Car commitments.

Canada and France saw Schumacher and Hill finish 1-2 with Lehto picking up a first point in the second Benetton car at Montreal. The two main adversaries finished 1-2 again in the British Grand Prix but, much to the delight of the home crowd, it was Hill who came home first. But again the critics were quick to point out that the major reason Hill won was due to a *stop and go* penalty

imposed on the German. The race, however, saw the beginning of major controversy as the German had ignored a black flag, was disqualified and had a two race ban imposed. As the German Grand Prix approached, Benetton were also in trouble over computer software enabling launch control systems to be operated at the start of races and there was further trouble in store for the outfit when they removed a fuel filter from a re-fuelling pump at Hockenheim resulting in a horrendous pit lane fire that engulfed Jos Verstappen.

With neither of the two title hopefuls being in

highly competitive Formula Ford at the age of 21 and took the Austrian, German and European Championships within three years. By 1987 he had moved up to F3 with the West Surrey Racing team and, after a further two seasons consolidating his trade, Roland looked to move his career upward again. He decided to try his luck in Japan, running initially in Saloon cars before graduating to Formula 3000 and sportscars where he triumphed in the Fuji 1000km in 1990. The following year he went on to success in the Suzuki 1000km before taking third place in the Daytona 24 hour classic in 1992.

Entry into Formula One is never easy but Roland was determined and thought he had a drive secured with the Eddie Jordan team in 1991 only to be thwarted by the last minute withdrawal of a sponsor. 1993, however, finally saw him make it when he signed up for the Simtek team which led him on his fateful trip to Imola. Sadly, his full potential will never be known but what was known of the man was his infectious humour and good natured charm. Roland Ratzenberger will be sadly missed around the Grand Prix circuits of the world. ◼

An appreciation by Mike Durcan

the points in Germany, Hungary was important to Schumacher as he still had his two race ban to serve. He made no mistake and now led Hill by 31 points and it seemed he had wrapped the title up prior to taking his enforced absence when he also won comfortably at Spa. But he was now disqualified in Belgium for contravening the skid block regulations and, with Hill taking both races that the German missed due to his suspensions, the lead was suddenly just one point. Schumacher took the European Grand Prix from Hill to give himself a safety net of five points but the best race of the season came in the worst conditions of the campaign when Hill drove like a man inspired to reduce the deficit back down to one point for the trip to Australia and the resulting anti-climax.

Whilst Williams and Benetton dominated the season, what of the other teams? Ferrari had been expected to come on strong in the latter half of the season but, in fact, their effort petered out somewhat after Berger's win in Germany and in the last seven races the Italians picked up only

19 points. Another outfit to get off to a bright start were Sauber, who were in the points in each of the first three Grand Prix but still only managed twelve points before the end of the season. McLaren, on the other hand, after taking only fourteen points from the first nine events, failed to figure in the points just once, at rain lashed Suzuka, in the last seven races. Lotus had an awful campaign, failing to score a point for the first time, but at least they saw the season out, something which looked unlikely when they went into administration in August. Outside of Williams, who took the manufacturers' title and Benetton, whose number one pilot won the drivers' championship, the happiest team was undoubtedly Jordan who easily won *the best of the rest* title with some highly promising performances from the young Barrichello.

But sadly, the 1994 season will be remembered more for the passing of Ayrton Senna and Roland Ratzenberger than for the technicalities which almost brought a fairy tale ending to the campaign for Damon Hill. ▓

Ayrton Senna.

Ayrton Senna (1962-1994)

For motor racing fans, the worst day of 1994, the First day of May, the San Marino Grand Prix at Imola, the death of Ayrton Senna. Nothing can change the grim finality of this simple statement and, in the world of motor sport, F1 the very pinnacle, will never seem the same again.

Motor racing has seen more than its fair share of tragedy with deaths of many of its greatest heroes, but nothing compares with the overwhelming sense of loss that accompanied Ayrton's death. Seeking adequate words to describe the stunning breadth of his talents and the range of his achievements is an almost impossible task which, in itself, only serves to further recall the sadness of the occasion.

Many great sportsmen and women have natural talent and skills which sometimes sadly are not nurtured and developed to their highest potential or which fade with pressures of life outside of their chosen sport. Ayrton Senna was hugely gifted with talent from an early age but, throughout his career, he displayed a single

Williams HQ, Didcot, in the aftermath of Imola.

mindedness and motivation which was legendary. He devoted his short life to motor sport.

Ayrton Senna da Silva was born 20th March 1960 in Sao Paulo, Brazil. His father was a wealthy businessman with a wide range of interests and he made his son's first go-kart when Ayrton was just four year's old. By the time he was thirteen, the youngster was racing and he went on to win the Brazilian National Championship four times in a row between 1978 and 1981. He came to England as a twenty one year old and progressed through Formula Ford and Formula 3, in which Formula he set a record of twelve wins in 1983 that was to stand until the year of his death. Armed with this success he made the move into F1 in 1984 and had his first success in the Portuguese Grand Prix of 1985 driving for Lotus. The following year he finished third in the World Championship. Moving to McLaren in 1988, Ayrton went on to capture his first of three World titles, recording no fewer than eight victories on his way. He followed up by taking the title again in both 1990 and 1991.

In his search for perfection in the ever changing world of F1, Ayrton felt that Williams would give him a more competitive car and in 1994 he signed up to become their number one driver. Sadly the car was not fast enough even with a talent as enormous as that of Ayrton behind the wheel and he died at Imola without scoring a solitary point for the Williams team.

In life, Ayrton Senna was a national hero in Brazil and in death he became even more so. Almost uniquely amongst sportsmen, he was honoured by the country of his birth with a state funeral and an unprecedented three days of national mourning which gave some measure of the esteem in which he was held. Sadly, all that remains are the memories. ▚

An appreciation by Mike Durcan

Grand Prix Record

Grand Prix Total	161	5th places	6
Wins	41	6th places	3
2nd places	23	Poles	65
3rd places	16	Fastest Laps	19
4th places	7	Total points	614

PPG *Indy Car* year

Preview...

Could Nigel Mansell retain his world crown or would the 'good ol' boys' of Indy Car wrestle it back from him?

1993 had seen Nigel Mansell become the first driver to pull off a hat-trick of F1/Indycar successes but would the Newman/Haas car be able to withstand a renewed challenge for supremacy from the Roger Penske outfit? Mansell's team mate at Newman/Haas would be veteran Mario Andretti who, during 1994, would drive in his 400th IndyCar race. After tasting success twice in the previous three campaigns, Newman/Haas had high hopes but were very wary, indeed, of the challenge to be posed by the Penske cars. Either way round, be it Mansell or Penske, Britain would have an interest for the Penske cars are built, by and large, at Poole, Dorset.

The Penske team looked a formidable outfit on paper having signed-up Emerson Fittipaldi, Al Unser Jnr and Paul Tracy. Fittipaldi had been runner-up to Mansell in 1993 and had 20 wins in 151 IndyCar starts in addition to his 14 successes in 144 F1 outings whilst Unser Jnr had won 19 of his 172 IndyCar races and had put his family name in the history books when winning the 1990 title, the first time anyone had emulated their father in winning an IndyCar Series.

Canadian Tracy had won the British Racing Driver's Club Bruce McLaren Trophy for the most promising Commonwealth driver and had fulfiled that potential with 1993 IndyCar victories at Long Beach, Cleveland, Toronto, Road America and Laguna Seca to finish third. Add to that little lot, Penske's own 79 IndyCar wins (a record) including nine Indianapolis 500's and Mansell was obviously going to have a difficult time in holding on to his title especially as Penske had instructed his company seven chassis for the three cars.

Another British interest would be the Bicester based Reynard company who were entering the IndyCar Series for the first time with its 941 chassis which would be used by the Chip Ganassi, Forsyth/Green, Vasser and Hayhoe teams. Further British connections were made by the Galles-Kraco team. Co-owner, Rick Galles, founded the chassis builder, Bicester based Galmer Engineering, and has been in IndyCar racing since 1983 but for the 1994 season he lost the services of Al Unser Jnr to Penske.

Continuing the British theme was Walker Motorsport. Derrick Walker, born in Edinburgh, began his racing career as a mechanic with Brabham's F1 team before being signed up as racing manager by Penske who then proceeded to win five IndyCar championships plus five Indianapolis 500s under his guidance before Walker decided, to set up on his own.

The Rahal/Hogan team along with Dale Coyne Racing were to provide new interest with the introduction of Honda engines to the IndyCar scene. Rahal/Hogan drivers would be Bobby Rahal himself who was the first IndyCar driver to earn over one million dollars when winning the IndyCar championship in 1986,1987 and 1992 after being *Rookie of the Year* in 1982, and newcomer Michael Groff ■

Nigel Mansell considers his chances for the forthcoming season.

Surfers Paradise

Queensland, Australia – 20 March 1994

Nigel Mansell got the season off to a flyer in every sense of the word when he began his defence of the title with an impressive pole position and the first point of the 1994 series. He was well over half a second faster than Michael Andretti and more than a second in front of third placed qualifier, Emerson Fittipaldi. Villeneuve, on his Indy debut, was on the fourth row but Mario Andretti got his final campaign underway in a disappointing nineteenth spot after his car caught fire midway through the last qualifying session. Teo Fabi, after a shunt, found himself in a back-up car in eleventh and last of the Reynard's which gave the Malcolm Ostler designed machine half a dozen entries in the top eleven grid positions. The race itself was run in conditions not quite typical of the average person's dream of Australia as the sea churned into massive breakers and the rain lashed down just as the race was about to get underway. The red flag came out and the race declared *wet*. A delay of forty-five minutes ensued but when the race started again Zampedri took a wrong line and caused a five car shunt involving Raul Boesel, Dominic Dobson,

Willy Ribbs, and Robbie Buhl. The red flag quickly appeared again and another lengthy delay ensued. The race eventually got underway some two hours after its scheduled start time with the track by now dry again!

At the third start, Zampedri again got it all wrong and took out Boesel and Rahal as well as dumping himself, Jones, Matsushita and Dobson into the sandtraps. All four in the sand recovered but up front, Michael Andretti powered his way past Mansell on the run to the first left-hander whilst Fernandez and Tracy, fourth and sixth placed on the grid, got in a mix up and dropped immediately to 18th and 27th respectively. Robby Gordon had made an impressive start and was up to third behind Andretti Jnr and Fittipaldi by lap six. Seven laps later, he was back down to fourth as Mansell got into the race and two laps later, the Briton was past Fittipaldi and into second. Gordon then made a mistake on lap seventeen and crashed out of the race with a full course yellow flag awaiting Andretti and the leaders. As the race began in earnest once more, Mansell skidded and fell back but perhaps some justice was done when Zampedri was collected

Michael Andretti chalks up the first win of the season.

by Mark Smith on lap 19 and dumped out.

By lap 30, Michael Andretti led Fittipaldi and Mario Andretti with Vasser the surprise package in fourth. Johansson and Villeneuve were disputing fifth but Mansell was back in thirteenth. Due to the late start, the evening gloom was now fast approaching and it was clear that the contest would not see the full 65 circuits. Johansson consolidated his fifth spot when Villeneuve crashed out on lap 36 by which time Mansell was up to ninth but a lap down on the leader who was still Michael Andretti.

On lap 50, with Andretti holding a four second lead it was announced that the race would now be one of 55 laps and Fittipaldi threw everything in as he desperately attempted to close the gap before he ran out of time. He succeeded to an extent, gaining almost a second a lap as Andretti made sure of lasting the remaining few laps and by the start of the last circuit there was little more than a second in it. Andretti then met up with Fabi who objected to being lapped and held up the leader to give Fittipaldi a glimmer of hope but once Andretti Jnr had got past Fabi, Fittipaldi found it equally difficult and there was still a second to spare for the leader at the line. The win gave Reynard the remarkable record of making a victorious debut in every formula in which it has competed and let Mansell know that he would have a fight on his hands to retain his title ◙

Points and Leaderboard

Position	Points	Driver
1	21	Mi. Andretti
2	16	E. Fittipaldi
3	14	Mario Andretti
4	12	J. Vasser
5	10	S. Johansson
6	8	M. Gugelmin
7	7	T. Fabi
=8	5	M. Groff
=8	5	N. Mansell
10	3	S. Goodyear
11	2	S. Sharp
12	1	D. Dobson

Race Placings

Pos	Driver	Team	Time	Diff	
1	M. Andretti	Chip Ganassi Reynard 94l Ford	1:53'52.770	–	
2	E. Fittipaldi	Penske Racing Penske PC23-Ilmor D	1:53'54.096	1.326	
3	Ma. Andretti	Newman/Hasse Lola T94/00 Ford	1;54'00.650	7.880	
4	J. Vasser	Hayhoe Reynard 94l Ford	1:54'34.577	41.807	
5	S. Johansson	Bettenhausen Penske PC22-Ilmor D	1:55'01.217	1'08.447	
6	M. Gugelmin	Chip Ganassi Reynard 94l Ford	1:55'22.328	1'29.558	
7	T. Fabi	Hall Reynard 94l-D	–	54 laps	
8	M. Groff	Rahal/Hogan Lola T94/00-Honda	–	54 laps	
9	N. Mansell	Newman/Haas Lola T94/00-Ford	–	54 laps	
10	S. Goodyear	Budweiser King Lola T94/00-Ford	–	53 laps	
11	S. Sharp	PacWest Lola T94/00-Ford	–	53 laps	
12	D. Dobson	PacWest Lola T94/00-Ford	–	52 laps	
13	A. Fernandez	Galles Reynard 94l-Ilmor D	–	52 laps	
14	Al Unser Jnr	Penske Racing Penske PC23-Ilmor D	–	51 laps	Electrical
15	H. Matsushita	Dick Simon Lola T94/00-Ford	–	48 laps	Running
16	P. Tracy	Penske Racing Penske PC23-Ilmor D	–	39 laps	Electrical
17	J. Villeneuve	Forsythe/Green Reynard 94l-Ford	–	36 laps	Accident
18	W. T Ribbs	Walker Lola T93/00-Ford	–	34 laps	Accident
19	D. Jones	AJ Foyt T94/00-Ford	–	31 laps	Transmission
20	R. Buhl	Dale Coyne Lola T93/00-Ford	–	30 laps	Low oil pressure
21	M. Smith	Walker Lola T94/00-Ford	–	19 laps	Accident
22	A. Zampedri	Euromotorsport Lola T93/00-Ilmor C	–	19 laps	Accident
23	R. Gordon	Walker Lola T94/00-Ford	–	16 laps	Accident
24	G. Brabham	Bettenhausen Penske PC22-Ilmor	–	10 laps	Transmission
25	A. Luyendyk	Indy Regency Lola T94/00-Ilmor D	–	8 laps	Transmission
26	B. Rahal	Rahal/Hogan Lola T94/00-Honda	–	0 laps	Accident
27	R. Boesel	Dick Simon Lola T94/00-Ford	–	0 laps	Accident
–	M. Greco	Arciero Lola T94/00-Ford	–	–	Did not start
–	B. Lazier	Leader Cards Lola T93/00-Ilmor C	–	–	Did not start
–	A. Montermini	Dale Coyne Lola T93/00-Ford	–	–	Did not start
–	D. Kudrave	Euromotorsport Lola T92/00-Ilmor A	–	–	Did not start

Average Speed of Winner: 80.994mph

Phoenix 200

Phoenix, Arizona, USA – 10 April 1994

Qualifying saw last year's winner, Mario Andretti, take fourth spot on the grid thus showing he was in the sort of form that gave him the record in last year's corresponding event of becoming, at the age of 53, the oldest driver ever to win an Indy Car race. Right behind him in sixth was 47 year old Emerson Fittipaldi as the Golden Oldies demonstrated they were still capable of producing the big one on the day. Mansell was third fastest but pole went appropriately to Paul Tracy who crashed out of the 1993 race when holding a lead of a full lap. Mansell, however, approached the race with some trepidation for the 1993 equivalent had witnessed his horrific crash in practice which put him out of action for some weeks. Indeed, he was quoted as saying *"I am not comfortable on this track. Believe me, after last year, I know that if anything goes wrong you are in the wall"*. Tracy's pole position, incidentally, was achieved by taking the lap record only just set by Jacques Villeneuve, who was to later have his car sandwiched between Mansell and the wall leaving him to race in a rebuilt, but untried, car the next day.

As a result, Villeneuve quickly lost his grid advantage as Tracy and Mansell battled it out up front. Mansell ate into Tracy's lead, slowly but surely, and on lap eleven overtook him. Lap 27 saw the first yellow when Ribbs was the victim of a tyre blow out which resulted in him slamming in to the wall. Mansell pitted during the yellow but then stalled and emerged a lap down in twelfth position with a lot of overtaking to do if he was to get back into contention. Lap 62, however, saved him the bother of getting past Tracy who, for the second year running, crashed out when in the lead. Fabi and Matsushita touched and went into the wall leaving Tracy with nowhere to go but into Matsushita just as he was about to lap him. Villeneuve then also piled into Matsushita whose car virtually blew to pieces. As the debris began to settle, Dominic Dobson was collected up in it and out he went, too. The fact that the race was run for the next 27 laps under a yellow whilst the wreckage was removed shows just how lucky Matsushita was to walk away with nothing more serious than a dislocated shoulder.

Nigel Mansell finished a lap down and in third place.

When the race got underway again, Mansell began making up ground but he also incurred the wrath of Scott Goodyear on lap 112 when the Brit came out of a pit stop with red hot rear tyres but cold front rubber. With little grip Mansell's slewed sideways and only righted itself immediately in front of Goodyear who was forced into evasive action before gesticulating at Nigel. The mishap cost Mansell another lap but up front Robby Gordon stormed into the lead when Fittipaldi and Al Unser Jnr pitted at the the three-quarter stage. Gordon, however, had not pitted since lap 82 and he slowed to a crawl on lap 154 in order to get round and refuel. This left Fittipaldi and Unser back in control with Mansell working his way through the field, albeit a lap adrift. With the leaders on lap 165 there was a devastating moment for the Andretti family when Mario's right front break exploded causing him to crash. Into this came Michael who walloped into John Paul Jnr with a wheel coming off and arcing spectacularly some 100ft into the air before landing on a hospitality complex. Miraculously only three people were injured, none seriously. The race was now a procession with too many lapped cars between Fittipaldi and Unser for the latter to make a race of it whilst Mansell was content to come home in one piece just one lap down in third ◼

Points and Leaderboard

Position	Points	Driver
1	37	Emerson Fittipaldi
=2	22	Stefan Johansson
=2	22	Jimmy Vasser
4	21	Michael Andretti
5	19	Nigel Mansell
6	16	Al Unser Jnr
7	14	Mario Andretti
8	13	Mike Groff
9	8	Maurice Gugelmin
=10	6	Teo Fabi
=10	6	Scott Sharp
=10	6	Robby Gordon

Race Placings

Pos	Driver	Team	Time	Diff	
1	E. Fittipaldi	Penske Racing Penske PC23-Ilmor D	1:51'41.615	–	
2	A. Unser Jnr	Penske Racing Penske PC23-Ilmor D	1:51'55.097	13.482	
3	N. Mansell	Newman Haas Lola T94/00-Ford	–	199 laps	
4	S. Johansson	Bettenhausen Penske PC22-Ilmor D	–	197 laps	
5	J. Vasser	Hayhoe Reynard 94I-Ford	–	197 laps	
6	M. Groff	Rahal/Hogan Lola T94/00-Honda	–	196 laps	
7	R. Gordon	Walker Lola T94/00-Ford	–	195 laps	
8	R. Boesel	Dick Simon Lola T94/00-Ford	–	195 laps	
9	S. Sharp	PacWest Lola T94/00-Ford	–	194 laps	
10	A. Fernandez	Galles Reynard 94I-Ilmor D	–	194 laps	
11	S. Goodyear	Budweiser King Lola T94/00-Ford	–	192 laps	
12	D. Jones	AJ Foyt Lola T94/00-Ford	–	190 laps	
13	B. Lazier	Leader Cards Lola T93/00-Ilmor C	–	190 laps	
14	B. Rahal	Rahal/Hogan Lola T94/00-Honda	–	188 laps	
15	M. Gugelmin	Chip Ganassi Reynard 94I-Ford	–	187 laps	
16	M. Greco	Arciero Lola T94/00-Ford	–	180 laps	
17	J. Andretti	Euromotorsport Lola T92/00-Ilmor A	–	179 laps	
18	J. Paul Jnr	Pro Formance Lola T93/00-Ilmor C	–	177 laps	
19	B. Till	Lola T93/00-Ford	–	168 laps	
20	Mi. Andretti	Chip Ganassi Reynard 94I-Ford	–	162 laps	Accident
21	Ma. Andretti	Newman/Haas Lola T94/00-Ford	–	156 laps	Accident
22	A. Luyendyk	Indy Regency Lola T94/00-Ilmor D	–	146 laps	Electrical
23	P. Tracy	Penske Racing Penske PC23-Ilmor D	–	62 laps	Accident
24	D. Dobson	PacWest Lola T94/00-Ford	–	61 laps	Accident
25	J. Villeneuve	Forsythe/Green Reynard 94I-Ford	–	61 laps	Accident
26	T. Fabi	Hall Reynard 94I-Ilmor D	–	60 laps	Accident
27	H. Matsushita	Dick Simon Lola T94/00-Ford	–	44 laps	Accident
28	W.T. Ribbs	Walker Lola T93/00-Ford	–	26 laps	Accident
–	D. Kudrave	Euromotorsport Lola T92/00-Ilmor A	–	–	Did not start
–	J. Unser	Dale Coyne Lola T93/00-Ford	–	–	Did not start
–	M. Smith	Walker Lola T94/00-Ford	–	–	Did not qualify

Average Speed of Winner: 107.437mph

Long Beach

Long Beach, California, USA – 17 April 1994

Al Unser Jnr came to the race with high hopes of getting back into the winning habit and with good reason. Not only had he finished second to team mate Emerson Fittipaldi at Phoenix but he is acknowledged as the *King of Long Beach* having won four consecutive times on the street circuit from 1988 to 1991. Certainly his Penske machine was flying in qualifying, as indeed were his team mates Emerson Fittipaldi and Paul Tracy and it was no surprise when they took 1-2-3 on the grid. Nearest to them was Nigel Mansell and, when the race started for real that was the way it stayed for the first twenty laps or so. The first to give way was Tracy who spun when his gearbox began to give trouble, enabling Unser to take control from Fittipaldi and then Mansell.

It was a lead that Unser was to hold for a further twenty laps but then, when he pitted, he earned a *stop and go* penalty by exiting at more than the statutory 60mph. This gave the lead to third member of the Penske outfit, Fittipaldi, who also held on to it for twenty or so laps before suddenly slowing with gearbox problems which were to eventually see him succumb after 66 laps having lost the lead back to Unser on lap 63. Mansell was still up with the pace but then on lap 67 had the bad luck to pick up a burst tyre. Even worse was the fact that he had just cleared the start/finish line and had to coast round for virtually a full lap before being able to pit for a replacement. The better news for the Briton, however, was that it was close enough to the finish of the race for him to get enough fuel on board to last the rest of the distance at the same time as the tyre was being changed. This enabled him to virtually make up all the lost ground when everybody else pitted around lap 80.

He was however, still over thirty seconds behind the leader, Unser, and his own position was more under threat from Robby Gordon who got the gap down on Mansell to seven seconds

at one time. Knowing he couldn't catch Unser barring a crash or mechanical problems, Mansell was able to concentrate on protecting his second place from Gordon and the three of them kept their positions through to the line giving Unser a fifth Long Beach success.

There was, however, an almighty battle going on behind them for fourth spot and no fewer than six drivers finished on the same lap whilst Johansson would have joined them except for running out of fuel on lap 102. Another to run out of fuel was Robbie Groff in his Indy Car debut when vying with another newcomer, Frank Freon, for the final point on offer leaving the latter with something to show after his first ever race. Another debutant, Claude Bourbonnais, got no further than 24 laps before retiring with a broken exhaust header in his team's spare car after he had crashed his original during qualifying.

Jimmy Vasser, though, had an even worse weekend than Bourbonnais. Coming in to the race in second place in the Championship, Vasser qualified only in 23rd spot and then suffered a flat tyre in the race itself and as he nursed his wounded car back to the pits he fell foul of a Mark Smith hat-trick. Following crashes in both earlier Rounds, Smith made it three out of three when he barged into Vasser, bringing about suspension trouble and an early retirement for one of the Championship contenders ❖

Points and Leaderboard

Position	Points	Driver
=1	37	E. Fittipaldi
=1	37	A. Unser Jnr
3	35	N. Mansell
4	29	Mi. Andretti
5	25	S. Johansson
6	24	Ma. Andretti
7	22	J. Vasser
8	20	R. Gordon
9	17	R. Boesel
10	14	M. Gugelmin

Al Unser Jnr celebrates victory at Long Beach and level pegging in the Championship points.

Race Placings

Pos	Driver	Team	Time	Diff	
1	A. Unser Jnr	Penske Racing Penske PC23-Ilmor D	1:40'53.582	–	
2	N. Mansell	Newman/Haas Lola T94/00Ford	1:41'32.689	39.107	
3	R. Gordon	Walker Lola T94/00-Ford	1:41'39.854	46.272	
4	R. Boesel	Dick Simon Lola T94/00-Ford	–	104 laps	
5	Ma. Andretti	Newman/Haas Lola T94/00-Ford	–	104 laps	
6	Mi. Andretti	Chip Ganassi Reynard 94l-Ford	–	104 laps	
7	M. Gugelmin	Chip Ganassi Reynard 94l-Ford	–	104 laps	
8	A. Fernandez	Galles Reynard 94l-Ilmor D	–	104 laps	
9	T. Fabi	Hall Reynard 94l-Ilmor D	–	104 laps	
10	S. Johansson	Bettenhausen Penske PC22-Ilmor D	–	102 laps	(Fuel)
11	A. Luyendyk	Indy Regency Lola T94/00-Ilmor D	–	102 laps	
12	F. Freon	Lola T93/00-Ford	–	101 laps	
13	R. Groff	Bettenhausen Penske PC22-Ilmor C	–	100 laps	(Fuel)
14	D. Jones	AJ Foyt Lola T94/00-Ford	–	100 laps	
15	J. Villeneuve	Forsythe/Green Reynard 94l-Ford	–	100 laps	
16	R. Buhl	Dale Coyne Lola T93/00-Ford	–	92 laps	(Transmission)
17	D. Dobson	PacWest Lola T94/00-Ford	–	91 laps	
18	W.T. Ribbs	Walker Lola T93/00-Ford	–	80 laps	(Exhaust)
19	S. Goodyear	Budweiser King Lola T94/00-Ford	–	80 laps	(Transmission)
20	P. Tracy	Penske Racing Penske PC23-Ilmor D	–	75 laps	(Transmission)
21	E. Fittipaldi	Penske Racing Penske PC23-Ilmor D	–	66 laps	(Transmission)
22	A. Zampedri	Euromotorsport Lola T93/00-Ilmor C	–	55 laps	(Exhaust)
23	M. Greco	Arciero Lola T94/00-Ford	–	40 laps	(Suspension)
24	J. Vasser	Hayhoe Reynard 94l-Ford	–	36 laps	(Accident)
25	M. Smith	Walker Lola T94/00-Ford	–	29 laps	(Accident)
26	C. Bourbonnais	Pro formance Lola T93/00-Ilmor C	–	24 laps	(Exhaust)
27	M. Groff	Rahal/Hogan Lola T94/00-Honda	–	19 laps	(Accident)
28	S. Sharpe	PacWest Lola T94/00-Ford	–	11 laps	(Engine)
29	B. Lazier	Leader Cards Lola T93/00-Ilmor C	–	6 laps	(Exhaust)
30	B. Rahal	Rahal/Hogan Lola T94/00-Honda	–	3 laps	(Oil)
–	H. Matsushita	Dick Simon Lola T94/00-Ford	–	–	Did not start
–	D. Kudrave	Euromotorsport Lola T92/00-Ilmor A	–	–	Did not start
–	J. Unser	Dale Coyne Lola T93/00-Ford	–	–	Did not start

Average Speed of Winner: 107.437mph.

Indy 500

Speedway, Indiana, USA – 29 May 1994

The title fight was now certainly hotting up with just three points separating Unser, Fittipaldi and Mansell. As qualifying for one of the world's most famous races got under way, all eyes were on Mario Andretti for whom this was to be his 29th and final Indy 500. He was to eventually finish in ninth place on the grid, indeed the Andretti clan had three of the top ten places. The first week's qualifying saw a Japanese, Hideshi Matsuda, become the first ever driver from that country to hold an Indy 500 pole but it was only a technicality as he was simply posting a time after being drawn first out of the hat in the qualifying order and his effort was soon passed. The surprise package was Lyn St James who put herself in front of such household names as Nigel Mansell, Eddie Cheever and Mario Andretti whilst Paul Tracy almost put himself out of the reckoning with a crash but recovered to lead the second day qualifiers, a poor placing for him but one he would be grateful to escape with following his bad accident. Up front, Al Unser Jnr grabbed his first ever Indy 500 pole but amongst the surprise non-qualifiers was Willy T. Ribbs.

Once the race was underway for real, it was dominated by the Penskes of Fittipaldi and Unser with the only other driver to lead on any of the 200 laps being Villeneuve who went to the front briefly on laps 62/63 and 125/129 after the leaders had made pit stops. By comparison, the 1993 race had witnessed no fewer than twelve different leaders. With less than forty miles remaining, however, Fittipaldi threw away his chance of a third success in the race when heading for a comfortable victory. He had led for 145 of the 184 laps he had completed when he attempted to lap his only rival, team mate Unser Jnr. The Brazilian misjudged his line at Turn Four to clip the curb and launch his car at the concrete wall which left the result a formality as Unser went on to complete his second success at Indianapolis in three years. It was Penske's tenth triumph in the event and their seventh in the last ten years demonstrating that, when it comes to the Indy 500, they have no peers.

But the major talking point was an accident that could have killed Mansell through no fault of

Villeneuve finished second and was the only other driver to complete the gruelling 200 laps.

his own. He had completed 92 laps when Hideshi Matsuda crashed at Turn One. John Paul Jnr picked up a puncture going through the debris and crashed at Turn Three. The field was waved down the warm up lane in order to allow officials to remove the debris and Mansell was minding his own business going slowly round in line with Brayton and John Andretti immediately behind him. At this juncture, Dennis Vitolo smacked full pelt into Andretti and was lifted over Brayton before landing on top of Mansell, only inches from the Briton's head. Severely shaken by the shock of being hit from nowhere when only cruising round, Mansell took some time to recover his senses, but was then aided by heat either from a methanol fire (which burns without flame) or steam. Either way, he was encouraged by the warm glow to evacuate at a quicker rate of knots than had hitherto been the case.

It was definitely a lucky escape for Mansell who was in third place at the time not far behind Fittipaldi and Unser. Away from the winner, perhaps the drive of the race came from Bobby Rahal who started 28th on the grid and blasted his way through the field to finish third. But there was to be no fairy tale ending for Mario Andretti whose last appearance in the Indy 500 finished as early as the 23rd lap when a broken pressure relief valve put paid to his hopes ◼

Points and Leaderboard

Position	Points	Driver
1	58	A. Unser Jnr
2	38	E. Fittipaldi
3	37	Mi. Andretti
4	35	N. Mansell
5	34	J. Vasser
6	30	R. Gordon
7	25	S. Johansson
8	24	Ma. Andretti
9	17	R. Boesel
=10	16	J. Villeneuve
=10	16	M. Gugelmin

Race Placings

Pos	Driver	Team	Time	Diff	
1	A. Unser Jnr	Penske Racing Penske PC23-Mercedes	3:6'29.006	–	
2	J. Villeneuve	Forsythe/Green Reynard 94l-Ford	–	200 laps	
3	B. Rahal	Rahal/Hogan Lola T93/00-Ilmor C	–	199 laps	
4	J. Vasser	Hayhoe Reynard 94l-Ford	–	199 laps	
5	R. Gordon	Walker Racing Lola T94/00-Ford	–	199 laps	
6	Mi. Andretti	Chip Ganassi Reynard 94l-Ford	–	198 laps	
7	T. Fabi	Hall Reynard 94l-Ilmor D	–	198 laps	
8	E. Cheever	Team Menard Lola T93/00-Menard	–	197 laps	
9	B. Herta	A.J.Foyt Lola T94/00-Ford	–	197 laps	
10	J. Andretti	A.J.Foyt Lola T94/00-Ford	–	196 laps	
11	M. Gugelmin	Chip Ganassi Reynard 94l-Ford	–	196 laps	
12	B. Till	Dale Coyne Racing Lola T93/00-Ford	–	194 laps	
13	S. Fox	Hemelgarn Racing Reynard 94l-Ford	–	193 laps	(Accident)
14	H. Matsushita	Simon Racing Lola T94/00-Ford	–	193 laps	
15	S. Johansson	Bettenhausen Penske PC22-Ilmor D	–	192 laps	
16	S. Sharp	PacWest Lola T94/00-Ford	–	186 laps	
17	E. Fittipaldi	Penske Racing Penske PC23-Mercedes	–	184 laps	(Accident)
18	A. Luyendyk	Indy Regency Lola T94/00-Ilmor D	–	179 laps	(Engine)
19	L. St James	Dick Simon Lola T94/00-Ford	–	170 laps	
20	S. Brayton	Team Menard Lola T93/00-Menard	–	116 laps	(Engine)
21	R. Boesel	Dick Simon Lola T94/00-Ford	–	100 laps	(Water Pump)
22	N. Mansell	Newman/Haas Lola T94/00-Ford	–	92 laps	(Accident)
23	P. Tracy	Penske Racing Penske PC23-Mercedes	–	92 laps	(Turbo)
24	H. Matsuda	Simon Racing/Beck Lola T93/00-Ford	–	90 laps	(Accident)
25	J. Paul Jnr	Pro Formance Lola T93/00-Ilmor D	–	89 laps	(Accident)
26	D. Vitolo	Dick Simon Lola T93/00-Ford	–	89 laps	(Accident)
27	M. Greco	Arciero/Simon Lola T94/00-Ford	–	53 laps	(Electrical)
28	A. Fernandez	Galles Reynard 94l-Ilmor D	–	30 laps	(Suspension)
29	D. Dobson	Pac West Lola T94/00-Ford	–	29 laps	(Accident)
30	S. Goodyear	Budweiser King Lola T94/00-Ford	–	29 laps	(Mechanical)
31	M. Groff	Rahal/Hogan Lola T93/00-Ilmor C	–	28 laps	(Accident)
32	Ma. Andretti	Newman/Haas Lola T94/00-Ford	–	23 laps	(Fuel System)
33	R. Guerrero	Pagan Racing Lola T92/00-Buick	–	20 laps	(Accident)

Average Speed of Winner: 80.994mph

Milwaukee

Milwaukee, Wisconsin, USA – 5 June 1994

The first anniversary of Nigel Mansell's initial oval track victory was not to be a happy one for the Champion despite setting the fastest time of the Friday practice session at 22.851, just pipping Boesel by 0.002secs. But Saturday was to prove a different tale in qualifying as his Lola struggled to find grip due to the excessive heat and Mansell was barely able to improve his practice time whereas several others did so by as much as four tenths of a second. So Mansell found himself down in ninth place on the grid but he wasn't on his own with Al Unser Jnr even further back than the Briton whilst Fittipaldi was only one place in front.

By lap seventeen, Unser and Fittipaldi had gone past everybody bar Tracy to make it a Penske 1-2-3.

When the race got underway, Boesel lost his pole advantage to Paul Tracy by Turn Three whilst Michael Andretti took the high road to move up quickly from twelfth to sixth. Unser was on Mansell's tail as the Briton failed to make any headway against Fittipaldi and by lap six Unser was past Mansell and alongside his Penske team-mate.

By lap seventeen, Unser and Fittipaldi had gone past everybody bar Tracy to make it a Penske 1-2-3. Lap 23 saw the first change of leader with Fittipaldi taking over from Tracy but eight laps later there was another lead man in Unser, although it was still a Penske 1-2-3.

The superiority of the Penskes was overwhelming. By the 36th circuit they had lapped everybody up to tenth place and, although Mansell overtook Michael Andretti to claim sixth spot, he too was soon to be lapped. By the one quarter stage, Villeneuve and Gordon capitulated and every other car in the race was at least a lap

down on the Penske flying machines. Even team-mate Tracy was beginning to find it difficult to hang on to the tails of Unser and Fittipaldi and their lead was such that even pit stops didn't stop one or the other of them from continuing to lead. Amazingly by lap 80, every car bar the Penskes had been lapped twice.

As the cars went through the halfway stage, it seemed the only hope anybody had of catching the Penskes was through retirement or accident. There was certainly every chance of an accident intervening as, incredibly, every car was still running which made the Penske advance through the field all the more remarkable. In fact, there was no accident and, amazingly, only one retirement, that of Stefan Johansson who succumbed on lap 163 with engine problems.

At the end it was a Penske 1-2-3 for the third time in Indy Car history and Unser's 22nd success leaving Mansell despondent in fifth place ▨

Points and Leaderboard

Position	Points	Driver
1	79	A. Unser Jnr
2	54	E. Fittipaldi
3	49	Mi. Andretti
4	45	N. Mansell
5	38	R. Gordon
6	36	J. Vasser
7	25	S. Johansson
8	24	Ma. Andretti
9	23	R. Boesel
=10	20	J. Villeneuve
=10	20	B. Rahal
=12	16	P. Tracy
=12	16	T. Fabi
=12	16	M. Gugelmin
15	15	M. Groff

Robbie Gordon in the Walker Racing
Lola T94/00-Ford finished sixth.

Race Placings

Pos	Driver	Team	Time	Diff	
1	Al Unser Jnr	Penske Racing Penske PC23-Ilmor D	1:36'57.964	–	
2	E. Fittipaldi	Penske Racing Penske PC23-Ilmor D	–	192 laps	
3	P. Tracy	Penske Racing Penske PC23-Ilmor D	–	190 laps	
4	Mi. Andretti	Chip Ganassi Reynard 94I-Ford	–	189 laps	
5	N. Mansell	Newman/Haas Lola T94/00-Ford	–	189 laps	
6	R. Gordon	Walker Racing Lola T94/00-Ford	–	189 laps	
7	B. Rahal	Rahal/Hogan Lola T94/00-Honda	–	189 laps	
8	R. Boesel	Dick Simon Lola T94/00-Ford	–	188 laps	
9	J. Villeneuve	Forsythe/Green Reynard 94I-Ford	–	187 laps	
10	B. Herta	AJ Foyt Lola T94/00-Ford	–	187 laps	
11	J. Vasser	Hayhoe Reynard 94I-Ford	–	187 laps	
12	S. Sharp	PacWest Lola T94/00-Ford	–	186 laps	
13	D. Dobson	PacWest Lola T94/00-Ford	–	185 laps	
14	Mario Andretti	Newman/Haas Lola T94/00-Ford	–	185 laps	
15	M. Gugelmin	Chip Ganassi Reynard 94I-Ford	–	184 laps	
16	A. Fernandez	Galles Reynard 94I-Ilmor D	–	184 laps	
17	T. Fabi	Hall Reynard 94I-Ilmor D	–	184 laps	
18	B. Lazier	Leader Cards Lola T93/00-Ilmor C	–	183 laps	
19	M. Groff	Rahal/Hogan Lola T94/00-Honda	–	181 laps	
20	M. Greco	Arciero/Simon Lola T94/00-Ford	–	181 laps	
21	A. Luyendyk	Indy Regency Lola T94/00-Ilmor D	–	180 laps	
22	S. Goodyear	Budweiser King Lola T94/00-Ford	–	178 laps	
23	H. Matsushita	Simon Racing Lola T94/00-Ford	–	178 laps	
24	M. Smith	Walker Lola T94/00-Ford	–	177 laps	
25	W. T. Ribbs	Walker Lola T94/00-Ford	–	174 laps	
–	S. Johansson	Bettenhausen Penske PC22-Ilmor D	–	163 laps	(Engine)

Average Speed of Winner: 118.804mph

Detroit

Al Unser Jnr came into the race as hot favourite on the back of his three straight victories in his previous three outings but Detroit in 1993 had seen Mansell take pole position before crashing his car in a controversial collision involving the *safety* car. The Briton needed a victory here if he was to stop the relentless advance of the Penskes and, for a time, it looked as if a return to a road course could have been the incentive he needed.

Friday saw Mansell set a time more than one second quicker than the Unser, Fittipaldi, and Tracy driven Penskes and, after the latter two had recovered to head him, Mansell then posted the only sub 70 second time to take pole position for the second consecutive year at Detroit. Ominously, however, Unser was second fastest with the other Penskes third and fourth on the grid to give Mansell every cause for worry.

When the race got away, Mansell held his lead from Unser but not for very long. Approaching the last three turns of the second lap, Unser came up to Mansell ready to pounce and when he was able to grab the inside line at turns 13 and 14 he was off into the distance. Within another two miles of the Belle Isle circuit, the second Penske driven by Tracy was through and away but at least Mansell was able to ward off the challenge of Fittipaldi in the third Penske. The first retirements came after seven laps had been completed with Boesel experiencing electrical problems and Groff's suspension affected by his collision with a tyre wall. The next to depart was Dominic Dobson, who spun on lap 20 and took out Zampedri who was having his debut drive for Dale Coyne. There were some amazing, lingering, times recorded at the first pit stops with Gugelmin and Danner both dropping five places as their crews were painfully slow in getting fuel aboard. Even worse, however, was Rahal's stop as he missed his mark in the pit lane, leaving his crew struggling to reach his car as a result of which he dropped from 13th to 21st!

Paul Tracy drove to victory and another success for the Penske team at Detroit.

Up front, the Penske's were still dominating with Fittipaldi now also past Mansell but lap 53 saw the Penske's self destruct. Unser appeared to be heading for his fourth straight victory and the Penske's for their second consecutive 1-2-3 but all that changed when his team mate, Paul Tracy braked later than Unser as they hit slower traffic in front. Just to prove that the only thing that can beat a Marlboro Penske is another Marlboro Penske, Tracy nudged Unser and sent the championship leader flying into a tyre wall to leave himself well in front of Fittipaldi. A couple of laps later an almost identical incident saw Mansell hit Fittipaldi as the Penske driver slowed a fraction of a second earlier because of catching up with slower cars. After striking the Penske's rear end, Mansell then slid into the tyres and he got out of the car and clambered over the tyres he had just re-arranged. On surveying the car, however, the Briton obviously decided it was still driveable and returned to the cockpit to rejoin the race. His effort, though, was to prove short-lived for he went out anyway after 65 laps when a broken throttle put paid to his hopes of collecting some consolation points.

Points and Leaderboard

Position	Points	Driver
1	83	Al Unser Jnr
2	70	E. Fittipaldi
3	59	Mi. Andretti
4	52	R. Gordon
5	46	N. Mansell
=6	36	J. Vasser
=6	36	P. Tracy
=8	28	T. Fabi
=8	28	B. Rahal
10	26	J. Villeneuve
11	25	S. Johansson
12	24	Ma. Andretti
13	23	R. Boesel
14	21	M. Gugelmin
15	13	M. Groff
16	11	B. Herta

Mansell's defection put Robby Gordon up to third behind Tracy and Fittipaldi with Unser back in the race but down to tenth due to suspension problems caused in his argument with the tyres. So it was Tracy's first victory of 1994 and his team's fifth success on the bounce ▓

Race Placings

Pos	Driver	Team	Time	Diff	
1	P. Tracy	Penske Racing Penske PC23-Ilmor D	1:52'29.642	–	
2	E. Fittipaldi	Penske Racing Penske PC23-Ilmor D	–	77 laps	
3	R Gordon	Walker Racing Lola T94/00-Ford	–	77 laps	
4	T. Fabi	Hall Reynard 94I-Ilmor D	–	77 laps	
5	Mi. Andretti	Chip Ganassi Reynard 94I-Ford	–	77 laps	
6	B. Rahal	Rahal/Hogan Lola T94/00-Honda	–	77 laps	
7	J. Villeneuve	Forsythe/Green Reynard 94I-Ford	–	77 laps	
8	M. Gugelmin	Chip Ganassi Reynard 94I-Ford	–	77 laps	
9	B. Herta	AJ Foyt Lola T94/00-Ford	–	77 laps	
10	Al Unser Jnr	Penske Racing Penske PC23-Ilmor D	–	77 laps	
11	S. Goodyear	Budweiser King Lola T94/00-Ford	–	76 laps	
12	C. Danner	Project Indy Lola T93/00-Ford	–	76 laps	
13	S. Sharp	PacWest Lola T94/00-Ford	–	76 laps	
14	M. Smith	Walker Lola T94/00-Ford	–	76 laps	
15	F. Ekblom	McCormack Lola T93/00-Ilmor D	–	76 laps	
16	W. T. Ribbs	Walker Lola T93/00-Ford	–	75 laps	
17	B.y Lazier	Leader Cards Lola T93/00-Ilmor D	–	75 laps	
18	Mario Andretti	Newman/Haas Lola T94/00-Ford	–	75 laps	
19	A. Luyendyk	Indy Regency Lola T94/00-Ilmor D	–	75 laps	
20	J. Vasser	Hayhoe Reynard 94I-Ford	–	74 laps	(Accident)
21	N. Mansell	Newman/Haas Lola T94/00-Ford	–	65 laps	(Broken Throttle)
22	S. Johansson	Bettenhausen Penske PC22-Ilmor D	–	51 laps	(Gearbox)
23	A. Fernandez	Galles Reynard 94I-Ilmor D	–	48 laps	(Accident)
24	M. Greco	Arciero/Simon Lola T94/00-Ford	–	30 laps	(Halfshaft)
25	D. Dobson	PacWest Lola T94/00-Ford	–	20 laps	(Accident)
26	A. Zampedri	Dale Coyne Lola T93/00-Ilmor C	–	20 laps	(Accident)
27	M. Groff	Rahal/Hogan Lola T94/00-Honda	–	7 laps	(Accident)
28	R. Boesel	Dick Simon Lola T94/00-Ford	–	7 laps	(Electrical)

Average Speed of Winner: 86.25mph

Portland

If Nigel Mansell, hunted by the Williams Grand Prix team to replace Ayrton Senna, had any doubts about returning to the F1 scene, they were presumably removed by the result of this race. Once again, the Briton had proved to be, more or less, the equal of the Penske's in qualifying and, although he hadn't grabbed pole as he had managed in the previous round at Detroit, he was at least on the front row, pipped by just 0.008sec by Unser's final lap. But whilst the speed of his Lola had proved equal over a few laps in qualifying quite clearly it could not hold the Penske's over the length of a race. Some twelve months earlier, Al Unser Jnr had not won an Indy Car event for over a year but at Portland he was to drive to his fourth success in five outings whilst the Penske super team were to register their second 1-2-3 of a campaign that they were dominating. Indeed, only the shunt that Paul Tracy gave team- mate Unser at Detroit deprived them of a hat-trick of clean sweeps.

Once more then, the closest Mansell got to Unser was at the start from where the American simply motored off, as far as the Briton was concerned, into the distance as he lapped at something like a second quicker than the 1993 Champion for much of the first fifteen laps. Unser, with a clear lead took his foot off a little to ensure a smooth passage and to conserve fuel. The gap remained fairly constant but Mansell had more to worry about than reducing Unser's advantage for Fittipaldi was, by lap twenty, right on the rear of the Briton and nine circuits later Penske were travelling 1-2-3 with both the Brazilian and Paul Tracy having gone past the Lola.

Just past the half-way stage on lap 58, a full course yellow to rescue Scott Goodyear allowed Fittipaldi to wipe out Unser's lead and Mansell was called in for a second pit stop in the hope of pinching some time during the yellow. The move paid temporary dividends when he managed to grab third place when Tracy stopped on lap 72.

Meanwhile, Unser had pitted on lap 69 and

Fittipaldi a lap later with the result that the Brazilian led by a matter of yards when he rejoined but Unser was not to be denied and, with his tyres a lap warmer than his team-mate's, he was soon back at the front of affairs. From here on in, it was a dog fight between the two Penskes with Unser going a couple of seconds up and then being hauled back in when he hit traffic before going clear again once through the hold ups whilst Fittipaldi negotiated the back markers, a situation that repeated itself time and again over the last thirty or so laps.

The race was finally decided when Unser easily got past Mario Andretti with just five circuits remaining whilst Fittipaldi got stuck behind him for over a lap which accounted for virtually all the 1.8 second gap between the two at the finish. Mansell, having given himself a chance of a podium appearance by pitting on the yellow, lost third place to Tracy with seven laps to go. The Briton then relinquished fourth spot to Robby Gordon when he wandered off course at turn three on lap 97 and, although he made a heroic effort to retrieve the situation, Mansell was still half a car length down at the line. Gordon's fine effort gave him his fifth successive top five finish and put him in third spot in the Championship whilst, of the others, Chip Ganassi's team failed to finish for the first time in the season when Gugelmin went out on lap 29 following Michael Andretti's exit after just eleven circuits ◼

Points and Leaderboard

Position	Points	Driver
1	105	A. Unser Jnr
2	86	E. Fittipaldi
3	64	R. Gordon
4	59	Mi. Andretti
5	56	N. Mansell
6	50	P. Tracy
7	36	J. Vasser
8	34	J. Villeneuve
9	30	S. Johansson
10	29	B. Rahal

The Newman/Haas team in pit stop action.

Race Placings

Pos	Driver	Team	Time	Diff	Grid
1	Al Unser Jnr	Penske Racing Penske PC23-Ilmor D	1:50'43.706	–	
2	E. Fittipaldi	Penske Racing Penske PC23-Ilmor D	–	102 laps	
3	P.l Tracy	Penske Racing Penske PC23-Ilmor D	–	102 laps	
4	R. Gordon	Walker Racing Lola T94/00-Ford	–	102 laps	
5	N. Mansell	Newman/Haas Lola T94/00-Ford	–	102 laps	
6	J. Villeneuve	Forsythe/Green Reynard 94I-Ford	–	101 laps	
7	A. Zampedri	Dale Coyne Lola T93/00-Ilmor D	–	101 laps	
8	S. Johansson	Bettenhausen Penske PC22-Ilmor D	–	101 laps	
9	Mario Andretti	Newman/Haas Lola T94/00-Ford	–	100 laps	
10	A. Fernandez	Galles Reynard 94I-Ilmor D	–	100 laps	
11	M. Groff	Rahal/Hogan Lola T94/00-Honda	–	99 laps	
12	B. Rahal	Rahal/Hogan Lola T94/00-Honda	–	99 laps	
13	R. Groff	Bettenhausen Penske PC23-Ilmor C	–	99 laps	
14	A. Luyendyk	Indy Regency Lola T94/00-Ilmor D	–	99 laps	
15	F. Freon	Lola T93/00-Ford	–	99 laps	
16	M. Smith	Walker Lola T94/00-Ford	–	99 laps	
17	D. Dobson	PacWest Lola T94/00-Ford	–	99 laps	
18	S. Sharp	PacWest Lola T94/00-Ford	–	98 laps	
19	P. Johnstone	Computech Lola T93/00-Honda	–	97 laps	
20	M. Greco	Arciero/Simon Lola T94/00-Ford	–	97 laps	
21	H. Matsushita	Simon Racing Lola T94/00-Ford	–	97 laps	
22	R. Bentley	Lola T92/00-Ilmor C	–	95 laps	
23	R. Boesel	Simon Racing Lola T94/00-Ford	–	94 laps	
24	B. Lazier	Leader Cards Lola T93/00-Ilmor C	–	91 laps	(Ran out of Fuel)
25	W. T Ribbs	Walker Lola T93/00-Ford	–	91 laps	
26	T. Fabi	Hall Reynard 94I-Ilmor D	–	85 laps	(Engine)
27	B. Herta	AJ Foyt Lola T94/00-Ford	–	85 laps	(Engine)
28	S. Goodyear	Budweiser King Lola T94/00-Ford	–	57 laps	(Accident)
29	J. Wood	Euromotorsport Lola T93/00-Ilmor C	–	52 laps	(Gearbox)
30	M. Gugelmin	Chip Ganassi Reynard 94I-Ford	–	29 laps	(Gearbox)
31	Mi. Andretti	Chip Ganassi Reynard 94I-Ford	–	11 laps	(Accident)
32	J. Vasser	Hayhoe Reynard 94I-Ford	–	11 laps	(Accident)

Average Speed of Winner: 107.777mph

Cleveland

Cleveland, Ohio, USA – 10 July 1994

The PPG Indycar Series arrived at Burke Lakefront Airport with most followers hoping that somewhere amidst the long straights, high speed corners and incredibly bumpy track, something could be found to negate the overwhelming supremacy that the Penske team had brought to bear on the 1994 Championship. On the other hand the headline writers were no doubt hoping for another Unser all the way victory so they could lead with *"Unser sails away again at Lakeside"* or *"Unser flies away again at Airport"*. Despite a brave and resilient effort by Mansell, the headline writers won.

Unser's team mate Paul Tracy, however, had

View from above – Nigel Mansell.

even more reason to want to win as he alone stood to scoop the one million dollar bonus on offer to any driver who won both the Detroit and Cleveland races plus at least one pole position at the two meetings. Having started the Detroit event from third place on the grid it was therefore vital to Tracy that he took pole at Cleveland in order to stay in contention of seriously improving his bank balance and he certainly made a crack at it when he set a target of 59.513 on his first lap. This time was eventually eclipsed in the second session by both Mansell and Fittipaldi only for Tracy, in the final minute, to hit back with a 59.342 time to keep his million dollar dream very much alive. But then Unser clocked 59.232 to gain his third pole of the season leaving Fittipaldi to bemoan, *"I can not believe it. A minute from the end I'm on pole and now I'm not even on the front row."*

So it was a Penske 1-2-3 on the starting line-up but if Tracy felt somewhat put out by his team mate pipping him it was probably nothing compared with the high feelings running in the Newman/Haas outfit after Mario Andretti left Nigel Mansell on the grass waving a fist at him. On exiting the pits side by side, Andretti on the inside lane had drifted wide and pushed Mansell off the track in a needless incident. Elsewhere, Mark Smith achieved his highest qualifying place to date of 12th but Raul Boesel, needing a shot in the arm to quell rumours that he was about to be replaced by the Dick Simon Racing Team, could only manage a disappointing 19th.

The first lap at Lakefront Airport is notorious for accidents and the 1993 event saw six cars damaged at the hairpin. This year there were just two as Michael Andretti, in attempting to evade Fabi, collected a totally innocent Scott Goodyear but both were able to continue though neither would recover to put in a challenge. The first car to go out was Jimmy Vasser on lap 7 and, after three top four places in the opening four rounds, his season was going rapidly downhill.

Up front, Mansell had moved up a place to third, but Unser enjoyed a five second lead over Penske team mate Paul Tracy by the end of lap 15. Mansell then overtook Tracy on lap 20 but was now seven seconds down on Unser. After the first lot of pit stops the advantage had grown to a massive twelve seconds but then, whatever chance Mansell had of winning disappeared when he was involved in his second shunt of the weekend with team mate Mario Andretti!

The Briton was able to continue but was never able to get a blow in at Unser although Mansell did actually manage to take the lead momentarily on lap 58 when Unser pitted before him in the second round of stops. Indeed that in itself was something of a rarity for it was only the second lap in 534 since Indianapolis that a Penske had not led the field! But once Mansell had pitted on lap 59, Unser regained the lead and increased it over the last 25 laps to almost 23 seconds. Fittipaldi's challenge ended on lap 65 with a burnt out engine leaving Tracy, Villeneuve and

Points and Leaderboard

Position	Points	Driver
1	127	A. Unser Jnr
2	86	E. Fittipaldi
3	72	N. Mansell
4	66	R. Gordon
5	64	P. Tracy
6	59	Mi. Andretti
7	46	J. Villeneuve
8	40	S. Johansson
9	36	J. Vasser
10	32	T. Fabi

Johansson to follow Mansell home. Boesel did his chances of keeping his job no harm at all by driving into sixth from 19th on the grid, Zampedri made it two top ten finishes in two outings for Dale Coyne and Willy T. Ribbs secured his first point of a disappointing campaign by finishing 12th. But the final word went to Mansell who said, *"With this Penske team in such form, finishing second is almost like winning"* ■

Race Placings

Pos	Driver	Team	Time	Diff	
1	A. Unser Jnr	Penske Racing Penske PC23-Ilmor D	1:27'32.000	–	
2	N. Mansell	Newman/Haas Lola T94/00-Ford	–	85 laps	
3	P. Tracy	Penske Racing Penske PC23-Ilmor D	–	85 laps	
4	J. Villeneuve	Forsythe/Green Reynard 94I-Ford	–	85 laps	
5	S. Johansson	Bettenhausen Penske PC22-Ilmor D	–	84 laps	
6	R. Boesel	Dick Simon Lola T94/00-Ford	–	84 laps	
7	A. Fernandez	Galles Reynard 94I-Ilmor D	–	84 laps	
8	M. Gugelmin	Chip Ganassi Reynard 94I-Ford	–	84 laps	
9	T. Fabi	Hall Reynard 94I-Ilmor D	–	83 laps	
10	A. Zampedri	Dale Coyne Lola T93/00-Ilmor C	–	83 laps	
11	R. Gordon	Walker Racing Lola T94/00-Ford	–	82 laps	
12	W.T. Ribbs	Walker Lola T93/00-Ford	–	82 laps	
13	B. Herta	A.J.Foyt Lola T94/00-Ford	–	82 laps	
14	S. Goodyear	Budweiser King Lola T94/00-Ford	–	81 laps	
15	H. Matsushita	Simon Racing Lola T94/00-Ford	–	81 laps	
16	A. Montermini	Budweiser King Lola T94/00-Ford	–	80 laps	
17	P. Johnstone	Computech Lola T93/00-Honda	–	80 laps	
18	Mi. Andretti	Chip Ganassi Reynard 94I-Ford	–	77 laps	(Engine)
19	M. Groff	Rahal/Hogan Lola T94/00-Honda	–	72 laps	(Fuel Pump)
20	E. Fittipaldi	Penske Racing Penske PC23-Ilmor D	–	65 laps	(Engine)
21	A. Luyendyk	Indy Regency Lola T94/00-Ilmor D	–	61 laps	(Turbo)
22	M. Smith	Walker Lola T94/00-Ford	–	61 laps	(Engine)
23	J. Wood	Euromotorsport Lola T93/00-Ilmor C	–	53 laps	(Exhaust)
24	S. Sharp	PacWest Lola T94/00-Ford	–	48 laps	(Suspension)
25	D. Dobson	PacWest Lola T94/00-Ford	–	48 laps	(Engine)
26	M. Greco	Arciero/Simon Lola T94/00-Ford	–	46 laps	(Suspension)
27	Ma. Andretti	Newman/Haas Lola T94/00-Ford	–	31 laps	(Suspension)
28	B. Rahal	Rahal/Hogan Lola T94/00-Honda	–	19 laps	(Engine)
29	R. Bentley	Lola T92/00-Ilmor C	–	19 laps	(Suspension)
30	G. Lavaggi	Lola T92/00-Ilmor C	–	12 laps	(Accident)
31	J. Vasser	Hayhoe Reynard 94I-Ford	–	6 laps	(Fuel Pump)

Average Speed of Winner: 138.026mph

Toronto

Toronto, Ontario, Canada – 17 July 1994

Nigel Mansell came into this race with the knowledge that, with the possible exception of Phoenix Raceway, no IndyCar circuit had given him more problems than the Toronto Molson track. In his 1993 debut year, the Briton had hit the walls in both practice and actual qualifying before retiring early in the race itself with a broken turbo.

For Mansell 1994 was to be an almost exact replica as he again hit the wall with an almighty bang, twisting the steering wheel and bending a wing. On this occasion, however, he had at least posted a time good enough to allow him to sit out the remainder of the qualifying session and nurse his swollen wrist in readiness for the race itself in which he was to start from second on the grid. He was joined on the front row by another Lola in the shape of Robby Gordon's Walker Racing car to give hope that the Penske march could be halted. Nevertheless, Unser, Fittipaldi and Tracy looked menacing in third, fourth and fifth with Michael Andretti putting his troubles of the previous Round behind him to line up sixth.

Among the big names down the list were Villeneuve in 15th and Boesel two places lower still but at least they were in the race. The same could not be said for promising youngster Bryan Herta who hit the wall at Turn 12 doing about 125mph to incur a broken right tibia, compression fractures to the pelvis and all sorts of internal injuries when a wheel thrust back off the wall into his cockpit.

Penske hopes took a dive very early in the race as Unser's engine began playing up immediately and forced his retirement after only two laps but even before that Michael Andretti had touched Tracy causing the second Penske to lose a lap whilst it pitted for repairs to a damaged wing. It could have been much worse except that the race was yellow flagged when five stragglers crashed together saving Tracy another lap. From pole, Gordon had made a flying start and was quickly some five seconds up on Mansell but, as Gordon received computer warnings about the amount of fuel he had used in gaining this advantage and slowed, the Briton began to close the gap. Gordon then had an even bigger problem when a rear tyre punctured and he slid off the track only to stall when he tried to return to the race on lap 12. This left Mansell in the lead and, with one Penske out and Tracy relegated to the back after his shunt with Andretti, there appeared to be a genuine hope of victory for the Brit.

Yet another full course yellow to remove debris from Gordon's burst tyre worked in Michael Andretti's favour and from the restart on lap 18 he overtook Fittipaldi to claim second spot behind Mansell. Things moved even further in Andretti's favour when Mansell also incurred a puncture on lap 26 and he had to coast for the best part of a lap before he could get back to the pits. Andretti now led from Fittipaldi and, apart from a pit exchange which surrendered the lead to Bobby Rahal on laps 39 and 40, he continued at the head of affairs for the remainder of the race. By lap 30 his lead had grown to over 11 seconds and by lap 43 it was up to almost 18 seconds with Rahal his nearest challenger followed by Fittipaldi.

> *"For Mansell a 66th lap retirement ensured a similar outcome to his 1993 Toronto experience."*

Pit stops by Mario Andretti and Johansson saw Fernandez take up a surprise fourth place for a time before falling back and two others having a good time of it were Gordon and Tracy who were carving their way back into contention for some points.

Andretti, meanwhile, continued to pull away and his lead was well over twenty seconds when, on lap 57, Bourbonnais spun and took

Matsushita out in the process. This ended the race for Bourbonnais whilst Matsushita lost several laps in attempting to get restarted. But for Andretti it was almost disastrous as a communication mix-up saw the pace car take to the track ahead of him. The leader reduced his speed to fall in unison with the pace car but there had been no full course yellow called and other cars began overtaking the nearest followers of Andretti. It was only now that Andretti, and the other leaders realised there had been a botch up by which time his lead was down to three seconds! Rahal, given renewed hope by the farcical situation, chased Andretti hard and by lap 81 had reduced the deficit to 2.7 seconds.

The leader, however, got back to his task and by lap 84 the advantage had grown to four seconds and it continued to increase until the finish. Fittipaldi was the first Penske home in third place whilst Mario completed a good day for the Andretti family by finishing fourth in his 400th IndyCar race. For Mansell, however, a 66th lap retirement through handling difficulties ensured a fairly similar outcome to his 1993 Toronto experience and it will surely not figure high on his list of places to revisit ▄

Points and Leaderboard

Position	Points	Driver
1	127	A. Unser Jnr
2	100	E. Fittipaldi
3	80	Mi. Andretti
4	75	R. Gordon
5	74	P. Tracy
6	72	N. Mansell
7	50	J. Villeneuve
8	45	B. Rahal
=9	40	Ma. Andretti
=9	40	S. Johansson
11	37	T. Fabi
12	36	J. Vasser
13	32	R. Boesel
14	26	M. Gugelmin
15	17	A. Fernandez
16	15	M. Groff

Race Placings

Pos	Driver	Team	Time	Diff	
1	Mi. Andretti	Chip Ganassi Reynard 94I-Ford	1:48'15.978	–	
2	B. Rahal	Rahal/Hogan Lola T94/00-Honda	–	98 laps	
3	E. Fittipaldi	Penske Racing Penske PC23-Ilmor D	–	98 laps	
4	Ma. Andretti	Newman/Haas Lola T94/00-Ford	–	98 laps	
5	P. Tracy	Penske Racing Penske PC23-Ilmor D	–	97 laps	
6	R. Gordon	Walker Racing Lola T94/00-Ford	–	97 laps	
7	A. Montermini	Budweiser King Lola T94/00-Ford	–	97 laps	
8	T. Fabi	Hall Reynard 94I-Ilmor D	–	97 laps	
9	J. Villeneuve	Forsythe/Green Reynard 94I-Ford	–	97 laps	
10	S. Goodyear	Budweiser King Lola T94/00-Ford	–	97 laps	
11	D. Dobson	PacWest Lola T94/00-Ford	–	97 laps	
12	R. Boesel	Dick Simon Racing Lola T94/00-Ford	–	97 laps	
13	A. Fernandez	Galles Reynard 94I-Ilmor D	–	97 laps	
14	S. Johansson	Bettenhausen Penske PC22-Ilmor D	–	97 laps	
15	M. Greco	Arciero/Simon Lola T94/00-Ford	–	96 laps	
16	S. Sharp	PacWest Lola T94/00-Ford	–	94 laps	(Exhaust)
17	A. Zampedri	Dale Coyne Lola T93/00-Ilmor C	–	93 laps	(Off-course)
18	H. Matsushita	Simon Racing Lola T94/00-Ford	–	85 laps	(Running)
19	R. Bentley	Lola T92/00-Ilmor C	–	81 laps	(Oil Pressure)
20	M. Gugelmin	Chip Ganassi Reynard 94I-Ford	–	69 laps	(Suspension)
21	W.T. Ribbs	Walker Lola T93/00-Ford	–	66 laps	(Accident)
22	M. Groff	Rahal/Hogan Lola T94/00-Honda	–	66 laps	(Gearbox)
23	N. Mansell	Newman/Haas Lola T94/00-Ford	–	66 laps	(Steering)
24	C. Bourbonnais	Forsythe/Green Lola T93/00-Ilmor D	–	57 laps	(Accident)
25	J. Vasser	Hayhoe Reynard 94I-Ford	–	43 laps	(Off-course)
26	M. Schiattarella	Lola T93/00-Ford	–	31 laps	(Gearbox)
27	P Johnstone	Computech Lola T93/00-Honda	–	30 laps	(Gearbox)
28	J. Wood	Euromotorsport Lola T93/00-Ilmor C	–	12 laps	(Electrical)
29	A. Unser Jnr	Penske Racing Penske PC23-Ilmor D	–	2 laps	(Engine)
30	M. Smith	Walker Lola T94/00-Ford	–	2 laps	(Engine)
31	A. Luyendyk	Indy Regency Lola T94/00-Ilmor D	–	1 lap	(Electrical)

Average Speed of Winner: 96.673mph

Michigan

Nigel Mansell returned to the scene of one of his most polished 1993 performances for he had led the corresponding race twelve months previously from start to finish to win by almost a lap. During qualifying it looked as if the Briton might well stage a repeat for he grabbed his first ever Speedway track pole with a speed of almost 234mph, only missing the lap record by 0.5 mph. The grid line up, incidentally, was three abreast with Mansell comfortably heading Raul Boesel and Michael Andretti with the second row consisting of Robbie Gordon, Mario Andretti and Stefan Johansson. So not a Penske in sight on the two front rows but Fittipaldi did line up seventh alongside Fabi and Dobson.

By a strange coincidence, when the race got underway there were to be two major factors that coincided with the German Grand Prix run on the same day thousands of miles across the Atlantic. Just as at Hockenheim, all the big names were to fall by the wayside leaving the lesser lights to grab a slice of the action. So, on a day that saw Panis and Bernard on the podium in Europe, the likes of Goodyear, Luyendyk and Dobson captured the honours at Michigan. Fourth placed Teo Fabi was even moved to say that he was grateful he didn't finish in the first three as he would have been embarrassed to mount the podium, Scott Goodyear accepted his good luck phlegmatically, saying *"Okay, we weren't the fastest but some days you don't have to be. You take it any way you can get it"*.

But, strangely, the coincidences didn't end there for, just as Verstappen had a lucky escape from a horrendous pit lane fire in Germany, Adrian Fernandez experienced a similar fright in the pit lane at Michigan when he stopped for fuel on his 65th lap. Occupying fifth place at the time of his stop after his best drive of the season thus far, Fernandez pulled away to rejoin the race with the fuel hose still attached to his Reynard. The hose ripped from the car spewing fuel which quickly ignited as another car sped past down the pit lane at the same moment and only quick action by the fire crews and team members prevented a disaster.

The race had been dogged by bad luck from the outset as both Vasser and Michael Andretti lost the left rear arms of what had previously been thought to be an indestructible Reynard chassis. But worse was to follow when all the Lolas in the race had to undergo installation of strengthening plates for the front sway bars after an inspection of the Walker Motorsport Lolas revealed a weakness. To complete a bleak picture, Alessandro Zampedri crashed in practice after a puncture, leaving his car in a mess every bit as bad as Herta's at Toronto but fortunately the Italian escaped lightly, in comparison to Herta, with a broken hip.

"This is the fastest track in the world bar none and they were the most frightening moments of my career. I was in big trouble"
– Nigel Mansell

When the race got underway, Mansell led for the first 26 laps to raise hopes of a repeat performance but there were signs of things to come as Luyendyk made headway to be up to 16th from 28th on the grid before five laps had passed. The first two cars to retire were the Rahal-Hogan Lolas but the third, unfortunately, was to be Mansell's Lola. The Briton had a couple of frightening experiences with the throttle jamming in the open position at 240mph but despite two pit stops to try to rectify the fault, the problem persisted and could have proved fatal.

Vasser's disappointing run continued as he was next to depart followed by Lazier just prior to the Fernandez fire incident. Then the big guns began to join Mansell on the sidelines with both Andretti's disappearing from the fray along with

Cheever, Villeneuve, Tracy, and Johansson. With 75 laps still to go, barely half the cars were still running. Back marker Luyendyk was now up to ninth but the race appeared to be a three way tryst between Unser, Boesel and Fittipaldi with Goodyear a lonely fourth (from 12th on the grid). Then Fittipaldi dropped out with a broken piston and Boesel's engine blew 25 laps from home. This appeared to leave the race at the mercy of Unser but his engine also packed in six laps later enabling Goodyear to lead from Luyendyk, Dobson and Fabi and that was the way it stayed leaving Goodyear, the winner in 1992, to become only the second driver besides Michael Andretti to have won twice at Michigan. All of which seemed peculiar when put by the fact that the Budweiser-King outfit announced in Toronto that they were to part company with Goodyear! Another to like Michigan is Arnie Luyendyk who virtually repeated his last to second 1991 drive to give his new outfit, Indy Regency not only a first ever podium position but their first ever top ten finish! ⬛

Points and Leaderboard

Position	Points	Driver
1	132	A. Unser Jnr
2	103	E. Fittipaldi
3	80	Mi. Andretti
4	75	R. Gordon
5	74	P. Tracy
6	73	N. Mansell
7	50	J. Villeneuve
8	49	T. Fabi
9	45	B. Rahal
=10	40	Ma. Andretti
=10	40	S. Johansson
12	37	R. Boesel
13	36	J. Vasser
14	30	S. Goodyear
15	26	M. Gugelmin
16	18	A. Luyendyk

Race Placings

Pos	Driver	Team	Time	Diff	Grid
1	S. Goodyear	Budweiser King Lola T94/00-Ford	3:07'04.099	–	
2	A. Luyendyk	Indy Regency Lola T94/00-Ilmor D	–	249 laps	
3	D. Dobson	Pac West Lola T94/00-Ford	–	248 laps	
4	T. Fabi	Hall Reynard 94l-Ilmor D	–	246 laps	
5	M. Smith	Walker Lola T94/00-Ford	–	240 laps	
6	H. Matsushita	Simon Racing Lola T94/00-Ford	–	239 laps	
7	W.T. Ribbs	Walker Lola T93/00-Ford	–	236 laps	
8	A. Unser Jnr	Penske Racing Penske PC23-Ilmor D	–	231 laps	(Engine)
9	R. Boesel	Dick Simon Lola T94/00-Ford	–	225 laps	(Engine)
10	E. Fittipaldi	Penske Racing Penske PC23-Ilmor D	–	209 laps	(Running)
11	M. Greco	Arciero/Simon Lola T94/00-Ford	–	195 laps	(Engine)
12	S. Sharp	PacWest Lola T94/00-Ford	–	185 laps	(Engine)
13	R. Gordon	Walker Racing Lola T94/00-Ford	–	182 laps	(Engine)
14	S. Johansson	Bettenhausen Penske PC22-Ilmor D	–	176 laps	(Engine)
15	M. Gugelmin	Chip Ganassi Reynard 94l-Ford	–	160 laps	(Accident)
16	P. Tracy	Penske Racing Penske PC23-Ilmor D	–	150 laps	(Fuel Pressure)
17	J. Wood	Euromotorsport Lola T93/00-Ilmor C	–	138 laps	(Overheating)
18	Ma. Andretti	Newman/Haas Lola T94/00-Ford	–	121 laps	(Engine)
19	R. Bentley	Lola T92/00-Ilmor C	–	116 laps	(Manifold)
20	J. Villeneuve	Forsythe/Green Reynard 94l-Ford	–	76 laps	(Accident)
21	E. Cheever	Forsythe Green Lola T93/00-Ilmor D	–	67 laps	(Electrical)
22	Mi. Andretti	Chip Ganassi Reynard 94l-Ford	–	66 laps	(Accident)
23	A. Fernandez	Galles Reynard 94l-Ilmor D	–	64 laps	(Fire)
24	B. Lazier	Lola T93/00-Ilmor C	–	55 laps	(Electrical)
25	J. Vasser	Hayhoe Reynard 94l-Ford	–	48 laps	(Wheel Bearing)
26	N. Mansell	Newman/Haas Lola T94/00-Ford	–	35 laps	(Throttle)
27	M. Groff	Rahal/Hogan Lola T94/00-Honda	–	24 laps	(Clutch)
28	B. Rahal	Rahal/Hogan Lola T94/00-Honda	–	9 laps	(Fuel Pump)
–	A. Zampedri	Dale Coyne Lola T93/00-Ilmor C	–	Did Not Start	

Average Speed of Winner: 159.800mph

Mid-Ohio

Lexington, Ohio, USA – 14 August 1994

From the start of practice there was never much doubt that the Mid-Ohio event would be anything other than another Penske benefit and so it proved to be with the flying machines cruising to yet another 1-2-3. The only car to get near them in practice, was Mansell's Lola with all four under 68secs whilst next best time was Michael Andretti at 68.549.

The story was repeated in the first qualifying session with all three Penske's under the 68 sec mark, Mansell at 68.185 and fifth place Gugelmin (his first time in the top five) over a second behind third place Fittipaldi. Elsewhere, Mauro Baldi's first single seat drive since 1985 saw him in next to last place whilst Arnie Luyendyk was quickly brought down to earth after finishing second in the previous race at Michigan when he just qualified in the last possible place!

The start at Ohio is made on the long back straight and leads in to a series of esses which somewhat negates the pole advantage so, although Unser had the inside line at the first corner, Tracy held the line at the second and used it to get past his team mate. They proceeded to leave Fittipaldi trailing by some two seconds a lap with Mansell trying, and failing, to hang on the tails of the Penskes. Just behind him was Gugelmin and these two led a bunch of twelve cars that were covered by only eight seconds after 25 laps. Following the first round of pit stops, Tracy and Unser led their Brazilian team mate by some fifteen seconds and after 40 laps the two leaders had lapped everybody up to eighth place.

The race had been pretty uneventful as the leaders entered lap 51 with just Groff, Rahal and Ribbs having retired by that stage but events

Scot Goodyear couldn't follow up his win in Michigan, slumping to 22nd place in Lexington.

then probably cost Tracy the race. Fabi and Villeneuve were involved in an incident that left the Italian spinning into the gravel. Whilst Fabi was being extracted, the yellow flags were out but the removal of Fabi was at a blind spot which Dobson, Gordon, Tracy and Unser approached in that order with the two Penskes, of course, about to lap the two other cars. Dobson was the first to see the removal lorry and slowed causing Gordon to take evasive action. Tracy went through and continued on his way but, of course, the yellows had been out and he was given a five second *stop and go* for overtaking which seemed a bit harsh given it was an evasive manoeuvre as much as anything. The decision gifted the race to Unser, his sixth success of the season.

Given this leeway, Unser simply made sure he stayed out of trouble and Tracy reduced the gap to under four seconds by lap seventy but then the Canadian hit trouble getting past Johansson. By the time he was able to make a decisive move, the race was in Unser's pocket and the championship leader was able to coast home with over a second and a half to spare despite easing right down. That left him 36 points clear with only 110 points remaining. But what of the 1993 Champion – Nigel Mansell? He had steering problems throughout and dropped to eighth place before catching Boesel close to home to elevate himself one place but as he said afterwards *"Let's just say it was a bad day at the office"* ⬛

Points and Leaderboard

Position	Points	Driver
1	153	A. Unser Jnr
2	117	E. Fittipaldi
3	91	P. Tracy
4	90	Mi. Andretti
5	87	R. Gordon
6	79	N. Mansell
7	54	J. Villeneuve
8	49	T. Fabi
9	45	B. Rahal
10	43	Ma. Andretti
11	42	R. Boesel
12	41	S. Johansson
13	36	J. Vasser
14	30	S. Goodyear
15	26	M. Gugelmin

Race Placings

Pos	Driver	Team	Time	Diff	
1	A. Unser Jnr	Penske Racing Penske PC23-Ilmor D	1:40'59.436	–	
2	P. Tracy	Penske Racing Penske PC23-Ilmor D	–	83 laps	
3	E. Fittipaldi	Penske Racing Penske PC23-Ilmor D	–	83 laps	
4	R. Gordon	Walker Racing Lola T94/00-Ford	–	82 laps	
5	Mi. Andretti	Chip Ganassi Reynard 94I-Ford	–	82 laps	
6	A. Fernandez	Galles Reynard 94I-Ilmor D	–	82 laps	
7	N. Mansell	Newman/Haas Lola T94/00-Ford	–	82 laps	
8	R. Boesel	Dick Simon Lola T94/00-Ford	–	82 laps	
9	J. Villeneuve	Forsythe/Green Reynard 94I-Ford	–	82 laps	
10	Ma. Andretti	Newman/Haas Lola T94/00-Ford	–	82 laps	
11	S. Sharp	PacWest Lola T94/00-Ford	–	82 laps	
12	S. Johansson	Bettenhausen Penske PC22-Ilmor D	–	81 laps	
13	A. Luyendyk	Indy Regency Lola T94/00-Ilmor D	–	81 laps	
14	J. Vasser	Hayhoe Reynard 94I-Ford	–	81 laps	
15	D. Dobson	PacWest Lola T94/00-Ford	–	81 laps	
16	M. Schiattarella	Lola T93/00-Ford	–	81 laps	
17	E. Cheever	Forsythe Green Lola T93/00-Ilmor D	–	80 laps	
18	H. Matsushita	Simon Racing Lola T94/00-Ford	–	80 laps	
19	M. Baldi	Lola T93/00-Ford	–	80 laps	
20	M. Smith	Walker Lola T94/00-Ford	–	80 laps	
21	T. Fabi	Hall Reynard 94I-Ilmor D	–	79 laps	
22	S. Goodyear	Budweiser King Lola T94/00-Ford	–	76 laps	
23	P. Johnstone	Comptech Lola T93/00-Honda	–	76 laps	
24	C. Bourbonnais	Team Losi Lola T93/00-Ilmor	–	59 laps	(Gearbox)
25	M. Gugelmin	Chip Ganassi Reynard 94I-Ford	–	55 laps	(Brakes)
26	M. Groff	Rahal/Hogan Lola T94/00-Honda	–	47 laps	(Engine)
27	B. Rahal	Rahal/Hogan Lola T94/00-Honda	–	46 laps	(Engine)
28	W.T. Ribbs	Walker Lola T93/00-Ford	–	4 laps	(Gearbox)

Average Speed of Winner: 110.387mph

New Hampshire

Loudon, New Hampshire, USA – 21 August 1994

Nigel Mansell, amid intensifying rumours that he would be quitting the IndyCar circuit at the end of the 1994 campaign, returned to the scene of possibly his best 1993 victory when arriving at Loudon to attempt to land his first success of 1994 against the Penske flying machines. As for qualifying, the Briton did well but was still almost a second behind Fittipaldi's Penske when he was knocked off the front row by the merest fraction when Boesel showed that he is something to be reckoned with on the oval tracks. His second place on the grid here followed pole position at Milwaukee. But at least Mansell was in front of Tracy in fourth and seven places up on Unser although he would have remembered that the first Penske 1-2-3 of the season had been at Milwaukee where their cars had started second, eighth and eleventh. For the record, Fittipaldi's pole was the first time in a thirty year career that he had landed pole on an oval track.

The race started in spectacular fashion with Fernandez slewing sideways causing a chain reaction that took out both Villeneuve and Luyendyk. The next attempt wasn't much more successful with Johansson and Cheever locking together in an incident that was to damage both suspensions and ultimately lead to both cars eventually retiring. If anybody thought it would be a case of third time lucky they would have been badly mistaken for Scott Sharp made a spectacular roll after going over Groff's front tyre. Remarkably, Sharp and his car were able to line up for the fourth start which got away without incident. Whilst the grid leaders all made decent starts to retain their positions the best get away was by Michael Andretti who moved quickly through the field to sixth spot from seventeenth within a matter of laps. A blistered tyre just past quarter distance cost Fittipaldi dearly as his stop dropped him down to fifth but team mate Unser had moved just as quickly through the field to push for third behind Tracy, Mansell and Boesel.

The latter gave up his third spot to Unser who then proceeded to battle it out with Mansell for second before their battle royale saw them first catch, and then pass, Tracy on lap 70. Mansell briefly led as pit stops took place but then he fell foul of team mate Mario Andretti at the halfway stage. Both Unser and Mansell came up to lap Andretti but neither could get past for three laps until Unser managed to squeeze his way through. Andretti, in a quite extraordinary show, had no intention of letting his British team mate follow suit after the leader. Mansell tried overtaking going into Turn One and, as Andretti closed the gate again, Mansell kept his line resulting in Andretti finishing in the wall. The incident, however, didn't do the Briton's car any good either and the damage inflicted caused him to retire later.

This left the race looking like another Penske 1-2-3 and when Tracy and Unser pitted on lap 151, Fittipaldi took over the lead which he appeared like keeping until he was forced to pit with just three miles left for a drop more fuel. This gave the lead back to Unser and the fourth Penske 1-2-3 was duly completed with just 1.7 seconds covering the three cars which, in turn, were two laps ahead of fourth place Boesel. It was the ninth Penske success of the campaign with the team missing just one podium finish (in (at Michigan). Elsewhere there was a welcome return to the points for Vasser whilst Fernandez kept up his improved form to finish eighth ◼

Points and Leaderboard

Position	Points	Driver
1	173	A. Unser Jnr
2	133	E. Fittipaldi
3	107	P. Tracy
4	100	Mi. Andretti
5	87	R. Gordon
6	79	N. Mansell
=7	54	J. Villeneuve
=7	54	R. Boesel
=9	49	B. Rahal
=9	49	T. Fab

Al Unser Jnr enjoyed another win to consolidate his lead in the Championship.

Race Placings

Pos	Driver	Team	Time	Diff	
1	A. Unser Jnr	Penske Racing Penske PC23-Ilmor D	1:43'31.594	–	
2	P. Tracy	Penske Racing Penske PC23-Ilmor D	–	200 laps	
3	E. Fittipaldi	Penske Racing Penske PC23-Ilmor D	–	200 laps	
4	R. Boesel	Dick Simon Lola T94/00-Ford	–	198 laps	
5	Mi. Andretti	Chip Ganassi Reynard 94I-Ford	–	198 laps	
6	D. Dobson	PacWest Lola T94/00-Ford	–	197 laps	
7	J. Vasser	Hayhoe Reynard 94I-Ford	–	195 laps	
8	A. Fernandez	Galles Reynard 94I-Ilmor D	–	195 laps	
9	B. Rahal	Rahal/Hogan Lola T94/00-Honda	–	193 laps	
10	W.T. Ribbs	Walker Lola T93/00-Ford	–	192 laps	
11	S. Goodyear	Budweiser King Lola T94/00-Ford	–	192 laps	
12	M. Smith	Walker Lola T94/00-Ford	–	192 laps	
13	R. Gordon	Walker Racing Lola T94/00-Ford	–	191 laps	
14	M. Gugelmin	Chip Ganassi Reynard 94I-Ford	–	188 laps	
15	J. Unser	Lola T93/00-Ford	–	185 laps	
16	M. Greco	Arciero Lola T94/00-Ford	–	184 laps	
17	H. Matsushita	Simon Racing Lola T94/00-Ford	–	153 laps	(Oil Pressure)
18	N. Mansell	Newman/Haas Lola T94/00-Ford	–	127 laps	(Handling)
19	Ma. Andretti	Newman/Haas Lola T94/00-Ford	–	107 laps	(Accident)
20	T. Fabi	Hall Reynard 94I-Ilmor D	–	88 laps	(Exhaust)
21	E. Cheever	Forsythe Green Lola T93/00-Ilmor D	–	80 laps	(Suspension)
22	R. Bentley	Lola T92/00-Ilmor A	–	37 laps	(Handling)
23	S. Johansson	Bettenhausen Penske PC22-Ilmor D	–	16 laps	(Handling)
24	S. Sharp	PacWest Lola T94/00-Ford	–	12 laps	(Accident)
25	M. Groff	Rahal/Hogan Lola T94/00-Honda	–	12 laps	(Accident)
26	J. Villeneuve	Forsythe/Green Lola Reynard 94I-Lola	–	0 laps	(Accident)
27	A. Luyendyk	Indy Regency Lola T94/00-Ilmor D	–	0 laps	(Accident)

Average Speed of Winner: 122.635mph

Vancouver

Vancouver, Canada – 4 September 1994

Despite being so ill that he could not even attend the track on the Friday prior to the race, Al Unser took another very positive step towards landing the 1994 title with a safety first routine that saw him outlast all his rivals. By the time of the race he reckoned he felt about 80% fit and, determined to finish in the points, his debilitation from food poisoning probably helped rather than hindered his tactics as he didn't have the strength to dispute any corners. With one of the most contact prone races going on all around him, Unser simply kept his nose clean to drift backwards initially from his starting place of eighth. But from the middle of the field he had a good view of most incidents and drove serenely round them to post his second successive Vancouver victory.

"Tracy and Michael Andretti's battle lost them $10,000 each!"

Qualifying had seen Mansell battling it out with Gordon for pole, the lead changing hands on several occasions before Gordon settled the matter with an explosive 54.570 to capture his second pole of the season, leaving the Briton with another fight, this time to hold off Michael Andretti who was beginning to threaten Mansell's 54.728. In the end, Nigel was successful but the drive of the final session belonged to Scott Goodyear who leap-frogged up the grid in the closing stages to grab fourth. Just behind Goodyear was Fabi who was in his highest grid placing since taking the ride in Jim Hall's Reynard. And the Penskes? The highest placed was Tracy in sixth, two places ahead of Unser with another four back to Fittipaldi.

Gordon made the most of his pole position on a track notorious as a single file circuit and led for the first 36 laps but before the major action got underway the plucky Alessandro Zampedri, back in racing just five weeks after breaking his pelvis at Michigan, had to make a hasty exit when his car burst into flames after only eight laps. Chasing Gordon hard was Mansell and his pressure paid off on lap 37 when the leader braked too late for the final corner and opted for the safety of a cruise down the pit road to gift the lead to the Brit.

"With this Penske team in such form, finishing second is almost like winning." – Nigel Mansell

---

Mansell continued to lead throughout the many contacts. Tracy and Michael Andretti led the way by clocking up no fewer than seventeen between them at the meeting with Tracy losing that particular battle by 11-6. The pair's last altercation cost them $10,000 each for *"taking unjustifiable risks and unsportsmanlike driving"*. When the Briton pitted, however, on lap 76 the lead passed momentarily to Fernandez only for him to promptly run out of fuel. The lead places now

Points and Leaderboard

Position	Points	Driver
1	193	A. Unser
2	137	C. Fittipaldi
3	114	Mi. Andretti
4	107	P. Tracy
5	104	S. Gordon
6	83	N. Mansell
7	55	B. Rahal
=8	54	J. Villeneuve
=8	54	R. Boesel
10	49	T. Fabi
11	45	Ma. Andretti
12	44	S. Goodyear
13	42	J. Vasser
14	41	S. Johansson
15	36	M. Gugelmin

had a familiar Penske look about them with only Gordon in amongst Unser, Tracy and Fittipaldi with Mansell rejoining in fifth. Although Mansell overtook Fittipaldi he was soon back in fifth when Michael Andretti, in turn, went past the Brit to set about Tracy on lap 93. The contact between these two also affected Mansell who dropped behind Fittipaldi, Gugelmin and Goodyear as a result, before mounting a last ditch effort to retrieve something. By the penultimate lap, Mansell was chasing Fittipaldi for fourth spot and made a highly optimistic dive inside the Brazilian who simply held his line to put both cars out.

Up front, Unser was out of any such trouble and went on to take his eighth victory of 1994 to equal Michael Andretti's record for a CART season and to leave him very close to the title 🏁

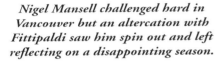

Nigel Mansell challenged hard in Vancouver but an altercation with Fittipaldi saw him spin out and left reflecting on a disappointing season.

Race Placings

Pos	Driver	Team	Time	Diff	
1	A. Unser	Penske Racing Penske PC23-Ilmor D	1:53'27.345	–	
2	R. Gordon	Walker Racing Lola T94/00-Ford	–	102 laps	
3	Mi. Andretti	Chip Ganassi Reynard 94I-Ford	–	102 laps	
4	S. Goodyear	Budweiser King Lola T94/00-Ford	–	102 laps	
5	M. Gugelmin	Chip Ganassi Reynard 94I-Ford	–	102 laps	
6	A. Luyendyk	Indy Regency Lola T94/00-Ilmor D	–	102 laps	
7	B. Rahal	Rahal/Hogan Lola T94/00-Honda	–	102 laps	
8	M. Smith	Walker Lola T94/00-Ford	–	102 laps	
9	E. Fittipaldi	Penske Racing Penske PC23-Ilmor D	–	101 laps	(Accident)
10	N. Mansell	Newman/Haas Lola T94/00-Ford	–	101 laps	(Accident)
11	Ma. Andretti	Newman/Haas Lola T94/00-Ford	–	101 laps	
12	S. Sharp	PacWest Lola T94/00-Ford	–	101 laps	
13	P. Johnstone	Comptech Racing Lola T93/00-Honda	–	101 laps	
14	M. Groff	Rahal/Hogan Lola T94/00-Honda	–	101 laps	
15	J. Vasser	Hayhoe Reynard 94I-Ford	–	101 laps	
16	M. Greco	Arciero Lola T94/00-Ford	–	100 laps	(Accident)
17	E. Cheever	Forsythe Green Lola T93/00 Ilmor D	–	99 laps	
18	T. Fabi	Hall Reynard 94I-Ilmor D	–	98 laps	
19	D. Dobson	PacWest Lola T94/00-Ford	–	96 laps	
20	P. Tracy	Penske Racing Penske PC23-Ilmor D	–	94 laps	(Suspension)
21	C. Bourbonnais	Forsythe/Green Lola T93/00-Ilmor D	–	88 laps	(Gearbox)
22	A. Fernandez	Galles Reynard 94I-Ilmor D	–	76 laps	(Ran out of fuel)
23	R. Boesel	Dick Simon Lola T94/00-Ford	–	68 laps	(Engine)
24	J. Villeneuve	Forsythe/Green Reynard 94I-Ford	–	53 laps	(Exhaust)
25	W.T. Ribbs	Walker Lola T93/00-Ford	–	52 laps	(Steering)
26	S. Johansson	Bettenhausen Penske PC22-Ilmor	–	45 laps	(Accident)
27	B. Lazier	Lola T93/00-Ilmor C	–	16 laps	(Halfshaft)
28	A. Zampedri	Lola T93/00-Ford	–	8 laps	(Fire)

Average Speed of Winner: 89.166mph

Road America

Road America belonged to the sons of famous fathers as Jacques Villeneuve captured his maiden IndyCar victory whilst, just over half a second later, Al Unser Jnr wrapped up the 1994 PPG IndyCar World Series title. The 23 year old Canadian, son of one of the best known F1 drivers of his generation, thus carved a niche in motor racing history in his own right by becoming the youngest driver to win a CART sanctioned IndyCar race. The 32 year old Unser Jnr took his second PPG title. The only thing missing was a podium finish from Michael Andretti whilst Mario looked on but that particular relationship was to founder as both retired within a lap of one another approaching the finish.

> *"The race had the mantle of procession written all over it but a massive shunt by Arnie Luyendyk on lap 32 brought out a full scale yellow."*

Nigel Mansell, meanwhile, had another disappointing day at the races. In qualifying, he had initially occupied a place on the front row but slipped to third, whilst in the race he was in a good fourth at the two-thirds stage only for a puncture to drop him out of contention. This left the Brit to come home just outside the points with his engine still running but sporting a cracked crank sensor device causing malfunction of his electrical system.

Of the others, Paul Tracy took pole from Villeneuve who made his time on the straights as he regularly clocked over 200mph on the radar screens but perhaps the most spectacular qualification was that of Robby Gordon who shot up from fifteenth in the first session to a final grid position of fifth after switching to the same setup as his team mate Mark Smith for the second session.

Also making big strides in the later period were Dominic Dobson, up eight places to twelfth, and Scott Sharp with the biggest leap of all from 26th to 13th after finding an incredible 4.5 seconds overnight improvement from somewhere. Where there are winners, however, there have to be losers and Rahal slipped from ninth to to sixteenth whilst Groff, who had been advised he would not be retained by the Rahal/Hogan outfit for 1995, dropped eight places from his first session tenth spot. A major shock was the sight of Michael Andretti languishing in twentieth spot in a time some two seconds slower than he had qualified in at the corresponding race in 1992.

Tracy used his pole position to good effect and pulled away from Villeneuve at almost a second per lap in the early exchanges with Unser, Gordon, and Mansell giving chase for third. Smith was consolidating his good eighth grid spot into a competitive racing position in the top ten when he hit engine problems on lap nine and retired three laps later with Gordon and Ribbs following suit shortly afterwards. After eleven laps, Tracy held a lead of approaching eight seconds, a lead he was to maintain through the first round of pit stops about the sixteen and seventeen lap mark.

Points and Leaderboard

Position	Points	Driver
1	209	A. Unser Jnr
2	151	E. Fittipaldi
3	114	Mi. Andretti
4	107	P. Tracy
5	104	R. Gordon
6	83	N. Mansell
7	74	J. Villeneuve
8	62	R. Boesel
9	61	T. Fabi
10	59	B. Rahal
11	50	S. Goodyear
12	46	S. Johansson
13	45	Ma. Andretti
14	42	J. Vasser
15	40	A. Fernandez

Meanwhile, Michael Andretti's dire weekend continued with two punctures in the first fifteen circuits.

The race had the mantle of procession written all over it but a massive shunt by Arnie Luyendyk on lap 32 brought out a full scale *yellow.* When the racing got underway again on lap 35, Tracy was almost on top of the pace car and, when the race cars accelerated, he hesitated for a moment to get a clear run which was immediately blocked by Villeneuve racing down the inside line. Once in front, Villeneuve's straight line speed gave him a big advantage although Tracy managed to stay on his tail by closing up on the corners.

Tracy's efforts, however, were all in vain for, on lap 43, his engine called it a day. This promoted Unser to second with Fittipaldi third ahead of Fabi. Prior to this Mansell had incurred a puncture on lap 36 that dropped him to seventeenth but the Andretti family suffered an even worse fate, both going out within a lap of one another less than twenty miles from home.

> *"The Andretti family suffered an even worse fate, both going out within a lap of one another less than twenty miles from home"*

Unser now experienced the same problem as his team mate Tracy had done in his efforts to catch Villeneuve. He could close on the corners but lost ground in the straights. As long as Villeneuve didn't make any mistakes, a maiden victory was his for the taking and the youngster was not going to make any errors although he did have a problem. He was, apparently, extremely low on fuel, so much so in fact that he actually switched off his engine to coast over the line some six tenths of a second ahead of the man who was about to claim his second Championship ◪

Race Placings

Pos	Driver	Team	Time	Diff	
1	J. Villeneuve	Forsythe/Green Reynard 94I-Ford	1:42'37.970	–	
2	A. Unser Jnr	Penske Racing Penske PC23-Ilmor D	–	50 laps	
3	E. Fittipaldi	Penske Racing Penske PC23-Ilmor D	–	50 laps	
4	T. Fabi	Hall Reynard 94I-Ilmor D	–	50 laps	
5	A. Fernandez	Galles Reynard 94I-Ilmor D	–	50 laps	
6	R. Boesel	Dick Simon Lola T94/00-Ford	–	50 laps	
7	S. Goodyear	Budweiser King Lola T94/00-Ford	–	50 laps	
8	S. Johansson	Bettenhausen Penske PC22-Ilmor D	–	50 laps	
9	B. Rahal	Rahal/Hogan Lola T94/00-Honda	–	50 laps	
10	S. Sharp	PacWest Lola T94/00-Ford	–	50 laps	
11	D. Dobson	PacWest Lola T94/00-Ford	–	50 laps	
12	C. Horner	Lola T93/00-Ford	–	50 laps	
13	N. Mansell	Newman/Haas Lola T94/00-Ford	–	50 laps	
14	H. Matsushita	Lola T94/00-Ford	–	49 laps	
15	G. Lavaggi	Lola T93/00-Ford	–	49 laps	
16	Ma. Andretti	Newman/Haas Lola T94/00-Ford	–	47 laps	(Engine)
17	Mi. Andretti	Chip Ganassi Reynard 94I-Ford	–	46 laps	(Exhaust)
18	P. Tracy	Penske Racing Penske PC23-Ilmor D	–	43 laps	(Engine)
19	M. Gugelmin	Chip Ganassi Reynard 94I-Ford	–	40 laps	(Engine)
20	M. Groff	Rahal/Hogan Lola T94/00-Honda	–	38 laps	(Engine)
21	M. Greco	Arciero Lola T94/00-Ford	–	38 laps	(Running)
22	A. Luyendyk	Indy Regency Lola T94/00-Ilmor D	–	30 laps	(Accident)
23	A. Zampedri	Lola T93/00-Ford	–	24 laps	(Gearbox)
24	W.T. Ribbs	Walker Lola T93/00-Ford	–	19 laps	(Engine)
25	R. Gordon	Walker Racing Lola T94/00-Ford	–	16 laps	(Gears)
26	M. Smith	Walker Racing Lola T94/00-Ford	–	12 laps	(Engine)
27	E. Cheever	Forsythe/Green Lola T93/00-Ilmor D	–	8 laps	(Engine)
28	J. Vasser	Hayhoe Reynard 94I-Ford	–	6 laps	(Handling)
29	F. Freon	Lola T93/00-Ilmor C	–	2 laps	(Electrical)
30	C. Bourbonnais	Forsythe/Green Lola T93/00-Ilmor D	–	0 laps	(Accident)
–	R. Bentley	Lola T92/00-Ilmor A	–	Did not start	

Average Speed of Winner: 116.92mph

Nazareth

The centre of attraction was Mario Andretti for whom this would be his last race at his hometown track and, for a time, it looked as if there could be a fairy tale ending as the veteran driver qualified in fifth place on the grid. Without making quite the same impact, Mark Smith also announced he would be retiring from the Indycar scene at the end of the 1994 campaign. With Nigel Mansell counting the days to the end of a disappointing season, there was an air of farewells about Nazareth, the track where Mansell twelve months previously had wrapped up the 1993 Championship at the first attempt when he won the race going away from the opposition.

> *"Tracy overtook poleman Fittipaldi as early as the second turn and then proceeded to drive a dominant race, leading for 192 of the 200 laps."*

But there was to be no repeat in 1994 despite the Briton qualifying in third, less than two-tenths of a second behind pole. Soon after the race began, Mansell was having big trouble with a

Al Unser Jnr

huge amount of oversteer and he quickly headed backwards down the field. Gordon, fourth on the grid, had overtaken Mansell on the first lap and, after just four circuits, the Brit was down to eighth. By the 20th lap, Mansell was eleventh whereupon he decided to make a pit stop to try to sort the problem. In fact he went on to make several pit stops, none of which cured the fault and by the time he decided to call it a day after only 87 laps, Mansell was a lowly seventeenth.

Meanwhile, qualifying had seen an all Penske front row of Fittipaldi and Tracy with the newly crowned Champion, Al Unser Jnr, somewhat surprisingly down in 18th due mainly to drawing the first spot in qualifying and having a slow track to contend with. Fittipaldi's pole was only the second time in his long career that he had captured pole at an oval raceway following his success at New Hampshire but he wasn't destined to win the actual race.

In fact Tracy overtook poleman Fittipaldi as early as the second turn and then proceeded to drive a dominant race, leading for 192 of the 200 laps. Also enjoying himself from way down the order was Tracy's team-mate, Unser who, amazingly, was in third place by lap 33. Another to be making ground hand over fist was former F1 star, Eddie Cheever who was up sixteen places to seventh when Mario Andretti brought the curtain down on his own farewell appearance at Nazareth, as well as signalling the demise of Cheever, when he clipped the Forsythe Green Lola on lap 40.

With Penske now installed in 1-2-3 the yellow that came out as a result of Andretti's clash with Cheever enabled Fittipaldi and Unser to close the gap on the team's third member, Tracy, and soon Unser would be in second when Fittipaldi slid on to the grass as he attempted to lap Villeneuve. Meanwhile, Johansson lost fourth spot to Boesel when he was given a *stop and go* penalty for crossing the grass between the pit entry lane and the track.

From the three-quarters stage, however, Tracy simply dominated as he increased his advantage over Unser by six seconds from two and a half seconds to win as hc liked by 8.459 seconds with Fittipaldi completing the fifth Penske 1-2-3 of the season a further five and a half seconds back. His third place in the race, however, was sufficient to ensure runners-up spot in the Championship with Tracy well placed to claim third in the last race of the series at Laguna Seca.

And the rest? They were nowhere with Boesel's fourth place being gained at a distance of four laps down, a fact which amply demonstrated the vast superiority of the Penskes ▨

Points and Leaderboard

Position	Points	Driver
1	225	A. Unser Jnr
2	166	E. Fittipaldi
3	130	P. Tracy
4	118	Mi. Andretti
5	104	R. Gordon
6	83	N. Mansell
7	80	J. Villeneuve
8	74	R. Boesel
9	69	T. Fabi
10	59	B. Rahal
11	56	S. Johansson
12	55	S. Goodyear
13	45	Ma. Andretti
14	42	J. Vasser
15	40	A. Fernandez

Race Placings

Pos	No	Driver	Team	Time	Diff	
1		P. Tracy	Penske Racing Penske PC23-Ilmor D	1:31'30.292	–	
2		A. Unser Jnr	Penske Racing Penske PC23-Ilmor D	–	200 laps	
3		E. Fittipaldi	Penske Racing Penske PC23-Ilmor D	–	200 laps	
4		R. Boesel	Dick Simon Lola T94/00 -Ford	–	196 laps	
5		S. Johansson	Bettenhausen Penske PC22-Ilmor D	–	195 laps	
6		T. Fabi	Hall Reynard 941-Ilmor D	–	194 laps	
7		J. Villeneuve	Forsythe/Green Reynard 941-Ford	–	193 laps	
8		S. Goodyear	Budweiser King Lola T94/00-Ford	–	191 laps	
9		Mi. Andretti	Chip Ganassi Reynard 941-Ford	–	191 laps	
10		M. Gugelmin	Chip Ganassi Reynard 941-Ford	–	190 laps	
11		M. Groff	Rahal/Hogan Lola T94/00-Honda	–	190 laps	
12		M. Smith	Walker Lola T94/00-Ford	–	189 laps	
13		J. Vasser	Hayhoe Reynard 941-Ford	–	189 laps	
14		B. Rahal	Rahal/Hogan Lola T94/00-Honda	–	189 laps	
15		S. Sharp	PacWest Lola T94/00-Ford	–	187 laps	
16		H. Matsushita	Lola T94/00-Ford	–	186 laps	
17		M. Greco	Arciero Lola T94/00-Ford	–	185 laps	
18		W.T. Ribbs	Walker Lola T93/00-Ford	–	182 laps	
19		D. Dobson	PacWest Lola T94/00-Ford	–	182 laps	
20		A. Zampedri	Lola T93/00-Ford	–	174 laps	
21		A. Fernandez	Galles Reynard 941-Ilmor D	–	134 laps	(Accident)
22		N. Mansell	Newman/Haas Lola T94/00-Ford	–	87 laps	(Handling)
23		R. Gordon	Walker Racing Lola T94/00-Ford	–	63 laps	(Wheel Bearing)
24		E. Cheever	Forsythe Green Lola T93/00-Ilmor D	–	45 laps	(Accident)
25		Ma. Andretti	Newman/Haas Lola T94/00-Ford	–	40 laps	(Accident)
26		A. Luyendyk	Indy Regency Lola T94/00-Ilmor D	–	23 laps	(Gearbox)

Average Speed of Winner: 131.41mph

Laguna Seca

Monterey, California, USA – 2 October 1994

Laguna Seca brought the curtain down not only on the season but on one of the most distinguished careers in motor racing history as Mario Andretti called it a day, after over thirty years of racing at the top. Sadly there was not to be a fitting finale to the tale as his car packed in with four of the 84 laps still to go to leave Andretti sat in the cockpit for an eternity as he reflected on climbing out for the last time. Besides his 1978 Formula One World Championship, 18 poles and twelve Grand Prix victories, Andretti had driven in 407 Indy Car races, taking pole in 67 of them and winning 52. The other farewell said was that of Nigel Mansell who had not seen success in his second Indy Car series after taking all before him in his first.

Back from a test drive in Europe for the Benetton Formula One team, Paul Tracy reckoned that the experience helped him land pole and the $25,000 prize that went with it as the reward for securing more poles than any other driver in the season. In taking his total of poles to four Tracy said *"You only usually have one chance over there to put down a fast time and that really helped me concentrate on my qualifying here"*. Indeed, his concentration must have been near perfect as he took his pole by the incredible margin of almost a second from Villeneuve and then Mansell but Mario was down in 12th to offer little hope for a memorable finish.

The race got away to a messy start with Robby Gordon and Al Unser Jnr banging wheels which dumped Unser, the Champion elect, unceremoniously in to the gravel. A few hundred yards further on at Turn Three, Michael Andretti and Fittipaldi collided and Rahal was unable to miss the stranded Chip Ganassi car. That left both Rahal and Michael Andretti out of the race before it had hardly started but Mario Andretti had a lucky escape and was able to continue. He had slowed to miss the carnage in front of him when he was rammed in the back and had to crawl in to the pits. Fortunately for the man who was centre of attraction, a full course yellow was called and his car was repaired without him losing a lap.

On the restart, Tracy confirmed that his pole time was no fluke by proceeding to drive away from Villeneuve and Mansell at a second a lap and that was that, as the Canadian led from start to finish with an amazing display of fearless driving that saw him average almost 0.3mph faster than his nearest challenger at the finish, Ralph Boesel. The major incident of the race took place in the pit lane when Johansson tried to leave his pit stall after completing a stop only to inadvertently nudge a mechanic in the next pit belonging to Adrian Fernandez who was in for a tyre change. The pit mechanic then threw the tyre he held at the front of Johansson's car resulting in both Fernandez and Johansson being given *stop and go* penalties but as Johansson exited after completing his penalty, he exceeded the 85mph pit lane speed restriction by one mph resulting in another penalty and then a fine for giving the Stewards an obscene gesture as he departed for a second time!

What little chance Mansell had of leaving the Indy Car scene on a high note disappeared when his team were unable to dislodge his right rear wheel leaving the Brit to soldier on for two thirds of the race on the same tyre. After a second lengthy pit stop to try to solve the problem had met with no more success than the first attempt, Mansell then had the misfortune to get stuck behind the pace car on a yellow to find himself a lap down on Tracy and six others. With twenty laps to go, however, the race had a familiar look about it with Penske once more driving 1-2-3 but Unser dropped out with gearbox problems whilst Fittipaldi was relieved of second place by a pair of daring moves instigated by Boesel and Villeneuve. But there was no way either of them could get near Tracy who thus finished the season with two wins in a row. Unfortunately for Tracy, all eyes were elsewhere as the Indy Car fraternity bade farewell to one of its legends ◆

Race Placings

Pos	Driver	Team	Time	Diff	
1	P. Tracy	Penske Racing Penske PC23-Ilmor	2:00'00.763	–	
2	R. Boesel	Dick Simon Lola T94/00-Ford	–	84 laps	
3	J. Villeneuve	Forsythe Green Reynard 94I-Ford	–	84 laps	
4	E. Fittipaldi	Penske Racing Penske PC23-Ilmor D	–	84 laps	
5	T. Fabi	Hall Reynard 94I-Ilmor D	–	84 laps	
6	A. Luyendyk	Indy Regency Lola T94/00-Ford	–	84 laps	
7	A. Fernandez	Galles Reynard 94I-Ilmor D	–	84 laps	
8	N. Mansell	Newman/Haas Lola T94/00-Ford	–	83 laps	
9	A. Montermini	King Lola T94/00-Ford	–	83 laps	
10	D. Dobson	PacWest Lola T94/00-Ford	–	83 laps	
11	W.T. Ribbs	Walker Lola T93/0-Ford	–	83 laps	
12	S. Johansson	Bettenhausen Penske PC22-Ilmor D	–	83 laps	
13	R. Gordon	Walker Racing Lola T94/00-Ford	–	82 laps	
14	M. Smith	Walker Lola T94/00-Ford	–	82 laps	
15	M. Groff	Rahal/Hogan Lola T94/00-Honda	–	82 laps	
16	A. Zampedri	Lola T93/00-Ford		82 laps	
17	P. Johnstone	Comptech Lola T93/00-Honda	–	81 laps	
18	F. Freon	Indy Regency Lola T94-Ilmor D	–	81 laps	
19	Ma. Andretti	Newman/Haas Lola T94/00-Ford	–	80 laps	(Engine)
20	A. Unser Jnr	Penske Racing Penske PC23-Ilmor D	–	74 laps	(Gearbox)
21	S. Sharp	PacWest Lola T94/00-Ford	–	59 laps	(Engine)
22	M. Gugelmin	Chip Ganassi Reynard 94I-Ford	–	51 laps	(Exhaust)
23	H. Matsushita	Lola T94/00-Ford		48 laps	(Electrical)
24	M. Greco	Arciero Lola T94/00-Ford	–	44 laps	(Gearbox)
25	E. Cheever	Forsythe/Green Lola T93/00-Ilmor D	–	36 laps	(Electrical)
26	J. Vasser	Hayhoe Reynard 94I-Ford	–	35 laps	(Accident)
27	S. Goodyear	Budweiser King Lola T94/00-Ford	–	16 laps	(Accident)
28	Mi. Andretti	Chip Ganassi Reynard 94I-Ford	–	0 laps	(Accident)
29	B. Rahal	Rahal/Hogan Lola T94/00-Ford	–	0 laps	(Accident)

Average Speed of Winner: 92.978mph

One of the most famous sights in Indy Car racing – the oval circuit of Indianapolis.

Review

The Penske team showed that winning was as easy as 1-2-3 – for the others second was as good as a win!

If the 1993 season had seen history made with Nigel Mansell winning the series in his "rookie" campaign to become the first driver to succeed in landing two F1 World titles back to back with an Indy Car Championship, then 1994 also made its fair share of history.

Roger Penske's team totally dominated the Championship and, between them, the Penske drivers Al Unser Jnr, Emerson Fittipaldi and Paul Tracy won an unprecedented twelve races in the season. Unser himself equalled Michael Andretti's total of eight wins in a CART campaign whilst the team registered an amazing five 1-2-3s at Milwaukee, Portland, Ohio, New Hampshire and Nazareth. Indeed, two of the races where the domination was most conspicuous, at Ohio and New Hampshire, were back to back but even prior to that, the Penskes were so superior to any of their rivals that when Mansell momentarily took the lead at Cleveland it was only the second circuit in over five hundred that a Penske had not been at the head of proceedings.

Although Unser took his second championship (following his 1990 success which made him the first driver to follow a father's footsteps) the Penske success was not just about the dual Champion and both Fittipaldi and Tracy had their moments, with the Brazilian ending a long wait by taking pole on an oval circuit for the first time in a thirty year career when posting the fastest qualifying time at New Hampshire. Tracy had a quiet start to the season with just two points from the first four races but thereafter was almost always a factor with eight top three finishes at the remaining twelve venues. With Unser finishing in the first three on eleven occasions as did Fittipaldi, the Penske drivers between them enjoyed 30 top three finishes out of a possible 48. Such was Tracy's late season form that Benetton lured the Canadian over the Atlantic to test drive for them to give rise to rumours that the driver, who was somewhat surprisingly deemed surplus to requirements by Roger Penske at the end of term, would be signed up for F1.

That little tryst, however, came to nought when Newman/Haas signed the newly released Penske pilot to partner Michael Andretti in 1995 as replacements for the departed Nigel Mansell and retired Mario Andretti.

Mario had announced twelve months earlier in Laguna Seca that he would be calling it a day at the end of the 1994 season. Nobody really believed him but he was true to his word and,

Final Placing and Points

Position	Points	Driver
1	225	A. Unser Jnr
2	178	E. Fittipaldi
3	152	P. Tracy
4	118	Mi. Andretti
5	104	R. Gordon
6	94	J. Villeneuve
7	90	R. Boesel
8	88	N. Mansell
9	79	T. Fabi
10	59	B. Rahal
11	57	S. Johansson
12	55	S. Goodyear
13	46	A. Fernandez
14	45	Mario Andretti
15	42	J. Vasser
16	39	M. Gugelmin
17	34	A. Luyendyk
18	30	D. Dobson
=19	17	M. Smith
=19	17	M. Groff
21	14	S. Sharp
22	12	W.T. Ribbs
23	11	B. Herta
24	10	A. Montermini
25	9	A. Zampedri
26	8	H. Matsushita
27	5	E. Cheever
28	3	J. Andretti
=29	2	M. Greco
=29	2	D. Danner
=31	1	F. Freon
=31	1	Jones
=31	1	Till

exactly a year later, at the same track in the hills overlooking Monterey, the legend's last Indy Car race came to a sad end when his timing chain broke four laps from the finish. So no fairy tale ending but a whole bag full of memories for him to look back on including his Formula One World title and a combined total of 64 F1 and Indy Car successes along with 85 poles.

And what of the other big name to call it quits, Nigel Mansell? After his fabulous debut in 1993 in which he won five races as well as the title with 191 points, 1994 was to prove a massive disappointment. Quite simply, his car was outclassed by the Penskes and the points chart seemed to indicate that Mansell accepted his fate a long way from the finishing straight. Certainly his Lola could compete with the Penskes in qualifying throughout the long summer to which two poles, three other front line starts, and seven second row starts in sixteen races bore testament. Indeed, his defence of his title had got off to a bright enough start in Australia where he captured pole. A disappointing ninth place there soon gave way to more hopeful signs and in the next seven races he had five top five placings including two seconds and a third. Not exactly unsuccessful by normal benchmarks, but by comparison to the points being amassed by Fittipaldi, Unser and Tracy, it was not going to bring a retention of the Championship.

The Brit's form fell badly away after his second at Cleveland in early July and he went on to score only 16 further points in the last eight races, a poor return by anybody's standards. Strangely, this downturn began at Toronto where in 1993 Mansell had hit the walls in both practice and qualifying. Twelve months later, he again hit the wall with some gusto and his season went downhill from that moment onwards.

Mansell's team mate Michael Andretti (although in several instances nobody would have described the pair in those terms) fared slightly better with seven top five positions but, away from the Newman/Haas and Penske outfits, the most impressive performance was given by Robbie Gordon in his Walker Racing Lola.

Gordon took pole at both Toronto and Vancouver and had six top five placings but, like Mansell, his season tailed off and he had only one point scoring finish in the last five races. Of

No paradise for Mansell in 1994 as he prepares for the start of the season at Surfers.

the others, Vasser and Johansson started off with excellent results being fourth and fifth at Surfers before reversing the places in the next race at Phoenix. There was also a fourth place for Vasser in the Indy 500 but, after taking 34 points in those three early outings, he only notched up a further eight in the remainder of the season.

Two of the strongest finishers in the seven month haul were Jacques Villeneuve and Ralph Boesel. Villeneuve collected 40 of his 94 points in the last three races including setting a record at Wisconsin when he became the youngest ever driver, at the age of 23, to win a CART sanctioned Indy Car race. Boesel captured 36 of his 90 points in those same three races but even this rich harvest paled into insignificance alongside the sheer and utter dominance of the Roger Penske dream machine throughout 1994 ■

TOCA British
Touring Car
year

Preview...

Two new manufacturers and twenty-one rounds of thrills, spills and appeals marked another exciting year.

Arguably the best and most spectacular form of motor racing ever seen in Great Britain continued to pack in the crowds at every BTCC meeting. Since 1991 when the championship became a solitary class for the two litre production cars, interest had increased each year and 1994, with no fewer than six former F1 drivers and an increase in participating manufacturers from eight to ten with the arrival of Alfa Corse and Volvo, would be no exception.

But with the two new manufacturers came the rub as the friendly atmosphere went out of the window. Alfa were known to be investing almost £6m in this bid to land the title at the first attempt and, given their reputation for stretching the rules to the limits, were eyed with some wariness from the very beginning by the likes of Ford's Andy Rouse, at 46 the oldest competitor in the cham-

pionship, and to whom the present format of BTCC racing owes so much. His voice spoke for many others in the arguments that were to rage over the Alfa's homologation. But, whatever the rights and wrongs of the Alfa homologation, surely it was either legal or not and the one black mark on the season was the car being declared legal prior to the season, then maybe not legal with the Alfa's contesting three races under appeal, then definitely not legal and excluded from an Oulton Park meeting with all points gained under appeal deducted, and then legal again with all points reinstated after a cobbled together compromise!

Volvo also showed that their entry of the 850 SE Estate was not just a gimmick to get publicity when they engaged the services of Tom Walkinshaw Racing to mastermind their bid. It is thought their budget was equal to Alfa's and

The colourful world of the BTCC was about to set forth on another spectacular season which saw big crowds and great action.

TWR, over a period of time, had gained the same sort of reputation as the Italians for seeing how far the rules could be pushed. The TWR connection continued with the appointment of driver Jan Lammers, a winner at Le Mans in a TWR Jaguar, but with no touring car experience. He would be partnered by Rick Rydell who, although a seasoned F3 driver in both Britain and Japan, also lacked experience.

So BMW, who had won the BTCC championship in all three years since its inception in 1991, knew they would have an almighty job on their hands to retain their standing in 1994. On paper their cars, prepared by the world famous German Schnitzer outfit, had the perfect back up of the 1993 World champion Jo Winkelhock, the vastly experienced Steve Soper and the Italian Roberto Ravaglia. But as the only rear drive car in the series the BMW outfit was hamstrung by a 100kg weight penalty in the first half of the season leaving it stranded in the title hunt.

Four times World champion Andy Rouse led the Ford attempt from the front in the sense that the present Mondeo racing car owes much of its life to development at the Coventry based Andy Rouse Engineering concern. The time he spent producing the car and arguing his corner in the disagreements over the Alfa homologation appeared to have reduced Rouse's winning opportunities out on the tarmac and the Mondeo's most realistic chance of success would lie with Kiwi Paul Radisich who had enjoyed a hat-trick of victories during the 1993 season. But could Ford add to their nine championships? Vauxhall were another outfit with an experienced driver combination. Scot John Cleland had won at least one race in each year since the beginning of the present two litre formula whilst, after Rouse, Jeff Allam was the BTCC's second highest winner.

Toyota put the preparation of their cars in the hands of the well respected and highly successful Norfolk based TOMS outfit and kept the driving team of 1993 of Julian Bailey and Will Hoy. After a highly successful two years in 1991 (when he was champion with BMW) and 1992 (runner up for Toyota), Hoy failed to win a race in 1993 so 1994 was looking very much like make or break time for him, a remark that applied even more to the team's third driver Tim Sugden who missed the entire 1993 campaign waiting for a Mercedes ride that never came.

Of the remaining outfits Renault appeared to harbour the best chance of success but its Laguna was untried. In 1993 the Renault 19 had twice won at Donington in the wet but failed on the dry tracks with the result that the French combine switched to the Laguna which had its racing engine and chassis designed by the company's Grand Prix division. Swiss star Alain Menu and Tim Harvey, who both won a race apiece in 1993 for Renault, were retained as their drivers.

Old Spice Nissan were again racing their Primeras but, with only one victory in three seasons, looked to have a daunting task to add to that figure. There is a strong O'dor family connection at Old Spice for the cars are prepared by Janspeed Engineering whose founder Jan O'dor is the father of team driver Kieth O'dor. The other drivers, Eric van de Poele and Top Gear's Tiff Needell both have F1 experience but the car looked to have a lot to do.

Perhaps the most interesting move was that of Patrick Watts from Team Mazda to Peugeot. He had driven quickly in 1993 but his team were clearly under financed and he suffered accordingly. The Peugeot 405 had undoubtedly underperformed in both 1992 and 1993 so the pairing certainly had possibilities. Watts would be backed up by Eugene O'Brien.

Mazda's cash problems in 1993 had not improved twelve months on. They replaced Watts with the 1993 Privateers champion Matt Neal, who at 15 stone 6lb, was the heaviest driver in the field which was just another handicap.

The privateers this year had their own championship sponsored by Total and the package for the private competitors ensured the winner would go home some £25,000 richer on top of TOCA's donation of £10,000 of start money to each privateer. The favourites for the top prize were the runaway 1993 National Saloon Car Champion James Thompson and 1992 TOCA Cup winner James Kaye. Other competitors included Nigel Smith who obviously had the blessing of Her Majesty – he was sponsored by HMSO – but the true privateer had to be Lincolnshire based Geoff Steel who prepares his BMW himself with sponsorship from his own motor business. ■

Thruxton

John Cleland's Vauxhall Cavalier came home second on the opening day.

With its bumps and very quick sweeps, Thruxton is not the easiest of tracks to make a BTCC debut which made Alfa driver Gabriele Tarquini's feat in claiming pole position from John Cleland's Cavalier all the more remarkable. There were just four drivers under 1min 20secs but it was noticeable that Alfa's second string, Giampiero Simoni was among them giving Alfa two of the first four four grid positions on their debut. The benefits of

the car's controversial aerodynamics was obviously playing its part. Third place was occupied by Paul Radisich's Mondeo whilst the best of the rest was BMW's reigning champion, Jo Winkelhock. The TWR Volvos had a horrendous time, however, and Jan Lammers and Rickard Rydell found themselves way down the field.

When the race itself got underway, Cleland was soon passed at the start by both Radisich and Winkelhock with Tarquini out in front but Cleland's Cavalier got by on the outside of the

1994 Grid Positions and Qualifying Times

Grid	Driver	Time	Grid	Driver	Time	Grid	Driver	Time
1	G. Tarquini	1'19.35	10	J. Allam	1'20.58	19	R. Rydell	1'22.65
2	J. Cleland	1'19.45	11	T. Harvey	1'20.58	20	J. Thompson*	1'22.68
3	P. Radisich	1'19.69	12	A. Menu	1'20.69	21	J. Lammers	1'23.56
4	G. Simoni	1'19.75	13	E. van de Poele	1'20.77	22	N. Albon*	1'23.64
5	J. Winkelhock	1'20.07	14	P. Watts	1'20.95	23	N. Smith*	1'24.11
6	W. Hoy	1'20.15	15	D. Leslie	1'20.99	24	I. Khan*	1'24.24
7	A. Rouse	1'20.16	16	E. O'Brien	1'21.36	25	G. Steel*	1'27.81
8	S. Soper	1'20.21	17	M. Neal	1'21.46	26	J. Kaye*	1'32.25
9	K. O'dor	1'20.40	18	J. Bailey	1'21.49		*Denotes Total Cup competitors	

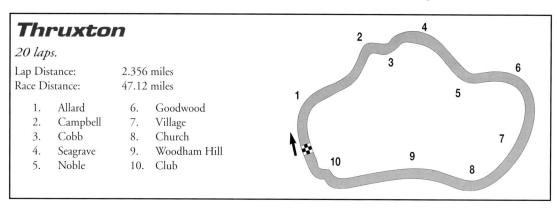

Thruxton

20 laps.

Lap Distance: 2.356 miles
Race Distance: 47.12 miles

1.	Allard	6.	Goodwood
2.	Campbell	7.	Village
3.	Cobb	8.	Church
4.	Seagrave	9.	Woodham Hill
5.	Noble	10.	Club

BMW at Church to reclaim third spot from Winkelhock. The second Alfa, driven by Simoni had experienced a bad start with a great deal of wheelspin and dropped back to sixth behind Hoy. The first crash of the season was merely a light brush between Rouse and Menu but it put paid to Rouse's chances. He made two stops and fell well behind. In the early stages, Tarquini was racing away from the field picking up about half a second a lap as Cleland could not get past

Radisich whilst his team mate, Simoni, was also beginning to recover. The Italian had got past Hoy on the second circuit and then went in front of Winkelhock on lap four but he, too, experienced difficulty in getting beyond Radisich. The Italian's exasperation caused him to bump with Radisich with the result that Winkelhock overtook both. The repercussions for Radisich, however, proved to be of the greater consequence as he retired a lap later.

Round One – Race Placings

Pos	Driver	Car	Time	Diff	Grid	
1	G. Tarquini	Alfa Romeo 155TS	27'19.12	–	1	
2	J. Cleland	Vauxhall Cavalier	–	0.56	2	
3	J. Winkelhock	BMW 318i	–	15.26	5	
4	S. Soper	BMW 318i	–	17.56	8	
5	W. Hoy	Toyota Carina E	–	17.91	6	
6	A. Menu	Renault Laguna	–	21.22	12	
7	P. Watts	Peugeot 405 Mi16	–	29.26	14	
8	D. Leslie	Mazda Xedos 6	–	32.85	15	
9	K. O'dor	Nissan Primera 2.0eGT	–	33.45	9	
10	T. Harvey	Renault Laguna	–	36.06	11	
11	G. Simoni	Alfa Romeo 155TS	–	37.86*	4	
12	M. Neal	Mazda Xedos 6	–	39.30	17	
13	E. van de Poele	Nissan Primera 2.0eGT	–	41.57	13	
14	J. Allam	Vauxhall Cavalier 16v	–	49.28	10	
15	R. Rydell	Volvo 850SE	–	1'01.24	19	
16	J. Kaye	Toyota Carina E	–	1'12.55	26	
17	N. Albon	Renault 19	–	1'16.46	22	
18	N. Smith	Vauxhall Cavalier 16v	–	1 lap down	23	
19	I. Khan**	Toyota Carina E	–	1 lap down	24	
20	J. Bailey	Toyota Carina E	–	1 lap down	18	
21	A. Rouse	Ford Mondeo Ghia	–	2 laps down	7	
22	G. Steel	BMW 318is	–	2 laps down	25	

Did Not Finish

–	P. Radisich	Ford Mondeo Ghia	–	16 laps	3	Accident damage
–	E. O'Brien	Peugeot 405Mi16	–	14 laps	16	Accident
–	J. Lammers	Volvo 850SE	–	4 laps	21	Mechanical
–	J. Thompson	Peugeot 405Mi16	–	1 lap	20	Mechanical

Fastest Lap: G. Tarquini – 1'20.20 (105.75mph) – Course Record

Average Speed of Winner: 103.48mph.

* includes 25 second time penalty.   ** denotes demoted one place

Simoni kept up his attack on Winkelhock and passed him to claim third place, or so he thought. Soper came in fifth after admitting he had had a battle royal with Andy Rouse because *"I didn't know he was two laps behind!"* O'dor reckoned he was heading for a top six finish until he collided with Menu half way through the race, a shunt which dropped him to 20th and he did well to recover into a top ten place but the worst accident befell Eugene O'Brien who hit the barriers at about 100mph on the fourteenth circuit. Thankfully, O'Brien was merely dazed.

Meanwhile up front, Tarquini was meeting the slower drivers and not always getting past as quick as he would have liked with the result that Cleland was definitely closing the gap on the leader. However, the line came soon enough with Cleland still almost a second down.

In the steward's room, a 25 second penalty was imposed on Simoni for his move on Radisich which had the effect of dropping the Italian youngster from third to eleventh and elevated Winkelhock to third, although not in sufficient time to share the champagne on the podium

In the privateer's Total Cup, James Kaye was

Championship Placings

Drivers' Points		Constructors' Points	
24	G. Tarquini	24	Alfa Romeo
18	J. Cleland	18	Vauxhall
12	J. Winkelhock	12	BMW
10	S. Soper	8	Toyota
8	W. Hoy	6	Renault
6	A. Menu	4	Peugeot
4	P. Watts	3	Mazda
3	D. Leslie	2	Nissan
2	K. O'dor		
1	T. Harvey		

TOTAL Cup

Position	Driver	Points
1st	J. Kaye	24
2nd	N. Albon	18
3rd	N. Smith	12
4th	I. Khan	10
5th	G. Steel	8

first home when he finished a creditable 16th in the overall race almost four seconds clear of his closest rival, Nigel Albon.■

Gabriele Tarquini's Alfa Romeo made a winning debut.

Brands Hatch

The Volvos of Lammers and Rydell finished in the second half of the field.

The first qualifying session was one of carnage as car after car met with disaster. Eventually the session was called to a halt with almost ten minutes left. Before the decision was taken, however, Steve Soper had started things rolling by spinning at Clearways quickly followed by Matt Neal incurring panel damage at Paddock.

The reigning champion, Jo Winkelhock joined in when he went wide at Surtees and hit a kerb resulting in a sideways dash into the approach to Clearways and then carouselling through the air before coming to rest against a barrier. Amazingly, Winkelhock, although temporarily knocked unconscious, walked away and his team performed wonders to get the car back into shape in time to take 18th position on the grid. The marshals at Clearways certainly had to keep their wits about them with cars raining down on them from all angles. Next it was the turn of both Watts and van de Poele. Watts was fortunate to have his car ready for the the next day but the Belgian's Nissan was never going to recover from the damage inflicted when the car smashed into the barriers having gone wide at the Clearways exit at over 100mph. Finishing the excitement was Tim Sugden who landed in the gravel at Paddock but up front there was no doubting the supremacy of the Alfa Romeos as they grabbed spots one and two under Tarquini and Simoni.

1994 Grid Positions and Qualifying Times

Grid	Driver	Time	Grid	Driver	Time	Grid	Driver	Time
1	G. Tarquini	46.64	11	W. Hoy	47.67	21	M. Neal	48.39
2	G. Simoni	46.86	12	J. Bailey	47.75	22	J. Kaye*	48.57
3	T. Harvey	47.15	13	K. O'dor	47.76	23	J. Lammers	48.66
4	A. Menu	47.25	14	T. Sugden	47.79	24	N. Albon*	49.43
5	J. Cleland	47 35	15	D. Leslie	47.83	25	G. Steel*	50.18
6	P. Radisich	47.39	16	R. Rydell	48.00			
7	S. Soper	47.46	17	N. Smith*	48.07	**Did Not Start**		
8	A. Rouse	47.48	18	J. Winkelhock	48.14	–	E. van de Poele	–
9	J. Allam	47.53	19	C. Goodwin*	48.36	–	I. Khan*	–
10	P. Watts	47.62	20	J. Thompson*	48.39	*Denotes Total Cup competitors		

Round Two – 30 laps

Tarquini held on to his front position from the start but his team mate, Simoni, relinquished his grid advantage when he slowed right up going into Druids on the first lap to let not only Harvey past but also Menu, Cleland and Watts. Harvey was now right on Tarquini's rear end but on his fourth lap his efforts found him resting in the gravel at Druids and his day had come to an early close as he did not start Race Two.

The seventh circuit claimed Winkelhock, who was not having a good weekend, when the German hit Bailey at Druids and was forced to retire. Bailey fared little better for, although he carried on, he was two laps down at the finish. Tarquini seized the opportunity to power ahead and by the end of the tenth lap was almost ten seconds clear of Simoni who had been busy picking off the men in front of him to get right back in the thick of things. Rouse and Cleland, meanwhile, were having a battle royal for third spot but Cleland just managed to hang on by the narrowest of margins. Radisich had an equally tough duel with Allam for fifth whilst Watts, in a

car that 24 hours earlier had looked too battered to continue, came home an excellent seventh. The unluckiest tale, however, surely belonged to Tim Sugden who was having his first outing for his new team. He was loathe to keep going when his oil pressure light came on intermittently and as a result pulled into the pits only to be told that this often happened on that particular car! The experience cost him two laps! In the Total Cup, Goodwin was passed by Smith five laps from home with nineteen year old James Thompson in third (16th overall)

Round Three – 30 laps

The race got off to a quite sensational start but then quickly became a procession. Simoni was obviously intent on averting a second consecutive bad start but as he dived to the right on the green light he found that Cleland had made an even quicker exit from the grid. This prevented Simoni making his intended manoeuvre and he went sideways across the track causing everyone to take evasive action. Everyone, apart from Matt Neal whose efforts to miss Simoni resulted in him

Round Two – Race Placings

Pos	Driver	Car	Time	Diff	Grid	
1	G. Tarquini	Alfa Romeo 155TS	24'04.82	–	1	
2	G. Simoni	Alfa Romeo 155TS	–	3.14 secs	2	
3	J. Cleland	Vauxhall Cavalier 16V	–	7.92 secs	5	
4	A. Rouse	Ford Mondeo Ghia	–	8.04 secs	8	
5	P. Radisich	Ford Mondeo Ghia	–	15.36 secs	6	
6	J. Allam	Vauxhall Cavalier 16V	–	15.77 secs	9	
7	P. Watts	Peugeot 405 Mi16	–	18.01 secs	10	
8	D. Leslie	Mazda Xedos 6	–	25.11 secs	15	
9	W. Hoy	Toyota Carina E	–	26.04 secs	11	
10	S. Soper	BMW 318i	–	26.34 secs	7	
11	K. O'dor	Nissan Primera 2.0eGT	–	26.99 secs	13	
12	J. Lammers	Volvo 850SE/GLT	–	44.50 secs	23	
13	N. Smith	Vauxhall Cavalier 16V	–	44.80 secs	17	
14	C. Goodwin	Vauxhall Cavalier 16V	–	45.73 secs	19	
15	M. Neal	Mazda Xedos 6	–	46.11 secs	21	
16	J. Thompson	Peugeot 405 Mi16	–	1 lap down	20	
17	J. Kaye	Toyota Carina E	–	1 lap down	22	
18	A. Menu	Renault Laguna	–	1 lap down	4	
19	J. Bailey	Toyota Carina E	–	2 laps down	12	
20	T. Sugden	Toyota Carina E	–	2 laps down	14	
21	G. Steel	BMW 318is	–	2 laps down	25	
22	R. Rydell	Volvo 850SE/GLT	–	10 laps down	16	

Did Not Finish

Pos	Driver	Car	Time	Diff	Grid	
–	N. Albon	Renault 19 16V	–	8 laps	24	Steering problems
–	J. Winkelhock	BMW 318i	–	6 laps	18	Accident damage
–	T. Harvey	Renault Laguna	–	3 laps	3	Gravel trap

Fastest Lap: G. Tarquini – 47.20 secs (91.80mph) – Course Record.

Average Speed of Winner: 89.96mph

The start of the Brands Hatch meeting – Tarquini was to make it three out of three wins.

spinning, successfully negotiated the melee which left Tarquini well clear and Simoni struggling. Indeed, after another spin on the second circuit, Simoni was plumb last before beginning an amazing ascent through the field to at least enliven a race which, up front, remained the same throughout with Tarquini, Cleland, Rouse, Radisich, Allam and Soper staying in the same positions from start to finish.

Simoni's reward for his gallant fightback was to eventually finish in eighth place only to find, for the second meeting in succession, the stewards being non too pleased with his aggression and excluding him from the race. Elsewhere, O'dor retired with differential problems after completing sixteen laps and Menu departed even earlier.

After a good start which saw the Swiss driver benefit from the melee at the beginning of the race which enabled him to move up to move up ten places from eighteenth at the line up, the Laguna developed engine problems to force Menu out after eleven laps. Lammers had looked likely to collect the Volvo Estate's first points only to be shunted by Bailey at Druids to drop back to sixteenth. In the Total Cup competition for the privateers, Goodwin took his revenge on Smith for his first race defeat whilst Thompson, Kaye and Steel filled the same three places as they had in the earlier duel but there was no doubting who was the happiest man leaving the track – Tarquini now had three wins out of three. ▨

Brands Hatch Indy

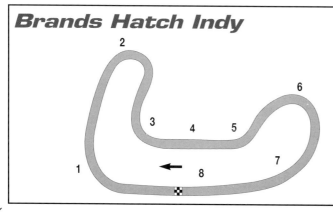

Lap Distance: 1.2 miles
Race Distance: 36 miles

1. Paddock
2. Druids
3. Graham Hill
4. Cooper Straight
5. Surtees
6. McLaren
7. Clark
8. Brabham Straight

Round Three – Race Placings

Pos	Driver	Car	Time	Diff	Grid	
1	G. Tarquini	Alfa Romeo 155TS	24'04.82	–	1	
2	J. Cleland	Vauxhall Cavalier 16V	–	5.42 secs	3	
3	A. Rouse	Ford Mondeo Ghia	–	6.19 secs	4	
4	P. Radisich	Ford Mondeo Ghia	–	10.40 secs	5	
5	J. Allam	Vauxhall Cavalier 16V	–	13.56 secs	6	
6	S. Soper	BMW 318i	–	15.20 secs	10	
7	J. Winkelhock	BMW 318i	–	24.32 secs	23	
8	P. Watts	Peugeot 405 Mi16	–	25.30 secs	7	
9	W. Hoy	Toyota Carina E	–	29.20 secs	9	
10	J. Bailey	Toyota Carina E	–	31.92 secs	19	
11	D. Leslie	Mazda Xedos 6	–	33.32 secs	8	
12	T. Sugden	Toyota Carina E	–	33.73 secs	20	
13	C. Goodwin	Vauxhall Cavalier 16V	–	37.74 secs	14	
14	N. Smith	Vauxhall Cavalier 16V	–	38.37 secs	13	
15	R. Rydell	Volvo 850SE/GLT	–	39.47 secs	22	
16	J. Lammers	Volvo 850SE/GLT	–	43.20 secs	12	
17	M. Neal	Mazda Xedos 6	–	1 lap down	15	
18	J. Thompson	Peugeot 405 Mi16	–	1 lap down	16	
19	J. Kaye	Toyota Carina E	–	1 lap down	17	
20	G. Steel	BMW 318is	–	5 laps down	21	

Did Not Finish

–	G. Simoni	Alfa Romeo 155TS	–	Excluded	2	
–	K. O'dor	Nissan Primera 2.0eGT	–	16 laps	11	Differential
–	A. Menu	Renault Laguna	–	11 laps	18	Engine

Fastest Lap: G. Tarquini – 47.22 secs (91.76mph) **Average Speed of Winner:** 89.96mph

Championship Placings

Drivers' Points		Constructors' Points	
72	G. Tarquini	72	Alfa Romeo
48	J. Cleland	48	Vauxhall
22	A. Rouse	22	Ford
18	G. Simoni	19	BMW
18	P. Radisich	12	Toyota
17	S. Soper	11	Peugeot
16	J. Winkelhock	6	Mazda
14	J. Allam	6	Renault
12	W. Hoy	2	Nissan
11	P. Watts		

TOTAL Cup

Position	Driver	Points
1st	N. Smith	54
2nd	J. Kaye	44
3rd	C. Goodwin	42
=4th	G. Steel	24
=4th	J. Thompson	24
6th	N. Albon	18
7th	I. Khan	10

Giampiero Simoni sees red.

Snetterton

The Alfa Romeos continue to dominate from the inside out.

The pre-race atmosphere was taut, to say the least, between the rival camps as protest was met by counter protest, appeals and controversy. Having passed the Alfa Romeo's rear wings which had been the source of argument thus far, FIA were now confronted with a protest regarding their front splitter. The Chief Scrutineer, Peter Riches, ruled the Alfas could not race but this decision was immediately protested by Alfa who impressed the Stewards of the meeting sufficiently to allow the Italian car to run. Ford then replied by lodging a further protest at the Stewards' decision with the consequence that Simoni and

Tarquini were allowed to participate *under appeal* which meant any points gained could be lost when the case was heard by the RACMSA's Eligibility Committee.

Alfa's Director of Motor Sport was not impressed. He said the authorities had picked on Simoni throughout the series and now they were doing as requested by Ford adding that *"It will be another 100 years before Alfas do another English Touring Car Championship"*. Meanwhile, a sideshow to the main event appeared when Rydell planted his Volvo wagon firmly in third place on the grid. Many teams had eyed the Volvo estate car with some suspicion but, whilst it

1994 Grid Positions and Qualifying Times

Grid	Driver	Time	Grid	Driver	Time	Grid	Driver	Time
1	G. Simoni	1'13.46	11	J. Cleland	1'14.09	21	T. Sugden	1'14.79
2	P. Radisich	1'13.64	12	J. Allam	1'14.10	22	J. Thompson*	1'15.68
3	R. Rydell	1'13.66	13	P. Watts	1'14.11	23	I. Khan*	1'15.72
4	A. Menu	1'13.67	14	W. Hoy	1'14.19	24	C. Goodwin*	1'15.84
5	G. Tarquini	1'13.70	16	J. Lammers	1'14.56	25	J. Kaye*	1'15.85
6	A. Rouse	1'13.81	15	J. Winkelhock	1'14.30	26	N. Smith*	1'16.00
7	T. Harvey	1'13.83	17	M. Neal	1'14.62	27	G. Steel*	1'18.30
8	K. O'dor	1'13.84	18	E. van de Poele	1'14.63	28	N. Albon*	no time
9	E. O'Brien	1'14.00	19	J. Bailey	1'14.64			
10	S. Soper	1'14.05	20	D. Leslie	1'14.71		*Denotes Total Cup competitors	

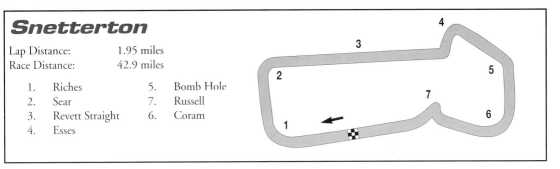

Snetterton

Lap Distance: 1.95 miles
Race Distance: 42.9 miles

1. Riches
2. Sear
3. Revett Straight
4. Esses
5. Bomb Hole
7. Russell
6. Coram

was chugging along at the back of the field, they were content to concentrate their attention on the Alfas. With a jump up the ladder of this magnitude, there was now suddenly a lot of talk about the Volvo's floorpans and undertrays.

If Rydell's presence on the second row had worried his opponents, then his start certainly did not for the 850 wouldn't fire at the green flag lap and the Swede was compelled to waste his big qualifying effort by setting off from the back of the grid. This gave Tarquini, down in fifth at the line up clear space into which he could sprint and he made the most of it to beat Menu into Riches.

The end of the first lap saw a first in the 1994 Championship as Simoni led – the first time that any lap had been completed without Tarquini at the head of affairs. Radisich overtook Simoni at Sears, as did Tarquini, on the second circuit and the lap ended with another first – the first lap of the 1994 calender to be completed without an Alfa in the lead! But normal service was soon to be resumed as Tarquini went past the New Zealander at the chicane after lifting Radisich's rear bumper off at The Esses. Another to pass Simoni at Sears was O'dor who was then up to third from eighth spot on the grid but Simoni was

Round Four – Race Placings

Pos	Driver	Car	Time	Diff	Grid	
1	G. Tarquini	Alfa Romeo 155TS	27'37.45	–	5	
2	P. Radisich	Ford Mondeo Ghia	–	1.00s	2	
3	G. Simoni	Alfa Romeo 155TS	–	2.97s	1	
4	K. O'dor	Nissan Primera 2.0eGT	–	16.68s	4	
5	P. Watts	Peugeot 405 Mi16	–	21.13s	13	
6	J. Allam	Vauxhall Cavalier 16V	–	22.26s	12	
7	E. O'Brien	Peugeot 405 Mi16	–	26.15s	9	
8	S. Soper	BMW 318i	–	26.54s	10	
9	E. van de Poele	Nissan Primera 2.0eGT	–	35.35s	18	
10	M. Neal	Mazda Xedos 6	–	38.37s	17	
11	J. Lammers	Volvo 850 SE/GLT 2.0	–	41.46s	16	
12	W. Hoy	Toyota Carina E	–	42.18s	14	
13	J. Kaye	Toyota Carina E	–	46.09s	25	
14	C. Goodwin	Vauxhall Cavalier 16V	–	47.63s	24	
15	N. Smith	Vauxhall Cavalier 16V	–	60.36s	26	
16	N. Albon	Renault 19 16V	–	1 lap down	28	
17	D. Leslie	Mazda Xedos 6	–	1 lap down	20	
18	G. Steel	BMW 318is	–	1 lap down	27	

Did Not Finish

–	T. Sugden	Toyota Carina E	–	19 laps	21	Accident
–	R. Rydell	Volvo 850 SE/GLT 2.0	–	19 laps	3	Accident
–	T. Harvey	Renault Laguna 850	–	15 laps	7	Differential
–	J. Thompson	Peugeot 405 Mi16	–	15 laps	22	Suspension
–	J. Cleland	Vauxhall Cavalier 16V	–	14 laps	11	Accident
–	I. Khan	Vauxhall Cavalier 16V	–	9 laps	23	Engine misfire
–	J. Bailey	Toyota Carina E	–	6 laps	19	Engine
–	J. Winkelhock	BMW 318i	–	6 laps	15	Accident
–	A. Menu	Renault Laguna	–	0 laps	4	Clutch
–	A. Rouse	Ford Mondeo Ghia	–	0 laps	6	Engine misfire

Fastest Lap: G. Tarquini – 1'13.83 (95.18mph) – Course Record

Average Speed of Winner: 93.27mph

TOTAL Cup		
Position	Driver	Points
1st	J. Kaye	66
2nd	N. Smith	64
3rd	C. Goodwin	30
4th	G. Steel	32
5th	N. Albon	28
6th	J. Thompson	24
7th	I. Khan	10

Championship Placings			
Drivers' Points		Constructors' Points	
96	Tarquini	96	Alfa Romeo
48	Cleland	62	Vauxhall
36	Radisich	43	Ford
30	Simoni	34	BMW
22	Rouse	30	Peugeot
20	Allam	23	Toyota
20	Soper	19	Mazda
19	Watts	18	Nissan
16	Winkelhock	9	Renault
12	Hoy	9	Volvo
12	O'dor		

soon to rest his third place back, with worse to follow for O'dor as his Nissan was also overtaken by both Harvey and O'Brien.

The day was to be quickly over for both Menu and Rouse, neither of whom were able to complete a lap due to clutch and engine problems respectively. With the front three up and away by the fourth circuit, Harvey was being jostled all the time and by the tenth lap, Cleland and Watts had joined O'dor and O'Brien in a five way battle for fourth. Harvey defended against Cleland for another four circuits before the Scot tried to overtake at Russell. Having successfully completed his attack, Cleland then found his car suffering from momentary fuel starvation coming out of the corner with the result that he slewed on Revetts Straight and collected Harvey. Although Harvey carried on, he survived for only another lap before

his differential called it a day. This left Watts in fifth behind O'dor and with the front three staying in convoy, that's the way it finished. Rydell's day, which had begun so promisingly, was now disappearing dismally. He had done well to climb through the field from his back mark but finished by smacking both Leslie and Sugden to complete a wretched half hour or so. Amongst the privateers, Thompson led from the off but soon hit suspension trouble which slowed him until he eventually retired on lap 15. Goodwin took over from him but was overtaken by Kaye at Sear on the final circuit with Smith third and Albon making light of his penalty to beat Steel for fourth. ❖

Radisich and Tarquini burn down the straight.

Silverstone

14-15 May 1994

David Leslie soldiers on, for now, in the under-financed Mazda.

Events leading up to Silverstone's double header were interesting with Ford testing Paul Radisich's car with a front splitter fixed a la Alfa Romeo style and with it in place, the New Zealander blasted round in 1'01.15, some 0.56 seconds faster than the eventual pole position and 0.84 seconds faster than his own qualifying time.

According to Ford, this definitely proved that Alfa were enjoying an unfair advantage with their front splitters. Meanwhile, in the light of later events, Alfa's announcement that it had decided against running a third car in the Championship appeared superfluous!

The qualifying sessions threw up another first for this season's championship when Alain

1994 Grid Positions and Qualifying Times

Grid	Driver	Time	Grid	Driver	Time	Grid	Driver	Time
1	A. Menu	1'01.71	11	J. Winkelhock	1'02.57	21	N. Smith*	1'03.17
2	G. Tarquini	1'01.93	12	E. O'Brien	1'02.57	22	E. van de Poele	1'03.25
3	P. Radisich	1'01.99	13	T. Sugden	1'02.60	23	J. Lammers	1'03.30
4	T. Harvey	1'02.13	14	R. Ravaglia	1'02.66	24	C. Goodwin*	1'03.56
5	A. Rouse	1'02.26	15	J. Allam	1'02.71	25	N. Albon*	1'03.81
6	G. Simoni	1'02.31	16	R. Rydell	1'02.78	26	J. Thompson*	1'04.01
7	J. Cleland	1'02.32	17	J. Bailey	1'02.84	27	H. Irvine*	1'06.92
8	W. Hoy	1'02.40	18	D. Leslie	1'02.93			
9	P. Watts	1'02.43	19	J. Kaye	1'02.98	*Denotes Total Cup competitors.		
10	K. O'dor	1'02.47	20	M. Neal	1'03.17			

Menu's Renault Laguna took pole thus breaking Alfa's grip on the position for the first time in 1994. Indeed, for a long period, it seemed that an all Renault Laguna front line was possible as Tim Harvey initially went a hundredth of a second faster than Tarquini before the Italian fought back. Andy Rouse, who was to play a controversial role in the second race, did well to claim a place on the third row as he only joined the first session with ten minutes to go after oil pressure problems and then crashed during the second session. But is Jeff Allam superstitious? He finished 13th on the grid after being 13th fastest on Friday the 13th!

Round Five – 18 laps

There was an exciting start to the race with Tarquini going past pole man Menu before the Italian went wide to allow Menu to regain the lead on the way to Becketts. Just behind, Harvey had also eclipsed Radisich to leave the Renaults one and three either side of the Championship leader. They were followed by Rouse, Simoni, Hoy, Cleland and Watts but by the time another circuit had elapsed, Hoy was past Simoni and Watts had overtaken Cleland at Copse.

After half a dozen laps, it seemed that Harvey was in trouble but Radisich could not get past him with the result that Menu and Tarquini began to open up a gap. The sixth lap witnessed another significant incident when Simoni completely misjudged Copse and spun into the air before crashing into the sleepers which wrote the Alfa off for the afternoon. Radisich managed to pass Harvey on the next lap and set off in pursuit of Tarquini who seemed content to bide his time just behind the Swiss driver. A fast closing Radisich was the incentive that Tarquini needed and he made his move at Luffield 2 on the fourteenth circuit. Menu waved Radisich into second a lap later but with open road in front of him Tarquini blasted for home.

Rouse was now setting sail for Menu's tail and would surely have succeeded in wrestling the third spot from the Swiss had the race not ended four laps prematurely when Matt Neal experienced a spectacular roll. Neal, van de Poele, Leslie, Goodwin and Winkelhock were all buzzing one another when Goodwin and Neal touched on the run down to Maggots. Neal's Mazda rolled over five or six times before coming to rest but fortunately the driver was unhurt. Meanwhile, Tarquini and Radisich quickly went through the debris but Radisich will have been very relieved that the race was called to a stand still as he picked up a front puncture in the mess strewn all over the track. Goodwin, who was involved in the race stopping incident, took the privateers top spot whilst down the field in the main race came a bit of trivia as David Leslie dead-heated with team mate Matt Neal. It was Leslie's second such result in his last three Silverstone starts, having finished level with Winkelhock in the previous year's GP support race. Newcomers Ravaglia and Irvine both had big disappointments with the former spinning out after 13 laps and the privateer finishing almost two laps down on his first attempt but up front it was five wins out of five for Tarquini and the Alfa.

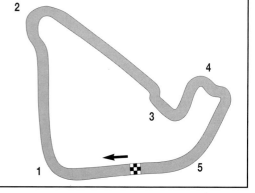

Silverstone

18 laps for Round 5 and 22 laps for Round 6.

Lap Distance:	1.650 miles
Race Distance:	Race One: 29.7 miles
	Race Two: 36.3 miles

1. Copse
2. Becketts
3. Brooklands
4. Luffield
5. Woodcote

Round Five – Race Placings

Pos	Driver	Car	Time	Diff	Grid	
1	G. Tarquini	Alfa Romeo 155TS	19'00.64	–	2	
2	P. Radisich	Ford Mondeo Ghia	–	2.67s	3	
3	A. Menu	Renault Laguna	–	3.17s	1	
4	A. Rouse	Ford Mondeo Ghia	–	4.41s	5	
5	P. Watts	Peugeot 405 Mi16	–	10.50s	9	
6	W. Hoy	Toyota Carina E	–	11.00s	8	
7	J. Cleland	Vauxhall Cavalier 16V	–	11.32s	7	
8	K. O'dor	Nissan Primera 2.0eGT	–	11.86s	10	
9	T. Sugden	Toyota Carina E	–	14.45s	13	
10	J. Bailey	Toyota Carina E	–	19.00s	17	
11	E. O'Brien	Peugeot 405 Mi16	–	20.78s	12	
12	J. Allam	Vauxhall Cavalier 16V	–	22.72s	15	
13	E. van de Poele	Nissan Primera 2.0eGT	–	26.07s	22	
14	J. Winkelhock	BMW 318i	–	26.27s	11	
15	M. Neal	Mazda Xedos 6	–	26.70s	20	
15	D. Leslie	Mazda Xedos 6	–	26.70s	18	
17	C. Goodwin	Vauxhall Cavalier 16V	–	26.84s	24	
18	J. Kaye	Toyota Carina E	–	27.17s	19	
19	R. Rydell	Volvo 850SE/GLT	–	32.62s	16	
20	N. Smith	Vauxhall Cavalier 16V	–	33.61s	21	
21	J. Thompson	Peugeot 405 Mi16	–	39.43s	26	
22	N. Albon	Renault 19 16V	–	50.64s	25	
23	H. Irvine	BMW 318is	–	1 lap down	27	

Did Not Finish

	Driver	Car	Time	Diff	Grid	
–	T. Harvey	Renault Laguna	–	16 laps	4	Differential
–	R. Ravaglia	BMW 318i	–	13 laps	14	Spin
–	J. Lammers	Volvo 850SE/GLT	–	9 laps	23	Accident
–	G. Simoni	Alfa Romeo 155TS	–	6 laps	6	Accident

Fastest Lap: P. Radisich – 1'02.38 (95.16mph)

Average Speed of Winner: 93.68mph

Round Six – 22 laps

The cars lined up for the second race of the afternoon without Simoni whose Alfa could not be got ready for racing after his earlier shunt and very soon, Alfa's (and Tarquini's) total domination of the Championship was also to be over. Radisich made a good start to get past Tarquini with Menu right behind the Italian when, at Luffield 1, it all happened. In plenty of congestion,

Watts appeared to nudge Cleland in the rear who, in turn touched Menu's back bumper. The Swiss driver couldn't help but touch Tarquini which spun the Italian round. This left O'dor with nowhere to go but into the Alfa broadside on. Away from all this confusion, Thompson and Winkelhock also collided and there was no option but to order a restart.

The race got away the second time without the Championship leader and Radisich took complete advantage to stay in front of Menu for the entire 22 laps. Rouse was third for five laps only to be black flagged for jumping the start and had to pay a visit to the pits as a penalty. He was furious and when he rejoined the race he cruised round until the leaders reappeared in his mirror. Rouse then proceeded to allow team mate Radisich through on lap 11 before starting to race again thus denying Menu the same clear passage he had allowed his team mate.

The Swiss did eventually get past Rouse but the Ford continued to sit on Menu's rear thus making the Swiss driver keep one eye on his mirror rather than being able to concentrate 100% on his pursuit of the leader. The tactics used by Rouse to ensure his team mate's victory were certainly not illegal but whether they were morally good for the sport was another question. With Menu finishing only a fifth of a second down on the New Zealander, he certainly had good reason

Menu races to second place in the Renault Laguna.

Round Six – Race Placings

Pos	Driver	Team	Time	Diff	Grid	
1	P. Radisich	Ford Mondeo Ghia	23'15.22	–	2	
2	A. Menu	Renault Laguna	–	0.21s	3	
3	P. Watts	Peugeot 405 Mi16	–	8.93s	5	
4	J. Cleland	Vauxhall Cavalier 16V	–	9.40s	7	
5	J. Bailey	Toyota Carina E	–	14.97s	10	
6	W. Hoy	Toyota Carina E	–	15.17s	6	
=7	T. Sugden	Toyota Carina E	–	15.94s	9	
=7	T. Harvey	Renault Laguna	–	15.94s	24	
9	J. Allam	Vauxhall Cavalier 16V	–	16.35s	12	
10	E. O'Brien	Peugeot 405 Mi16	–	18.92s	11	
11	D. Leslie	Mazda Xedos 6	–	21.76s	16	
12	E. van de Poele	Nissan Primera 2.0eGT	–	27.74s	13	
13	R. Rydell	Volvo 850SE/GLT	–	28.06s	19	
14	J. Winkelhock	BMW 318i	–	28.20s	14	
15	J. Kaye	Toyota Carina E	–	29.99s	18	
16	J. Lammers	Volvo 850SE/GLT	–	32.76s	25	
17	C. Goodwin	Vauxhall Cavalier 16V	–	39.29s	17	
18	N. Albon	Renault 19 16V	–	46.34s	22	
19	A. Rouse	Ford Mondeo Ghia	–	1 lap down	4	
20	H. Irvine	BMW 318is	–	2 laps down	23	

Did Not Finish

Pos	Driver	Team	Time	Diff	Grid	
–	N. Smith	Vauxhall Cavalier 16V	–	11 laps	20	Accident
–	R. Ravaglia	BMW 318i	–	11 laps	26	Accident
–	G. Tarquini	Alfa Romeo 155TS	–	0 laps	1	Accident
–	K. O'dor	Nissan Primera 2.0eGT	–	0 laps	8	Accident
–	J. Thompson	Peugeot 405 Mi16	–	0 laps	21	Accident

Fastest Lap: A. Menu – 1'02.29 (95.30mph)

Average Speed of Winner: 93.60mph

Championship Placings

Drivers' Points		Constructors' Points	
120	G. Tarquini	120	Alfa Romeo
78	P .Radisich	85	Ford
62	J. Cleland	78	Vauxhall
39	P. Watts	56	Peugeot
36	A. Menu	40	Toyota
32	A. Rouse	39	Renault
30	G. Simoni	37	BMW
24	W. Hoy	28	Mazda
22	J. Allam	26	Nissan
20	S. Soper	14	Volvo

TOTAL Cup

Position	Driver	Points
1st	J. Kaye	110
2nd	C. Goodwin	102
3rd	N. Smith	78
4th	N. Albon	48
5th	J. Thompson	34
6th	G. Steel	32

to think Rouse's tactics had contributed much to his failure to get past Radisich.

Watts came home in third, a respectful distance down on the front two, and he was followed home by Cleland.

One of the drives of the second race was by Tim Harvey who, having started from the back of the grid, got up as high as fifth place at one stage before having to eventually settle for a dead heat seventh with Sugden.

The debut's of Ravaglia and Irvine didn't get any better with the former crashing with Smith after eleven circuits whilst Hamish Irvine this time finished two laps down as the privateers race went to Kaye. ◈

Championship leader Tarquini.

Oulton Park

The race is on as the crowds continue to flock to see the BTCC action.

The story of this round was not what happened on the track but what went on off it as the season long argument of whether the Alfa Romeo cars were legal or not was forced to a climax by the Italian manufacturer.

After the Snetterton scenario, where the Chief Scrutineer's decision that the Alfas had to race with their front spoilers pushed back had been overruled by the Stewards of that Meeting and with the cars still running at Silverstone under appeal, a decision had been made three days prior to the Oulton Park event by the Eligibility Appeal Panel that the Alfa Romeos should not be allowed to race with their front spoilers in a forward position.

The Alfa team, however, still smarting from the decision and the knock on effect of having their points (and those of Tarquini) deducted for the two wins at Snetterton and Silverstone, submit-

ted their cars to the scrutineer with the spoilers still extended. They were excluded and went home saying *"The British authorities have given us no option but to withdraw from the meeting and to return home to consider all the possible options prior to the next round at Donington"*.

With no Alfas to contend with, Alain Menu grabbed pole and was joined on the front row by his Renault team-mate, Tim Harvey whilst in third came the new (after the decision to deduct Tarquini's points) Championship leader Paul Radisich. Having taken the front row, the Renault pairing of Menu and Harvey must have been shocked to see Radisich fly between them as the light turned to green. The New Zealander later described it as *"the best start I've ever made"*. Another to get off to a flyer was Steve Soper who was up alongside Harvey from seventh on the grid but one driver who didn't was Nigel Albon whose car never left the line after breaking a dri-

1994 Grid Positions and Qualifying Times

Grid	Driver	Time	Grid	Driver	Time	Grid	Driver	Time
1	A. Menu	1'43.43	10	W. Hoy	1'44.27	19	N. Smith*	1'45.47
2	T. Harvey	1'43.60	11	J. Winkelhock	1'44.31	20	C. Goodwin*	1'45.53
3	P. Radisich	1'43.62	12	K. O'dor	1'44.51	21	D. Leslie	1'45.56
4	P. Watts	1'43.66	13	E. O'Brien	1'44.51	22	E. van de Poele	1'45.85
5	J. Cleland	1'43.84	14	J. Bailey	1'44.58	23	N. Albon*	1'46.10
6	R. Rydell	1'43.90	15	J. Lammers	1'45.07	24	I. Khan*	1'47.02
7	S. Soper	1'43.90	16	J. Kaye*	1'45.13	25	H. Irvine*	1'51.59
8	J. Allam	1'44.08	17	T. Sugden	1'45.23	26	G. Steel*	1'51.65
9	A. Rouse	1'44.15	18	T. Needell	1'45.36		*Denotes Total Cup competitors	

veshaft at the start. Menu, recovered from the shock of being left by Radisich, was now busy fighting back but he lost team-mate Harvey as early as the second lap when his Laguna blew its engine at the top of Clay Hill.

Lap three saw the move of the race as Menu darted for the narrowest of gaps on the inside of Radisich at Cascades. Both cars touched and, had Radisich not been aware of the fact that both would finish in the gravel trap if he maintained his line, the leaders could have both disappeared. Thereafter there was no change in the first four with Menu, Radisich, Watts (driving a great race in his 93 Peugeot), and Soper went round in Indian file. Cleland was initially in fifth but then hit the oil spilled by Harvey and took a back seat for a while before fighting his way back to eventually finish seventh. Rydell was going well and he drove his Volvo to fifth, its highest ever finish. In fact, the Estate had proved to be unpassable once entrenched in fifth with Winkelhock, Allam and Cleland all attempting to pass without success. Indeed, the German's efforts gave him a quick burst of grasscutting as he came off at Old Hall. Bailey was waved past by stricken team-mate Will Hoy who then held up the opposition before retiring after 14 laps and the Toyota took the last point on offer in tenth spot. ◼

Round Seven – Race Placings

Pos	Driver	Car	Time	Diff	Grid	
1	A. Menu	Renault Laguna	28'22.23	–	1	
2	P. Radisich	Ford Mondeo Ghia	–	1.95s	3	
3	P. Watts	Peugeot 405 Mi16	–	5.66s	4	
4	S. Soper	BMW 318i	–	6.71s	7	
5	R. Rydell	Volvo 850SE/GLT	–	12.29s	6	
6	J. Allam	Vauxhall Cavalier 16V	–	12.71s	8	
7	J. Cleland	Vauxhall Cavalier 16V	–	14.47s	5	
8	J. Winkelhock	BMW 318i	–	15.65s	11	
9	E. O'Brien	Peugeot 405 Mi16	–	17.64s	13	
10	J. Bailey	Toyota Carina E	–	18.23s	14	
11	K. O'dor	Nissan Primera 2.0eGT	–	24.58s	12	
12	T. Sugden	Toyota Carina E	–	35.50s	17	
13	J. Lammers	Volvo 850SE/GLT	–	35.67s	15	
14	E. van de Poele	Nissan Primera 2.0eGT	–	41.51s	22	
15	C. Goodwin	Vauxhall Cavalier 16V	–	41.99s	20	
16	N. Smith	Vauxhall Cavalier 16V	–	43.44s	19	
17	T. Needell	Nissan Primera 2.0eGT	–	55.63s	18	
18	G. Steel	BMW 318is	–	1 lap down	26	

Did Not Finish

–	W. Hoy	Toyota Carina E	–	14 laps	10	Exhaust
–	D. Leslie	Mazda Xedos 6	–	11 laps	21	Loose wheel
–	I. Khan	Vauxhall Cavalier 16V	–	9 laps	24	Ignition
–	J. Kaye	Toyota Carina E	–	8 laps	16	Exhaust
–	H. Irvine	BMW 318is	–	7 laps	25	Gearbox
–	A. Rouse	Ford Mondeo Ghia	–	3 laps	9	Engine
–	T. Harvey	Renault Laguna	–	1 lap	2	Engine
–	N. Albon	Renault 19 16V	–	Did not start	23	Driveshaft

Fastest Lap: A. Menu – 1'45.06 (95.08mph) – Course Record **Average Speed of Winner:** 93.90mph

Oulton Park

16 laps.

Lap Distance: 2.780 miles
Race Distance: 44.48 miles

1.	Old Hall	6.	Knickerbrook
2.	Cascades	7.	Clay Hill
3.	Island	8.	Druids
4.	Shell	9.	Lodge
5.	Foulston's	10.	Deer Leep

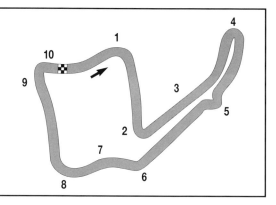

Championship Placings

Drivers' Points		Constructors' Points	
108	P. Radisich	115	Ford
72	G. Tarquini	88	Vauxhall
68	J. Cleland	72	Alfa Romeo
66	A. Menu	72	Peugeot
57	P. Watts	69	Renault
34	A. Rouse	50	BMW
33	S. Soper	47	Toyota
32	J. Allam	37	Nissan
27	W. Hoy	33	Mazda
24	K. O'dor	24	Volvo

TOTAL Cup

Position	Driver	Points
1st	C. Goodwin	126
2nd	J. Kaye	110
3rd	N. Smith	96
4th	N. Albon	48
5th	G. Steel	44
6th	J. Thompson	34

Below: Alain Menu, making a meal of things, got his just-deserts and served up a win for Renault, after trailing Radisich.

Donington

A top three finish for Allam's Vauxhall in round nine.

After all the appeals and counter appeals that had dogged the Autotrader BTCC virtually all season, the Alfas were back with their points reinstated following a directive issued by FIA saying *"It is our view that, due to the different interpretations that can be made of the regulations, any car currently homologated (for example, the Alfa Romeos) with adjustable bodywork have a valid claim to be racing with the bodywork in any position. However, this is not the intention and manufacturers must indicate the entirely completed position of any adjustable aerodynamic bodywork and will only be allowed to compete with adjustable bodywork in the entirely completed position"*. So, in the end, com-

1994 Grid Positions and Qualifying Times

Grid	Driver	Time	Grid	Driver	Time	Grid	Driver	Time
1	P. Radisich	1'39.69	11	J. Winkelhock	1'40.77	21	J. Kaye*	1'41.83
2	G. Tarquini	1'39.86	12	J. Bailey	1'40.83	22	N. Smith*	1'42.19
3	J. Cleland	1'40.01	13	W. Hoy	1'40.96	23	C. Goodwin*	1'42.53
4	A. Menu	1'40.03	14	E. van de Poele	1'41.17	24	N. Albon*	1'43.32
5	A. Rouse	1'40.09	15	T. Sugden	1'41.24	25	I. Khan*	1'44.01
6	T. Harvey	1'40.09	16	K. O'dor	1'41.24	26	G. Steel*	1'47.00
7	G. Simoni	1'40.11	17	J. Lammers	1'41.24	27	H. Irvine*	1'48.55
8	P. Watts	1'40.31	18	D. Leslie	1'41.34			
9	J. Allam	1'40.42	19	R. Ravaglia	1'41.40		*Denotes Total Cup competitor.	
10	R. Rydell	1'40.49	20	E. O'Brien	1'41.56			

promise was reached although neither side in the dispute was happy. Alfa made the point that they had not competed at Oulton Park and therefore lost vital points whilst Ford said *"It's a case of having to accept it and putting up with it"*. Missing from the line up at Donington was the reigning privateer's Champion, Matt Neal. The Mazda team confirmed it was doubtful whether Neal would be driving for them again in the present campaign as their budget had gone out of the window when he crashed the Xedos 6 at Silverstone in May when apparently all that was salvaged was a door!

Former World and European Champion, Roberto Ravaglia, however was back for a sec-

ond stand in drive for Steve Soper, although he was not to enjoy his weekend out. Also racing was privateer, Ian Khan, despite coming straight from his Class success in the 24 hour Nuburgring race. The strangest occurrence during qualifying was Tim Harvey borrowing team-mate Alain Menu's Renault Laguna and then proceeding to roll it.

Harvey did the decent thing and offered his car to the Swiss driver but the offer was declined and Menu promptly plonked himself on the second row! Ravaglia, meanwhile, found himself down in 19th after a spin which damaged his oil cooler whilst up front it was business as usual with Radisich and Tarquini on the the front row.

Round Eight – 15 laps

Tarquini not only failed to make headway against poleman Radisich at the start but lost second place to Cleland on the run to the Craner. Rouse gained a place from his fifth spot on the grid but was overtaken on the second lap by both Renault Lagunas before fighting back well to regain fifth from Harvey. He then set about tackling Menu, tackling being the operative word.

Lap eight saw the two combatants alongside each other at the Esses when they touched sending the Laguna in a nice airborne loop before landing some way behind Rouse and carrying on at a respectful distance for the rest of the race. Harvey had been busy keeping the chasing pack off his team mate with Watts, Simoni and Allam all trying to pass in order to get in a blow.

Just as Simoni did get past, his afternoon came to a premature end when his engine blew on lap nine to make it five engine failures this sea-

son for the Alfas. He was the second retirement with Winkelhock already having departed on the second circuit with bent steering following a collision with Sugden at Melbourne. This would have been a massive blow for the German as it was the corresponding meeting in 1993 that set him on the way to his run of victories that eventually landed him the title. But it was not to be this time round, although he did manage eighth place in the second race.

Ravaglia's disappointing weekend continued when he and O'dor brushed swords at Goddards on the penultimate lap which cost him any chance he had of getting amongst the points.

Harvey was definitely slowing and Watts, Allam and Bailey also overtook him and, up front, the order was also to change at Coppice on the ninth circuit when Cleland darted inside Radisich, almost went on the grass and then recovered to

Donington

15 laps.

Lap Distance: 2.50 miles
Race Distance: 37.5 miles

1.	Redgate	6.	Coppice
2.	Craner Corner	7.	Esses
3.	Old hairpin	8.	Melbourne
4.	Starkeys	9.	Goddard
5.	McLeans		

take a slender advantage that widened slightly with the each passing lap.

Tarquini was, like team mate Simoni, having engine trouble and was prepared to coast round in third. In fact, that is precisely how he crossed the finishing line with his engine having packed up at Goddards from where he was able to roll home a much relieved third. There were, however, to be no Alfa's in the second race line up. In the privateers race, there were celebrations for Irvine who didn't finish last for the first time since he joined the circuit but he was helped in his cause by Steel's spin at Goddard's early in the race. Steel resumed the race well behind Irvine and had almost caught him by the finish when he was just three seconds down.

Round Eight – Race Placings

Pos	Driver	Car	Time	Diff	Grid	
1	J. Cleland	Vauxhall Cavalier 16V	25'31.99	–	3	
2	P. Radisich	Ford Mondeo Ghia	–	4.37s	1	
3	G. Tarquini	Alfa Romeo 155TS	–	8.02s	2	
4	A. Rouse	Ford Mondeo Ghia	–	10.49s	5	
5	A. Menu	Renault Laguna	–	17.08s	4	
6	J. Allam	Vauxhall Cavalier 16V	–	17.25s	9	
7	P. Watts	Peugeot 405 Mi16	–	18.97s	8	
8	J. Bailey	Toyota Carina E	–	21.93s	12	
9	T. Harvey	Renault Laguna	–	23.77s	6	
10	W. Hoy	Toyota Carina E	–	27.41s	13	
11	R. Rydell	Volvo 850SE/GLT 2.0	–	29.02s	10	
12	R. Ravaglia	BMW 318i	–	29.21s	19	
13	K. O'dor	Nissan Primera 2.0eGT	–	30.07s	16	
14	J. Lammers	Volvo 850SE/GLT 2.0	–	35.54s	17	
15	T. Sugden	Toyota Carina E	–	39.59s	15	
16	E. O'Brien	Peugeot 405 Mi16	–	40.86s	20	
17	E. van de Poele	Nissan Primera 2.0eGT	–	42.76s	14	
18	J. Kaye	Toyota Carina E	–	44.11s	21	
19	C. Goodwin	Vauxhall Cavalier 16V	–	45.50s	23	
20	N. Smith	Vauxhall Cavalier 16V	–	52.37s	22	
21	I. Khan	Vauxhall Cavalier 16V	–	69.11s	25	
22	N. Albon	Renault 19 16V	–	70.63s	24	
23	H. Irvine	BMW 318is	–	1 lap down	27	
24	G. Steel	BMW 318is	–	1 lap down	26	

Did Not Finish

–	D. Leslie	Mazda Xedos 6	–	11 laps	18	Oil pump
–	G. Simoni	Alfa Romeo 155TS	–	9 laps	7	Engine
–	J. Winkelhock	BMW 318i	–	2 laps	11	Accident

Fastest Lap: J. Cleland – 1'40.32 (89.71mph) – *Course Record*

Average Speed of Winner: 88.12mph

Round Nine – 15 laps

The second race, with the Alfa's absent for the second time in three outings, albeit not by choice this time, turned out to be a benefit for Cleland and Radisich who were to finish 1-2 for the second time in the afternoon. On this occasion, however, they were to steamroller the opposition, finishing a massive 17 seconds in front of third place Jeff Allam. In fact at the start, it was Radisich who sprinted away after overtaking Cleland at Coppice on the very first circuit and the Ford was clear at the half way stage. The Scot dug in and began to make in roads and by lap nine had come alongside the leader to make the decisive move of the race at Goddards. Behind the leaders, and well behind at that, Menu overhauled Rouse also at Goddards but on the second circuit.

There appeared to be shades of Oulton Park all over again as Rouse held up the chasing pack of Watts, Harvey, Bailey and Allam but in a melee, the Ford suddenly was nudged out of the way and, whilst Rouse went cutting the grass, all four

Round Nine – Race Placings

Pos	Driver	Team	Time	Diff	Grid	
1	J. Cleland	Vauxhall Cavalier 16V	25'22.11	–	1	
2	P. Radisich	Ford Mondeo Ghia	–	1.95s	2	
3	J. Allam	Vauxhall Cavalier 16V	–	18.83s	6	
4	A. Menu	Renault Laguna	–	22.51s	5	
5	J. Bailey	Toyota Carina E	–	25.46s	8	
6	A. Rouse	Ford Mondeo Ghia	–	27.23s	4	
7	W. Hoy	Toyota Carina E	–	29.77s	10	
8	J. Winkelhock	BMW 318i	–	30.48s	27	
9	R. Ravaglia	BMW 318i	–	31.14s	12	
10	T. Harvey	Renault Laguna	–	31.79s	9	
11	P. Watts	Peugeot 405 Mi16	–	32.64s	7	
12	K. O'dor	Nissan Primera 2.0eGT	–	34.67s	13	
13	E. van de Poele	Nissan Primera 2.0eGT	–	36.45s	17	
14	T. Sugden	Toyota Carina E	–	39.22s	15	
15	J. Lammers	Volvo 850SE/GLT 2.0	–	42.76s	14	
16	J. Kaye	Toyota Carina E	–	51.33s	18	
17	C. Goodwin	Vauxhall Cavalier 16V	–	53.45s	19	
18	N. Smith	Vauxhall Cavalier 16V	–	54.27s	20	
19	I. Khan	Vauxhall Cavalier 16V	–	65.56s	21	
20	E. O'Brien	Peugeot 405 Mi16	–	88.57s	16	
21	G. Steel	BMW 318is	–	94.98s	24	

Did Not Finish

–	N. Albon	Renault 19 16V	–	3 laps	22	Clutch
–	H. Irvine	BMW 318is	–	3 laps	23	Gearbox
–	R. Rydell	Volvo 850SE/GLT 2.0	–	1 lap	11	Electrical

Fastest Lap: P. Radisich – 1'40.35 (89.68mph)

Average Speed of Winner: 88.89mph

Championship Placing

Drivers' Points		Constructors' Points	
132	G. Tarquini	134	Ford
132	P. Radisich	132	Alfa Romeo
114	J. Cleland	132	Vauxhall
78	A. Menu	85	Renault
55	P. Watts	82	Peugeot
48	A. Rouse	60	Toyota
46	J. Allam		

TOTAL Cup

Position	Driver	Points
1st	C. Goodwin	162
2nd	J. Kaye	158
3rd	N. Smith	150
=4th	N. Albon	56
=4th	G. Steer	56
6th	J. Thompson	34

moved past him. Allam was having a great drive and now passed Bailey on lap six and then on the eighth circuit he overtook both Watts and Harvey at Goddards. His sights were now set on Menu who made a mistake at Coppice on lap 12 and Allam was through, although Radisich in second was nowhere to be seen. It was Allam's first visit to the podium in 1994.

Another first was Ravaglia who had the consolation of picking up his first points of the British season when he came home in ninth but out of the points for the first time in 1994 was Patrick Watts who couldn't compete with a massive brake problem.

The result really set up the Championship with Radisich and Tarquini left absolutely level on 132 points with Cleland breathing down their necks whilst the manufacturer's title was just as close with only two points separating Ford, Alfa, and Vauxhall! ☒

Brands Hatch GP

25-26 June 1994

A familiar sight as Simoni and Tarquini line up amo e due on the Grand Prix circuit of Brands Hatch

The 1993 Champion, Jos Winkelhock, was on the starting line despite having made a flying visit to Japan to stand in for Team Schnitzer's Prince Leopold van Bayern at the Tokachi round of the Japanese Touring Car Championship and he was now in the middle of a three month spell that would see him either competing or testing in six different countries. Not yet back in the line up, however, was Matt Neal who was still suffering from the financial consequences of his almighty roll at Silverstone. Practice was delayed when an overnight thunderstorm turned parts of the track into muddy skating rinks but when it did get underway it was the Alfa's Red Army that once again led the way. The big surprise, however, was

1994 Grid Positions and Qualifying Times

Grid	Driver	Time	Grid	Driver	Time	Grid	Driver	Time
1	G. Simoni	1'30.86	11	K. O'dor	1'32.34	21	W. Hoy	1'33.25
2	G. Tarquini	1'31.35	12	J. Cleland	1'32.39	22	N. Smith *	1'33.89
3	P. Radisich	1'31.81	13	R. Rydell	1'32.56	23	C. Goodwin *	1'33.94
4	P. Watts	1'31.82	14	E. O'Brien	1'32.69	24	J. Kaye *	1'34.40
5	A. Menu	1'31.82	15	T. Needell	1'32.71	25	I. Khan *	1'35.04
6	A. Rouse	1'31.83	16	J. Allam	1'32.80	26	N. Albon *	1'35.20
7	S. Soper	1'31.85	17	E. van de Poele	1'32.83	27	H. Irvine *	1'39.23
8	T. Harvey	1'31.90	18	J. Bailey	1'32.85			
9	J. Lammers	1'31.98	19	D. Leslie	1'33.12		*Denotes Total Cup competitors.		
10	J. Winkelhock	1'32.01	20	J. Thompson *	1'33.17			

the performance of Giampiero Simoni who outscored his partner, Gabriele Tarquini, by half a second. Without these two, it would have been close for pole as less than one tenth of a second separated the next six but they were, in turn, a full second behind Simoni! Another surprise was the sight of Will Hoy down amongst the privateers in his Toyota which equalled his pole time of two years ago but was now only good enough for 21st!

Round Ten – 18 laps

Having grabbed both front row places the Alfa team, with Tarquini only level with Radisich on points in the championship, were in no mood to lose the opportunity to take full advantage to increase the Italian's lead and Simoni was quite clearly under instructions to make way for his team mate.

With Simoni away slowly to allow Tarquini into the lead, the following cars were well packed together until Watts got past Radisich and put some daylight between himself and the New Zealander. But Watts could not make any impression on Simoni and began to fall back to find Radisich back in his mirrors.

By lap eight, Radisich had taken Watts at Dingle Dell but all eyes were on Rouse and Menu, the chief protagonists in the Oulton Park fracas, who were circuiting nose to tail in sixth and seventh behind Steve Soper. But they let bygones be bygones before Menu dropped away with oversteer which he incurred in a startline knock with Soper.

Meanwhile, Cleland was making headway from his poor twelfth line up spot and Menu was swallowed up before he tackled the oldest man on the circuit. Rouse was passed but Soper was out of reach and it looked like a sixth place for the flying Scot whilst both Lammers and

Winkelhock overtook the slowing Menu. However, the struggle for third between Watts and Radisich was to improve everybody's standing by one place on the last lap when the New Zealander tried to defend himself at Druids and found himself in the gravel as a result of a nudge from Watts.

The Race Director excluded Watts but Peugeot immediately appealed to the Stewards who re-instated him after taking into account the position of the damage on the cars involved. Radisich, the joint leader prior to the race was not amused – not only was he now 24 points behind Tarquini, who had gone on to register a bloodless victory, the New Zealander also had the indignity of having to start from the back of the grid in the second race as a penalty for not completing the first event!

Also of note were the Volvos both finishing in the points together for the first time with Lammers, in seventh, producing his best finish of the first half of the campaign. In the privateers race, James Kaye not only won but wrestled the Championship lead from Chris Goodwin.

Brands Hatch GP

18 laps.

Lap Distance:	2.60 miles
Race Distance:	46.8 miles

1.	Paddock	6.	Westfield
2.	Druids	7.	Dingle Dell
3.	Graham Hill	8.	Stirlings
4.	Surtees	9.	Clearways
5.	Hawthorn	10.	Clark

Patrick Watts finished third in the Peugeot 405.

Round Ten – Race Placings

Pos	Driver	Car	Time	Diff	Grid	
1	G. Tarquini	Alfa Romeo 155TS	28'02.22	–	2	
2	G. Simoni	Alfa Romeo 155TS	–	0.20s	1	
3	P. Watts	Peugeot 405 Mi16	–	4.38s	4	
4	S. Soper	BMW 318i	–	4.55s	7	
5	J. Cleland	Vauxhall Cavalier 16V	–	6.57s	12	
6	A. Rouse	Ford Mondeo Ghia	–	11.97s	6	
7	J. Lammers	Volvo 850SE/GLT 2.0	–	15.88s	9	
8	J. Winkelhock	BMW 318i	–	17.27s	10	
9	A. Menu	Renault Laguna	–	19.80s	5	
10	R. Rydell	Volvo 850/GLT 2.0	–	20.24s	13	
11	J. Bailey	Toyota Carina E	–	21.64s	18	
12	K. O'dor	Nissan Primera eGT	–	25.70s	11	
13	E. O'Brien	Peugeot 405 Mi16	–	28.56s	14	
14	E. van de Poele	Nissan Primera eGT	–	29.37s	17	
15	J. Kaye	Toyota Carina E	–	37.24s	24	
16	N. Smith	Vauxhall Cavalier 16V	–	37.68s	22	
17	C. Goodwin	Vauxhall Cavalier 16V	–	43.83s	23	
18	J. Thompson	Peugeot 405 Mi16	–	46.87s	20	
19	J. Allam	Vauxhall Cavalier 16V	–	53.18s	16	
20	I. Khan	Vauxhall Cavalier 16V	–	60.99s	25	
21	H. Irvine	BMW 318is	–	1 lap down	27	

Did Not Finish

–	P. Radisich	Ford Mondeo Ghia	–	17 laps	3	Accident
–	W. Hoy	Toyota Carina E	–	13 laps	21	Gearbox
–	T. Harvey	Renault Laguna	–	12 laps	8	Tyres
–	T. Needell	Nissan Primera eGT	–	12 laps	15	Fractured sump
–	D. Leslie	Mazda Xedos 6	–	0 laps	19	Electrics

Did Not Start

–	N. Albon	Renault 19 16V	–	–	26	Engine

Fastest Lap: G. Tarquini – 1'31.96 (101.79mph)

Average Speed of Winner: 100.16mph

Round Eleven – 18 laps

By virtue of their 1-2 in the first race, Tarquini and Simoni held the front row of the grid for the second skirmish of the afternoon and Simoni should therefore, in theory, have been able to shield Tarquini from the rest of the field as he had done in the earlier confrontation. It didn't, however, work out quite like that although the end result was another 1-2 for the Alfas.

Simoni got a dreadful start through wheelspin, which allowed both Watts and Soper to promote themselves from the second row and on to the tail of Tarquini whilst by Druids, Lammers, in an amazing drive from seventh on the grid, had also passed the second Alfa. Simoni then got his act together and by lap three had retaken Lammers and was after Soper in fourth. Tarquini, meanwhile, was demonstrating that he didn't need any help from his team mate as he began to pull away from Watts at the front.

Before the half way stage, Simoni was in third and closing on Watts and on lap nine made his move at Surtees to overtake the Peugeot thus regaining his starting position. Behind the lead-

ers, events took a disappointing turn for Lammers and Soper at Druids on the seventh circuit when Cleland hit Soper who, in turn, ricocheted into the Dutchman which dropped the BMW and Volvo 850 well down the field and out of contention for points.

Rouse and Menu were having their now customary tete-a-tete and, although they had managed to miss one another in the first race, they didn't at Druids on lap four in the second contest when Rouse found himself on the grass after contact with Menu's Renault.

This allowed both Winkelhock and van de Poele through to put Rouse down to tenth. He did extremely well to recover from this to eventually finish a very creditable fifth, retaking Menu in the process. But the afternoon was rapidly becoming a nightmare for Radisich who had started the day on level points with Tarquini. Starting from the back of the grid following his first race collision with Watts, the New Zealander went past no fewer than eight cars on one lap but his speed only served to strip his tyres of their

After their success at Donington, the Cavaliers were off the pace at Brands.

Round Eleven – Race Placings

Pos	Driver	Team	Time	Diff	Grid	
1	G. Tarquini	Alfa Romeo 155TS	28'00.41	–	1	
2	G. Simoni	Alfa Romeo 155TS	–	0.26s	2	
3	P. Watts	Peugeot 405Mi16	–	1.95s	3	
4	J. Cleland	Vauxhall Cavalier 16V	–	6.73s	5	
5	A. Rouse	Ford Mondeo Ghia	–	12.76s	6	
6	A. Menu	Renault Laguna	–	13.63s	9	
7	J. Winkelhock	BMW 318i	–	16.47s	8	
8	R. Rydell	Volvo 850SE/GLT 2.0	–	18.22s	10	
9	J. Bailey	Toyota Carina E	–	19.50s	11	
10	J. Allam	Vauxhall Cavalier 16V	–	20.34s	19	
11	T. Harvey	Renault Laguna	–	24.04s	24	
12	E. van de Poele	Nissan Primera eGT	–	25.30s	14	
13	K. O'dor	Nissan Primera eGT	–	25.65s	12	
14	S. Soper	BMW 318i	–	25.74s	4	
15	J. Thompson	Peugeot 405 Mi16	–	29.97s	18	
16	J. Lammers	Volvo 850SE/GLT 2.0	–	35.88s	7	
17	W. Hoy	Toyota Carina E	–	37.78s	23	
18	T. Needell	Nissan Primera eGT	–	45.24s	25	
19	D. Leslie	Mazda Xedos 6	–	46.07s	26	
20	N. Smith	Vauxhall Cavalier	–	51.33s	16	
21	J. Kaye	Toyota Carina E	–	69.13s	15	
22	I. Khan	Vauxhall Cavalier 16V	–	70.33s	20	

Did Not Finish

–	P. Radisich	Ford Mondeo Ghia	–	13 laps	22	Tyres
–	H. Irvine	BMW 318is	–	13 laps	21	Retired
–	E. O'Brien	Peugeot 405 Mi16	–	11 laps	13	Puncture
–	C. Goodwin	Vauxhall Cavalier 16V	–	0 laps	17	Accident

Did Not Start

–	N. Albon	Renault 19 16V	–	–	–	Engine

Fastest Lap: G. Tarquini – 1'31.78 (101.99mph)

Average Speed of Winner: 100. 26mph

laminate to leave them bulging and forcing him to retire after 13 circuits. A pointless weekend for Radisich was made worse by the news up front that Tarquini was taking his 48th point of the double header to really rub salt in the wounds!

The hardest earned point, however, was probably that of Jeff Allam who, having started off from the back of the grid, had to contend with Chris Goodwin being spun round by O'dor on the first lap before making his way through the field to grab the last point on offer.

In the Total Cup, James Thompson finished well clear of Nigel Smith, indeed, the youngster showed his tail to the works cars of Lammers, Hoy, Needell, and Leslie but Kaye's chances of repeating his first race success were scuppered by a misfiring engine. ♦

Championship Placings

Drivers' Points		Constructors' Points	
180	G. Tarquini	180	Alfa Romeo
132	P. Radisich	157	Ford
132	J. Cleland	154	Vauxhall
86	A. Menu	118	Peugeot
79	P. Watts	97	Renault
66	G. Simoni	76	BMW
62	A. Rouse	66	Toyota
47	J. Allam	39	Nissan
40	S. Soper	39	Volvo
29	J. Winkelhock	29	Mazda
29	W. Hoy		

TOTAL Cup

Position	Driver	Points
1st	J. Kaye	194
2nd	C. Goodwin	174
3rd	N. Smith	156
4th	J. Thompson	68
=5th	N. Albon	56
=5th	G. Steel	56

Silverstone GP

Ready for the off at Silverstone with the BMWs taking prime position on the starting grid.

If there was to be one particular meeting where the Tarquini/Alfa charge could be halted in its tracks, many critics considered the Silverstone GP Support race to be the best opportunity offered. The Alfa's straightline speed was not its strongest point and the car was therefore thought to be vulnerable to the long straights whilst the meeting was also the first to take place since the 1st July homologation date which saw the BMW's rear drive weight reduced by 25 kgs whilst the same amount was added to its front wheel drive opponents leaving the Germans some 50 kgs better off than they had hitherto been.

In addition, the BMW's were debuting a new rear wing and front airdam but Renault made their second homologation blunder of the campaign and were ordered to remove their newly installed front undertray.

At the end of the first qualifying session, however, it was service as normal with Tarquini in provisional pole with BMW drivers, Ravaglia and Winkelhock, back in fourth and sixth respectively. Saturday, however, was to prove a different matter with the BMW pair both clipping Tarquini's best effort when Ravaglia joined Winkelhock on the front row with just seconds of the session left. At the end of qualifying, just six-hundredths of a second separated the first three with the Lagunas of Harvey and Menu coming next. Julian Bailey qualified in the top six for the first time in 1994, Simoni was seventh, and the last two to be within a second of pole were Radisich and Watts who both clocked identical times of 2'00.08secs. Amongst the surprises was Andy Rouse down in 15th, over two seconds behind Winkelhock, whilst the lone Mazda of David Leslie struggled again to finish last of the works cars amidst

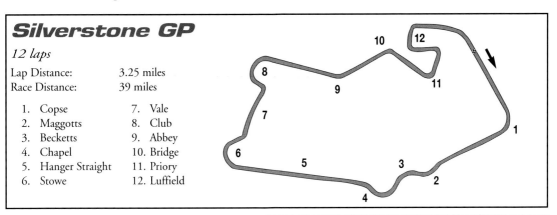

Silverstone GP

12 laps

Lap Distance:	3.25 miles
Race Distance:	39 miles

1. Copse
2. Maggotts
3. Becketts
4. Chapel
5. Hanger Straight
6. Stowe
7. Vale
8. Club
9. Abbey
10. Bridge
11. Priory
12. Luffield

1994 Grid Positions and Qualifying Times

Grid	Driver	Time	Grid	Driver	Time	Grid	Driver	Time
1	J. Winkelhock	2'00.01	11	R. Rydell	2'01.43	21	D. Leslie	2'03.15
2	R. Ravaglia	2'00.04	12	K. O'dor	2'01.45	22	J. Kaye *	2'03.29
3	G. Tarquini	2'00.07	13	T. Needell	2'01.77	23	J. Thompson *	2'03.29
4	T. Harvey	2'00.22	14	W. Hoy	2'01.97	24	C. Goodwin *	2'03.80
5	A. Menu	2'00.34	15	A. Rouse	2'02.01	25	N. Smith *	2'04.61
6	J. Bailey	2'00.76	16	J. Allam	2'02.12	26	N. Albon *	2'06.76
7	G. Simoni	2'00.86	17	J. Lammers	2'02.21	27	H. Irvine *	2'09.66
8	P. Watts	2'00.88	18	E. O'Brien	2'02.30		*Denotes Total Cup competitors	
9	P. Radisich	2'00.88	19	E. van de Poele	2'02.39			
10	J. Cleland	2'01.40	20	T. Sugden	2'02.50			

rumours that the Xedos might not last the season out due to a lack of funds.

On such a big day and with most of the Grand Prix crowd staying on to watch the BTCC showpiece race of the season, the Tourers could certainly have done without the accident extravaganza they put on at the start. Winkelhock was the quickest of the BMW's into Copse but a poor getaway by Tarquini allowed both Menu and Bailey past.

The Swiss driver then touched Bailey who spun in front of the chasing pack. Cleland, van de Poele, Needell, O'dor, and Goodwin joined Bailey on the sidelines whilst Simoni and O'Brien were to retire from the restarted race as a direct result of damage incurred in this rendition of the *Keystone Copse.* Menu was deemed to be the culprit and was fined £3,000 with his licence endorsed but his opinion as he went to pay BTCC'S highest ever fine was *"I still think it was 50:50 but, unfortunately, nobody else does!"*. The biggest sufferers in all this were Nissan who, in 1993, had enjoyed a 1-2 at the GP meeting. Now they had a 1-2-3 of a different nature as all the Old Spice cars were put out at a stroke.

The restarted race was shortened by three laps to twelve but that was a dozen too many for Ravaglia whose BMW, having sat in a hot temperature on the grid for ten minutes whilst the new line up sorted itself out, refused to start. To complete a miserable second start for the German outfit, Winkelhock lost his pole advantage as Tarquini overtook at Copse and proceeded to put some daylight between his Alfa and the rest of the field. Watts had made an excellent start and was up to third but Lammers smote Rouse an almighty whack in the rear to put the Ford man out at Abbey. With Simoni calling it a day due to damage received in the original race, Leslie's Mazda had a rare excursion in to top ten territory by the end of the first circuit. Albon joined the sidelines after just one lap when his manifold broke and when O'Brien went out after four laps, just sixteen competitors were left from the original field of 27.

The last car to retire was Tim Sugden's Carina on lap eight after his engine had been misfiring for four laps. Sugden must have been particularly sorry to see the original race halted as he had been up to sixth from twentieth on the grid. The

TOTAL Cup

Position	Driver	Points
1st	J. Kaye	204
2rd	C. Goodwin	174
2nd	N. Smith	174
4th	J. Thompson	92
=5th	N. Albon	56
=5th	G. Steel	56

Championship Placings

Drivers' Points		Constructors' Points	
198	G. Tarquini	198	Alfa Romeo
144	P. Radisich	169	Ford
132	J. Cleland	160	Vauxhall
94	A. Menu	120	Peugeot
85	P. Watts	107	Renault
66	G. Simoni	100	BMW
62	A. Rouse	69	Toyota
53	J. Winkelhock	43	Volvo
51	J. Allam	39	Nissan
40	S. Soper	31	Mazda

crowd, presumably, could not have been over impressed with the show thus far but, up front, at least Tarquini and Winkelhock were putting on a battle. After making an attempt to pass Tarquini at Becketts on lap nine and failing,

Winkelhock managed to pass his quarry on exiting Hangar Straight on the same circuit and managed to sustain his lead long enough to secure his first BTCC win since Oulton Park eleven months earlier. The rest of the field tracked round in procession whilst in the Total Cup, the competition leader James Kaye had to nurse his

car through the entire race due to high engine temperature which left the youngest competitor, James Thompson, to win unchallenged. But of even more satisfaction to Thompson was his tenth place in the overall race and an entry in the record books as the first Total Cup runner to score a point in the overall series in 1994. ∎

Round Twelve – Race Placings

Pos	Driver	Car	Time	Diff	Grid	
1	J. Winkelhock	BMW 318i	24'40.26	–	1	
2	G. Tarquini	Alfa Romeo 155TS	–	1.96s	3	
3	P. Radisich	Ford Mondeo Ghia	–	8.05s	9	
4	T. Harvey	Renault Laguna	–	12.26s	4	
5	A. Menu	Renault Laguna	–	13.68s	5	
6	P. Watts	Peugeot 405 Mi16	–	15.20s	8	
7	J. Allam	Vauxhall Cavalier 16V	–	15.97s	16	
8	R. Rydell	Volvo 850SE/GLT 2.0	–	27.79s	11	
9	W. Hoy	Toyota Carina	–	29.39s	14	
10	J. Thompson	Peugeot 405 Mi 16	–	31.75s	23	
11	D. Leslie	Mazda Xedos 6	–	33.98s	21	
12	J. Lammers	Volvo 850SE/GLT 2.0	–	43.08s	17	
13	N. Smith	Vauxhall Cavalier 16V	–	47.53s	25	
14	H. Irvine	BMW 318is	–	1 lap down	27	
15	J. Kaye	Toyota Carina E	–	1 lap down	22	
Did Not Finish						
–	T. Sugden	Toyota Carina E	–	8 laps	20	Engine
–	E. O'Brien	Peugeot 405 Mi16	–	4 laps	18	Accident
–	N. Albon	Renault 19 16V	–	1 lap	26	Exhaust
–	A. Rouse	Ford Mondeo Ghia	–	0 laps	15	Accident
–	G. Simoni	Alfa Romeo 155TS	–	0 laps	7	Accident
Did Not Start						
–	R. Ravaglia	BMW 318i	–	–	2	Electrical
–	J. Bailey	Toyota Carina E	–	–	6	Accident
–	J. Cleland	Vauxhall Cavalier 16V	–	–	10	Accident
–	K. O'dor	Nissan Primera 2.0eGT	–	–	12	Accident
–	E. van de Poele	Nissan Primera 2.0eGT	–	–	19	Accident
–	T. Needell	Nissan Primera 2.0eGT	–	–	13	Accident
–	C. Goodwin	Vauxhall Cavalier 16V	–	–	24	Accident

Fastest Lap: G. Tarquini – 2' 01.76 (92.89mph)

Average Speed of Winner: 91.09mph

Knockhill

30-31 July 1994

Tim Harvey in the Renault 19 – disqualified for tipping Tarquini.

The entourage arrived in Scotland minus the one surviving Mazda of David Leslie as the Japanese firm withdrew from the 1994 competition. The parent company was in a great deal of financial trouble created mainly by the value of the yen on the world's money markets which had left the budget for BTCC wafer thin. The other major news as the convoy headed north came from the Old Spice Nissan outfit who confirmed it had replaced Eric van de Poele with Tiff Needell *"until further notice"*. Needell had been turning out occasionally as a third driver for the Nissan team and had usually managed to outqualify van de Poele. Meanwhile Julian Bailey travelled north

with high hopes – in 1993 he had crashed in the Silverstone GP support race and then gone to Scotland two weeks later to win after qualifying in pole. Would history be repeated?

The answer to that question was quickly revealed to be *"No"* as both Toyota's struggled to get much straightline speed and languished way down the grid which Radisich headed despite a bad viral infection. The BMWs continued their resurgence with Winkelhock on the front row and Soper on the second just behind Menu who climbed from seventh in the second session. If the big surprise was the sight of the Alfas down in fifth and eighth then at least Rydell raised a few eyebrows when he plonked his Volvo estate on

1994 Grid Positions and Qualifying Times

Grid	Driver	Time	Grid	Driver	Time	Grid	Driver	Time
1	P. Radisich	54.68	9	P. Watts	55.08	17	W. Hoy	55.71
2	J. Winkelhock	54.75	10	K. O'dor	55.14	18	J. Thompson *	55.92
3	A. Menu	54.75	11	J. Allam	55.21	19	T. Needell	56.28
4	S. Soper	54.81	12	J. Cleland	55.24	20	N. Albon *	56.61
5	G. Simoni	54.98	13	A. Rouse	55.24	21	N. Smith *	56.72
6	R. Rydell	55.00	14	E. O'Brien	55.31	22	J. Kaye *	57.02
7	T. Harvey	55.01	15	J. Lammers	55.53	23	H. Irvine *	57.46
8	G. Tarquini	55.04	16	J. Bailey	55.55		*Denotes Total Cup competitors.	

the third row. Watts, who was expected to debut a new car, stuck with his old one but spoiled his chances by hitting some debris on the track which resulted in his suspension being damaged. Allam outqualified his Vauxhall team-mate, John Cleland for the first occasion in a long time but they were still nowhere near the front whilst Needell must have been wishing van de Poele had kept his drive as the *Top Gear* presenter languished in nineteenth place!

Round Thirteen – 32 laps

Radisich got away to a flyer to hold his pole position into the first corner from Winkelhock whilst Soper, in the other BMW on the second row, experienced the same treatment from Menu. Behind the leading quartet, Simoni was holding fifth but falling behind with each passing lap. The first car to depart the race was the Vauxhall of privateer Nigel Smith who called it a day after four laps, having had his steering badly damaged in a first lap shunt with fellow Total Cup competitor Nigel Albon. But next to go on lap seven was Championship leader Gabriele Tarquini who did it in some style thanks to a little help from Tim Harvey who tried to get past the Italian on the inside only to clip the Alfa's rear end, tipping Tarquini into a spectacular roll which saw the car written off and the Italian extremely lucky to walk away unscathed. Harvey was excluded from the race by officials for *careless driving*. Renault Racing appealed against the decision but lost which then caused Harvey's team to appeal against that verdict as well. This appeal allowed Harvey to start the second race but Tarquini's Scottish trip was over. Meanwhile, Harvey was indignant, saying *"It was at least 50% Tarquini's fault but the officials have tried to suspend me without any evidence such as TV replays or any witnesses other than the observer's report"*.

Up front, the leading four remained in grid order for 16 circuits before Winkelhock first of all slowed and then, two laps later, pitted with differential trouble. This left the Swiss driver with a clear run at Radisich but he couldn't get past the Ford until the penultimate circuit at just the same time as Soper looked likely to pounce on the pair of them. Although outmanoeuvred, Soper played his part to the full in one of the best finishes of the season with less than half a second covering first to third. A bad day for Alfa, however, continued with Simoni pulling in with engine problems

The car in front is Bailey in the Toyota Carina on two wheels.

Round Thirteen – Race Placings

Pos	Driver	Car	Time	Diff	Grid	
1	A. Menu	Renault Laguna	30'00.26	–	3	
2	P. Radisich	Ford Mondeo	–	00.35s	1	
3	S. Soper	BMW 318i	–	00.45s	4	
4	J. Allam	Vauxhall Cavalier 16V	–	11.54s	11	
5	J. Cleland	Vauxhall Cavalier 16V	–	16.68s	12	
6	R. Rydell	Volvo 850E/GLT 2.0	–	21.49s	6	
7	E. O'Brien	Peugeot 405 Mi16	–	22.31s	14	
8	J. Bailey	Toyota Carina	–	22.82s	16	
9	W. Hoy	Toyota Carina	–	23.15s	17	
10	T. Needell	Nissan Primera 2.0eGT	–	30.21s	19	
11	A. Rouse	Ford Mondeo	–	31.94s	13	
12	J. Kaye	Toyota Carina	–	55.05s	22	
13	H. Irvine	BMW 318is	–	1 lap down	23	
14	K. O'dor	Nissan Primera 2.0eGT	–	2 laps down	10	
15	P. Watts	Peugeot 405 Mi16	–	11 laps down	9	

Did Not Finish

–	N. Albon	Renault 19 16V	–	25 laps	20	Gearbox
–	G. Simoni	Alfa Romeo 155TS	–	23 laps	5	Engine
–	J. Thompson	Peugeot 405 Mi16	–	20 laps	18	Gearbox
–	J. Winkelhock	BMW 318i	–	19 laps	2	Differential
–	J. Lammers	Volvo 850SE/GLT 2.0	–	16 laps	15	Black flagged
–	G. Tarquini	Alfa Romeo 155TS	–	6 laps	8	Accident
–	N. Smith	Vauxhall Cavalier 16V	–	4 laps	21	Steering

Disqualified

–	T. Harvey	Renault Laguna	Excluded for careless driving	7	

Fastest Lap: S. Soper – 54.99 secs (85.10mph)   **Average Speed of Winner:** 83.18mph

allowing Allam to pip team mate Cleland for fourth ahead of Rydell's Volvo. The other Volvo, driven by Jan Lammers, was involved with O'Brien to earn a black flag whilst others to have a less than enjoyable race were Andy Rouse down in eleventh and Patrick Watts who spent most of the race in the pits trying to repair a leaking brake system. In the Total Cup, Albon led for the first time since April before retiring on lap 25 leaving Kaye to win from Hamish Irvine.

Round Fourteen – 32 laps

Harvey was allowed to start from his original fourth place on the grid due to his appeal which put Allam and Cleland down to fifth and sixth despite their first race placings. The race, however, due to the difficulty of overtaking at the Scottish track became somewhat of a procession with the first six on the grid being the first six home although not quite in grid order. The BMW of Soper, which had clocked the quickest lap in the earlier race, again demonstrated it was the fastest car on the straights and Menu must have been pleased to see in his mirror that Soper could not get past Radisich. Lap 17, however, saw Menu's hopes dashed when the BMW flashed past the Ford and set off in pursuit of the Renault. It took Soper nine laps to get into a position to challenge but when Menu left a gap,

the BMW was through and gone leaving Menu to attempt to hold on to second on tyres that were fast wearing out.

There were two laps left when he lost his battle with Radisich which gave the New Zealander back to back seconds and reduced Tarquini's championship lead to just 18 points. Soper, meanwhile, was celebrating his first victory for over thirteen months. Alfa's difficult weekend continued with Simoni coming home a distant ninth whilst Harvey made the most of his appeal by holding on to fourth.

The Nissans had a poor time of it in the second race after Needell had grabbed a point for finishing tenth in the opener. This time round Needell could only manage 16th two places behind O'dor, who had smacked Kaye's Toyota

Round Fourteen – Race Placings

Pos	Driver	Team	Time	Diff	Grid	
1	S. Soper	BMW 318i	29'54.21	–	3	
2	P. Radisich	Ford Mondeo	–	1.49s	2	
3	A. Menu	Renault Laguna	–	2.65s	1	
4	T. Harvey	Renault Laguna	–	3.16s	4	
5	J. Allam	Vauxhall Cavalier 16V	–	3.64s	5	
6	J. Cleland	Vauxhall Cavalier 16V	–	3.92s	6	
7	J. Bailey	Toyota Carina	–	5.31s	9	
8	W. Hoy	Toyota Carina	–	9.01s	10	
9	G. Simoni	Alfa Romeo	–	16.49s	20	
10	R. Rydell	Volvo 850SE/GLT 2.0	–	28.37s	7	
11	J. Winkelhock	BMW 318i	–	29.00s	19	
12	J. Lammers	Volvo 850SE/GLT 2.0	–	31.05s	18	
13	E. O'Brien	Peugeot 405 Mi16	–	32.18s	8	
14	K. O'dor	Nissan Primera 2.0eGT	–	33.02s	15	
15	A. Rouse	Ford Mondeo	–	33.74s	12	
16	T. Needell	Nissan Primera 2.0eGT	–	43.04s	11	
17	N. Smith	Vauxhall Cavalier 16V	–	2 laps down	17	
18	J. Kaye	Toyota Carina	–	8 laps down	13	

Did Not Finish

–	H. Irvine	BMW 318is	–	24 laps	14	Engine
–	P. Watts	Peugeot 405 Mi16	–	9 laps	16	Puncture

Fastest Lap: S. Soper – 55.02 (85.05mph)   **Average Speed of Winner:** 83.46mph

Championship Placings

Drivers' Points		Constructors' Points	
198	G. Tarquini	205	Ford
180	P. Radisich	204	Alfa Romeo
146	J. Cleland	180	Vauxhall
130	A. Menu	143	Renault
85	P. Watts	136	BMW
76	S. Soper	129	Peugeot
69	J. Allam	81	Toyota
68	G. Simoni	55	Volvo
62	A. Rouse	44	Nissan
53	J. Winkelhock	31	Mazda

TOTAL Cup

Position	Driver	Points
1st	J. Kaye	246
2nd	N. Smith	198
3rd	C. Goodwin	174
4th	J. Thompson	92

at the start but the most disappointed man of the afternoon besides Tarquini must have been Patrick Watts. After finishing the first outing some eleven laps down, the second race gave him his first retirement of the season. The Total Cup was even more lacklustre with just three cars lining up on the grid. Irvine departed on lap 25 whilst Kaye, after his opening lap shunt, spent a long time in the pits administering repairs leaving Smith, whose engineers had welded together his steering rack, to crawl round to his second Total Cup victory of the campaign. ◼

Knockhill

32 laps.

Lap Distance: 1.30 miles
Race Distance: 41.6 miles

1.	Duffus	5.	Clark
2.	McIntyre	6.	Railway
3.	Butcher's	7.	Taylor's
4.	Chicane	8.	Stewart Straight

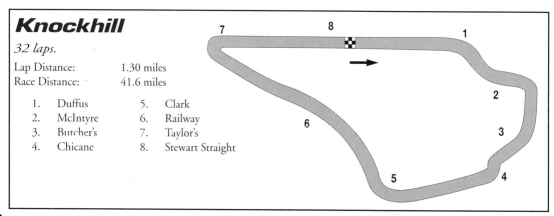

Oulton Park

Winkelhock made it three wins from the last four Oulton Park appearances.

With two wins from his last three races at Oulton Park there was little doubt that Jos Winkelhock was the driver most looking forward to the 15th Round of the series at the Cheshire track. One regular missing from the starting line up, however, was Tim Sugden whose Toyota Carina was still in its Spa 24 hour specification and obviously therefore not able to take part in a BTCC sprint. If Winkelhock

thought it would be easy, he was soon put in place by a blistering qualifying lap from Alain Menu which gave the Swiss driver pole position by the massive margin of almost four-fifths of a second from the reigning champion. But before this we had the unusual sight of privateers Hamish Irvine and Nigel Albon taking turns to head the timesheets, not because of a sudden surge of power from their cars, however, but because the rest of the field were twiddling their

1994 Grid Positions and Qualifying Times

Grid	Driver	Time	Grid	Driver	Time	Grid	Driver	Time
1	A. Menu	1'41.93	10	R. Rydell	1'44.07	19	W. Hoy	1'45.68
2	J. Winkelhock	1'42.70	11	K. O'dor	1'44.17	20	C. Goodwin*	1'46.15
3	J. Cleland	1'43.07	12	A. Rouse	1'44.22	21	J. Kaye*	1'46.34
4	R. Ravaglia	1'43.20	13	J. Lammers	1'44.27	22	N. Albon*	1'46.77
5	G. Tarquini	1'43.23	14	J. Bailey	1'44.46	23	N. Smith*	1'47.78
6	G. Simoni	1'43.43	15	T. Needell	1'44.51	24	H. Irvine*	1'48.92
7	T. Harvey	1'43.64	16	J. Allam	1'44.82	25	G. Steel*	1'50.27
8	P. Radisich	1'43.83	17	J. Thompson*	1'44.98		*Denotes Total Cup competitors	
9	P. Watts	1'43.89	18	E. O'Brien	1'45.47			

Race Placings

Pos	Driver	Car	Time	Diff	Grid	
1	J. Winkelhock	BMW 318i	28'09.63	–	2	
2	A. Menu	Renault Laguna	–	2.95s	1	
3	G. Tarquini	Alfa Romeo 155TS	–	8.61s	5	
4	G. Simoni	Alfa Romeo 155TS	–	9.03s	6	
5	R. Ravaglia	BMW 318i	–	9.31s	4	
6	T. Harvey	Renault Laguna	–	16.66s	7	
7	J. Lammers	Volvo 850SE/GLT 2.0	–	20.10s	13	
8	P. Watts	Peugeot 405 Mi16	–	29.95s	9	
9	J. Bailey	Toyota Carina E	–	34.73s	14	
10	K. O'dor	Nissan Primera 2.0eGT	–	34.92s	11	
11	W. Hoy	Toyota Carina E	–	41.71s	19	
12	J. Allam	Vauxhall Cavalier 16V	–	46.20s	16	
13	T. Needell	Nissan Primera 2.0eGT	–	47.67s	15	
14	E. O'Brien	Peugeot 405 Mi16	–	48.91s	18	
15	N. Albon	Renault 19 16V	–	90.03s	22	
16	H. Irvine	BMW 318i	–	1 lap down	24	
17	N. Smith	Vauxhall Cavalier 16V	–	2 laps down	23	
18	C. Goodwin	Vauxhall Cavalier 16V	–	3 laps down	20	

Did Not Finish

	Driver	Car	Time	Diff	Grid	
–	A. Rouse	Ford Mondeo Ghia	–	12 laps	12	Oil pressure
–	P. Radisich	Ford Mondeo Ghia	–	10 laps	8	Oil pressure
–	J. Thompson	Peugeot 405 Mi16	–	5 laps	17	Gearbox
–	G. Steel	BMW 318is	–	4 laps	25	Suspension
–	R. Rydell	Volvo 850SE/GLT 2.0	–	3 laps	10	Overheating
–	J. Cleland	Vauxhall Cavalier 16V	–	0 laps	3	Accident
–	J. Kaye	Toyota Carina E	–	0 laps	21	Accident

Fastest Lap: J. Winkelhock – 1'44.16 (95.91mph) – Course Record

Average Speed of Winner: 94.60mph

thumbs in the pits due to an oil slick at Foulstons. When the rest of the bunch did venture out, Cleland took third ahead of the second BMW in which Ravaglia, again deputising for Steve Soper, had a superb time in his first ever run on the circuit. The Alfas were back on the third row but Simoni was, in fact, lucky to be driving at all just 24 hours after a big shunt at Island in practice which left him nursing a very sore and stiff neck.

Perhaps the most disappointed driver was Tim Harvey who, after setting the fastest test time, could only qualify in seventh but the Ford pairing of Radisich and Rouse would also have been unhappy with the performance of their respective Mondeos. The only driver to go faster in the second session was Eugene O'Brien but he still languished down behind leading privateer, James Thompson.

After gaining pole position with a show of incredible speed, Menu threw his advantage away with a dreadful start. So bad, in fact, that not only did Winkelhock take the lead but Cleland demoted the Swiss driver to third by Old Hall. Another to drop two places courtesy of a poor start was Ravaglia who saw both Simoni and Radisich go past. Not content with this, Simoni quickly overhauled Menu and Cleland to take an amazing second spot by the end of the first circuit in what must have been one of the most spectacular starts of the campaign.

By now, Menu was down to fifth but Cleland was not to see the end of the first lap. At Druids he was touched into the tyres by Bailey, with Rydell an innocent victim as he was taken by surprise and severely damaged his radiator against the Volvo's boot. The Swede's race ended after three laps with his radiator badly leaking.

Another first lap incident saw the demise of leading privateer James Kaye who crashed in to Chris Goodwin after his Cavalier had gone on the grass and returned to the track in a sideways position. Out in front, Winkelhock was well out of any danger and making the most of the clear road to press home his advantage. After taking a three second lead by the end of the first lap, he increased this by posting a lap record on the third tour before easing off to make sure he lasted home. Simoni's fast start, meanwhile, was petering out as his tyres failed to reach temperature as quickly as the others and, by the end of the fifth circuit, Menu had regained second having overtaken Radisich at Old Hall and the Italian at Knickerbrook.

Menu set off after Winkelhock and actually posted faster laps than the leader on four of the next six circuits but the gap never shrank to less than two seconds. Tarquini was the next to pass Simoni which left Radisich in his sights but there was no need for the Italian to exert himself to catch the Mondeo as the New Zealander capitulated with falling oil pressure on lap ten, a fate his team mate,

Andy Rouse, was also to suffer two circuits later. And that's the way it stayed with Italians filling third, fourth and fifth behind the German winner and Swiss runner-up. With Dutchman Jan Lammers finishing in the top seven for the first time, it was left to Tim Harvey to save British blushes by getting home in sixth.

In the Privateers race, Nigel Albon scored his first success of the season but the day belonged to the reigning BTCC Champion, Jos Winkelhock, who made it three wins out of his last four Oulton Park starts as well as joining the illustrious names of Stirling Moss and Jim Clark as only the third driver ever to win successive Oulton Park Gold Cups. ◼

Championship Placings

Drivers' Points		Constructors' Points	
210	G. Tarquini	216	Alfa Romeo
180	P. Radisich	205	Ford
148	A. Menu	183	Vauxhall
146	J. Cleland	161	Renault
88	P. Watts	160	BMW
78	G. Simoni	140	Peugeot
77	J. Winkelhock	87	Toyota
76	S. Soper	65	Volvo
69	J. Allam	48	Nissan
62	A. Rouse	31	Mazda

TOTAL Cup

Position	Driver	Points
1st	J. Kaye	246
2nd	N. Smith	210
3rd	C. Goodwin	184
4th	J. Thompson	92
5th	N. Albon	80
6th	H. Irvine	76

Tiff Needell in the Nissan.

Brands Hatch Indy

28-29 August 1994

Radisich about to make an enemy of Peugeot's O'Brien.

Privateer Chris Goodwin, a test driver for Vauxhall, was probably the most disappointed driver in the week prior to the Brands Hatch double header. It had been understood prior to the start of the season that he would graduate to a third Vauxhall works car to join Cleland and Allam for the last few races of the championship but this move was put on the back burner on the Monday prior to the race leaving Goodwin to continue in the privateer's Total Cup. Another disappointed man was Toyota's Tim Sugden who sat the event out as the team's three Carinas had only two new Japanese specification suspensions and reverse head engines between them with the vote going to Will Hoy and Julian Bailey.

The BMWs were certainly once more to the fore as they made the most of their revised weight concession introduced two months earlier and, at the end of the first qualifying session, both Winkelhock and Soper were over a quarter of a second ahead of the opposition leaving Alfa's Tarquini bemoaning *"Early in the year everybody was complaining about us but look at the BMWs.*

1994 Grid Positions and Qualifying Times

Grid	Driver	Time	Grid	Driver	Time	Grid	Driver	Time
1	J. Winkelhock	47.08	10	P. Watts	47.62	19	N. Smith *	48.11
2	S. Soper	47.09	11	E. O'Brien	47.74	20	J. Allam	48.28
3	G. Simoni	47.36	12	A. Rouse	47.79	21	C. Goodwin *	48.47
4	G. Tarquini	47.39	13	J. Cleland	47.79	22	J. Kaye *	48.66
5	R. Rydell	47.43	14	J. Bailey	47.80	23	N. Albon *	49.22
6	A. Menu	47.44	15	K. O'dor	47.91	24	H. Irvine *	50.04
7	T. Harvey	47.54	16	T. Needell	47.93	25	G. Steel *	50.56
8	J. Lammers	47.56	17	W. Hoy	47.95			
9	P. Radisich	47.57	18	J. Thompson *	47.97		*Denotes Total Cup competitors		

The weight gap is too little". Certainly Team Schnitzer were confident their BMWs wouldn't be caught as they didn't even bother sending Winkelhock out for the second session whilst Soper ventured only briefly on to the track to scrub his tyres. The all white front row gave way to an all red Alfa second row. The Volvos put in one of their best qualifying displays to see Rydell in fifth and Lammers in eighth but the best second session performance undoubtedly belonged to Alain Menu who moved up eight places from his first session fourteenth when he was experiencing problems with his differential.

Round Sixteen – 32 laps

All of the grid leaders got away well, apart from Simoni who tried too hard and suffered wheelspin to drop to fifth. Team mate Tarquini, however, made the best start of all and slipped inside Soper at Surtees to take second behind Winkelhock. Soper was then to lose further ground to Menu at Druids whilst Lammers, in inspirational mood, went past Simoni in to fifth at Clearways on lap three. He, however, headed a group of traffic jam proportions and a contact seemed inevitable. Sure enough, Rydell and Watts (who was possibly suffering from lack of sleep with his wife having given birth to a daughter just a few days earlier) touched, which cost Rydell not only several places but also a damaged front end which ultimately caused all sorts of understeering problems for the remainder of the meeting.

Simoni retook Lammers and set about Soper who was having problems with a broken damper on the right rear which was making it almost impossible to negotiate left handers at speed. The Italian caught Soper and then passed Menu for good measure.

Another making solid headway was Harvey and on lap 25 he also overtook both Menu and Soper but, up front, there was less action. Winkelhock was never going to be caught by Tarquini who was similarly untroubled to hold second. Radisich's chances of the title were all

Round Sixteen – Race Placings

Pos	Driver	Car	Time	Diff	Grid	
1	J. Winkelhock	BMW 318i	25'52.01	–	1	
2	G. Tarquini	Alfa Romeo 155TS	–	25'52.60	4	
3	G. Simoni	Alfa Romeo 155TS	–	25'55.56	3	
4	T. Harvey	Renault Laguna	–	26'02.26	7	
5	S. Soper	BMW 318i	–	26'07.15	2	
6	P. Watts	Peugeot 405 Mi16	–	26'08.06	10	
7	A. Menu	Renault Laguna	–	26'08.19	6	
8	E. O'Brien	Peugeot 405 Mi16	–	26'08.34	11	
9	J. Lammers	Volvo 850SE/GLT 2.0	–	26'11.17	8	
10	J. Bailey	Toyota Carina E	–	26'11.43	14	
11	A. Rouse	Ford Mondeo Ghia	–	26'12.18	12	
12	W. Hoy	Toyota Carina E	–	26'13.43	17	
13	J. Allam	Vauxhall Cavalier16V	–	26'13.68	20	
14	P. Radisich	Ford Mondeo Ghia	–	26'15.75	9	
15	R. Rydell	Volvo 850SE/GLT 2.0	–	26'16.37	5	
16	K. O'dor	Nissan Primera eGT	–	26'18.74	15	
17	T. Needell	Nissan Primera eGT	–	26'22.25	16	
18	J. Kaye	Toyota Carina E	–	26'27.10	22	
19	N. Smith	Vauxhall Cavalier16V	–	26'28.19	19	
20	J. Thompson	Peugeot 405 Mi16	–	26'39.73	18	
21	H. Irvine	BMW 318i	–	31 laps	24	
22	C. Goodwin	Vauxhall Cavalier16V	–	30 laps	21	
23	G. Steel	BMW 318i	–	30 laps	25	

Did Not Finish

–	N. Albon	Renault 19 16v	–	14 laps	23	Spin
–	J. Cleland	Vauxhall Cavalier	–	1 lap	13	Engine

Fastest Lap: J. Winkelhock – 47.50 secs (91.22mph)   **Average Speed of Winner:** 89.33mph

but extinguished with a poor 14th whilst Rydell's problems saw him drop rapidly away to finish one place behind Radisich.

In the Total Cup, Goodwin's disappointment in not getting a works drive, was compounded when, after leading in the early stages, he suffered a suspension collapse and trailed in two laps down leaving the two competition leaders James Kaye and Nigel Smith to consolidate their advantage over him.

Round Seventeen – 29 laps

At the start of the second race, Winkelhock, Tarquini and Simoni kept formation but Soper got past Harvey off the line only to see his fast get away count for nought due to the action behind him. Watts and Hoy touched at Clearways which turned the Peugeot round. O'dor hit Watts leaving the Nissan a write off and then the privateer Hamish Irvine joined the pile up. The race was stopped and a restart over a reduced 29 laps ordered. This would begin with six fewer drivers than the first race of the afternoon for, in addition to the accident victims, Hoy, Watts, O'dor and Irvine, the engines of both Rouse and Cleland had given.

The restart saw more incident, albeit of a controversial type, as Radisich knocked Allam off the track at Cooper Straight and in to the barriers causing the Vauxhall's retirement. The Kiwi was later to send O'Brien flying off at Graham Hill Bend on lap 13 causing the Peugeot driver with a wild reputation to complain *"It was blatant. I just hope he is punished in the same way as I have been in the past"*.

He wasn't but, to complete an eventful afternoon for the Kiwi, Radisich was disqualified for his part in the Allam incident and fined £500 to boot. Following his 14th place in the first race, Radisich's disqualification left him trailing Tarquini

Round Seventeen – Race Placings

Pos	Driver	Car	Time	Diff	Grid	
1	J. Winkelhock	BMW 318i	23'27.38	–	1	
2	G. Tarquini	Alfa Romeo 155TS	–	23'28.01	2	
3	G. Simoni	Alfa Romeo 155TS	–	23'29.64	3	
4	S. Soper	BMW 318i	–	23'34.28	5	
5	J. Lammers	Volvo 850SE/GLT 2.0	–	23'38.21	9	
6	J. Bailey	Toyota Carina E	–	23'38.37	10	
7	A. Menu	Renault Laguna	–	23'41.92	7	
8	R. Rydell	Volvo 850SE/GLT 2.0	–	23'48.21	15	
9	T. Needell	Nissan Primera eGT	–	23'54.43	17	
10	N. Smith	Vauxhall Cavalier 16V	–	24'05.91	19	
11	C. Goodwin	Vauxhall Cavalier 16V	–	24'09.02	22	
12	N. Albon	Renault 19 16v	–	28 laps	24	
13	G. Steel	BMW 318i	–	28 laps	23	

Disqualified

–	P. Radisich	Ford Mondeo Ghia – had finished eighth			14	

Did Not Finish

–	J. Kaye	Toyota Carina E	–	20 laps	18	Accident
–	T. Harvey	Renault Laguna	–	17 laps	4	Throttle cable
–	E. O'Brien	Peugeot 405 Mi16	–	13 laps	8	Accident
–	J. Thompson	Peugeot 405 Mi16	–	12 laps	20	Steering rack
–	J. Allam	Vauxhall Cavalier 16V	–	1 lap	13	Accident

Did Not Start

–	A. Rouse	Ford Mondeo Ghia	–	–		Engine
–	W. Hoy	Toyota Carina E	–	–		Accident
–	P. Watts	Peugeot 405 Mi16	–	–		Accident
–	K. O'dor	Nissan Primera eGT 2.0	–	–		Accident
–	H. Irvine	BMW 318i	–	–		Accident
–	J. Cleland	Vauxhall Cavalier 16V	–			Engine from first race

Fastest Lap: G. Tarquini – 47.61 secs (91.00mph)   **Average Speed of Winner:** 89.28mph

You can with a Nissan as O'dor proved!

by some 66 points and with just 96 points left to play for the incident, almost certainly gave the title to the Italian.

Winkelhock, meanwhile, had made his third superb getaway of the afternoon whilst the other BMW of Soper also got a flyer, overtaking both Harvey and Simoni on the startline as the Italian experienced his second wheelspinning start of the meeting. Winkelhock then overtook Tarquini up Hailwood Hill to put the BMWs in a 1-2 position.

Simoni's bad start saw him drop to sixth as the Renaults of Menu and Harvey also went past

TOTAL Cup

Position	Driver	Points
1st	J. Kaye	270
2nd	N. Smith	252
3rd	C. Goodwin	210
4th	J. Thompson	104
5th	N. Albon	92
6th	H. Irvine	86

him but his team mate, Tarquini, was doing somewhat better. He regained second from Soper at Clearways on the seventh tour.

In the Total Cup, Goodwin started from the pits after a hasty repair job to his suspension and Nigel Smith did likewise after being involved in the first lap shunt which, conversely, gave Goodwin sufficient time to line up on the grid!

The Total Cup championship leader, Kaye, spun off on lap twenty to join Thompson on the sidelines and, with Goodwin's car still suffering from the first race damage, Smith took full advantage to grab victory. He also benefited from the major race retirements to capture a point in the overall race by taking tenth although he didn't actually finish in front of any works cars that were still running at the end of an eventful race. ◪

Championship Placings

Drivers' Points		Constructors' Points	
246	G. Tarquini	252	Alfa Romeo
180	P. Radisich	215	Ford
156	A. Menu	208	BMW
146	J. Cleland	186	Vauxhall
125	J. Winkelhock	181	Renault
102	G. Simoni	153	Peugeot
94	P. Watts	103	Toyota
94	S. Soper	85	Volvo
64	J. Allam	54	Nissan
62	A. Rouse	31	Mazda

Silverstone GP

Menu leads Radisich and pinches the Championship Runners-up spot from the Kiwi.

One of the biggest stories of the meeting was the announcement of Andy Rouse's retirement from driving. The 46 year old had 60 overall wins plus a further 84 class victories to mark the Midlands based driver as the most successful ever BTCC pilot. It was revealed that his successor would be the 1993 British F3 champion Kelvin Burt who was immediately put into the third Mondeo whilst another announcement confirmed that Patrick Watts would be staying with Peugeot after rumours that he was off to pastures new. Elsewhere, Nissan gave Kieth O'dor first crack in its latest Primera and Rick Rydell had a breathless weekend that, in the end, yielded him just one point. He left Silverstone on the Friday prior to the race in order to be present at the birth of his daughter in Sweden but missed

1994 Grid Positions and Qualifying Times

Grid	Driver	Time	Grid	Driver	Time	Grid	Driver	Time
1	T. Harvey	2'00.52	10	A. Rouse	2'01.68	19	E. O'Brien	2'03.08
2	J. Winkelhock	2'00.81	11	J. Allam	2'02.05	20	C. Goodwin *	2'03.63
3	G. Tarquini	2'00.86	12	W. Hoy	2'02.18	21	J. Kaye *	2'03.68
4	G. Simoni	2'00.91	13	P. Watts	2'02.35	22	J. Thompson *	2'03.72
5	S. Soper	2'00.96	14	K. Burt	2'02.41	23	N. Smith *	2'04.27
6	J. Cleland	2'01.11	15	T. Sugden	2'02.61	24	K. O'dor	2'04.83
7	A. Menu	2'01.13	16	R. Rydell	2'02.73	25	N. Albon *	2'05.51
8	P. Radisich	2'01.38	17	J. Lammers	2'02.78	26	H. Irvine *	2'08.55
9	J. Bailey	2'01.67	18	T. Needell	2'02.96			

Denotes Total Cup competitors

that event by some two hours. With his flight back to Britain delayed, he also very nearly missed qualifying and had just seven minutes to register a time. Fortunately he managed to get in one good lap which saw him start sixteenth. Champion elect, Gabriele Tarquini, meanwhile was doubtful for most of the week with a bout of nausea on Tuesday giving way to a raging sore throat that saw him complete just eight laps in total during both qualifying sessions. His third place on the grid, therefore, was a quite remarkable achievement.

Tim Harvey who had not held such an elevated position for over two, years Pembrey 1992 to be exact. He was three-tenths of a second faster than Winkelhock's BMW and the two of them headed an all red Alfa second row.

Round Eighteen – Nine laps

Harvey had been busy all week practising his starts and it paid rich dividends for him once he had gained pole. Winkelhock made a poor getaway leaving Harvey's Renault a clear leader whilst the Alfas made the most of the German's sluggishness with teamwork ensuring a smooth passage for a still far from fit Tarquini. Simoni whipped past Winkelhock and then allowed his team mate past on the outside before making sure he then held everybody else at bay. The BMW threat never materialised with Soper banging a kerb on the first lap resulting in a slow tour round and a pit stop which relegated him to last.

Despite then going on to register the fastest lap of the race, Soper was so far behind that he could still only manage to finish 22nd. Winkelhock didn't even finish as his engine blew in a big way after completing just three laps and another regular points scorer to bite the dust was Patrick Watts whose new Peugeot refused to start either race with a fuel injection problem. Simoni was beginning to experience some trouble with his tyres and, although trying desperately to protect his team mate's second spot, he was unable to repulse third lap attacks by both Menu and, more importantly, Radisich.

Round Eighteen – Race Placings

Pos	Driver	Car	Time	Diff	Grid	
1	T. Harvey	Renault Laguna	18'36.68	–	1	
2	G. Tarquini	Alfa Romeo 155TS	–	0.75s	3	
3	A. Menu	Renault Laguna	–	3.50s	7	
4	J. Cleland	Vauxhall Cavalier 16V	–	7.31s	6	
5	J. Bailey	Toyota Carina E	–	10.94s	9	
6	G. Simoni	Alfa Romeo 155TS	–	12.21s	4	
7	W. Hoy	Toyota Carina E	–	14.63s	12	
8	J. Allam	Vauxhall Cavalier 16V	–	14.87s	11	
9	T. Sugden	Toyota Carina E	–	20.24s	15	
10	R. Rydell	Volvo 850SE/GLT 2.0 2	–	21.29s	16	
11	K. O'dor	Nissan Primera 2.0eGT	–	22.66s	24	
12	E. O'Brien	Peugeot 405 Mi16	–	23.89s	19	
13	A. Rouse	Ford Mondeo Ghia	–	24.85s	10	
14	K. Burt	Ford Mondeo Ghia	–	26.81s	14	
15	T. Needell	Nissan Primera 2.0eGT	–	28.97s	18	
16	J. Lammers	Volvo 850SE/GLT 2.0	–	34.30s	17	
17	N. Smith	Vauxhall Cavalier 16V	–	34.63s	23	
18	J. Thompson	Peugeot 405 Mi16	–	36.51s	22	
19	C. Goodwin	Vauxhall Cavalier 16V	–	37.44s	20	
20	J. Kaye	Toyota Carina E	–	38.88s	21	
21	N. Albon	Renault 19 16V	–	41.76s	25	
22	S. Soper	BMW 318i	–	84.02s	5	
23	H. Irvine	BMW 318is	–	3 laps down	26	

Did Not Finish

–	P. Radisich	Ford Mondeo	–	8 laps	8	Engine
–	J. Winkelhock	BMW 318i	–	3 laps	2	Engine
–	P. Watts	Peugeot 405 Mi 16	–	0 laps	13	Fuel injection

Fastest Lap: S. Soper – 2'01.78 (92.88mph)   ***Average Speed of Winner:*** 91.16mph

The New Zealander needed to gain at least one more place if he was to take the championship to the following race but, after completing eight laps, a tell tale puff of smoke announced an unwanted hat-trick for the challenger. He was out of the race, the meeting and the Championship with the afternoon's eventual results rubbing salt in his wounds by also depriving him of second place in the title race as Menu scored sufficient points to overtake the Ford man. With Tarquini seeing Radisich out of the race, the situation was tailor made for Harvey to make the most of the situation. Tarquini was certainly not going to risk anything silly by having a battle with the leader nor was he going to let anybody past him. Harvey made no mistakes but was probably pleased, anyway, to see the red flags come out with three laps remaining after backmarkers, Albon and Irvine, had mated their cars at Club.

Rydell got a consolation point for his travels in tenth place, O'dor's new Nissan performed better than Watts' new Peugeot but he still missed the points by a place with Burt, on his debut, down in fourteenth. In the Total Cup, Nigel Smith took the honours and, by doing so, closed to within four points of the privateer's leader, James Kaye.

Round Nineteen – 12 laps

Four of the first race starters, Radisich, Winkelhock, Albon and Irvine, failed to make the second race line up and Watts quickly joined them when his new car refused to move off for the second time in the afternoon. O'Brien was another who didn't see the completion of a full lap as he clashed on Hangar Straight with O'dor who was reprimanded and his licence endorsed by the Stewards for his part in the incident. In another first lap incident, Harvey's dreams of completing a double were just that when Tarquini nudged him at Copse. When the first race winner rejoined, it was immediately in front of the two leaders, Tarquini and Menu and, bearing in mind that Harvey was fined a massive £2,000 for shunting Tarquini off at Knockhill in July, the crowd sensed trouble but there wasn't as Harvey moved aside to allow the frontrunners through.

The best start was made by Julian Bailey whose Toyota fairly flew leaving him looking at only Tarquini in front by the time he had cleared Copse. He had almost caught Tarquini by Club

Round Nineteen – Race Placings

Pos	Driver	Car	Time	Diff	Grid	
1	G. Tarquini	Alfa Romeo 155TS	24'43.95	–	2	
2	A. Menu	Renault Laguna	–	1.99s	3	
3	G. Simoni	Alfa Romeo 155TS	–	3.49s	6	
4	J. Cleland	Vauxhall Cavalier 16V	–	5.69s	4	
5	S. Soper	BMW 318i	–	12.12s	23	
6	J. Bailey	Toyota Carina E	–	14.17s	5	
7	W. Hoy	Toyota Carina E	–	14.59s	7	
8	A. Rouse	Ford Mondeo Ghia	–	17.54s	13	
9	J. Allam	Vauxhall Cavalier 16V	–	17.77s	8	
10	T. Sugden	Toyota Carina E	–	23.76s	9	
11	K. Burt	Ford Mondeo Ghia	–	24.58s	14	
12	R. Rydell	Volvo 850 SE/GLT 2.0	–	31.25s	10	
13	J. Kaye	Toyota Carina E	–	36.76s	20	
14	T. Needell	Nissan Primera 2.0eGT	–	37.92s	15	
15	C. Goodwin	Vauxhall Cavalier 16V	–	39.62s	19	
16	N. Smith	Vauxhall Cavalier 16V	–	39.90s	17	
17	J. Lammers	Volvo 850 SE/GLT 2.0	–	52.50s	16	
18	T. Harvey	Renault Laguna	–	1 lap down	1	

Did Not Finish

Pos	Driver	Car	Time	Diff	Grid	
–	J. Thompson	Peugeot 405 Mi16	–	9 laps	18	Handling
–	K. O'dor	Nissan Primera 2.0eGT	–	3 laps	11	Radiator
–	E. O'Brien	Peugeot 405 Mi16	–	0 laps	12	Accident
–	P. Watts	Peugeot 405 Mi16	–	0 laps	22	Fuel injection

Fastest Lap: G.Tarquini – 2'01.61 (93.01mph)   **Average Speed of Winner:** 91.46mph

Nigel Albon steps closer to winning the privateers' trophy.

but couldn't quite get in to position to challenge for a surprise lead after which his tyres began to give him trouble. Menu regained second place from Bailey and, after four laps, Simoni and Cleland were also through. Before the end of the race, Bailey had lost another place as Soper blitzed his way through the field from last place on the grid to finish a most creditable fifth. But the leaders were now spreadeagled with Tarquini going on to celebrate his Championship victory in some style with two seconds to spare from Menu and similar margins splitting the second, third and fourth cars before a massive six second gap to Soper in fifth. Burt's debut came to a disappointing end when Sugden got past him on the

TOTAL Cup

Position	Driver	Points
1st	J. Kaye	304
2nd	N. Smith	288
3rd	C. Goodwin	240
4th	J. Thompson	122
5th	N. Albon	100
6th	H. Irvine	92

final lap to grab the last point on offer whilst Menu's second place (and his fifteenth consecutive scoring race) was just enough to put him into second place in the Championship ahead of Radisich.

With the main Championship all sewn up, eyes were on the Total Cup entrants, especially Kaye and Smith. This time, Kaye made no mistake as he made a flying start to quickly gain ground. After overtaking Goodwin, he found Thompson dropping out and then moved past his arch rival Smith. When he also got past Needell to give himself a buffer between himself and the rest of the privateers, Kaye was virtually assured of maximum points but he then received a bonus when Goodwin deprived Smith of second which increased the points difference to sixteen going in to the final meeting at Donington. ◼

Championship Placings

Drivers' Points		Constructors' Points	
288	G. Tarquini	294	Alfa Romeo
186	A. Menu	223	Renault
180	P. Radisich	220	BMW
166	J. Cleland	218	Ford
125	J. Winkelhock	210	Vauxhall
120	G. Simoni	154	Peugeot
102	S. Soper	121	Toyota
94	P. Watts	87	Volvo
74	J. Allam	65	Nissan
68	T. Harvey	31	Mazda

Donington

The pack race flat out down the straight.

Gabriele Tarquini, and Alfa Romeo had the Drivers' and Manufacturers' Championships all sewn up prior to the last meeting of the season but second place in both was up for grabs at Donington. Radisich's failure to score in any of the previous five rounds had seen him slip to third but only six points behind Menu whilst in the Manufacturers' title, just thirteen points separated Renault, BMW, Ford and Vauxhall. The Total

Cup Championship was also still undecided with James Kaye in pole position enjoying a lead of sixteen points over his only challenger Nigel Smith. So there was still plenty to play for as the Autotrader BTCC headed to its conclusion. But more than that, the crowds turned up to see a BTCC finale from Andy Rouse for whom this would be his last drive in the Championship after landing 60 race victories and over eighty Class wins on his way to four titles during his twenty-

1994 Grid Positions and Qualifying Times

Grid	Driver	Time	Grid	Driver	Time	Grid	Driver	Time
1	J. Winkelhock	1'39.66	10	J. Bailey	1'40.79	19	T. Needell	1'41.94
2	P. Radisich	1'39.76	11	A. Rouse	1'40.82	20	C. Goodwin *	1'42.19
3	S. Soper	1'39.81	12	R. Rydell	1'40.92	21	J. Thompson *	1'42.44
4	G. Simoni	1'40.02	13	W. Hoy	1'41.02	22	J. Kaye *	1'42.59
5	A. Menu	1'40.13	14	J. Lammers	1'41.06	23	N. Smith *	1'42.73
6	T. Harvey	1'40.21	15	J. Allam	1'41.27	24	N. Albon *	1'44.76
7	J. Cleland	1'40.45	16	R. Gravett	1'41.35	25	H. Irvine *	1'49.05
8	G. Tarquini	1'40.53	17	T. Sugden	1'41.40		*Denotes Total Cup competitors	
9	P. Watts	1'40.65	18	K. O'dor	1'41.81			

one year association with the BTCC. Sadly, there was to be no fairy tale ending but, just as Rouse was making his farewell, Rob Gravett was making a comeback after a twelve month absence to get some practice in ready for the FIA World Touring Car Cup.

Qualifying was badly hindered by a Hillman Imp competing in the ICS Historic Cars Championship shedding its entire oil capacity all over the track from McLeans to Coppice with the result that there was the most unusual sight of privateers Nigel Smith and Hamish Irvine heading the grid after almost twenty minutes of the first session. But when the big guns decided it was safe to venture out, the picture quickly changed with the BMW's of Winkelhock and Soper taking first and third whilst Radisich, needing to beat Menu by seven points to grab the runners-up spot, did his chances no harm by splitting the two BMW's. Simoni outqualified Tarquini to take fourth but the third row was the all yellow of the Renault camp. Gravatt's come back found him languishing in sixteenth whilst in the Total Cup, leader Kaye had the drop on Smith.

Round Twenty – 18 laps

Winkelhock used his pole position to stay ahead of Radisich through Redgate followed by in grid order by Soper, Simoni and Menu but just behind these, Cleland was a most unhappy chappy after an altercation with Tim Harvey. *"He doesn't deserve to have a licence. His £2,000 Knockhill fine hasn't made any difference to him"* fumed the Scot but Harvey countered *"John was well out of order. He just pushed me out and I clipped his back bumper"*. Simoni then touched Soper on his way to the third but the clip also resulted in Menu getting past. The two bumps allowed the front two to get away but on the second lap Tarquini, released from the need to ensure finishing in the points, was prepared to take chances to finish the season off in style. His bravado, however, proved to be his undoing as he went off at Old Hairpin. With Radisich apparently out of reach, Menu was desperate to at least take third and he pushed past Simoni at the end of the

Round Twenty – Race Placings

Pos	Driver	Car	Time	Diff	Grid	
1	P. Radisich	Ford Mondeo Ghia	30'26.79	–	2	
2	A. Menu	Renault Laguna	–	3.90s	5	
3	G. Simoni	Alfa Romeo 155TS	–	10.09s	4	
4	J. Winkelhock	BMW 318i	–	12.33s	1	
5	T. Harvey	Renault Laguna	–	24.57s	6	
6	J. Bailey	Toyota Carina E	–	26.90s	10	
7	P. Watts	Peugeot 405 Mi16	–	28.55s	9	
8	J. Cleland	Vauxhall Cavalier 16v	–	35.12s	7	
9	J. Allam	Vauxhall Cavalier 16v	–	35.88s	15	
10	R. Rydell	Volvo 850 SE/GLT 2.0	–	38.70s	12	
11	R. Gravett	Ford Mondeo Ghia	–	38.70s	16	
12	S. Soper	BMW 318i	–	41.43s	3	
13	J. Lammers	Volvo 850 SE/GLT 2.0	–	42.50s	14	
14	C. Goodwin	Vauxhall Cavalier 16v	–	57.91s	20	
15	T. Needell	Nissan Primera 2.0 eGT	–	60.49s	19	
16	J. Thompson	Peugeot 405 Mi16	–	61.25s	21	
17	J. Kaye	Toyota Carina E	–	61.71s	22	
18	W. Hoy	Toyota Carina E	–	75.39s	13	
19	T. Sugden	Toyota Carina E	–	93.39s	17	
20	A. Rouse	Ford Mondeo Ghia	–	1 lap down	11	
21	H. Irvine	BMW 318is	–	1 lap down	25	
22	K. O'dor	Nissan Primera 2.0 eGT	–	2 laps down	18	
23	N. Smith	Vauxhall Cavalier 16v	–	3 laps down	23	

Did Not Finish

–	N. Albon	Renault 19 16v	–	3 laps	24	Accident
–	G. Tarquini	Alfa Romeo 155TS	–	1 lap	8	Spin

Fastest Lap: P. Radisich – 1'40.50 (89.55mph)   ***Average Speed of Winner:*** 88.68mph

Simoni

second circuit which, if the positions remained the same, would take the two second place contenders into the last race dead level.

A mistake from Winkelhock, also at Old Hairpin, saw him onto the grass from which he emerged fourth behind Radisich, Menu and Simoni whilst the BMW team's day worsened when Soper's fuel pump began missing, dropping him to nineteenth. By the time he got the problem sorted out, Soper was out of contention despite passing no fewer than seven cars to get back up to twelfth place by the finish. Rouse, in his penultimate race, then went broadside into Hoy and forced the Ford man to stop. When he returned to the fray, he quickly allowed teammate Radisich through which gave Rouse the chance to defend Radisich's position from Menu. By the time the Swiss driver managed to overtake Rouse, Radisich was clear and could afford to ease up before crossing the line. With Menu second, it meant that the two of them went into the final race of the campaign on 204 points apiece to set up a straight shoot-out.

In the Total Cup, leader Kaye was third but was denied the title by Albon being shunted out by Sugden early in the race which allowed Smith to coast round after a pit stop to claim eight points, albeit three laps down which reduced Kaye's lead to 20 points with 24 to drive for in the second race.

Round Twentyone – 18 laps

Radisich's chances disappeared on the formation lap when his car's six cylinders were reduced to five and, although the problem was cured, it was only done so at the penalty of the Kiwi having to start from the pit lane, effectively putting the runners-up spot in the hands of Menu barring a retirement. So when Simoni made a powerful start, Menu did not respond, knowing that all he virtually had to do was finish in the points to take runners-up spot. If Menu didn't have to take any chances, neither did Tarquini and he enjoyed himself starting from the back of the field after his first race demise. The Champion put on a memorable display to be up to fifth by the end of the twelfth lap with a fourth place his final destiny.

Radisich, too, had some motoring to do after eventually setting off some thirty seconds behind the field. He obviously could not hope to catch Menu and his strategy had to be to capture at least a single point and then hope that some misfortune befell his Swiss rival. With a clear road in front of him, Radisich soon set a lap record to help him close on the rest of the field. He would, in fact, become the last man to overtake Andy Rouse in a BTCC race to take two points as the Ford man's last race at least had the consolation of one final point for tenth place. Up front, however, Menu was not making any errors and, with the second place man playing safe, Simoni made the best of the situation to record his first BTCC victory in the last race of the season. Indeed, the Italian's victory was only the second major success of his career, the first being an Italian F3 victory at Magione in 1992.

With Menu's success in outscoring Radisich, the Manufacturers' runners-up spot went to Renault in front of Ford, BMW and Vauxhall. In the Total Cup, Smith's outside chance of catching the Championship leader, Kaye, quickly disappeared when, in an understandable hurry, he put his car on the grass after a spin. This gifted the title and the £25,000 first prize for the Privateer's Cup to Kaye who couldn't help but comment on how even the Privateer's competition has come on by leaps and bounds, saying *"The last time I won this title, I was given a coat but Total's sponsorship has ensured that it has become a prestigious event within the overall series"*.

So, the curtain came down on yet another exceptional Autotrader BTCC Championship. ◼

Round Twentyone – Race Placings

Pos	Driver	Car	Time	Diff	Grid	
1	G. Simoni	Alfa Romeo 155TS	30'30.75	–	3	
2	Al. Menu	Renault Laguna	–	3.13s	2	
3	J. Winkelhock	BMW 318i	–	8.20s	4	
4	G. Tarquini	Alfa Romeo 155TS	–	11.41s	25	
5	J. Cleland	Vauxhall Cavalier 16V	–	18.24s	8	
6	J. Bailey	Toyota Carina E	–	18.73s	6	
7	W. Hoy	Toyota Carina E	–	19.27s	18	
8	T. Harvey	Renault Laguna	–	20.29s	5	
9	P. Radisich	Ford Mondeo Ghia	–	20.38s	1	
10	A. Rouse	Ford Mondeo Ghia	–	22.14s	20	
11	P. Watts	Peugeot 405 Mi16	–	24.64s	7	
12	R. Rydell	Volvo 850 SE/GLT 2.0	–	27.84s	10	
13	J. Allam	Vauxhall Cavalier 16V	–	28.85s	9	
14	T. Sugden	Toyota Carina E	–	33.39s	19	
15	T. Needell	Nissan Primera 2.0 eGT	–	42.08s	15	
16	J. Lammers	Volvo 850 SE/GLT 2.0	–	45.88s	13	
17	J. Kaye	Toyota Carina E	–	53.19s	17	
18	K. O'dor	Nissan Primera 2.0 eGT	–	53.99s	22	
19	J. Thompson	Peugeot 405 Mi16	–	56.05s	16	
20	N. Smith	Vauxhall Cavalier 16V	–	56.67s	23	
21	C. Goodwin	Vauxhall Cavalier 16V	–	61.18s	14	
22	N. Albon	Renault 19 16v	–	91.22s	24	
23	H. Irvine	BMW 318is	–	1 lap down	21	

Did Not Finish

–	S. Soper	BMW 318i	–	4 laps	12	Gears
–	R. Gravett	Ford Mondeo Ghia	–	2 laps	11	Accident

Fastest Lap: P. Radisich – 1'39.89 (90.09mph)

Average Speed of Winner: 88.48mph

"Smoking" Tim Sugden locks it up!

Review

Alfa ruled the roost in another frenetic packed season which was packed with controversy and large crowds!

The all-conquering Alfa Romeo 155 TS of Gabriele Tarquini.

Once again, the BTCC proved that it has the package the fans want with over 420,000 turning out to watch the 1994 Championship. This represented an increase of some 30% over the previous year and an amazing upturn of 70% over 1992. Alan Gow, Managing Director of TOCA, said *"These figures underline the spiralling popularity of the AutoTrader British Touring Car Championship. It now regularly draws crowds of more than 25,000 which puts it on a par with FA Premiership football and Test Match cricket".* Certainly it is packed with action and with its increasing television coverage can only gain further appeal.

In the early part of the season, BTCC bore a striking resemblance to Formula One with the Alfa Romeo's dominance threatened only by the authorities claiming *foul* in much the same way that FIA levelled matters in F1 off the track by penalising Benetton. Just as Schumacher's lead in F1 was reduced from overwhelming to one that could be overtaken, so was Tarquini's in the BTCC. With the pot of money that the Italians were prepared to throw at taking the title, they were always going to be favourites, but after winning the first four races, Tarquini already had twice as many points on the board (96) as his nearest challenger, John Cleland. He took the fifth race at Silverstone as well, but in the second of that afternoon's races came the first glimmer of hope for his rivals when the Italian was hit amidships by an innocent O'dor. Tarquini's lead was now only 42 points!

By Round Seven at Oulton Park, the row over the homologation of the Alfas was reaching a cli-

Drivers – Final Placings

Drivers' Points

298	G. Tarquini	27	R. Rydell
222	A. Menu	20	K. O'dor
206	P. Radisich	18	J. Lammers
177	J. Cleland	15	E. O'Brien
156	G. Simoni	10	R. Ravaglia
147	J. Winkelhock	9	T. Sugden
102	S. Soper	6	D. Leslie
98	P. Watts	3	T. Needell
76	J. Allam	2	E. van de Poele
75	T. Harvey	1	M. Neal
66	A. Rouse	1	J. Thompson
65	J. Bailey	1	N. Smith
48	W. Hoy		

Constructors' Placings

Position	Points	Constructor
1st	330	Alfa Romeo
2nd	259	Renault
3rd	248	Ford
4th	242	BMW
5th	224	Vauxhall
6th	167	Peugeot
7th	137	Toyota
8th	103	Volvo
9th	69	Nissan
10th	31	Mazda

TOTAL Cup – Final

Position	Driver	Points
1st	J. Kaye	340
2nd	N. Smith	308
3rd	C. Goodwin	274
4th	J. Thompson	158
5th	N. Albon	108
6th	H. Irvine	108

max. The Italians had raced under appeal at both Snetterton and Silverstone and, at the latter track, Ford's Radisich tested with a front splitter fitted in the same style as the Alfa Romeo. He blasted round almost nine tenths of a second faster than when it was removed leaving Ford claiming that it proved beyond any doubt that the Italians were enjoying an unfair advantage. The Appeals committee agreed with Ford and told the Alfa management they could not run their cars without modifying them. The points won under appeal were withdrawn, the Italians went home without racing and Paul Radisich's second place at the Cheshire circuit put him in the lead by 36 points over Tarquini whose points total was now down to 72!

When Rounds Eight and Nine at Donington arrived, the position had shifted yet again with FIA now getting involved and appearing to say that the fracas all seemed to be a genuine misunderstanding of the regulations. Alfa would in future run in accordance with how the regulations had been meant to read but would not lose the points gained for the races won under appeal. Neither Alfa or Ford were happy but both accept-ed the situation. Strangely, after all this, the Alfas were again absent in Round Nine but on this occasion it was engine problems to both cars that put them out. So, with not having competed for totally different reasons in two races, Tarquini was now exactly level at the top of the leaderboard with Ford's Paul Radisich on 132 points.

Rounds Ten and Eleven at Brands Hatch appeared to virtually seal the title for Tarquini for, as he was making the best of his way home in both races to take 48 points, Radisich was experiencing a nightmare and failed to complete in either event. The next race, the British GP Support spectacular, threw an extra dimension into the equation with the decision to effectively reduce the BMW's weight penalty by 50kgs. The 1993 Champion, Jo Winkelhock, had not been able to compete on equal terms because of the penalty hitherto but now promptly took both pole and the actual race but Tarquini still increased his overall lead by finishing second to the German.

The entourage now moved north to Scotland, apart from the Mazda outfit who called it a day due to a lack of budget. Matt Neal had not raced since he wrapped his car up in May and David Leslie's unequal struggle was now at an end. The meeting signalled yet another turning point in the Championship with Tarquini crashing spectacularly in the first of the afternoon's races. Unable to continue in the second feature, the Italian was grateful to BMW's Steve Soper and Renault's Alain Menu for denying Radisich full points. However, the Kiwi's two second places at Knockhill reduced the deficit to just 18 points.

That, however, was the end of the road for Radisich in the BTCC, although he would have the ample compensation of taking the World title

Above: Round Twelve – O'Brien, Cleland and O'dor all know a man who can!

at Donington in October. The New Zealander would now remain pointless over the next five races, a period which would also see Tarquini with only one success. This was mainly due to the new dominance of the BMW as Jo Winkelhock took three races on the bounce. Tarquini, however, was still picking up points in second and his advantage soon gave him the Championship at the first attempt. Radisich's disastrous run even saw him lose second spot to Renault's Menu who became easily the most consistent driver in the later stages of the championship with 17 consecutive point scoring appearances after failing to get on the scoreboard in three of the first four!

Like Radisich, another to fade was John Cleland who, after harvesting 132 points in the first eleven races, mustered only a further 45 in the remaining ten. Patrick Watts suffered similarly with 85 points in the first twelve races before tailing off to finish with just 98 but he had done enough in his first season with Peugeot to warrant another crack in 1995. But what would have happened had the BMWs been allowed to run from the *off* with the reduced weight penalty allowed them for the second half of the campaign? Winkelhock picked up no fewer than 118 points in the last ten races whilst team mate Steve Soper also won a race giving the BMWs a 50% success rate in the last ten outings.

The Total Cup for the privateers went right down to the last race before James Kaye could claim his £25,000 prize following his tenth win of the campaign. He had been chased all the way by Nigel Smith in his HMSO backed Cavalier with this pair clear of Chris Goodwin who was bitterly disappointed not to have got the works drive with Vauxhall late in the season that he appeared to be being groomed for.

But, long after the dust has settled on Tarquini's and Alfa's Championship victories, 1994 will be remembered for another reason. It marked the final season for the most famous name in BTCC – Andy Rouse who, although he will be around masterminding Ford's efforts in future, signed off as a driver after 60 overall wins commenting *"60 seems to be about the right number to retire on, I don't think I would have made it to 65."* ◪

Le Mans

24-Hour Race

Le Mans, France – 18/19 June 1994

Before Le Mans, Derek Bell announced that his 24th start would be his last – again!

Emotions were running high for the 61st running of the most famous 24 hour race on the calender. It was Derek Bell's 24th and final start in the event and, whilst it was sad to say goodbye to the five times winner, it was the SARD Toyota of Eddie Irvine, Mauro Martini and Jeff Krosnoff that brought a tear to the eye as it hurtled round carrying the name of Roland Ratzenberger who would have been contesting his fourth Le Mans race with the team but for his ill-fated F1 crash at the San Marino GP six weeks earlier. Certainly Irvine, Martini and Krosnoff paid a fitting tribute to the Austrian as they took the car to within sight of ending Toyota's nineteen year wait for victory. With only an hour and a half of the race remaining and with Krosnoff at the wheel, the 94CV was in the lead only to come grinding to a halt as its gear selector developed a fault. Krosnoff nursed the stricken vehicle back to the pits where fast repairs got the car back on the track with Irvine at the controls but the stop of over twelve minutes had not only cost them the lead, they had dropped to third behind the two Dauer Porsches.

> *"To win the race with a GT car is quite extraordinary. I actually cried when we won. I've never, ever, done that before."*
> *– Max Welti*

The stop was to produce one of the most exciting finishes, albeit for second spot, in the history of the race as the man from Ulster set sail after Thierry Boutsen in the second of the Dauers although Dalmas was beyond recall in first place.

Race Placings

First named driver commenced race

Pos	No	Drivers	Car	Laps		Class
1	36	Baldi/Dalmas/Haywood	Dauer Porsche 962GT LM	344		LM GT1
2	1	Martini/Irvine/Krosnoff	SARD Toyota CV94	343		LMP1/C90
3	35	Stuck/Sullivan/Boutsen	Dauer Porsche 962GT LM	343		LM GT1
4	4	Wollek/Andskar/Fouche	Trust Toyota CV94	328		LMP1/C90
5	75	Millen/O'Connell/Morton	Cunningham Nissan 300ZX	317		IMSA GTS
6	5	D. Bell/Donovan/Lassig	Kramer Porsche CK8	316		LMP1/C90
7	9	Ricci/Evans/Olczyk	Courage C32 LM	310		LMP1/C90
8	52	Dupuy/Pareja/Palau	Larbre Porsche 911RSR	307		LM GT2
9	54	Calderari/Bryner/Mastropietro	Biennoise Porsche 911RSR	299		LMP1/C90
10	59	Euser/Huisman/Tomlje	Konrad Porsche 911RSR	295		LMP1/C90
11	57	Saldana/d'Orleans Borbon/Vilarino	Repsol Ferrari 348LM	276		LMP1/C90
12	40	Arnoux/J. Bell/Balas	Dodge Viper	273		LM GT1
13	60	Roy/Police/Galmard	Legeay Alpine A610	272		LM GT2
14	48	Hahne/Gachot/Bouchet	Kremer Honda NSX	257		LM GT2
15	74	Terada/de Thoisy/Freon	Artnature Mazda RX-7	250		IMSA GTS
16	46	Favre/Shimizu/Okada	Kremer Honda NSX	240		LM GT2
17	68	Sirera/Camp/Puig	Agusta Venturi 400LM	225		LM GT2
18	47	Takahashi/Tsuchiya/Iida	Kremer Honda NSX	222		LM GT2

Finished but Not Classified

	No	Drivers	Car	Laps		Class
–	41	Migault/Morin/Gache	Dodge Viper	225		LM GT1
–	30	Maury-Larybiere/Poulain/Chauvin	BBA Venturi 500LM	221		LM GT1
–	37	Chappell/Baker/Andrews	ADA de Tomaso Pantera	210		LM GT1
–	6	Harada/Yoshikawa/Kondo	ADA Porsche 962	189		LMP1/C90
–	65	Ratel/Chaufour/Hunkeler	Agusta Venturi 400LM	137		LM GT2

Did Not Finish

	No	Drivers	Car	Laps		Class
–	34	Cudini/Helary/Boullion	Bugatti EB110S	227	(24th hour)	LM GT1
–	55	Otha/Smith/"Stingbrace"	Simpson Ferrari 348LM	57	(12th hour)	LM GT2
–	31	Agusta/Coppelli/Krine	Agusta Venturi 600LM	115	(12th hour)	LM GT1
–	8	Bourdais/Couvreur/Minassian	Alpa LM	64	(12th hour)	LMP1/C90
–	38	M.Ferte/Neugarten/Grouillard	Jacadi Venturi 500LM	107	(12th hour)	LM GT1
–	7	Boulay/Robin/Lacaud	ALD C90	96	(12th hour)	LMP1/C90
–	21	Regout/Yvon/Libert	WR LM93	86	(11th hour)	LMP2
–	22	Gonin/Petit	WR LM93	104	(11th hour)	LMP2
–	59	Konrad/Sommer/Azevedo	Konrad Porsche 911RSR	100	(11th hour)	LM GT2
–	3	A.Ferte/Pescarolo/Lagorce	Courage C32 LM	142	(11th hour)	LMP1/C90
–	20	Santal/Tassier/Dro	Debora LMP294	79	(11th hour)	LMP2
–	63	Wilson/Hewland/Brodie	Harrier LR9	45	(11th hour)	LMP2
–	49	Laffite/JM.Almeras/J.Almeras	Porsche 911RSR	94	(10th hour)	LM GT2
–	2	Raphanel/Fabre/Robert	Courage C32 LM	107	(9th hour)	LMP1/C90
–	58	Bscher/Nielsen/Owen-Jones	Seikel Porsche 968	84	(9th hour)	LM GT2
–	29	Olofsson/della Noce/Angelastri	Obermaier Ferrari F40	51	(9th hour)	LM GT1
–	56	Haberthur/Gouselard/Vuillaume	Chicco D'Oro Porsche 911RSR	56	(8th hour)	LM GT2
–	61	Thyrring/Zwart/Fuchs	Lotus Sport Esprit 300	28	(7th hour)	LM GT2
–	62	Piper/Hardman/Iacobelli	Lotus Sport Esprit 300	59	(6th hour)	LM GT2
–	50	Yver/Leconte/Chereau	Larbre Porsche 911RSR	62	(6th hour)	LM GT2
–	45	Richter/Ebeling/Wiazik	Heico Porsche 911RSR	57	(6th hour)	LM GT2
–	64	Larrauri/Mancini/Gouhier	Repsol Ferrari 348LM	23	(5th hour)	LM GT2
–	66	Bellm/Nuttall/Rickett	Henriksen Porsche 911	34	(4th hour)	LM GT2
–	76	van de Poele/Kasuya/Gentilozzi	Cunningham Nissan 300ZX	25	(4th hour)	IMSA GTS

Disqualified

	No	Drivers	Car	Laps		Class
–	51	Said/Maisonneuve/Jeliski	Callaway Corvette	142	(14th hour)	LM GT2

Did Not Start

	No	Drivers	Car	Laps		Class
–	39	de Lesseps/Tropenat/Belmondo	Venturi 600LM	–		LM GT1

Did Not Qualify

	No	Drivers	Car	Laps		Class
–	53	Hugenholtz/Heinkele/Kuster	Magnani Lotus Sport Esprit 300	–	–	LM GT2

Fastest Lap: Thierry Boutsen – 3'52.54 (130.832mph)

Irvine restarted 14 seconds down on Boutsen and was handicapped by the lack of third gear but his opponent also had problems as he desperately needed a tyre change but couldn't afford the time with Irvine putting in five consecutive laps under four minutes. At the start of the penultimate circuit, the gap had shrunk to less than two seconds and by now Boutsen was in desperate need of tyres and a clear road. He couldn't afford to stop for the former and, just when he needed it most, he didn't get the latter as entering the Ford Chicane for the last time he came upon no fewer than three struggling back markers. Boutsen was forced to slow fractionally to get past and Irvine was up to him. As the cars emerged on to the straight, the Toyota's grip enabled it to slip into the lead and get over the line less than a car length in front after 24 hours of racing!

If they were disappointed to have lost out on a 1-2 by the smallest of margins, the Dauer Porsche driven by Mauro Baldi, Yannick Dalmas and Hurley Haywood gave team boss Max Welti the great satisfaction of winning the overall race with a GT car. As he celebrated the 13th victory of a Porsche at Le Mans, Welti said *"To win the race with a GT car is quite extraordinary. I actually cried when we won. I've never, ever, done that before"*. The car had never been out of the top six and had been second for four of the first six hours until Dalmas ran out of fuel approaching the pits. This delay, coupled with a replacement driveshaft being required, dropped the car back to sixth from where it gradually made progress throughout the night. By the end of the fourteenth hour, the eventual winning car was in third place behind its sister vehicle and when Boutsen experienced a broken wishbone at Mulsanne immediately after setting the fastest lap time, Baldi and Co were up to second which became first when Krosnoff had the wind taken out of his sails with his gear selector fault.

Bell, meanwhile, starting from second place on the grid was allowed to take the cars over the startline and led for the first half lap of his final appearance before quickly dropping to motor round in eighth or ninth place for six hours or so. The car suffered so badly from a vibration problem which eventually caused the mirrors to become merely blurs that the rear wing had to be

Class Winners

Class	Drivers	Overall
LMP1/C90	Martini/Irvine/Krosnoff	2
LMP2	No finishers	–
LMGT1	Baldi/Dalmas/Haywood	1
LM GT2	Dupuy/Pareja/Palau	8
IMSA GTS	Millen/O'Connell/Morton	5

replaced and then the throttle stuck in the *open* position as Bell braked into Indianapolis, one of the sharpest corners on the circuit in the middle of the night. Being thrown all over, Bell managed to switch the engine off but then had no lights on restarting it. The lights were to be a constant source of trouble until daylight broke and the dismal run of pit stops they caused put paid to any serious challenge being mounted by Bell or his colleagues. The Briton, however, was given a standing ovation on climbing into the Porsche K8 for his final stint at the wheel as he brought his distinguished career to an end with a highly creditable sixth place. Bell, who won the race three times with Jackie Ickz and twice with Hans Stuck, was adamant that this was his farewell, quoting the fatal accidents in F1 as the deciding factor. *"How many more miles have I driven than Ayrton Senna? I must have driven more miles than anybody else still racing and it makes you think"*.

Of the other cars, the Trust Toyota looked as likely to win the race as did its SARD counterpart. Indeed, for much of the first half of the race, the two cars swopped places at the head of events in accordance with their pit stops. When the SARD Toyota stopped at around midnight to bleed their brake system, the Trust car assumed a comfortable lead until a succession of pit stops to investigate rear end vibration and a delay of an hour to fit a new drivetrain dropped it back to fifth and out of all contention before coming back well to take fourth spot ahead of one of the Cunningham Nissan 300ZXs which had arrived at Le Mans very much favoured as a dark horse for outright victory. The American driving team of Steve Millen, Johnny O'Connell and John Morton were trying for a unique endurance treble having earlier secured victory at both Daytona and Sebring but during warm up it was the second 300ZX that set the track alight when Paul Gentilozzi had to eject swiftly due to an electrical fire! Whilst the first car experienced a good run, however, the second car became the race's first retirement due basically to the damage the earlier fire had caused. With the car low on power and a long way behind after only four hours a decision to withdraw was taken. Meanwhile, Morton had to do most of the driving in the first car as O'Connell felt unwell and Millen, having had his crash helmets stolen, found the borrowed replacement too tight. Despite these setbacks, the car was comfortable in fourth at the 20 hour mark but a pit stop of 25 minutes to have a new camshaft fitted was enough to drop it to fifth where it stayed until the end of the race well ahead of the only other finisher in the IMSA GTS Class, an Artnature Mazda RX-7 of 1990 vintage.

The local French Courage cars had entered with high hopes but both of its lead vehicles were out of the contest inside the first eight hours despite Alain Ferte taking pole position during

Hour by Hour Positions

Pos/hour	1	2	3	4	5	6	7	8	9	10	11	12	13	14	15	16	17	18	19	20	21	22	23	24
1	35	35	1	1	4	4	4	1	4	4	4	4	4	1	1	1	1	1	1	1	1	1	36	36
2	1	36	36	36	36	1	1	4	35	1	1	1	1	35	35	36	36	36	36	36	36	36	35	1
3	4	1	4	4	1	2	35	35	1	35	35	35	35	36	36	35	35	35	35	35	35	35	1	35
4	2	4	2	3	35	35	2	2	2	2	2	36	36	36	75	75	75	75	75	75	4	4	4	4
5	36	2	3	3	3	2	36	36	36	75	75	75	5	4	4	4	4	4	4	4	75	75	75	75
6	3	3	35	35	2	36	36	75	75	75	5	52	52	52	34	52	5	5	6	5	5	5	5	5
7	75	75	75	75	75	75	75	3	5	5	52	34	34	34	5	5	52	52	9	9	9	9	9	9
8	76	5	5	5	5	5	34	52	52	52	34	5	5	5	52	9	9	9	52	52	52	52	52	52
9	5	33	29	51	52	51	51	5	51	34	54	54	54	9	9	54	54	54	54	54	54	54	54	54
10	38	29	52	52	33	52	52	34	34	9	51	9	9	54	54	34	59	59	59	59	59	59	59	59
11	33	51	59	33	51	74	33	51	9	51	9	30	30	30	30	30	30	30	40	57	57	57	57	57
12	51	52	33	74	74	33	5	6	74	54	30	59	59	59	59	59	34	40	57	40	40	40	40	40
13	29	59	45	6	34	34	6	54	54	30	59	40	40	68	68	68	68	34	40	60	60	60	60	60
14	48	66	51	45	6	6	74	74	6	74	40	68	68	40	40	40	40	57	60	30	74	74	74	48
15	66	50	50	29	50	54	54	9	30	40	68	51	74	74	74	57	57	60	34	74	48	48	48	74
16	52	45	74	50	59	59	49	38	38	59	74	60	57	60	60	60	60	68	74	68	30	30	46	46
17	50	74	6	34	49	49	38	30	40	68	60	57	60	57	57	74	74	74	68	48	68	46	34	68
18	59	48	54	54	54	30	9	33	68	48	74	51	6	6	6	6	6	6	48	34	34	68	41	41
19	54	54	47	59	58	58	30	49	59	6	57	48	6	48	48	48	48	48	46	46	46	41	30	47
20	49	47	34	49	9	38	59	68	33	60	31	6	48	46	46	46	46	46	6	41	41	34	68	30
21	64	61	49	58	30	30	40	58	40	60	57	6	31	41	41	41	41	41	47	6	47	47	47	37
22	34	6	9	62	57	9	40	59	48	38	38	41	47	47	47	47	47	47	41	47	6	37	37	6
23	45	49	57	48	38	68	68	48	57	21	46	46	46	37	37	37	37	37	37	37	37	6	6	65
24	47	65	58	57	48	48	48	60	21	31	41	38	37	65	65	65	65	65	65	65	65	65	65	
25	8	34	40	60	40	57	47	47	49	33	7	47	65											
26	74	31	21	9	62	47	60	57	31	46	47	37												
27	61	57	48	40	68	60	57	58	47	7	37	8												
28	60	76	60	30	60	31	31	21	22	47	8	55												
29	57	58	62	68	45	21	21	31	46	41	55	65												
30	62	60	30	38	47	7	7	22	7	22	65													
31	65	40	68	21	31	22	46	7	41	20														
32	31	30	66	47	29	46	22	46	20	8														
33	40	62	63	31	21	29	41	41	8	37														
34	58	34	38	63	7	41	29	20	37	55														
35	6	63	56	7	22	56	20	8	63	63														
36	55	68	61	56	46	63	8	29	55	65														
37	30	9	31	8	63	20	56	37	65															
38	63	21	7	46	56	8	63	63																
39	68	38	8	22	41	61	37	55																
40	21	8	65	61	8	65	65	65																
41	22	22	76	41	61	37	55																	
42	7	56	37	65	20	55																		
43	9	7	64	37	65																			
44	41	37	22	64	37																			
45	37	46	41	55	55																			
46	56	55	46	20																				
47	46	41	55																					
48	20	20	20																					

Notes
Refer to race result details for number of car.
Read down for race position and across for hours completed.

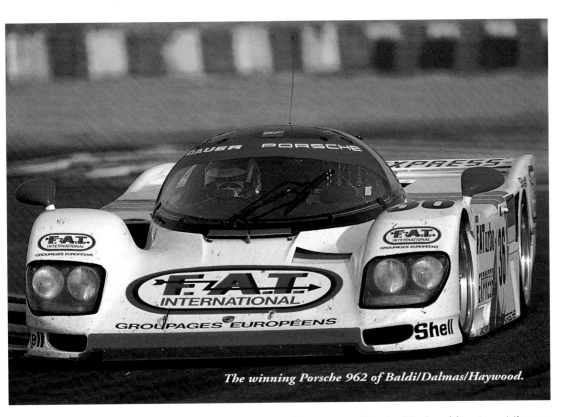

The winning Porsche 962 of Baldi/Dalmas/Haywood.

qualifying, leaving just the third entry to motor on. In this car, Andy Evans showed remarkable endurance having jetted home to the States on the Thursday to see to some personal business before arriving back at Le Mans in time to see team mate Jean-Louise Ricci start the race. Ricci, however, was soon in trouble with an unscheduled stop in the gravel on lap two which necessitated a pit stop to clear the dirt out of the system. This, in turn, resulted in a time penalty being imposed as more than four mechanics were spotted working on the car at the same time. With Olczyk also visiting the gravel and a new starter motor being required, the car did well to finish seventh.

The all Japanese driving team of Harada, Yoshikawa and Kondo could have done with an interpreter as Harada was forced to start in last place from the pits despite having qualified in 13th spot on the grid when he mislaid his gloves and couldn't find them in time for the parade lap whilst Yoshikawa radioed in during the night that she was stranded at the Dunlop chicane when, in fact, she was at Mulsanne! Further language difficulties were experienced as instructions were

given to cure the electrical problem to get the car started and back to the pit for attention. A cracked cylinder head was the next problem which put the ADA Porsche 962 out of the race – or so it seemed but the Japanese are a persistent lot and the car reappeared with just fifteen minutes left to be still running at the finish. Another motor to come out for the formality of being able to say it completed was the Ratel/Chaufour/Hunkeler driven Austa Venturi 400LM which was out of the race from 18:00 until 03:45 from when it lapped at about six circuits per hour before spending most of Sunday in the pits prior to rolling out as flag time approached.

But if Derek Bell's last appearance brought a sad farewell, spare a thought for the Callaway Corvette of Boris Said, Michel Maisonneuve, and Frank Jelinski. They led the LM GT2 Class from the start until the early hours of Sunday morning when it ran out of fuel at Indianapolis and was got going again by adding the contents of a fuel can in direct contravention of the rules and was disqualified! ❖

Formula 3
Grand Prix
year

Preview...

Expanding grids and three new teams helped boost the series after some years in the doldrums.

With both F1 and Touring Car racing continuing to dominate public interest in British motor racing, F3 has taken something of a back seat in recent years. Although Italy enjoyed a 60 strong competition in 1993 and the German equivalent also attracted a healthy number of entrants, the British 1993 F3 Championship had seen just twelve competitors commence the Class A series. Fortunately for 1994 this number was almost doubled to 22 brought about, in the main, by the introduction of three new outfits.

Having helped Fiat's first entry into British F3 in 1993, Warren Hughes, the most experienced F3 driver in the competition would now be debuting the TOM's Toyota whilst Renault chose West Surrey Racing to mastermind the entrance of two cars under the Racing for Spain banner with Ivan Arias and Pedro de la Rosa driving. The third newcomers were Mitsubishi who based themselves with Alan Docking Racing and named ex-Formula Ford competitor, Marc Gene as driver. On the chassis front, Reynard had opted to take a season off leaving only the Toyota's not using Dallara F394's whilst Mugen were the most numeric of engines. Paul Stewart Racing would be using both as it commenced its attempt to land a hat-trick of Championships. The surprise from PSR was their failure to name an experienced F3 man as a driver to replace 1993 Champion Kelvin Burt who had moved on to higher things. Team Manager Andy Miller, however, announced he was more than happy with the selection of Dane Jan Magnussen, and Dario Franchitti, the 1993 Formula Vauxhall Champion. Events were to confirm his thoughts.

The biggest challenge to the Mugen engines in 1993 came from Edenbridge Racing who used Vauxhall. Edenbridge secured five successes in 1993 and their drivers in 1994 would be the Brazilian pairing of Marcos Gueiros and Luiz Garcia Jnr. Also using Vauxhall in 1994 would be DAW Racing with South African Garth Waberski making his debut. The main challenge, however, to the recent PSR domination of F3 was expected to come from another Mugen powered outfit in West Surrey Racing where Dick Bennetts was predicting big things for Belgian Vincent Radermecker, another recruit from Formula Vauxhall/Opel. He would be joined by Gualter Salles who had some F3 experience in 1993 at Edenbridge. Another expected to mount a serious challenge to PSR was Gareth Rees who had switched from Fortec to Alan Docking Racing. The 1992 Vauxhall Euroseries winner had had a disappointing 1993 but looked likely to be more competitive in the "Docs" Dallara than he had been in Fortec's Reynard. Fortec meanwhile, anxious to prove their two 1992 debut season victories were no flash in the pan, turned to youngsters Jeremie Dufour and Christian Horner and the Frenchman, in particular, was not to let them down.

With a new points system rewarding all top ten finishers, the Championship seemed wide open. Then the actual racing began and Mr Magnussen had something to say about the title heading anywhere else other than to himself and PSR. ▰

Silverstone

Round One – 27 March 1994

Dario Franchitti started the campaign as though he meant to carry on in the footsteps of the previous Paul Stewart Racing drivers, Gil de Ferran and Kelvin Burt, who had finished up as Champions. He took pole position, having jumped from fifth in the final session, for the first race on the calender and was never headed. The other PSR driver, Jan Magnussen, was in fourth after failing to appear in the second session following a crash five minutes from the end of the first session. The qualifying was so tight that Gareth Rees was in third on 55.51secs with Jeremy Dufour ninth on 55.66 secs. Renault entered British Formula Three with two cars racing under the Racing for Spain banner with Ivan Arias and Pedro de la Rosa driving.

The race saw Franchitti almost relinquish his pole position when he virtually stalled at the start but nobody behind was quick enough to seize on the error and the cars went into Copse in grid order. Magnussen and Rees both went past Lakin as he slid wide at Becketts but these tussles were allowing Franchitti to open up some leeway. Cunningham managed what Franchitti had almost achieved and stalled at the start to leave himself last whilst Cotterill and Salles touched at Becketts resulting in Cotterill's retirement after completing six laps. Up front Lakin regained second by going past Rees on lap two and then Magnussen on lap three, both manoevres coming at Brooklands. Lap seven saw the hopes of Warren Hughes disappear when he nudged Gueiros which dropped Hughes to fourteenth from eighth and the Geordie eventually retired near the end of the race from the damage sustained. Lakin, meanwhile, was reducing Franchitti's lead of about a second by one tenth each circuit until lap ten when his car developed gear change problems and effectively put paid to a close finish.

An enthralling battle had developed, however, for the minor placings with Radermecker and Morelli going at it nip and tuck until their two cars collided at Woodcote on lap ten. Morelli lost his front wing and finished last, seven laps behind the winner. The nineteenth lap saw the makings of a nasty accident when Xavier's engine blew and dropped oil. He spun and was met head on by Ivan Arias but miraculously neither driver was hurt. The top places were all held to the finish as everybody settled for what they had got whilst the Class B event was easily taken by Duncan Vercoe. ⚑

Race Placings – Round One (25 laps)

Pos	Driver	Time	Diff	Pos	Driver	Time	Diff
1	D. Franchitti	23'29.76	–	18	S. Allen*	24 laps	–
2	S. Lakin	23'32.06	2.3s	19	P. Dawson*	24 laps	–
3	J. Magnussen	23'34.98	5.22s	20	C. Lazarakis*	24 laps	–
4	G. Rees	23'36.12	6.36s	21	D. Morelli	18 laps	–
5	S. Arnold	23'36.69	6.93s				
6	V. Radermecker	23'37.68	7.92s	**Failed to Finish**			
7	J. Dufour	23'41.48	11.72s	–	W. Hughes	23 laps	accident
8	M. Gueiros	23'44.17	14.41s	–	C. Horner	22 laps	accident
9	R. Rosset	23'46.60	16.84s	–	R. Xavier	19 laps	accident
10	G. Salles	23'47.30	17.54s	–	I. Arias	19 laps	accident
11	B. Cunningham	23'57.41	27.65s	–	C. Clark*	14 laps	spin
12	L. Garcia Jnr	23'58.64	28.88s	–	J. Cotterill	6 laps	accident
13	S. Watson	24'02.23	32.47s				
14	G. Waberski	24'03.17	33.41s	**Fastest Laps:**			
15	D. Vercoe*	24.04.40	34.64s	A	V. Radermecker	55.60s	106.76mph
16	P. de la Rosa	24'10.07	40.31s	B	D. Vercoe	56.65s	104.79mph
17	G. Hedley*	24 laps	–	*Denotes Class B competitors.			

Donington

Round Two – 10 April 1994

The Paul Stewart Racing team stamped their authority on the British Formula Three scene when Jan Magnussen emulated team mate Dario Franchitti's Silverstone win by taking Round Two with a convincing margin to spare. Franchitti, in turn, occupied third place as Magnussen had in the opener to leave the two PSR drivers locked together on 32 points. The Dane declared his intent in the second qualifying session when he clocked 1'30.15, almost half a second better than Luiz Garcia Jnr as between them, PSR and Edenbridge monopolised the first four grid positions. Jeremy Dufour, who had finished seventh in the Round One, hit the Coppice tyre wall which resulted in him sustaining a wrist injury that prevented him participating in the actual race itself whilst reigning Class B champion, Jamie Spence, was supposed to be making his Class A debut only to find his Fred Goddard Dallara F394 was not quite ready and a decision not to race was taken after Spence had qualified in 21st spot.

Just as Renault had entered British Formula Three at Silverstone for the first time in the opening round, so did Mitsubishi at Donington with young Spanish driver, Marc Gene, also making his debut in the Formula. Class B performer Duncan Vercoe qualified in front of seven Class A competitors to underline his dominance of the subsidiary competition.

Having struggled at the start of the First Round race, Dario Franchitti again experienced difficulties this time round and dropped to fifth from third. Gueiros, however, had an even worse time of it, touching team mate Garcia on the first circuit at McLeans before rolling. The car was badly damaged but the driver unhurt. Up front, Magnussen wasn't hanging around and made the most of pole by building an astonishing lead of over two seconds at the end of the first tour. By the end of the second circuit, PSR were sitting back enjoying a one-two as Franchitti fought back but there was a massive five seconds between the two cars.

Xavier's engine blew for the second race in succession and the oil dropped proved to be Clark's undoing as he crashed after completing seven laps. Waberski also couldn't handle the oil slick and came off on both lap eight and for the second and last time on lap sixteen. Franchitti, meanwhile, was making little impression on team mate Magnussen and lost second spot on lap 17 when he had two wheels on the grass to allow Garcia through.

Race Placings – Round Two (20 laps)

Pos	Driver	Time	Diff	Pos	Driver	Time	Diff
1	J. Magnussen	30'33.68	–	18	P. Dawson*	19 laps	–
2	L. Garcia Jnr	30'36.03	2.35s		**Failed to Finish**		
3	D. Franchitti	30'36.35	2.67s	–	G. Waberski	15 laps	spin
4	S. Lakin	30'43.15	9.47s	–	M. dos Santos	15 laps	spin
5	G. Rees	30'44.50	10.82s	–	S. Allen	12 laps	spin
6	S. Arnold	30'57.42	23.74s	–	R. Xavier	7 laps	engine
7	D. Morelli	31'03.01	29.33s	–	C. Clark	7 laps	spin
8	B. Cunningham	31'03.33	29.65s	–	V. Radermecker	1 lap	spin
9	S. Watson	31'07.64	33.96s	–	M. Gueiros	–	accident
10	R. Rosset	31'07.99	34.31s	–	J. Dufour	Did not start	
11	P. de la Rosa	31'10.01	36.42s				
12	G. Salles	31'22.85	49.17s		**Fastest Laps:**		
13	M. Gene	31'28.21	54.53s	A	L. Garcia Jnr	1'30.56	99.38mph
14	C. Horner	31'31.71	58.03s	B	D. Vercoe	1'31.80	98.03mph
15	I. Arias	31'32.58	58.90s	*Denotes Class B competitors.*			
16	D. Vercoe*	31'42.81	69.13s				
17	G. Hedley*	19 laps	–				

Brands Hatch Indy

Rounds Three and Four – 24 April 1994

Round Three – 15 laps

For the first time in British Formula Three the crowds at Brands Hatch witnessed a double header, a bill which was to benefit Magnussen and Radermecker in particular. Indeed, Rees, Dufour and Gueiros also would have appreciated the change to two races as they added plenty of points to their tally. Two who wouldn't have thought much of the idea were Lakin and Franchitti, neither of whom could muster a solitary point between them despite commencing the day in two of the top three Championship positions.

Qualifying saw an all Paul Stewart Racing front row whilst Jamie Spence, the Class B Champion finally making his bow in Class A, lined up in eleventh. Vercoe again demonstrated his Class B superiority by being quicker than no fewer than ten Class A contestants. But the main drama was still to unfold as Franchitti's car failed to fire and although the PSR camp got it going, it was after the five minute board and he was off the front row and on the back! His team mate, Jan Magnussen, however, did start as scheduled and once again pulled away to make the most of his pole position. The best first lap though was achieved by Warren Hughes who was up to eighth from 17th after just the one circuit but he was not to make any further progress throughout the remainder of the race. The three points for this achievement, however, were the first for March Racing Organisation's Ralt.

Franchitti, meanwhile, was making up his lost ground and had moved into 14th but on the eighth tour he clipped the kerb at Paddock resulting in a broken ballpoint in the front right suspension and no points which dropped him from joint first to fourth in the overall standings. Roberto Xavier, whose engine had blown in each of the two previous rounds, didn't give it chance this time when he collided as early as the third lap with Ivan Arias forcing the retirement of both machines. Having seen nearest Championship rival Franchitti disappear from the race, Magnussen's cause was then helped further when his next nearest challenger in the title race, Scott Lakin also retired. His problem had arisen when he hit Salles on lap four and he eventually gave up the unequal struggle after completing 12 laps presumably to give his team more time to complete necessary repairs for the second race.

Race Placings – Round Three (15 laps)

Pos	Driver	Time	Diff	Pos	Driver	Time	Diff
1	J. Magnussen	10'49.23	–	18	M. Gene	11'21.16	31.93s
2	V. Radermecker	10'50.33	1.10s	19	G. Hedley*	11'23.38	34.15s
3	G. Rees	10'51.33	2.10s	20	S. Watson	11'31.26	42.03
4	J. Dufour	10'51.89	2.66s	21	P. Dawson*	14 laps	–
5	M. Gueiros	10'52.06	2.83s	22	S. Allen*	14 laps	–
6	R. Rosset	10'53.00	3.77s				
7	J. Spence	10'53.75	4.52s	**Failed to Finish**			
8	W. Hughes	10'57.02	7.79s	–	S. Lakin	12 laps	accident
9	G. Salles	10'59.87	10.64s	–	D. Franchitti	8 laps	suspension
10	L. Garcia Jnr	11'00.06	10.83s	–	I. Arias	2 laps	accident
11	B. Cunningham	11'01.84	12.61s	–	R. Xavier	2 laps	accident
12	G. Waberski	11'02.52	13.29s	–	D. Morelli	Did not start	
13	S. Arnold	11'02.64	13.41s				
14	C. Horner	11'04.07	14.84s	**Fastest Laps:**			
15	D. Vercoe*	11'05.42	16.19s	A	J. Magnussen	42.48 secs	102.00mph
16	P. de la Rosa	11'05.73	16.50s	B	D. Vercoe	43.14 secs	100.43mph
17	C. Clark*	11'21.05	31.82s	*Denotes Class B competitors.			

Magnussen came home unchallenged with Radermecker equally secure in second. Rees, Dufour and Gueiros in the next three positions were, however, covered by less than three quarters of a second whilst Spence claimed his first Class A points in seventh. Vercoe slaughtered his Class B opposition coming home a whopping 15 seconds clear of Clark.

Round Four – 15 laps

The second race over the Brands Indy circuit saw Waberski stall on the line but Radermecker had no such trouble and got a real flyer to head Magnussen with Hughes also getting away to an excellent start going into fourth from eighth spot on the grid. Druids witnessed Magnussen try to regain the lead but as he tried to dive inside Radermecker, the Belgian closed the gap and a mighty shunt occurred which left the Dane with a damaged wing to nurse home if he was to score points. Salles also spun at Druids on the same lap which put him amongst the back runners whilst Franchitti's unhappy weekend continued when he tangled with Horner, again at Druids, on lap six. Meanwhile, Rees had overtaken the slowing Magnussen and was chasing Radermecker hard whilst lap seven witnessed Dufour also going past Magnussen. The race then took a rest for a couple of laps when Garcia struck into De La Rosa on lap nine and with the car in a dangerous position, the Clerk of the Course had no hesitation in calling for the pace car.

Vital laps ticked by for those intent on making headway and by the time the pace car pulled off there were just three laps left by which time Hughes was out of the race due to low fuel pressure. Magnussen was by now having great trouble with his engine overheating but he managed to nurse it home as Radermecker hung on to his lead to become the first driver from outside the Paul Stewart Racing stable to win a 1994 Round. Rees followed him home to add a third to his first race second whilst Dufour added a third to his earlier fourth leaving Gueiros to double up his fifth placings. Spence, on his debut day, improved from seventh to sixth whilst Class B competitor, Duncan Vercoe finished an overall eighth to make it a maximum in all four races to date leaving him a massive 30 points clear of Hedley in that Class.

Jan Magnussen.

Race Placings – Round Four (15 laps)

Pos	Driver	Time	Diff
1	V. Radermecker	12'52.20	–
2	G. Rees	12'52.78	0.58s
3	J. Dufour	12'53.10	0.90s
4	J. Magnussen	12'53.26	1.06s
5	M. Gueiros	12'53.55	1.35s
6	J. Spence	12'55.26	3.06s
7	B. Cunningham	12'56.12	3.92s
8	D. Vercoe*	12'59.01	6.81s
9	P. de la Rosa	13'00.00	7.80s
10	R. Rosset	13'00.33	8.13s
11	S. Watson	13'01.56	9.36s
12	M. Gene	13'01.96	9.76s
13	I. Arias	13'02.59	10.39s
14	S. Lakin	13'02.97	10.77s
15	R. Xavier	13'03.79	11.59s
16	C. Clark*	13'06.91	14.71s
17	G. Salles	13'08.02	15.82s
18	G. Hedley*	13'11.17	18.97s
19	S. Allen*	13'11.47	19.27s
20	P. Dawson*	13'11.70	19.50s

Failed to Finish

Pos	Driver	Time	Diff
–	W. Hughes	11 laps	mechanical
–	S. Arnold	9 laps	mechanical
–	L. Garcia Jnr	8 laps	spin
–	C. Horner	5 laps	accident
–	D. Franchitti	5 laps	accident
–	G. Waberski	Did not start	stalled

Fastest Laps:

A	J. Dufour	42.48 secs	102.00mph
B	D. Vercoe	43.30 secs	100.06mph

Denotes Class B competitors.

Silverstone

Rounds Five and Six – 2 May 1994

Round Five – 12 laps

This was the day that Jan Magnussen stamped his authority on the Championship as he totally dominated the proceedings to win both races in the double header to make it four wins from six outings. Qualifying was overshadowed by the tragic news of Ayrton Senna's death at Imola and the drivers found it difficult to motivate themselves for the Bank Holiday double bill.

However, for the second time in the 1994 Championship, there was an all PSR front line on the grid with Gueiros taking third, his best effort thus far, ahead of Radermecker by the merest time of 0.01 seconds. Lying second in the Championship coming up to the twin races was Gareth Rees who was therefore far from happy with sixth place in the starting line up. Both Rosset and Lakin would have been higher up the grid had they not suffered from sticking throttles (Lakin had been as high as second).

When the race got underway, Maghussen got away smartly but his stable mate, Franchitti didn't and was almost immediately overtaken by Radermecker. After his pointless double header at Brands Hatch, Franchitti must have found it

difficult to believe what happened next as Radermecker clipped the Scot at Copse, leaving him to retire on lap three contemplating a back line start in the second race. Franchitti was raging but the the Belgian was unrepentant saying *"He hit me, not the other way round"*. Although the Scot was the only retirement of the first race, Steve Arnold also suffered from a damaged nose section received in a first lap shunt at Beckett's and he eventually finished last having completed only nine laps.

Salles finished in eleventh spot but the placing hid the fact that he had received a crack off Dufour on the final circuit and he was unable to start the following race. Up at the front Magnussen led from start to finish whilst Radermecker never relinquished second after his splendid start. Gueiros held on to his third place but Rosset was held up by a slowing Franchitti and Rees never recovered from a bad start due to a grip problem.

In the Class B race, Duncan Vercoe scored another effortless victory as he continued to run-away from his rivals, the best of whom was again Chris Clark.

Race Placings – Round Five (12 laps)

Pos	Driver	Time	Diff	Pos	Driver	Time	Diff
1	J. Magnussen	11'22.13	–	18	S. Watson	11'45.18	23.05s
2	V. Radermecker	11'22.64	0.51s	19	G. Waberski	11'46.67	24.54s
3	M. Gueiros	11'23.20	1.07s	20	M. Gene	11'46.80	24.67s
4	S. Lakin	11'23.72	1.59s	21	C. Clark*	11'53.95	31.82s
5	D. Morelli	11'25.48	3.35s	22	P. Dawson*	11'54.50	32.37s
6	R. Rosset	11'26.59	4.46s	23	G. Hedley*	11'57.07	34.94s
7	G. Rees	11'28.37	6.24s	24	S. Allen*	11'58.71	36.58s
8	B. Cunningham	11'32.78	10.65s	25	S. Arnold	9 laps	–
9	L. Garcia Jnr	11'34.20	12.07s				
10	J. Spence	11'38.61	16.48s	**Failed to Finish**			
11	G. Salles	11'41.76	19.63s	–	D. Franchitti	3 laps	accident
12	I. Arias	11'42.08	19.95s				
13	J. Dufour	11'42.17	20.04s	**Fastest Laps:**			
14	P. de la Rosa	11'42.30	20.17s	A	S. Lakin	55.91 secs	106.17mph
15	D. Vercoe*	11'42.49	20.36s	B	D. Vercoe	56.82 secs	104.47mph
16	C. Horner	11'42.78	20.65s	*Denotes Class B competitors.			
17	R. Xavier	11'44.96	22.83s				

Round Six – 12 laps

Magnussen again dominated his opponents from the green light but behind him it was Lakin who this time got off to a flyer to move from fourth on the grid to second in the race with the main sufferer being Marcos Gueiros. He had a dreadful start, dropping down to fifth. Although there had only been one retirement in the first race, it wasn't long before that number had been quadrupled in the second with Arnold and Gene colliding at Brooklands on the second circuit and collecting the unfortunate De La Rosa on the way.

Franchitti, meanwhile, was having a super stab at getting at least some points from the day's work despite having to start from the back row after his first race retirement. By lap four he was up to 13th from 26th place on the grid and on the next tour he achieved the fastest lap of 55.54 to get a consolation point which was supplemented by him being awarded the Shell Driver of the Meeting Award. He moved past Vercoe on the way to Copse on lap six and then it was the turn of Garcia to feel the blast of air as the Scot left him in his wake at Becketts on lap nine. Probably the hardest earned point of the season came the Scot's way when he passed Dufour on lap ten at the Complex but it was all of little matter to the disconsolate Franchitti who was seeing his Championship aspirations diminish at the double headers.

Barely one and a half seconds separated the first five home and it was as close as that throughout the race. Despite this apparent closeness, however, there was little excitement for the near proximity of the cars to one another never spilled into overtaking manoevres.

Normally a driver would have been happy with a second and a third from a double headed bill of fare but in Radermecker's case the success in claiming these spots actually saw him fall further behind Magnussen in the chase for the title. But if Magnussen was looking strong, what about Vercoe in Class B? He made it a straight six out of six with another facile victory. ◪

Jan Magnussen.

Race Placings – Round Six (12 laps)

Pos	Driver	Time	Diff	Pos	Driver	Time	Diff
1	J. Magnussen	11'22.03	–	18	G. Waberski	11'43.01	20.98s
2	S. Lakin	11'22.41	0.38s	19	C. Clark*	11'50.01	27.98s
3	V. Radermecker	11'22.88	0.85s	20	P. Dawson*	11'52.04	30.01s
4	R. Rosset	11'23.29	1.26s	21	G. Hedley*	11'54.72	32.69s
5	M. Gueiros	11'23.53	1.50s	22	S. Allen*	11'55.48	33.45s
6	D. Morelli	11'25.69	3.66s				
7	B. Cunningham	11'26.38	4.35s	**Failed to Finish**			
8	J. Spence	11'27.49	5.46s	–	P. de la Rosa	2 laps	accident
9	G. Rees	11'27.78	5.75s	–	M. Gene	2 laps	accident
10	D. Franchitti	11'28.43	6.40s	–	S. Arnold	2 laps	accident
11	J. Dufour	11'28.71	6.68s	–	G. Salles	Did not start	
12	L. Garcia Jnr	11'29.56	7.53s				
13	D. Vercoe*	11'30.89	8.86s	**Fastest Laps:**			
14	C. Horner	11'31.52	9.49s	A	S. Lakin	55.54 secs	106.88mph
15	I. Arias	11'38.12	16.09s	B	D. Vercoe	56.34 secs	105.36mph
16	R. Xavier	11'39.87	17.84s	*Denotes Class B competitors.*			
17	S. Watson	11'40.22	18.19s				

Brands Hatch

Round Seven – 8 May 1994

Scott Lakin could have been forgiven for thinking everything was coming up roses prior to the start of the seventh round of the Championship. It was announced that his Intersport car was to receive additional backing from the Japanese Middlebridge organisation for future races and, doubtless anxious to prove to the new backers that they had invested wisely, he then proceeded to collect his first ever F3 pole ahead of the PSR pair, Jan Magnussen and Dario Franchitti who had recorded exactly the same times just 0.05 seconds behind Lakin. Meanwhile, Jamie Spence stated he had switched from Fred Goddard Racing to PTM Motorsport for the remainder of the Championship whilst two regular Class B competitors, Chris Clark and runaway leader, Duncan Vercoe, were missing. Clark was said to be still too upset from the tragic events at Imola to resume racing whilst Vercoe had no option but to sit this one out after a massive shunt in testing.

Making their seasonal debuts were Piers Hunnisett and Italian Davide Campana who, in the absence of Vercoe were to take their Bowman cars to a 1-2 in the Class B category. In the case of Hunnisett, his victory made it two wins from two appearances in F3 Class B competition leaving the Eastbourne youngster hoping for more opportunities during the rest of the season.

Spence was to have a nightmare debut for his new outfit as his car packed up in the first qualifying session and then experienced a broken battery lead in the second leaving him amongst the backmarkers on the grid. When the race did get underway for real, Spence stalled and was whacked up the back by Dawson who was put out of the race through no fault of his own. The red flags were out and three laps were lost which was initially in favour of Lakin. He had made a bad start at the first green light and lost his advantage but at the second *off* he was much quicker and led from Magnussen. The Dane, however, got past at Paddock on the second lap whilst the next change saw Radermecker move into fourth past Gueiros. Franchitti headed Lakin at Surtees on lap ten and the manoeuvre caused Lakin to understeer as he tried to fend off the Scot which let in both Radermecker and Gueiros.

There were no further changes amongst the leaders but Dufour had the bad luck to experience a misfire after setting a lap record of almost 116mph. But it was still Magnussen who made it five wins out of the last six races as the PSR stable took the honours with a 1-2. ✪

Race Placings – Round Seven (17 laps)

Pos	Driver	Time	Diff	Pos	Driver	Time	Diff
1	J. Magnussen	23'20.62	–	17	D. Campana*	24'22.46	61.84s
2	D. Franchitti	23'20.73	0.11s	18	G. Hedley*	16 laps	–
3	V. Radermecker	23'21.16	0.54s	19	S. Allan*	16 laps	–
4	M. Gueiros	23'21.60	0.98s	20	J. Dufour	14 laps	–
5	S. Lakin	23'27.00	6.38s				
6	G. Rees	23'27.29	6.67s	**Failed to Finish**			
7	G. Salles	23'31.03	10.41s	–	R. Rosset	15 laps	spin
8	D. Morelli	23'34.52	13.90s	–	J. Spence	8 laps	retired
9	B. Cunningham	23'34.52	13.90s	–	M. Gene	1 lap	spin
10	S. Arnold	23'35.42	14.80s	–	P. de la Rosa	1 lap	suspension
11	C. Horner	23'37.96	17.34s	–	P. Dawson	0 laps	accident
12	L. Garcia Jnr	23'38.41	17.79s				
13	S. Watson	23'38.84	18.22s	**Fastest Laps:**			
14	I. Arias	23'46.54	25.92s	A	J. Dufour	1'20.83	115.80mph
15	R. Xavier	24'13.06	52.44s	B	P. Hunnisett	1'24.16	111.22mph
16	P. Hunnisett*	24'13.08	52.46s	*Denotes Class B competitors.*			

Thruxton

Round Eight – 30 May 1994

With Magnussen having dominated the Formula Three scene to such an extent that it was difficult to see where a serious challenge to his supremacy could be mounted from, it was a pleasant surprise to see the Dane down in fourth place on the grid. There were two main contributory factors to this as Magnussen was suffering from the after effects of flu but, more importantly, Warren Hughes was back. The Geordie had been without a drive since his Ralt team had withdrawn and P1 Engineering moved quickly to snap him up putting him in Dino Morelli's Dallara F394-Fiat. In his first drive for his new outfit, Hughes claimed pole almost one year after his first ever number one starting position. The other front line starter was Gareth Rees whilst Vincent Radermecker completed the first four in the line up but two of them were not to figure in the race itself. Hughes got clear at the off and went into Allard clear but Radermecker was pushing Rees hard just behind as the cars entered the Complex. Radermecker touched Hughes' car causing both to spin. Garcia could not avoid Radermecker and after the dust settled, Magnussen was back in his accustomed position at the head of affairs. The

Marshals, however, had little alternative but to bring out the red flags and have a restart over 17 laps as opposed to the original twenty. From the restart, Rees and Dufour touched which allowed Magnussen to claim the lead with Paul Stewart Racing team mate Franchitti in second. Somewhat surprisingly, however, Franchitti had no intention of driving as a team and dived inside the Dane at the chicane on the second circuit on his way to claiming the fastest lap.

Not to be outdone, Magnussen pulled the same stunt on lap four to regain the lead and Franchitti also lost second place to Rees as he struggled with a lack of grip. By the time Rees had got past Franchitti, however, the race was over for Magnussen had flown and Franchitti realised belatedly that his job was now to prevent Rees making any further ground on his team mate. He wrested back second spot and then made sure there was always distance between him and Magnussen. Rees made two serious attempts to get by at the chicane without success. In turn, Lakin was pushing hard for third but never got there and in the end had more on his mind in keeping Dufour out rather than catching Rees. ✖

Race Placings – Round Eight (17 laps)

Pos	Driver	Time	Diff	Pos	Driver	Time	Diff
1	J. Magnussen	19'59.40	–	18	J. Mowlem*	20'36.74	37.34s
2	D. Franchitti	20'00.45	1.05s	20	G. Hedley*	16 laps	–
3	G. Rees	20'00.72	1.32s	24	S. Allen*	16 laps	–
4	S. Lakin	20'01.89	2.49s		**Failed to Finish**		
5	J. Dufour	20'02.32	2.92s				
6	R. Rosset	20'09.45	10.05s	–	B. Cunningham	6 laps	fuel pump
7	M. Gueiros	20'14.65	15.25s	–	P. Dawson*	1 lap	spin
8	G. Salles	20'15.91	16.51s	–	C. Clark*	1 lap	electrics
9	S. Watson	20'17.54	18.14s	–	W. Hughes	Did not start	accident
10	S. Arnold	20'23.60	24.20s	–	V. Radermecker	Did not start	accident
11	D. Vercoe*	20'24.34	24.94s	–	L. Garcia Jnr	Did not start	accident
12	M. Gene	20'24.74	25.34s		**Fastest Laps:**		
13	R. Xavier	20'26.65	27.25s				
14	G. Waberski	20'28.56	29.16s	A	D. Franchitti	1'09.57	121.91mph
15	P. de la Rosa	20'29.15	29.75s	B	D. Vercoe	1'10.57	120.18mph
16	I. Arias	20'29.57	30.17s		*Denotes Class B competitors.*		
17	C. Horner	20'33.67	34.27s				

Oulton Park

Round Nine – 5 June 1994

The race saw another twist in the Warren Hughes/Dino Morelli saga at P1 Engineering with the manufacturer re-instating Morelli into their Dallara Fiat leaving Hughes out of a ride again following his races with both P1 and March. His reaction was to immediately sign up to race in Japan for HKS Mitsubishi. Another driver to miss out on Round Nine was Garth Waberski whose team, DAW, announced that they, and their South African driver, were side stepping Oulton Park in order *"to take stock of our position as we don't feel we should be languishing around 14th position"*. One driver with no such worries was Jan Magnussen who took his sixth pole of the season without any undue fuss but the surprise package was Marc Gene in his HKS Mitsubishi. The Spaniard drove the car to its best ever start position of sixth whilst in the Class B section Duncan Vercoe was again streets ahead of the opposition.

Rees, in second spot on the grid, blasted away at the start to try to get in front of Magnussen but was not successful as the Dane held his line. Behind came Dufour, Radermecker and Franchitti but the latter came unstuck when he tried to move through at Cascades. As he tried to pass Dufour on the outside, his rear wheels locked putting him into the grit and causing a spin. By the time he was able to rejoin the race, Franchitti was plumb last and facing yet another drive through the field. In taking avoiding action, Radermecker lost a couple of seconds on Dufour and was left with a lonely drive for the rest of the race.

On the thirteenth circuit Gueiros tried the same move at Cascades that Franchitti had made earlier in the race with same result, only to a much more marked degree as he slid across the gravel trap and whacked into the tyres. The pace car was scrambled and everybody assumed the cars would carry on round in convoy for the final two laps. The pace car, however, failed to pick up Magnussen, choosing instead one of the back markers, Gray Hedley, causing some confusion not least to Luiz Garcia Jnr who, in his haste, hit Class B leader Duncan Vercoe to the extent that Vercoe's right rear tyre punctured causing him to limp round to the finish, being overtaken in the process by Clark who had been literally miles adrift when the pace car intervened. At the end of all the excitement, however, it was very much still Magnussen with seven wins out of nine starts. 🏁

Race Placings – Round Nine (15 laps)

Pos	Driver	Time	Diff		Pos	Driver	Time	Diff
1	J. Magnussen	25'34.52	–		18	C. Clark*	25'47.23	12.71s
2	G. Rees	25'34.71	0.19s		19	D. Vercoe*	26'40.14	1'5.62
3	J. Dufour	25'34.97	0.45s		20	G. Hedley*	29'40.89	1'6.37
4	V. Radermecker	25'36.15	1.63s		21	P. Dawson*	29'44.03	1'9.51
5	R. Rosset	25'36.52	2.00s		22	S. Allen*	29'45.44	1'10.92
6	J. Spence	25'36.75	2.23s		23	J. Williams*	14 laps	–
7	M. Gene	25'37.38	2.86s					
8	D. Morelli	25'37.77	3.25s		**Failed to Finish**			
9	B. Cunningham	25'39.11	4.59s		–	M. Gueiros	11 laps	accident
10	L. Garcia Jnr	25'39.46	4.94s		–	S. Lakin	5 laps	accident
11	R. Xavier	25'40.26	5.74s		–	I. Arias	2 laps	spin
12	S. Arnold	25'42.33	7.81s					
13	D. Franchitti	25'44.19	9.67s		**Fastest Laps:**			
14	C. Horner	25'44.53	10.01s		A	J. Magnussen	1'33.68	106.63mph
15	S. Watson	25'46.56	12.04s		B	D. Vercoe	1'34.96	105.20mph
16	P. de la Rosa	25'46.63	12.11s		*Denotes Class B competitors.*			
17	G. Salles	25'46.92	12.40s					

Vincent Radermecker prepares for the start of another race.

Gareth Rees.

Donington

Donington Park will have its own special little place in the heart of Jan Magnussen when he eventually retires and not just because this success made it eight wins out of ten in the 1994 F3 Championship. It was at the Leicestershire track that the flying Dane notched his maiden F3 victory and he left Donington following this win with a posse of F1 teams, contracts in hand, chasing him. He also very nearly had another cause for celebration when, in qualifying, he almost became the first F3 driver to lap at 100mph (1'30.00) just failing by 0.04 of a second to claim the honour. His time, however, obviously gave him pole and he was joined by Paul Stewart Racing team-mate, Dario Franchitti on the front row.

There was a sensational start to the race when Lakin appeared to stall and, whilst most of the entourage managed to get by, Chris Clark drove straight into the back of the stationary Intersport car whilst Brown's maiden voyage came to an abrupt end within yards as he also failed to miss the melee. But, whilst there were casualties (thankfully, not amongst the drivers), there were definite beneficiaries with Dario Franchitti, in particular, welcoming the red flag. He had made a complete hash of the first lap by going too fast at the Old Hairpin and spinning off. By the time he got back on the track he was well down the field and very grateful to see a restart ordered.

Franchitti made a far better start the second time round and was pushing Magnussen hard with Rees and Gueiros in third and fourth. Behind these, Garcia was having problems and dropped from fourth on the grid down to eighth but, when Salles tried to demote him one more place, the WSR car spun off and found itself at the back of the field from where Salles did well to recover to finish an eventual 14th.

Up front, there was no change in the order except for Franchitti making a mistake in trying to pass team-mate, Magnussen, at the Old Hairpin on the 12th circuit. The Dane closed the door as Franchitti tried to get through resulting in Franchitti hitting a kerb and letting Rees through into second, a placing which, at the finishing line, also hauled him up to second in the overall points standings but he needed a telescope to see Magnussen who now held an 85 point lead as he announced that he had signed for McLaren to help in their test and development programme. ▮

Race Placings – Round Ten (17 laps)

Pos	Driver	Time	Diff	Pos	Driver	Time	Diff
1	J. Magnussen	25'54.91	–	18	D. Vercoe*	27'09.53	1'14.62
2	G. Rees	25'55.55	0.64s	19	G. Hedley*	16 laps	–
3	D. Franchitti	25'56.07	1.16s	20	P. Dawson*	16 laps	–
4	M. Gueiros	25'56.52	1.61s	–	S. Allen*	27'06.62	Excluded
5	R. Rosset	25'59.54	4.63s				
6	V. Radermecker	26'00.61	5.70s	**Failed to Finish**			
7	J. Dufour	26'01.08	6.17s	–	R. Xavier	15 laps	spin
8	L. Garcia Jnr	26'10.99	16.08s	–	G. Waberski	7 laps	spin
9	B. Cunningham	26'18.97	24.06s	–	P. de la Rosa	6 laps	suspension
10	J. Spence	26'23.50	28.59s	–	S. Lakin	Did not start	accident
11	D. Morelli	26'25.90	30.99s	–	C. Clark*	Did not start	accident
12	S. Watson	26'26.03	31.12s	–	Z. Brown*	Did not start	accident
13	C. Horner	26'32.06	37.15s				
14	G. Salles	26'39.05	44.14s	**Fastest Laps:**			
15	S. Arnold	26'42.49	47.58s	A	R. Rosset	1'30.80	99.11mph
16	M. Gene	26'43.23	48.32s	B	D. Vercoe	1'31.06	98.83mph
17	I. Arias	26'43.94	49.03s	*Denotes Class B competitors.*			

Silverstone

Round Eleven – 10 July 1994

The British GP Meeting witnessed not only an exciting qualifying contest for the major players but an equally enthralling F3 qualifying. The first F3 session ended with Rees on provisional pole ahead of Radermecker and the PSR pair, Jan Magnussen and Dario Franchitti. The evening session however, saw Magnussen immediately lower Rees' time only for Rosset post an even faster one. The Dane recaptured pole and was joined by Franchitti but then Italian F3 hot shot, Gianicarlo Fisichella dislodged Franchitti who hit back immediately to regain the place he had just lost. With less than three minutes remaining, however, Radermecker put in a storming lap to go under 1 min 47 and dragged Jeremie Dufour through the barrier with him. So there were now six different nationalities in the first six grid positions but Rees, having held provisional pole would have been disappointed to line up seventh.

When the actual race got underway both Steve Arnold and the European Karting Championship leader, Jarno Trulli, would start from the back of the field after experiencing electrical problems on the warm up lap. Up front the leading three qualifiers all made good getaways

but Magnussen immediately lost his fourth spot to Rosset on the run down to Copse where the Dane hit the back of Rosset to spin the Brazilian into the gravel. The incident put paid to any hopes Magnussen had of a seventh success due to the damage his car sustained but Rosset was out of the race altogether. The collision allowed Rees and Fisichella through into fourth and fifth but the carnage continued at Stowe when Cunningham was touched into a spin leaving him the wrong way round to watch helplessly as the rest of the field bore down on him. Arnold went one side of him and de la Rosa the other, but Arias was left with nowhere to go and to hit Cunningham head on.

At the front it was like procession like stuff with the same order of Radermecker, Dufour, Franchitti, Rees and Fisichella being maintained throughout. Or almost. With the finishing line in sight, Franchitti's engine cut out and he was fortunate to have just sufficient momentum to roll past the chequered flag although he lost three places in the process. Magnussen nursed his damaged car home in seventh whilst Garcia and Arnold motored their way into the points from 19th and 28th place on the grid.

Race Placings – Round Eleven (15 laps)

Pos	Driver	Time	Diff
1	V. Radermecker	27'15.14	–
2	J. Dufour	27'16.20	1.06s
3	G. Rees	27'22.74	7.60s
4	G. Fisichella	27'23.16	8.02s
5	M. Gueiros	27'28.08	12.94s
6	D. Franchitti	27'29.02	13.88s
7	J. Magnussen	27'29.47	14.33s
8	L. Garcia	27'38.62	23.48s
9	S. Arnold	27'46.92	31.78s
10	C. Horner	27'49.19	34.05s
11	P. de la Rosa	27'49.82	34.68s
12	S. Watson	27'54.63	39.49s
13	D. Vercoe*	27'56.49	41.35s
14	R. Xavier	28'07.02	51.88s
15	J. Trulli	28'13.77	58.63s
16	Z. Brown*	28'27.76	1'12.62
17	F. Balletti	28'27.99	1'12.85
18	S. Allen*	28'28.53	1'13.39
19	D. Morelli	28'56.85	1'41.71
20	G. Hedley*	1 lap down	–
21	P. Dawson*	1 lap down	–

Failed to Finish

Pos	Driver	Time	Diff
–	G. Salles	11 laps	accident
–	J. Spence	10 laps	accident
–	M. Gene	2 laps	gearbox
–	G. Waberski	1 lap	spin
–	B. Cunningham	0 laps	accident
–	I. Arias	0 laps	accident
–	R. Rosset	0 laps	accident

Fastest Laps:

A	J. Dufour	1.47.89	104.84mph
B	D. Vercoe	1.49.15	103.67mph

*Denotes Class B competitors.

Snetterton

Round Twelve – 24 July 1994

Amongst the drivers hoping to do well in qualifying were Dario Franchitti, who had never failed to claim pole in any of the competitions he had participated in at the Norfolk venue, and Ricardo Rosset who had qualified in second at Snetterton in 1993 before finishing third in the actual race. The happier of the pair turned out to be Rosset, who in the first session, set not only provisional pole but also two other times that would have landed him the same result. Franchitti, despite being the top Briton, languished in seventh as the Boys from Brazil amazingly packed three drivers in to the top five. In addition to Rosset, Salles gained his first ever top four grid position whilst Gueiros equalled Salles' time. Meanwhile, Magnussen quietly qualified in second with Salles and Radermecker constituting an all West Surrey Racing second row. In Class B, Vercoe once more pulverised his opposition but was still disappointed to finish 16th overall after earlier being ten places higher before blowing a head gasket. There was, however, to be even worse news for the Class B runaway leader as his car could not be got ready in time for Sunday's race.

For once, the Paul Stewart Racing regime had a dreadful start as Franchitti's Dallara cut out temporarily at the Esses on the first circuit dropping him back a couple of places but team mate Magnussen was not even that lucky as the Dane came off attempting to overtake Rosset at Riches. Another to make an early exit was Horner who, after gleaning his first point of the season in the previous round, was punted off the track at Sear on the first circuit whilst, on a hot and sticky afternoon, Arias became the first of several drivers to suffer from overheating. Franchitti was also dropping out of contention with overheating and Rees lost four laps when he was forced to pit on lap nine with fuel injection problems. Up front Rosset, who had extended his lead to a comfortable two seconds, had a big fright when a Class B competitor hit the kerb just as the race leader was about to lap him forcing the Brazilian almost to stop before regaining his composure to keep his lead and land only the second race victory of his career. Certainly he will have fond memories of Snetterton having finished third and first inside twelve months! Others to enjoy themselves Salles with his first ever F3 top three finish, Steve Arnold who finished in the top six for the second time in 1994, Marc Gene who was in the points for only the second time in the campaign and, of course, Rosset's AJS Team for whom it was a first ever British F3 success. ◼

Race Placings – Round Twelve (25 laps)

Pos	Driver	Time	Diff
1	R. Rosset	28'31.74	–
2	V. Radermecker	28'32.32	0.58s
3	G. Salles	28'33.73	1.99s
4	M. Gueiros	28'34.38	2.64s
5	J. Dufour	28'36.03	4.29s
6	S. Arnold	28'46.83	15.09s
7	J. Spence	28'49.83	18.09s
8	M. Gene	28'52.28	20.54s
9	L. Garcia Jnr	28'53.83	22.09s
10	D. Franchitti	28'54.22	22.48s
11	P. de la Rosa	29'01.56	29.82s
12	S. Watson	29'02.12	30.38s
13	F. Beletti	29'29.82	58.08s
14	G.Hedley*	1 lap down	–
15	P. Dawson*	1 lap down	–
16	G. Rees	3 laps down	–

Failed to Finish

–	B. Cunningham	17 laps	spin
–	D. Morelli	13 laps	overheating
–	R. Xavier	13 laps	accident
–	G. Waberski	13 laps	accident
–	J. Magnussen	1 lap	spin
–	I. Arias	1 lap	overheating
–	C. Horner	0 laps	spin
–	D. Vercoe*	Did not Start	electrics

Fastest Laps:

A	R. Rosset	1'07.28	104.44mph
B	P. Dawson	1'0952	101.08mph

*Denotes Class B competitors.

*Vincent Radermecker, mobbed by fans,
awaits the start of the race.*

Magnussen powers on, Radermecker gives chase.

Pembrey

Rounds Thirteen and Fourteen – 21 August 1994

Round Thirteen – 17 laps

taly's Fabiano Beletti didn't even make the qualifying sessions as he suffered a horrendous crash during the Friday test day when he went wide at Honda Curve which protects the entrance to the pit straight. His Intersport Dallara rolled three times before coming to rest but thankfully the driver, although taken to hospital, escaped with comparatively light injuries. When qualifying got underway, Radermecker knew he had to win at Pembrey to stand any realistic chance of catching the flying Dane Jan Magnussen whilst hoping at the same time that the Championship leader came unstuck. The Belgian certainly did his best in qualifying and grabbed his second pole of the season from qualifying (as opposed to the pole he had obtained for the second race at Brands Hatch which was his reward for winning the first race in a double bill). But right behind him was Magnussen whilst third place man in the championship, Gareth Rees, was also third on the grid. The shock of the qualifying sessions was undoubtedly Christian Horner's seventh place. Horner had never really been at the races during the previous four months but a two week sojourn in the Greek Islands appeared to have given him

a tonic. The most disappointed team must have been Edenbridge Racing who had won at Pembrey in 1993 but were left scratching their heads with Gueiros in 13th and Garcia in 17th.

The two races themselves had been extended at the last minute from fifteen laps to twenty but a massive first lap shunt saw the initial race reduced back down to seventeen. Magnussen had caught and passed Radermecker at the first corner but, at the back of the field, there was the sight of Ivan Arias in his WSR Racing for Spain car flying through the air. He had been pushed into Jamie Spence's vehicle which launched the Spaniard in to mid-air. His car was left almost beyond recognition and he was somewhat fortunate to escape serious injury. The car, incidentally, was virtually written off for the second time in the season as it was the vehicle that Lakin had been using in his Donington starting line up shunt!

When the race re-started, Magnussen again shot away faster than Radermecker leaving the Belgian to reflect afterwards that this was where his last chance of making up points on the championship leader disappeared. *"I lost it at the start"* he bemoaned after chasing the Dane relentlessly

Race Placings – Round Thirteen (17 laps)

Pos	Driver	Time	Diff	Pos	Driver	Time	Diff
1	J. Magnussen	15'11.52	–	17	R. Xavier	15'44.43	32.82s
2	V. Radermecker	15'11.72	0. 20s	18	J. Spence	15'53.72	42.20s
3	D. Franchitti	15'13.87	2.35s	19	P. Dawson*	1 lap down	–
4	R. Rosset	15'16.20	4.68s	20	N. Greensall*	1 lap down	–
5	G. Rees	15'16.63	5.11s				
6	C. Horner	15.22.00	10.48s	**Failed to Finish**			
7	D. Morelli	15'22.36	10.84s	–	G. Hedley*	15 laps	accident
8	G. Salles	15'23.86	12.34s	–	G. Waberski	4 laps	spin
9	D. Vercoe*	15'25.93	14.41s	–	J. Dufour	2 laps	accident
10	M. Gene	15'26.55	15.03s	–	I. Arias	0 laps	accident
11	M. Gueiros	15'27.04	15.52s				
12	L. Garcia Jnr	15'28.12	16.60s	**Fastest Laps:**			
13	B. Cunningham	15'30.11	18.59s	A	D. Franchitti	52.88	99.12mph
14	S. Arnold	15'30.33	18.81s	B	D. Vercoe	53.45	98.06mph
15	S. Watson	15'33.42	21.90s	*Denotes Class B competitors.*			
16	P. de la Rosa	15'36.92	23.40s				

but unsuccessfully throughout the entire race. The second row of Dufour and Rees, meanwhile, had a head to head at the appropriately named Hatchetts which caused Dufour to drop to ninth but Rees was luckier and lost only two places. The incident, however, was to cost the Frenchman dearly for in trying too hard to make up lost ground, he went off at Honda and gave the tyres an almighty whack that not only ended his participation in the first race but put him out of the second event as well. The incident benefited Rosset who was up to fourth from ninth and Horner, who was now fifth, but Rees claimed a place back when he out manoeuvred Horner at Hatchetts. And that's the way things stayed with Horner obtaining a top six place for the first time whilst the Class B race went, surprise, surprise to Duncan Vercoe by the proverbial mile.

Round Fourteen – 20 laps

Radermecker saw his last glimpse of the title slip away with an even worse start than his poor effort in the first race. In fact, his second get away was so bad that by Hatchetts he was in fifth place behind Franchitti, Rosset and Rees as well as Magnussen. But at least he was still in the race which was more than could be said for South African Stephen Watson who failed to complete the first lap when he went off at the Esses as he tried to pass Arnold. Gueiros slid off at Honda on the fourth circuit effectively ending his race as he then proceeded to cruise round before retiring whilst Arnold and Waberski completed the non-finishers around the half way stage.

But up front, the crucial blow had been struck with Radermecker's bad start allowing Magnussen's team mate Franchitti in to second place, a dream position for Magnussen to be in as he edged ever closer to the Championship. With Franchitti riding shotgun for him, the Dane was never under any pressure. But Radermecker was and he tried desperately to recover some of his lost ground by overtaking Rees on the eleventh circuit only to spin round allowing Morelli through to leave the Belgian a place worse off rather than a position better off! Some seven laps later, Radermecker regained fifth from Morelli but it was too little, too late.

Almost everybody in the race held their own station throughout bar retirements and it was a boring race which brought Magnussen his tenth win of the campaign whilst Franchitti gave Paul Stewart Racing their second one-two of the season. Another happy driver was Salles who finished in the points for the third race running but Horner couldn't repeat his first race charge and finished ninth, a placing he would have been happy with prior to the earlier event.

And so it looked like history would repeat itself for the third year running as the results in Wales made it almost certain that Magnussen would wrap up the title for Paul Stewart Racing at the end of August at Silverstone just as PSR had in 1992 and 1993! ■

Race Placings – Round Fourteen (20 laps)

Pos	Driver	Time	Diff	Pos	Driver	Time	Diff
1	J. Magnussen	15'11.52	–	16	N. Greensall*	1 lap down	–
2	D. Franchitti	15'12.37	0.85s	17	G. Hedley*	1 lap down	–
3	R. Rosset	15'12.88	1.36s	18	P. Dawson*	1 lap down	–
4	G. Rees	15'13.87	2.35s				
5	V. Radermecker	15'18.27	6.75s	**Failed to Finish**			
6	D. Morelli	15'19.72	8.20s	–	G. Waberski	10 laps	handling
7	G. Salles	15'20.68	9.16s	–	S. Arnold	9 laps	gearbox
8	D. Vercoe*	15'21.12	9.60s	–	M. Gueiros	4 laps	handling
9	C. Horner	15'21.92	10.40s	–	S. Watson	0 laps	spin
10	M. Gene	15'22.66	11.14s				
11	B. Cunningham	15'28.11	16.59s	**Fastest Laps:**			
12	L. Garcia Jnr	15'30.37	18.85s	A	V. Radermecker	52.97s	98.95 mph
13	P. de la Rosa	15'35.15	23.63s	B	D. Vercoe*	53.36s	98.23mph
14	J. Spence	15'38.26	26.74s	*Denotes Class B competitors.*			
15	R. Xavier	15'43.27	31.75s				

Silverstone

Rounds Fifteen and Sixteen – 29 August 1994

Round Fifteen – 15 laps

Jan Magnussen went in to the last double header of the season needing just twelve points to wrap up the Championship a long way from the finishing line. In the event, he not only collected the twelve points but claimed the title with nonchalant ease by taking pole and never being headed in either race. In Class B, Duncan Vercoe required only four points to seal his title and, like Magnussen, completed the task in style, taking not only both races but also adding the two fastest laps to his tally, setting new record times for the Class on both occasions.

Elsewhere, Alex Postan raced Fred Goddard's old 913 Reynard-Mugen for the sole purpose of keeping his licence up whilst Warren Hughes, who left the British F3 scene earlier in the campaign to race in Japan, paid a fleeting visit and caused some consternation. He actually had to pay to get in but when Roberto Xavier fell out with the P1 team over the performance of his car in qualifying, the P1 team manager Roly Vincini quickly persuaded Hughes, who had raced for the outfit at Thruxton in May, to try his hand. Hughes had to borrow Magnussen's spare helmet, de la Rosa's spare racesuit and an assortment of gear from Dario Franchitti. The man of all clothes took to the track for the second session and registered the tenth fastest time to qualify sixteenth, only to be ruled out of the race by the authorities who stated the proper procedures for a change of driver had not been followed and Hughes returned to his role of spectator!

Radermecker's last forlorn hope of the title disappeared altogether in qualifying when Magnussen took pole with the Belgian challenger a lowly fifth behind the Dane's team mate Dario Franchitti. In Class B, Johnny Mowlem, having only his second outing of the season for Mark Bailey Racing, briefly challenged Vercoe for top spot but eventually had to settle for lining up three places adrift whilst Postan was well back.

When the race got underway, both Franchitti and Rees didn't as they both stalled at the start leaving Magnussen to drive away from Gueiros. The gap was a full second at the end of the first circuit and almost two seconds after four laps. The lead expanded to almost three seconds by the end of ten circuits and the Dane eased off to make sure there were no mishaps which reduced

Race Placings – Round Fifteen (15 laps)

Pos	Driver	Time	Diff	Pos	Driver	Time	Diff
1	J. Magnussen	14'24.69	–	18	C. Horner	14'50.31	25.62s
2	M. Gueiros	14'26.64	1.95s	19	J. Mowlem*	14'56.63	31.94s
3	R. Rosset	14'27.26	2.57s	20	Z. Brown*	15'02.34	37.65s
4	J. Dufour	14'27.87	3.18s	21	G. Hedley*	15'28.74	64.05s
5	G. Rees	14'30.65	5.96s	22	A. Postan*	1 lap down	–
6	V. Radermecker	14'31.24	6.55s				
7	G. Salles	14'34.60	9.91s	**Failed to Finish**			
8	D. Morelli	14'35.99	11.30s	–	S. Arnold	14 laps	accident
9	L. Garcia Jnr	14'36.48	11.79s	–	P. de la Rosa	14 laps	accident
10	M. Gene	14'43.64	18.95s	–	R. Xavier	Did not start	
11	J. Spence	14'43.36	19.17s	–	W. Hughes	Did not start	
12	B. Cunningham	14'44.85	20.16s	–	P. Dawson	Did not start	
13	D. Vercoe*	14'46.32	21.70s				
14	D. Franchitti	14'47.35	22.66s	**Fastest Laps:**			
15	S. Watson	14'48.09	23.40s	A	G. Rees	56.73s	104.19mph
16	G. Waberski	14'49.84	25.15s	B	D. Vercoe	57.87s	102.14mph
17	I. Arias	14'50.31	25.62s	*Denotes Class B competitors.*			

his winning margin to just under two seconds at the flag which was also confirmation of his title. But the drive of the race belonged to Gareth Rees who, after stalling, had rejoined the race with only fellow staller Franchitti, and two Class B competitors, Hedley and Postan behind him. In an amazing drive that must have left him pondering *"If only..."*, Rees overtook no fewer than seventeen cars as he ploughed his way through the field to fifth. Gueiros made the most of his high qualifying place and the plight of Franchitti and Rees to produce his best finish to date and which saw his team, Edenbridge Racing, equal their best of the year achieved when Garcia had finished second at Donington in May. In Class B Vercoe duly completed his task with as much panache as Magnussen in Class A whilst Mowlem made it two seconds in two outings.

Round Sixteen – 15 laps

This race was even less keenly fought than the first. If anybody thought that Magnussen, having secured his title, would ease up then they were right. Unfortunately for the other competitors, it was only when he also had the second race well and truly wrapped up that his foot came off and he coasted to another effortless triumph having gone one and a half seconds clear at the end of the first circuit which increased to more than four seconds before the Dane allowed the field to close somewhat. He had strolled to win number twelve to equal Ayrton Senna's record (which the great Brazilian set in twenty races). His success also gave his team, Paul Stewart Racing, their third successive title following the victories of Gil de Ferran in 1992 and Kelvin Burt in 1993, the first occasion a team has ever achieved a hat-trick in British F3. In fact, it was very nearly a four timer following David Coulthard's second place in 1991. Vercoe's two wins gave him thirteen victories and fourteen fastest laps.

Elsewhere in the race, Spence spun off on the first lap and both Waberski and Cunningham retired with engine problems. Franchitti made up six places from his starting place of fourteenth but Gueiros made a bad start getting involved with Rosset and dropping to fifth from second as a consequence. Dufour, meanwhile, suffered an even worse fate as he set off amongst the backmarkers after stalling before battling his way through the field in much the same style that Rees had done in the opener to finish seventh. After only one finish in the points in the first eleven races, Marc Gene also had reason to feel pleased with his day's work as his ninth and tenth spots made it five consecutive point scoring races for him in his Alan Docking car.

But the day belonged to Magnussen and Vercoe. Magnussen said *"It's unbelievable. I've had a good car and a good team and I've learned a lot. But I'm really pleased for the team who have now won the title three times in a row"*. Vercoe was a little more restrained, saying *"It feels good and this time next year I hope to be doing the same thing in Class A"*. ▪

Race Placings – Round Sixteen (15 laps)

Pos	Driver	Time	Diff	Pos	Driver	Time	Diff
1	J. Magnussen	14'24.99	–	16	J. Mowlem*	14'51.69	26.70s
2	R. Rosset	14'27.18	2.19s	17	Z. Brown*	14'55.87	30.88s
3	G. Rees	14'28.00	3.01s	18	G. Hedley*	1 lap down	–
4	D. Morelli	14'29.72	4.73s	19	A. Postan*	1 lap down	–
5	M. Gueiros	14'30.07	5.08s				
6	V. Radermecker	14'30.62	5.63s	**Failed to Finish**			
7	J. Dufour	14'31.11	6.12s	–	B. Cunningham	11 laps	engine/gearbox
8	D. Franchitti	14'35.41	10.42s	–	G. Waberski	9 laps	engine
9	M. Gene	14'35.96	10.97s	–	J. Spence	1 lap	spin/accident
10	L. Garcia Jnr	14'42.75	17.76s				
11	C. Horner	14'43.66	18.67s	**Fastest Laps:**			
12	S. Watson	14'44.50	19.51s	A	J. Dufour	56.70s	104.25mph
13	D. Vercoe*	14'46.60	21.61s	B	D. Vercoe	57.71s	102.42mph
14	I. Arias	14'49.25	24.26s	*Denotes Class B competitors.*			
15	G. Salles	14'50.31	25.32s				

Thruxton

Round Seventeen – 11 September 1994

With no replacement driver having been found for Roberto Xavier who walked out on the P1 team at Silverstone, the team ran just one car which was one more than PTM whose driver, Jamie Spence had also departed, although this break was amicable and mutual due to a lack of money. Yet another absentee was the Class B Champion Duncan Vercoe who, having wrapped up his title, was saving his budget to carry over to 1995. Vercoe's drive was offered to Jason Weller but when he declined, Brazilian Thomas Erdos stepped in very late for his F3 debut.

In an amazing coincidence, Radermecker, who has a good record at Thruxton just pipped Magnussen in both qualifying sessions by the same margin of 0.01 seconds whilst the second row belonged to two of the biggest jumpers, Rosset and Dufour. The latter found a monumental improvement of 0.63 seconds on his first session whilst Rosset improved by 0.33 secs. The biggest shock was Gareth Rees in ninth place whilst Erdos took over from where Vercoe left off to gain an unchallenged Class B pole.

If the race had lost much of its appeal with Magnussen having wrapped up the title at Silverstone, there was still the question of whether the flying Dane could capture Ayrton Senna's 1983 record of 12 wins outright having equalled it in the previous round. The Dane did, in fact, succeed in his bid and, in typical fashion, he produced probably the manoeuvre of the season to capture the record. As the leaders entered the Complex, Magnussen drove into it in third but emerged in first! Both Radermecker and Rosset took an inside line whilst Magnussen went outside, beating them for speed and braking power.

Magnussen, once in the lead, didn't waste any time in stamping his authority on the proceedings and, free of traffic, put in some quick laps. Rees, meanwhile, wanted a good points finish to secure third place overall in the Championship and he moved quietly through the field from his low starting line up to take sixth spot, sufficient to clinch the third place but not enough to enable him to catch Radermecker whose second place in the race guaranteed him second place in the Championship. Erdos won the Class B race in very much the same style as Vercoe but the second debutant, Tim Pearson, found it hard going and finished last.

But, at the end of the race, it was another Magnussen benefit and this time it was the coveted prize of Senna's record that he took home with him. ◼

Race Placings – Round Seventeen (20 laps)

Pos	Driver	Time	Diff	Pos	Driver	Time	Diff
1	J. Magnussen	23'43.47	–	17	F. Beletti	24'44.78	61.31s
2	V. Radermecker	23'44.36	0.89s	18	G. Hedley*	24'57.56	74.09s
3	R. Rosset	23'44.67	1.20s	19	S. Allen*	1 lap down	–
4	J. Dufour	23'45.13	1.66s	20	P. Dawson*	1 lap down	–
5	D. Franchitti	23'48.13	4.66s	21	T. Pearson	1 lap down	–
6	G. Rees	23'49.46	5.99s				
7	D. Morelli	23'56.64	13.12s	**Failed to Finish**			
8	L. Garcia Jnr	23'57.81	14.34s	–	G. Salles	18 laps	accident
9	M. Gueiros	23'57.95	14.48s		B. Cunningham	0 laps	accident
10	M. Gene	24'03.47	20.00s		S. Watson	0 laps	accident
11	C. Horner	24'09.25	25.78s				
12	I. Arias	24'09.95	26.48s	**Fastest Laps:**			
13	T. Erdos*	24'10.41	26.94s	A	J. Dufour	1'10.18	120.85mph
14	G. Waberski	24'17.13	33.66s	B	T. Erdos	1'11.46	118.69mph
15	S. Arnold	24'23.98	40.51s	*Denotes Class B competitors.			
16	P. de la Rosa	24'26.72	42.25s				

Silverstone

Round Eighteen – 2 October 1994

The morning's first qualifying session had been shortened due to the amount of water on the track with almost everybody, including the new champion Jan Magnussen, spinning. Without exception, every driver complained about being unable to get up full throttle but, despite the many spins there was remarkably little damage with only Ivan Arias and Paul Dawson being unable to take part in the second session. This was a particular blow to Arias who was lying in seventh when he went out, easily his best performance of the year.

Another to produce his best qualifying round of the year was Marcos Gueiros who lined up on the front row having equalled Vincent Radermeckers pole time.

After the race itself had been delayed for almost an hour and a half because of standing water on the track the decision was made to go ahead with the contest reduced by a fifth down to twelve circuits. Radermecker got away well but was helped into a clear lead by Gueiros who wasted his best qualifying effort of the campaign with a start that was as appalling as the weather. He selected fourth instead of second and was immediately consumed by six cars. Radermecker's cause was also helped by Rees nudging Magnussen at Stowe but perhaps the most amazing thing about the first lap was that everybody completed it apart from the two non-starters.

But the good luck was not to hold and the second circuit soon began to claim spinners with Radermecker a victim at Priory. Garcia went at Copse where Dawson joined him but Cunningham got away with his show of aquaplaning to continue and ultimately claim his best finish of the season in fifth place, albeit over half a minute down on the winner. After the promise of his best qualifying position, Gueiros' day was rapidly coming apart and, following his poor start to the race, he spun out for good at Priory on the fourth tour. Rosset set the fastest time of the race thus far but then paid the penalty as he went skidding off at Copse on the seventh tour. His time was superseded by Dufour but he also was to fail to finish as he was involved in a controversial incident towards the end of the race with Morelli who was fined for his part in the altercation. All of which allowed the unflappable Magnussen to splash his way through the water to his fourteenth victory of a memorable summer for the Dane. ❖

Race Placings – Round Eighteen (12 laps)

Pos	Driver	Time	Diff
1	J. Magnussen	26'03.08	–
2	G. Rees	26'07.03	3.95s
3	D. Morelli	26'17.65	14.57s
4	D. Franchitti	26'19.56	16.48s
5	B. Cunningham	26'34.03	30.95s
6	G. Salles	26'38.02	34.94s
7	M. Gene	26'38.08	35.20s
8	P. de la Rosa	26'42.61	39.53s
9	S. Watson	26'44.38	41.30s
10	F. Beletti	26'52.88	49.80s
11	C. Horner	26'54.47	51.39s
12	T. Erdos*	27'05.41	62.33s
13	G. Waberski	27'15.76	72.68s
14	S. Allen*	1 lap down	–
15	J. Clermont*	1 lap down	–

Failed to Finish

	Driver		
–	J. Dufour	11 laps	accident
–	B. Verdon-Roe*	10 laps	spin
–	R. Rosset	6 laps	spin
–	M. Gueiros	3 laps	spin
–	S. Arnold	2 laps	spin
–	V. Radermecker	1 lap	spin
–	L. Garcia	1 lap	spin
–	P. Dawson*	1 lap	spin
–	I. Arias	Did not start	
–	G. Hedley*	Did not start	

Fastest Laps:

	Driver	Speed
A	J. Dufour	88.91mph
B	B. Verdon-Roe	88.06mph

*Denotes Class B competitors.

Review

With more cars and a new points system, the 1994 F3 season was expected to be more open than for some years and the first race at Silverstone in March, gave no clue to the dominance that one man was about to impose on the series. The opening Round's qualifying saw Jan Magnussen fourth on the grid, a position he would improve on by one place in the actual race itself. Not a poor performance by any means, but no indication of the stranglehold that the Dane was about to exert on the championship. In the remaining 17 races, he was to win fourteen times, breaking in the process, Ayrton Senna's long standing F3 record of twelve successes in 1983. His potential for higher things had not gone unnoticed and by the end of the season he was testing in F1 for McLaren. Putting things even more in perspective, Vincent Radermecker was the next most successful driver with two victories whilst the only others to win were Magnussen's team mate Dario Franchitti, who took the opening race of the campaign, and Ricardo Rosset who won at Snetterton when Magnussen spun off at the end of the first lap.

So Magnussen helped the Paul Stewart Racing outfit to their third successive championship but Dario Franchitti was nowhere near as consistent in the second car. After taking 32 points from the first two races, he secured just one in his next four outings before recovering to enjoy five top three finishes in the final eleven races. The main threat to Magnussen had been expected to come from Radermecker and the Belgian did indeed finish second in the title race, albeit the proverbial miles behind, or to be exact, 125 points. With a maximum of 21 points on offer for each race, Magnussen's winning margin was such that he could virtually have gone home two-thirds of the way through the season!

Without Magnussen, it could have been an exciting championship with only eighty points separating Radermecker from Jeremie Dufour in seventh. The Belgian, in fact, secured runner's-up

The Championship
Final Placings and Points

Pos'n	Class A Driver	Points	Class B Driver	Points
1	Magnussen	308	Vercoe	289
2	Radermecker	183	Hedley	202
3	Rees	171	Dawson	145
4	Franchitti	133	Allen	113
5	Rosset	132	Clark	80
6	Gueiros	107	Mowlem	45
7	Dufour	103	Erdos	41
8	Lakin	69	Brown	39
9	Morelli	63	Greensall	27
10	Salles	39	Hunnisett	21
11	Garcia	34	Postan	16
12	Cunningham	29	Campana	15
13	Spence	25	Clermont	12
14	Arnold	24	Lazarakis	8
15	M.Gene	19	Pearson	8
16	Horner	10	Williams	6
17	Fisichella	10	Verdon-Roe	1
18	Watson	7		
19	de la Rosa	6		
20	Hughes	3		
21	Beletti	1		

spot by just twelve points from Gareth Rees who had led the Belgian by two points after the second Donington meeting at the end of June. It was at this meeting that the season came to a premature end for Scott Lakin who had been in fourth place in the title hunt at the half-way stage of the campaign. Lakin was hit by Class B competitors Chris Clark and Zak Brown causing extensive damage to Lakin's Dallara-Mugen – "About £10,000 worth of damage. If I can't get some sponsorship that's my season over". He didn't, and it was.

Of the others, Rosset must have wished the season had begun at Snetterton where not only did he enjoy his first F3 victory but his AJS Team were also enjoying a first ever F3 success. After Snetterton, Magnussen won all five remaining races but such was Rosset's consistency over the last third of the campaign that despite this nap hand from the Dane, the Brazilian actually

Dario Franchitti

outscored Magnussen by 82 points to 80 over the last six races!

The Edenbridge outfit, who had secured five victories in 1993, saw their two drivers, Luis Garcia and Marcos Gueiros experience vastly conflicting campaigns with Garcia making just one appearance in the top seven, and that was in the second race of the season. Gueiros, however, was much more consistent, failing to score on only four occasions and having ten top five finishes. Fortec's newcomer, Jeremie Dufour, was another to improve in the second half of the season when he was hardly ever out of the top five

after picking up only 28 points in the first seven rounds. The Frenchman also had the satisfaction of picking up a nice fat cheque when he won the big money seven lap Avon F3 Supersprint at Donington in June.

If the Class A winner Magnussen could have gone home with time to spare, Class B winner, Duncan Vercoe did. The runaway secondary competition winner didn't bother competing again once he wrapped his title up at Silverstone at the end of August on the same weekend that Magnussen confirmed his own championship status. It was really that easy for both of them. ❖

Championship Winning Teams/Chassis by Class

Class A			Class B	
Driver	*Team/Chassis*		*Driver*	*Team/Chassis*
J. Magnussen	PSR Dallara F394-Mugen		D. Vercoe	DAW Racing Dallara F393-Vauxhall
V. Radermecker	WSR Dallara F394-Mugen		G. Hedley	GH Racing Dallara F393-Mugen/Fiat
G. Rees	ADR Dallara F394-Mugen		P. Dawson	ADR Dallara F393-Mugen
D. Franchitti	PSR Dallara F393/4-Mugen		S. Allen	Reynard 933-Mugen
R. Rosset	Team AJS Dallara F394-Mugen		C. Clark	PTM Motorsport Dallara F393-Fiat
M. Gueiros	Edenbridge Dallara F394-Vauxhall		J. Mowlem	MBR Dallara F393-Mugen
J. Dufour	Fortec Mtrsport Dallara F394-Mugen		T. Erdos	DAW Dallara F393-Vauxhall/
S. Lakin	Intersport Racing Dallara F393-Mugen		T. Erdos	PTM Motorsport Dallara F393-Fiat

FIA European Formula 3000 year

Round One – Silverstone, 2 May 1994 (38 laps)

Pos	Driver	Time	Pos	Driver	Time
1	F. Lagorce	1:01'56.79	11	G. Gomez	1:02'59.72
2	D. Coulthard	1:02'00.89	12	K. Brack	1:03'00.45
3	G. de Ferran	1:02'04.31	13	T. Marques	1:03'15.85
4	V. Sospiri	1:02'37.98	14	J. Policand	1 lap down
5	H. Noda	1:02'39.77	15	T. Inque	1 lap down
6	D. Cottaz	1:02'40.65	16	F. de Simone	2 laps down
7	M. Papis	1:02'41.18	17	S. Nardozi	3 laps down
8	J. Boullion	1:02'41.64			
9	J. Gene	1:02'58.80			
10	O. Gavin	1:02'59.43			

Failed to Finish

N. Leboissetier 32 laps electrics

E. Clerico	22 laps	engine
M. Goossens	21 laps	spin
C. Pescatori	20 laps	driver ill
P. Diniz	14 laps	wheel nut
R. Stirling	12 laps	clutch
W. Eyckmans	9 laps	engine
P. delle Piane	5 laps	accident

Fastest Lap:

F. Lagorce 120.91mph

Round Two – Pau, 23 May 1994 (71 laps)

Pos	Driver	Time	Pos	Driver	Time
1	G. de Ferran	1:25'39.269	9	J. Gene	1 lap down
2	V. Sospiri	1:25'44.741	10	F. de Simone	2 laps down
3	D. Cottaz	1:25'51.117			
4	J-C. Boullion	1:25'52.825			
5	F. Lagorce	1:26'23.343			
6	G. Gomez	1 lap down			
7	C. Pescatori	1 lap down			
8	J. Policand	1 lap down			

Failed to Finish

P. Crinelli	45 laps	accident
M. Papis	32 laps	accident
E. Clerico	32 laps	accident
T. Marques	30 laps	accident

M. van Hool	25 laps	suspension
H. Noda	16 laps	accident
M. Goossens	15 laps	clutch
A. McNish	7 laps	spin
N. Leboissetier	1 lap	accident
P. Diniz	1 lap	accident

Fastest Lap:

V. Sospiri 86.483mph

Round Three – Barcelona, 30 May 1994 (41 laps)

Pos	Driver	Time	Pos	Driver	Time
1	M. Papis	1:05'41.393	10	P. Diniz	1:06'56.321
2	F. de Simone	1:06'04.825	11	K. Brack	1:07'06.618
3	V. Sospiri	1:06'05.302	12	M. van Hool	1:07'08.876
4	J. Gene	1:06'13.991	13	T. noue	1 lap down
5	F. Lagorce	1:06'15.529			
6	M. Goossens	1:06'27.295			
7	D. Cottaz	1:06'28.129			
8	G. Gomez	1:06'28.552			
9	C. Pescatori	1:06'36.333			

Failed to Finish

P.G. de Ferran	35 laps	engine
W. Eyckmans	30 laps	gearbox
J. Policand	25 laps	spin

S. Nardozi	25 laps	gearbox
P. delle Piane	12 laps	disqualified
O. Gavin	10 laps	suspension
J-C. Boullion	10 laps	spin
E. Clerico	6 laps	engine
H. Noda	5 laps	spin
T. Marques	DNS	accident

Fastest Lap:

J-C. Boullion 112.205mph

Round Four – Enna, 17 July 1994 (40 laps)

Pos	Driver	Time	Pos	Driver	Time
1	G. de Ferran	57'41.731	10	G. Gomez	58'52.277
2	F. Lagorce	57'52.357	11	K. Brack	58'53.989
3	H. Noda	57'55.845	12	T. Marques	59'41.027
4	M. Papis	58'13.860	13	T. Inoue	1 lap down
5	J. Policand	58'19.358	14	J-C. Boullion	1 lap down
6	C. Pescatori	58'24.122	15	J. Taylor	3 laps down
7	M. Goossens	58'35.804			
8	P. delle Piane	58'41.497			
9	D. Cottaz	58'52.095			

Failed to Finish

V. Sospiri 22 laps accident

E. Clerico	20 laps	suspension
P. Diniz	9 laps	spin
N. Leboissetier	6 laps	spin
N. Matubara	5 laps	accident
O. Gavin	1 lap	throttle cable
F. de Simone	0 laps	accident
M. van Hool	0 laps	clutch

Fastest Lap:

C. Pescatori 130.04mph

Round Five – Hockenheim, 31 July 1994 (29 laps)

Pos	Driver	Time	Pos	Driver	Time
1	F. Lagorce	58'07.686	11	D. Cottaz	59'22.125
2	J-C. Boullion	58'15.484	12	T. Inoue	59'23.136
3	G. de Ferran	58'28.089	13	M. van Hool	59'33.010
4	V. Sospiri	58'38.724	14	F. de Simone	60'05.428
5	M. Goossens	58'46.652	15	E. Clerico	1 lap down
6	W. Eyckmans	58'55.587	16	S. Nardozi	2 laps down
7	J. Policand	58'56.576			
8	C. Pescatori	59'01.188	**Failed to Finish**		
9	K. Brack	59'11.806			
10	T. Marques	59'21.338	H. Noda	24 laps	engine
			M. Papis	21 laps	accident

P. Diniz	20 laps	accident
J. Taylor	17 laps	spin
G. Gomez	16 laps	accident
N. Leboissetier	4 laps	accident
P. delle Piane	1 lap	accident
O. Gavin	DNS	gearbox

Fastest Lap:

F. Lagorce   127.962mph

Round Six – Spa, 28 August 1994 (29 laps)

Pos	Driver	Time	Pos	Driver	Time
1	J-C. Boullion	1:11'34.525	10	C. Pescatori	1:13'00.873
2	D. Cottaz	1:11'51.464	11	M. Papis	1:13'09.627
3	K. Brack	1:12'12.698	12	J. Policand	1:13'31.258
4	G. Gomez	1:12'22.004	13	F. Lagorce	1:14'09.070
5	G. de Ferran	1:12'26.697	14	T. Inoue	3 laps down
6	F. de Simone	1:12'38.048	15	E. Julian	3 laps down
7	H. Noda	1:12'39.759	16	S. Nardozi	3 laps down
8	T. Marques	1:12'46.253			
9	P. Diniz	1:12'48.168	**Failed to Finish**		

P. delle Piane	19 laps	retired
N. Leboisettier	10 laps	accident
M. Goossens	6 laps	accident
J. Taylor	3 laps	differential
M. van Hool	2 laps	brakes
E. Clerico	0 laps	accident
V. Sospiri	0 laps	accident

Fastest Lap:

T. Marques   102.77mph

Round Seven – Estoril, 25 September 1994 (44 laps)

Pos	Driver	Time	Pos	Driver	Time
1	J-C. Boullion	1:08'11.419	11	M. van Hool	1:09'20.911
2	V. Sospiri	1:08'32.879	12	T. Marques	1:09'38.843
3	G. Gomez	1:08'35.054	13	M. Papis	1 lap down
4	P. Dinez	1:08'37.572	14	E. Julian	1 lap down
5	D. Cottaz	1:08'38.358	15	J. Taylor	1 lap down
6	K. Brack	1:08'40.463	16	H. Noda	2 laps down
7	E. Clerico	1:08'41.114	17	J. Policand	3 laps down
8	F. Lagorce	1:08'59.898			
9	T. Inoue	1:09'15.069	**Failed to Finish**		
10	N. Leboisettier	1:09'20.397	C. Pescatori	27 laps	spin

F. de Simone	23 laps	fire
M. Rostan	15 laps	electrics
P. delle Piane	9 laps	electrics
P. Carcasci	8 laps	electrics
G. de Ferran	2 laps	accident
M. Goossens	0 laps	accident
W. Eyckmans	0 laps	electrics

Fastest Lap:

E. Clerico   106.95mph

Round Eight – Magny Cours, 2 October 1994 (48 laps)

Pos	Driver	Time
1	J-C. Boullion	1:10'41.298
2	F .Lagorce	1:10'45.661
3	G. Gomez	1:10'53.138
4	T. Marques	1:11'51.018
5	V. Sospiri	1:11'56.800
6	M. Papis	1:12'03.743
7	D. Cottaz *	1:13'00.576
8	P. delle Piane	1 lap down
9	C. Pescatori	1 lap down
10	K. Brack	1 lap down
11	H. Noda	1 lap down
12	N. Leboissetier	1 lap down
13	E. Julian	2 laps down
14	M. Rostan	3 laps down
15	S. Nardozi	5 laps down

Failed to Finish

E. Clerico	31 laps	engine
W. Eyckmans	30 laps	engine
P. Diniz	28 laps	spin
T. Inoue	26 laps	spin
J. Policand	19 laps	Spin
M. Goossens	1 lap	accident
G. de Ferran	1 lap	accident
F. de Simone	O laps	accident
M. van Hool	0 laps	accident

Fastest Lap:

F. Lagorce   109.02mph

* includes 60 second time penalty

The Championship

Pos'n	Driver	Points
1	J-C. Boullion	36
2	F. Lagorce	34
3	G. de Ferran	28
4	V. Sospiri	24
=5	D. Cottaz	13
=5	M. Papis	13
7	G. Gomez	12
8	F de Simone	7
=9	H. Noda	6
=9	D. Coulthard	6
11	K. Brack	5
=12	M. Goossens	3
=12	P. Diniz	3
=12	T. Marques	3
=12	J. Gene	3
16	J. Policand	2
=17	W. Eyckmans	1
=17	C. Pescatori	1

National Formula Ford year

Formula Ford racing provides grass-roots level thrills and spills for the wanna-bes of motorsport over sixteen exciting rounds.

Round One – Thruxton, 3 April 1994

Pos	Driver	Time	Pos	Driver	Time
1	Jonny Kane	12'11.89	6	Omar Bettin	12'44.61
2	Nick Fleming	12'30.55	7	Martin Byford	12'44.95
3	Jonathan Milicevic	12'39.14	8	Marcello Battistuzzi	13'02.82
4	Jiri de Veirman	12'41.23	9	Stephen White	13'07.08
5	Rob Barff	12'44.42	10	John Warrington	13'09.57

Fastest Lap:
Jonny Kane — 105.68mph

Raced over 8 laps

Round Two – Brands Hatch, 17 April 1994

Pos	Driver	Time	Pos	Driver	Time
1	Jonny Kane	15'53.04	6	Jason Watt	16'12.25
2	Justin Keen	15'57.95	7	Stephen White	16'13.62
3	Geoffrey Horion	16'03.63	8	Vincent Vosse	16'13.68
4	Martin Byford	16'06.51	9	Omar Bettin	16'13.80
5	Nick Fleming	16'06.95	10	Jiri de Veirman	16'14.41

Fastest Lap:
Jonny Kane — 92.30mph

Raced over 20 laps

Round Three – Snetterton, 2 May 1994

Pos	Driver	Time	Pos	Driver	Time
1	Geoffrey Horion	22'36.75	6	Giorgio Vinella	23'00.24
2	Omar Bettin	22'37.42	7	Marcelo Battistuzzi	23'04.22
3	Peter Duke	22'42.53	8	Nigel Greensall	23'07.70
4	Vincent Vosse	22'46.55	9	Jonathan Milicevic	23'11.69
5	Nick Fleming	22'55.17	10	Jiri de Veirman	23'11.70

Fastest Lap:
Jonny Kane — 94.97mph

Raced over 18 laps

Round Four – Snetterton, 2 May 1994

Pos	Driver	Time	Pos	Driver	Time
1	Jonny Kane	22'22.35	6	Vincent Vosse	22'38.18
2	Jason Watt	22'23.18	7	Omar Bettin	22'38.18
3	Justin Keen	22'30.82	8	Giorgio Vinella	22'45.67
4	Geoffrey Horion	22'31.72	9	Peter Duke	22'50.88
5	Martin Byford	22'35.54	10	Stephen White	22'57.46

Fastest Lap:
Jason Watt — 95.21mph

Raced over 18 laps

Round Five – Silverstone, 16 May 1994

Pos	Driver	Time	Pos	Driver	Time
1	Jonny Kane	12'39.90	6	Stephen White	12'49.35
2	Justin Keen	12'46.32	7	Martin Byford	12'50.16
3	Jason Watt	12'46.58	8	Vincent Vosse	12'51.30
4	Geoffrey Horion	12'46.81	9	Jonathan Milicevic	12'54.18
5	Peter Duke	12'48.98	10	Nigel Greensall	12'54.41

Fastest Lap:
Jonny Kane — 94.95mph

Raced over 12 laps

Round Six – Oulton Park, 30 May 1994

Pos	Driver	Time	Pos	Driver	Time
1	Jonny Kane	14'07.38	6	Geoffrey Horion	14'18.52
2	Jason Watt	14'08.11	7	Omar Bettin	14'24.46
3	Vincent Vosse	14'14.76	8	Martin Byford	14'27.00
4	Stephen White	14'15.90	9	Nick Fleming	14'30.80
5	Narain Karthikeyan	14'16.38	10	Giorgio Vinella	14'31.98

Fastest Lap:
Jason Watt — 96.11mph

Raced over 8 laps

Round Seven – Donington, 12 June 1994

Pos	Driver	Time	Pos	Driver	Time
1	Jonny Kane	13'40.05	6	Jiri de Veirman	13'58.27
2	Stephen White	13'43.02	7	Peter Duke	13'59.69
3	Geoffrey Horion	13'47.42	8	Martin Byford	14'03.08
4	Vincent Vosse	13'50.58	9	Giorgio Vinella	14'06.18
5	Neil Cunningham	13'51.48	10	Jonathan Milicevic	14'11.71

Fastest Lap:
Stephen White — 89.59mph

Raced over 8 laps

Round Eight – Donington, 12 June 1994

Pos	Driver	Time	Pos	Driver	Time
1	Jason Watt	20'09.56	6	Omar Bettin	20'43.16
2	Jonny Kane	20'10.65	7	Giorgio Vinella	20'44.16
3	Geoffrey Horion	20'28.50	8	Jonathan Milicevic	20'44.46
4	Vincent Vosse	20'36.84	9	Peter Duke	20'44.98
5	Martin Byford	20'42.82	10	Marcelo Battistuzzi	20'52.45

Fastest Lap:
Jason Watt — 89.86mph

Raced over 8 laps

Round Nine – Brands Hatch, 26 June 1994

Pos	Driver	Time	Pos	Driver	Time
1	Jason Watt	13'56.12	6	Peter Duke	14'05.03
2	Justin Keen	14'00.62	7	Vincent Vosse	14'05.36
3	Jonny Kane	14'00.68	8	Nick Fleming	14'07.31
4	Geoffrey Horion	14'03.80	9	Narain Karthikeyan	14'08.80
5	Andrew McAuley	14'04.12	10	Martin Byford	14'15.16

Fastest Lap:
Jason Watt — 101.73mph

Raced over 9 laps

Round Ten – Knockhill, 31 July 1994

Pos	Driver	Time	Pos	Driver	Time
1	Jonny Kane	18'26.06	6	Justin Keen	18'58.01
2	Jason Watt	18'34.97	7	Vincent Vosse	18'58.55
3	Peter Duke	18'35.56	8	Nick Fleming	19'00.72
4	Stephen White	18'35.71	9	Geoffrey Horion	19'07.27
5	Giorgio Vinella	18'52.13	10	Marcelo Battistuzzi	19'17.89

Fastest Lap:
Jonny Kane — 85.46mph

Raced over 20 laps

Round Eleven – Knockhill, 31 July 1994

Pos	Driver	Time	Pos	Driver	Time
1	Jonny Kane	13'48.93	6	Justin Keen	14'00.45
2	Jason Watt	13'52.97	7	Jiri de Veirman	14'02.91
3	Peter Duke	13'53.29	8	Omar Bettin	14'04.13
4	Stephen White	13'53.50	9	Giorgio Vinella	14'04.71
5	Martin Byford	14'00.34	10	Vincent Vosse	14'05.02

Fastest Lap:
Stephen White — 85.79mph

Raced over 15 laps

Round Twelve – Oulton Park, 14 August 1994

Pos	Driver	Time	Pos	Driver	Time
1	Jonny Kane	20'47.09	6	Martin Byford	21'07.20
2	Jason Watt	20'48.90	7	Jiri de Veirman	21'14.78
3	Peter Duke	20'58.72	8	Nick Fleming	21'15.27
4	Justin Keen	21'00.66	9	Narain Karthikeyan	21'28.38
5	Stephen White	21'07.04	10	John Loebell	21'29.14

Fastest Lap:
Jonny Kane — 96.84mph

Raced over 12 laps

Round Thirteen – Brands Hatch, 29 August 1994

Pos	Driver	Time	Pos	Driver	Time
1	Jonny Kane	13'39.96	6	Martin Byford	13'47.73
2	Geoffrey Horion	13'40.14	7	Giorgio Vinella	13'48.28
3	Stephen White	13'40.29	8	Omar Bettin	13'51.14
4	Vincent Vosse	13'42.84	9	Patrick Simon	13'55.15
5	Jason Watt	13'43.20	10	Jiri de Veirman	13'55.98

Fastest Lap:

Jonny Kane — 91.29mph

Raced over 17 laps

Round Fourteen – Brands Hatch, 29 August 1994

Pos	Driver	Time	Pos	Driver	Time
1	Jonny Kaye	13'38.0	6	Jiri de Veirman	13'43.65
2	Andy Charsley	13'39.66	7	Omar Bettin	13'49.02
3	Geoffrey Horion	13'41.49	8	Stephen White	13'50.04
4	Jason Watt	13'41.54	9	Martin Byford	13'51.56
5	Vincent Vosse	13'43.57	10	Robert d'Ercole	13'51.56

Fastest Lap:

Stephen White — 91.37mph

Raced over 17 laps

Round Fifteen – Silverstone, 11 September 1994

Pos	Driver	Time	Pos	Driver	Time
1	Jonny Kaye	20'34.69	6	Peter Duke	20'46.58
2	Geoffrey Horion	20'36.76	7	Stephen White	20'47.44
3	Jason Watt	20'38.30	8	Martin Byford	20'55.17
4	Justin Keen	20'44.38	9	Naoki Kurose	20'55.60
5	Vincent Vosse	20'46.26	10	Omar Bettin	21'03.21

Fastest Lap:

Geoffrey Horion — 92.60mph

Raced over 10 laps

Round Sixteen – Donington, 18 September 1994

Pos	Driver	Time	Pos	Driver	Time
1	Jonny Kane	20'11.88	6	Stephen White	20'30.70
2	Justin Keen	20'18.19	7	Martin Byford	20'31.20
3	Jason Watt	20'20.08	8	Peter Duke	20'37.76
4	Geoffrey Horion	20'20.24	9	Mario Haberfield	20'43.60
5	Narain Karthikeyan	20'21.49	10	Giorgio Vinella	20'47.46

Fastest Lap:

Jonny Kane — 89.76mph

Raced over 12 laps

The Championship

Pos'n	Driver	Points	Pos'n	Driver	Points
1	Jason Watt*	186	4	Stephen White*	97
2	Geoffrey Horion	155	5	Vincent Vosse	93
3	Justin Keen	106	6	Jonny Kane*	89

Points totals for Watt, White and Kane all adjusted for points deductions.

Avon Young Drivers Championship

Pos'n	Driver	Points
1	Peter Duke	202
2	Omar Bettin	174
3	Giorgio Vinella	148

Championship Points Grids

Formula 1 Grand Prix Points Grid – Drivers

	Brazil	Pacific	San Marino	Monaco	Spain	Canada	France	Britain	Germany	Hungary	Belgium	Italy	Portugal	European	Japan	Australia	Total
M. Schumacher	10	10	10	10	6	10	10	–	–	10	–	–	–	10	6	–	92
D. Hill	6	–	1	–	10	6	6	10	–	6	10	10	10	6	10	–	91
G. Berger	–	6	–	4	–	3	4	–	10	–	–	6	–	2	–	6	31
J. Alesi	4	–	–	2	3	4	–	6	–	–	–	–	–	–	4	1	24
U. Katayama	2	–	2	–	–	–	–	1	–	–	–	–	–	–	–	–	5
M. Blundell	–	–	–	–	4	–	–	–	–	2	2	–	–	–	–	–	8
J.J. Lehto	–	–	–	–	–	1	–	–	–	–	–	–	–	–	–	–	1
M. Hakkinen	–	–	4	–	–	–	–	4	–	–	6	4	4	4	–	–	26
M. Brundle	–	–	–	6	–	–	–	–	–	3	–	2	1	–	–	4	16
C. Fittipaldi	–	3	–	–	–	–	–	–	3	–	–	–	–	–	–	–	6
R. Barrichello	3	4	–	–	–	–	–	3	–	–	–	3	3	–	–	3	19
E. Irvine	–	–	–	–	1	–	–	–	–	–	–	–	–	3	2	–	6
E. Comas	–	1	–	–	–	–	–	–	1	–	–	–	–	–	–	–	2
M. Alboreto	–	–	–	1	–	–	–	–	–	–	–	–	–	–	–	–	1
P. Martini	–	–	–	–	2	–	2	–	–	–	–	–	–	–	–	–	4
E. Bernard	–	–	–	–	–	–	–	–	4	–	–	–	–	–	–	–	4
O. Panis	–	–	–	–	–	–	–	–	6	1	–	–	–	–	–	2	9
K. Wendlinger	1	–	3	–	–	–	–	–	–	–	–	–	–	–	–	–	4
H.H. Frentzen	–	2	–	–	–	–	3	–	–	–	–	–	–	1	1	–	7
N. Larini	–	–	6	–	–	–	–	–	–	–	–	–	–	–	–	–	6
A. de Cesaris	–	–	–	3	–	–	1	–	–	–	–	–	–	–	–	–	4
D. Coulthard	–	–	–	–	–	2	–	2	–	–	3	1	6	–	–	–	14
G. Morbidelli	–	–	–	–	–	–	–	–	2	–	1	–	–	–	–	–	3
J. Verstappen	–	–	–	–	–	–	–	–	–	4	4	–	2	–	–	–	10
N. Mansell	–	–	–	–	–	–	–	–	–	–	–	–	–	–	3	10	13

Formula 1 Grand Prix Points Grid – Constructors

	Brazil	Pacific	San Marino	Monaco	Spain	Canada	France	Britain	Germany	Hungary	Belgium	Italy	Portugal	European	Japan	Australia	Total
Benetton	10	10	10	10	6	11	10	–	–	14	4	–	2	10	6	–	103
Williams	6	–	1	–	10	8	6	12	–	6	13	11	16	6	13	10	118
Ferrari	4	6	6	6	3	7	4	6	10	–	–	6	–	2	4	7	71
Jordan	3	4	–	3	1	–	–	3	–	–	–	3	3	3	2	3	28
Tyrrell	2	–	2	–	4	–	–	1	–	2	2	–	–	–	–	–	13
McLaren	–	–	4	6	–	–	–	4	–	3	6	6	5	4	–	4	42
Footwork	–	3	–	–	–	–	–	–	5	–	1	–	–	–	–	–	9
Sauber	1	2	3	–	–	–	4	–	–	–	–	–	–	1	1	–	12
Ligier	–	–	–	–	–	–	–	–	10	1	–	–	–	–	–	2	13
Minardi	–	–	–	1	2	–	2	–	–	–	–	–	–	–	–	–	5
Larrousse	–	1	–	–	–	–	–	1	–	–	–	–	–	–	–	–	2

Current Formula 1 All Time Statistics

Constructor	GP's	Wins	Poles	Points
Ferrari	537	104	113	2752
McLaren	410	104	79	1907.5
Williams	329	78	73	1512.5
Lotus	490	79	107	1352
Tyrell	352	23	14	605
Benetton	201	15	9	526.5
Ligier	293	8	9	349
Footwork/Arrows	255	–	–	125
Jordan	64	–	1	45
Minardi	155	–	–	26
Sauber	32	–	–	24
Larrousse	127	–	–	23
Simtek	16	–	–	–
Pacific	16	–	–	–

Driver	GP's	Wins	Poles
N. Mansell	185	31	32
M. Schumacher	52	10	6
D. Hill	33	9	4
G. Berger	162	9	10
M. Alboreto	193	5	2
R. Barrichello	32	–	1
J. Alesi	85	–	1
A. de Cesaris	208	–	1

NB Pacific's total includes GP's they have failed to qualify to race in.

AutoTrader BTCC Points Grid

	Thruxton	Brands Hatch	Brands Hatch	Snetterton	Silverstone	Silverstone	Oulton Park	Donington	Donington	Brands Hatch	Brands Hatch	Silverstone	Knockhill	Knockhill	Oulton Park	Brands Hatch	Brands Hatch	Silverstone	Silverstone	Donington	Donington	Total
G. Tarquini	24	24	24	24	24	–	–	12	–	24	24	18	–	–	12	18	18	18	24	–	10	298
P. Radisich	–	8	10	18	18	24	18	18	18	–	–	12	18	18	–	–	–	–	–	24	2	206
A. Menu	6	–	–	–	12	18	24	8	10	2	6	8	24	12	18	4	4	12	18	18	18	222
J. Winkelhock	12	–	4	–	–	–	3	–	3	3	4	24	–	–	24	24	24	–	–	10	12	147
S. Soper	10	1	6	3	–	–	10	–	–	10	–	–	12	24	–	8	10	–	8	–	–	102
J. Cleland	18	12	18	–	4	10	4	24	24	8	10	–	8	6	–	–	–	10	10	3	8	177
J. Bailey	–	–	1	–	–	8	1	3	8	–	2	–	3	4	2	1	6	8	6	6	6	65
W. Hoy	8	2	2	–	6	6	–	1	4	–	–	2	2	3	–	–	–	4	4	–	4	48
D. Leslie	3	3	–	–	–	–	–	–	–	–	–	–	–	–	–	–	–	–	–	–	–	6
J. Allam	–	6	8	6	–	2	6	6	12	–	1	4	10	8	–	–	–	3	2	2	–	76
T. Harvey	1	–	–	–	–	–	2	1	–	–	10	–	10	6	10	–	24	–	8	3	–	75
M. Neal	–	–	–	1	–	–	–	–	–	–	–	–	–	–	–	–	–	–	–	–	–	1
E. O'Brien	–	–	–	4	1	1	2	–	–	–	–	–	4	–	–	3	–	–	–	–	–	15
J. Lammers	–	–	–	–	–	–	–	–	4	–	–	–	–	4	2	8	–	–	–	–	–	18
R. Rydell	–	–	–	–	–	8	–	–	1	3	3	6	1	–	–	3	1	–	1	–	–	27
P. Watts	4	4	3	8	8	12	12	4	–	12	12	6	–	–	3	6	–	–	–	4	–	98
J. Thompson	–	–	–	–	–	–	–	–	–	–	–	1	–	–	–	–	–	–	–	–	–	1
K. O'dor	2	–	–	10	3	4	–	–	–	–	–	–	–	–	–	1	–	–	–	–	–	20
A. Rouse	–	10	12	–	10	–	–	10	6	6	8	–	–	–	–	–	–	–	3	–	1	66
R. Ravaglia	–	–	–	–	–	–	–	2	–	–	–	–	–	–	8	–	–	–	–	–	–	10
E. v'Poele	–	–	–	2	–	–	–	–	–	–	–	–	–	–	–	–	–	–	–	–	–	2
T. Needell	–	–	–	–	–	–	–	–	–	–	–	–	1	–	–	–	2	–	–	–	–	3
G. Simoni	–	18	–	12	–	–	–	–	–	18	18	–	–	2	10	12	12	6	12	12	24	156
T. Sugden	–	–	–	–	2	4	–	–	–	–	–	–	–	–	–	–	–	2	1	–	–	9
N. Smith	–	–	–	–	–	–	–	–	–	–	–	–	–	–	–	1	–	–	–	–	–	1

Formula 3 Points Grid

	Silverstone	Donington	Brands Hatch	Brands Hatch	Silverstone	Silverstone	Brands Hatch	Thruxton	Oulton Park	Donington	Silverstone	Snetterton	Pembrey	Pembrey	Silverstone	Silverstone	Thruxton	Silverstone	Total
D. Franchitti	20	12	–	–	1	1	15	16	–	12	6	1	13	15	–	3	10	8	133
S. Lakin	15	10	–	–	10	16	8	10	–	–	–	–	–	–	–	–	–	–	69
J. Magnussen	12	20	21	10	20	20	20	20	21	20	4	–	20	20	20	20	20	20	308
G. Rees	10	8	12	15	4	2	6	12	15	15	12	–	8	10	9	12	6	15	171
S. Arnold	8	6	–	–	–	–	1	1	–	–	2	6	–	–	–	–	–	–	24
V. Radermecker	7	–	15	20	15	12	12	–	10	6	20	15	15	9	6	6	15	–	183
J. Dufour	4	–	10	13	–	–	1	8	12	4	16	8	–	–	10	5	11	1	103
M. Gueiros	3	–	8	8	12	8	10	4	–	10	8	10	1	–	15	8	2	–	107
R. Rosset	2	1	6	2	6	10	–	6	8	9	–	21	10	12	12	15	12	–	132
G. Salles	1	–	2	–	–	–	4	3	–	–	–	12	3	4	4	–	–	6	39
L. Garcia Jnr	–	16	1	–	2	–	–	–	1	3	3	2	–	–	2	1	3	–	34
D. Morelli	–	4	–	–	8	6	3	–	3	–	–	–	4	6	3	10	4	12	63
B. Cunningham	–	3	–	4	3	4	2	–	2	2	–	–	–	1	–	–	–	8	29
S. Watson	–	2	–	–	–	–	–	2	–	–	–	–	–	–	–	–	–	2	7
J. Spence	–	–	4	6	1	3	–	–	6	1	–	4	–	–	–	–	–	–	25
W. Hughes	–	–	3	–	–	–	–	–	–	–	–	–	–	–	–	–	–	–	3
P. de la Rosa	–	–	–	2	–	–	–	–	–	–	–	–	–	–	–	–	–	3	6
M. Gene	–	–	–	–	–	–	–	–	4	–	–	3	2	2	1	2	1	4	19
G. Fisichello	–	–	–	–	–	–	–	–	–	–	10	–	–	–	–	–	–	–	10
C. Horner	–	–	–	–	–	–	–	–	–	–	1	–	6	3	–	–	–	–	10
F. Belletti	–	–	–	–	–	–	–	–	–	–	–	–	–	–	–	–	–	1	1

PPG IndyCar Points Grid

	Surfers Paradise	Pheonix 200	Long Beach	Indy 500	Milwaukee	Detroit	Portland	Cleveland	Toronto	Michigan	Mid-Ohio	New Hampshire	Vancouver	Road America	Nazareth	Laguna Seca	Total
N. Mansell	5	14	16	–	10	1	10	16	–	1	6	–	4	–	–	5	88
Ma. Andretti	14	–	10	–	–	–	4	–	12	–	3	–	2	–	–	–	45
E. Fittipaldi	16	21	–	1	16	16	16	–	14	3	14	16	4	14	15	12	178
P. Tracy	–	1	1	–	14	20	14	14	10	–	17	16	–	2	21	22	152
A. Unser Jnr	–	16	21	21	21	4	22	22	–	5	21	20	20	16	16	–	225
B. Rahal	–	–	–	14	6	8	1	–	16	–	–	4	6	4	–	–	59
Mi. Andretti	21	–	8	8	12	10	–	–	21	–	10	10	14	–	4	–	118
M. Gugelmin	8	–	6	2	–	5	–	5	–	–	–	–	10	–	3	–	39
T. Fabi	6	–	4	5	1	12	–	4	5	12	–	–	–	12	8	–	79
S. Johansson	10	12	3	–	–	–	5	10	–	–	1	–	–	5	10	1	57
J. Villeneuve	–	–	–	16	4	6	8	12	4	–	4	–	–	20	6	14	94
R. Boesel	–	5	12	–	6	–	–	8	1	5	5	12	–	8	12	16	90
R. Gordon	–	6	14	10	8	14	12	2	9	–	12	–	17	–	–	–	104
J. Vasser	12	10	–	12	2	–	–	–	–	–	–	–	6	–	–	–	42
S. Goodyear	3	2	–	–	–	2	–	–	3	20	–	2	12	6	5	–	55

Motor Racing
Diary 1995

FIA Formula 1 Grand Prix

12th	March	Argentina		30th	July	Germany
26th	March	Brazil		13th	August	Hungary
16th	April	Pacific		27th	August	Belguim
30th	April	San Marino		10th	September	Italy
14th	May	Spain		24th	September	Portugal
28th	May	Monaco		8th	October	Europe
11th	June	Canadian		29th	October	Japan
2nd	July	France		12th	November	Australia
16th	July	Britain				

PPG IndyCar World Series

5th	March	Miami		9th	July	Road America
19th	March	Surfer's Paradise		16th	July	Toronto
2nd	April	Phoenix		23rd	July	Cleveland
9th	April	Long Beach		30th	July	Michigan
23rd	April	Nazereth		13th	August	Mid-Ohio
28th	May	Indianapolis		20th	August	New Hampshire
4th	June	Milwaukee		3rd	September	Vancouver
11th	June	Detroit		10th	September	Laguna Seca
25th	June	Portland				

British Touring Car Championship

5th	March	Miami		25th	June	Donington Park
2nd	April	Donington Park		9th	July	Silverstone GP
17th	April	Brands Hatch		30th	July	Knockhill
30th	April	Thruxton		13th	August	Brands Hatch
14th	May	Silverstone		28th	August	Snetterton
29th	May	Oulton Park		10th	September	Oulton Park
11th	June	Brands Hatch GP		24th	September	Silverstone

NB All dates are provisional.